Photographer's Guide to the
Nikon Coolpix P950

Photographer's Guide to the Nikon Coolpix P950

Getting the Most from Nikon's Superzoom Digital Camera

Alexander S. White

WHITE KNIGHT PRESS
HENRICO, VIRGINIA

Copyright © 2020 by Alexander S. White.

All rights reserved.

No part of this publication may be reproduced, stored in a retrieval system or transmitted in any form or by any means, electronic, mechanical, photocopying, recording or otherwise, without the prior written permission of the copyright holder, except for brief quotations used in a review.

The publisher does not assume responsibility for any damage or injury to property or person that results from the use of any of the advice, information, or suggestions contained in this book. Although the information in this book has been checked carefully for errors, the information is not guaranteed. Corrections and updates will be posted as needed at whiteknightpress.com.

Product names, brand names, and company names mentioned in this book are protected by trademarks, which are acknowledged.

Published by
White Knight Press
9704 Old Club Trace
Henrico, Virginia 23238
www.whiteknightpress.com
contact@whiteknightpress.com

ISBN: 978-1-937986-86-5 (paperback)
978-1-937986-87-2 (ebook)

To my wife, Clenise.

Contents

Introduction 1

CHAPTER 1: PRELIMINARY SETUP 3

Setting Up the Camera 3
    Charging and Inserting the Battery 3
    Inserting the Memory Card. 4
Introduction to Main Controls 6
    Top of Camera 6
    Back of Camera 6
    Front and Sides of Camera 7
    Bottom of Camera 8
Setting the Date, Time, and Language 9

CHAPTER 2: BASIC OPERATIONS 11

Fully Automatic—Auto Mode 11
Other Settings in Auto Mode 12
    Focus 13
        Autofocus Options. 13
        Manual Focus 13
    Exposure Compensation 13
    Flash. 14
Motion Picture Recording 15
Viewing Pictures and Movies 16
    Review While in Shooting Mode 17
    Reviewing Images in Playback Mode 17
    Playing Movies 17

CHAPTER 3: THE SHOOTING MODES 19

Auto Mode 19
Program Mode 20
Shutter Priority Mode 20
Aperture Priority Mode 22
Manual Exposure Mode 24

Scene Modes. 26
    Moon Mode. 27
    Bird-watching Mode 28
    The SCENE Setting on the Mode Dial 29
        Portrait 30
        Landscape 30
        Sports 30
        Night Portrait 31
        Party/Indoor 31
        Beach. 31
        Snow 31
        Sunset 32
        Dusk/Dawn. 32
        Night Landscape. 32
        Close-up 33
        Food 33
        Fireworks Show 34
        Backlighting/HDR 34
        Easy Panorama. 36
        Pet Portrait 37
        Selective Color. 37
        Multiple Exposure Lighten 38
        Time-lapse Movie 38
Creative Mode 39
User Settings Mode 41

Chapter 4: The Shooting Menu   43

Image Quality 45
Image Size 47
Picture Control. 49
    Standard 49
    Neutral 49
    Vivid 50
    Monochrome 50
    Adjustments to Picture Control Settings 50
Custom Picture Control 51
White Balance 52
Metering 54
Continuous. 56
ISO Sensitivity 59
    Minimum Shutter Speed 61
Exposure Bracketing. 62
AF Area Mode 63
    Face Priority 63
    Manual (Spot, Normal or Wide). 63
    Subject Tracking 64
    Target Finding AF 64
Autofocus Mode 65
Flash Exposure Compensation 65
Noise Reduction Filter 66
Long Exposure NR 66
Active D-Lighting 66
Multiple Exposure 68
Save User Settings 69
Reset User Settings 69
Zoom Memory and Startup Zoom Position 69

Contents | ix

    Manual Exposure Preview 71

Chapter 5: Physical Controls   72

    Power Switch. 72
    Shutter Release Button 72
    Mode Dial 73
    Zoom Lever 73
    Function Button 73
    Microphone and Speaker 74
    Flash Pop-up Button 74
    Side Zoom Control. 75
    Snap-back Zoom Button 75
    Side Dial 75
    External Microphone Jack 75
    Accessory Terminal 76
    Viewfinder, Eye Sensor, and Monitor Button 76
    Diopter Adjustment Wheel 76
    AE-L/AF-L Button 76
    Focus Mode Selector 76
        Autofocus 76
        Manual Focus 77
    Movie Button 78
    Playback Button 78
    Display Button 78
    Command Dial 79
    Menu Button 79
    Delete/Trash Button 80
    Multi Selector and its Buttons and Dial 80
        Multi Selector Dial 80
        OK Button 81
        Direction Buttons 81
            Up Button: Flash Mode 82
            Right Button: Exposure Compensation 85
            Down Button: Focus Mode 85
            Left Button: Self-timer; Smile Timer; Pet Portrait Release 86
    Self-timer/AF Assist/Red-eye Reduction Lamp 87
    USB Port and HDMI Port 88
    Tilting and Swiveling LCD Screen 88

Chapter 6: Playback   90

    Normal Playback 90
        Index Views, Calendar View, and Enlarging Images 90
        Various Playback Screens. 91
        Viewing Shots Taken in a Sequence 93
    The Playback Menu 94
        Mark for Upload. 95
        Quick Retouch 95
        D-Lighting. 96
        Skin Softening 96
        Filter Effects 96
        Slide Show 99
        Protect. 99
        Rotate Image 100
        Small Picture 100
        Sequence Display. 101

Key Picture Selection 101

Chapter 7: The Setup Menu 102

Time Zone and Date 102
Slot Empty Release Lock 103
Monitor Settings 104
EVF Auto Toggle 105
Date Stamp 106
Self-timer: After Release 106
Vibration Reduction 106
AF Assist 108
Digital Zoom 108
Assign Side Zoom Control 110
Snap-back Zoom 110
Assign Side Dial 110
AE/AF Lock Button 111
Sound Settings 111
Auto Off 112
Format Card 112
Language 112
HDMI 113
Charge by Computer 113
Image Comment 114
Copyright Information 114
Location Data 114
Toggle Av/Tv Selection 115
Reset File Numbering 115
Peaking 116
Reset All 116
Conformity Marking 116
Firmware Version 117

Chapter 8: Motion Pictures 118

Movie-making Overview 118
Quick Guide to Recording a Movie Clip 118
Other Settings for Movies 119
    White Balance, Picture Control, and Creative and Scene Mode Options 119
    Focus and Focus Lock 119
    Exposure, Exposure Compensation, and Exposure Lock 120
    Self-timer 120
    Vibration Reduction 120
    Zoom 121
Taking Still Images During Movie Recording 121
Pausing Recording with the OK Button 122
Fn Button: Does Not Operate During Video Recording 122
Limits on Length of Video Recording 122
The Movie Menu 123
    Frame Rate 123
    Movie Options 124
        HS (High-Speed) Movie Options 124
    Autofocus Mode 126
    Electronic VR (Vibration Reduction) 127
    Wind Noise Reduction 127
    Zoom Microphone 127
    Frame Rate 128

Contents | xi

      External Microphone Sensitivity 128
   Movie Manual Mode. 128
      Movie Manual Menu 128
         Exposure Mode 129
         Picture Control and Custom Picture Control 129
         White Balance 130
         ISO Sensitivity 130
         Other Items on Movie Manual Menu 130
   Recording to an External Video Recorder. 130
   Movie Playback and Editing. 131
      Playback. 131
      Editing. 131

Chapter 9: Wireless Features, Superzoom Lens, and Other Topics   134

   SnapBridge App 134
      Initial Connection and Transferring Images from Camera to Smart Device 134
      Remote Control of Camera Using SnapBridge App 138
      Adding Location Data to Images. 138
      Summary of Options for Transferring Images and Movies to a Smart Device Wirelessly 139
   Network Menu 140
      Airplane Mode 140
      Choose Connection 140
      Connect to Smart Device. 140
      Connection to Remote 140
      Send While Shooting 141
      Wi-Fi 141
      Bluetooth 141
      Restore Default Settings 142
   Using the Superzoom Lens 142
   Macro (Close-up) Photography 145
   Infrared Photography 147
   Street Photography 148
   Connecting to a Television Set 149

Appendix A: Accessories   150

   Cases 150
   Batteries and Chargers 150
   AC Adapter. 151
   Remote Controls 152
   Dot Sight 153
   External Flash 154
   External Microphones 154
   Filters 155
   Lens Hood 156

Appendix B: Quick Tips   157

Appendix C: Resources for Further Information   160

   Photography Books 160
   Digital Photography Review 160
   Reviews of the Coolpix P950 160

The Official Nikon Site	160
Videos	161
Photography Information	161

Index 162

Introduction

The Nikon Coolpix P950 continues Nikon's approach of combining excellent photography and video features with the telephoto performance of a small telescope, as with earlier superzoom models, including the P900 and P1000. In fact, it could be said that the P950 combines the best features of those two models. It provides an amazing 83x optical zoom capability equivalent to 24mm to 2000mm, but it is fairly compact and light in weight. It adds the ability to shoot still images using a Raw format for flexibility in post-processing, and it offers improved optical stability and autofocus, as well as a brighter, larger viewfinder than that in the P900. It also provides a 4K option for video recording, and a jack for connecting an external microphone. It has an accessory shoe for attaching a microphone, flash, or other device.

The P950 is not the perfect camera, of course; no camera can serve as the ideal tool for all situations. Because of the design of its superzoom lens, the camera has a limited range of aperture settings available: from f/2.8 to f/8.0 at the widest focal length, and only from f/6.5 to f/8.0 when the lens is zoomed in fully. This narrow range can limit the ability to make certain kinds of shots, such as those calling for a wide aperture. And, although the P950 has a swiveling LCD monitor, it does not provide any touchscreen capabilities. It also does not include a built-in GPS capability for adding location data to images, although this can be done using Nikon's SnapBridge app and a smartphone or tablet.

This discussion of the camera's features is not complete, but it serves to illustrate that the Coolpix P950 has capabilities that should be attractive to serious amateur photographers—those who want a camera that has many options for creative control of images without needing to change lenses, and that is compact enough to be carried around at all times, so it will be available when a good picture-taking opportunity arises. In particular, if you want a fixed-lens camera that will pull in distant scenes without resorting to measures such as digital zoom or connecting the camera to a spotting scope or telescope, the P950 offers a great combination of superzoom focal length and advanced features such as a Raw format and 4K video capture.

My goal with this guide is to provide a thorough introduction to the camera's features, explaining how they work and when you might use them. The book is intended largely for beginning and intermediate photographers who are not satisfied with the documentation provided with the camera and who need a more user-friendly explanation of its controls and menus. For those seeking more advanced information, I discuss some topics that go beyond the basics, and I include information in the appendices to help you uncover additional resources. This book is not a replacement for the official Nikon Coolpix P950 Reference Manual, which contains a great deal of useful information; my book should be viewed as a supplementary resource to illustrate and explain the use of the camera's features.

One note on the scope of this guide: I live in the United States, and I bought my camera here. I am not familiar with any variations for cameras sold in Europe, the United Kingdom, or elsewhere, such as different batteries or chargers. The photographic functions are not different, though, so this guide should be useful to photographers in all locations, apart from that narrow range of issues. I have stated measurements in both the Imperial and metric systems for the benefit of readers in various countries around the world.

If you find any problems in this book, including typographical errors or information that appears to be confusing or incorrect, please let me know by e-mail to contact@whiteknightpress.com. Feedback from readers is the best source of information for improving books such as this one. If you have general comments or feedback to provide, you also may want to post a review of the book at Amazon.com or another site that sells the book.

Chapter 1: Preliminary Setup

Setting Up the Camera

The box for the Nikon Coolpix P950 should contain the camera itself, Nikon lithium-ion battery, battery terminal cover, charging adapter, neck strap, USB cable, lens cap, lens hood, and the brief "Quick Start Guide" pamphlet. There also should be a registration card and one or two other items, such as an advertising sheet or safety notice. Nikon does not include an HDMI cable for connecting the camera to a TV set, and it does not include the full instruction manual or software on a disc. The full Nikon reference manual is available for download as a PDF document from the following website: http://nikonimglib.com/manual/. You also can view the manual in an online format at https://onlinemanual.nikonimglib.com/p950/en/. The Nikon software for viewing and editing images and videos, ViewNX-i, Capture NX-D, and ViewNX-Movie Editor, is available at https://downloadcenter.nikonimglib.com.

It is a good idea to attach the neck strap to the camera right away, because the camera is fairly heavy and you are likely to want to let it hang around your neck when you are walking around with it. With this camera, you have to be careful to keep track of the lens cap and put it in a safe place when it's off the lens. There is no way to secure the cap to the camera.

Charging and Inserting the Battery

The Nikon battery for the Coolpix P950 is the EN-EL20a. The standard procedure is to charge the battery while it's inside the camera. To do this, you use the supplied USB cable to connect the camera to an AC outlet using the supplied charger, or to a USB port on a computer or other device. There are pluses and minuses to this approach to battery-charging. On the positive side, the battery can charge automatically when the camera is connected to your computer to upload images, and you need only one cable for both charging the battery and connecting the camera to the computer. Also, you don't have to remove the battery from the camera to recharge it. You can refresh its charge by just plugging the camera into a power source.

The main drawbacks are that you cannot use the camera while the battery is charging, and you cannot charge another battery outside the camera. Once the battery dies, you cannot readily replace the battery; you have to stop and recharge the battery. The solution to this situation is to purchase extra batteries and a device that will charge those batteries outside the camera. I'll discuss batteries and other accessories in Appendix A.

To charge the battery, open the door on the bottom of the camera and put in the battery. You can only insert it fully into the camera one way. Look for the four gold-colored contacts at one edge of the battery, and insert the battery so those contacts are next to the outside edge of the camera, under the trash-can icon on the camera's back, as it goes into the compartment. Figure 1-1 shows the battery lined up to go into the camera.

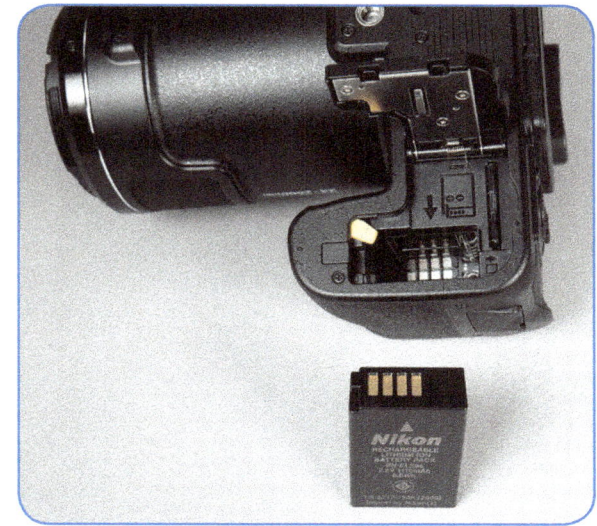

Figure 1-1. Battery Lined Up to Go into Camera

If the battery will not go all the way down into the compartment, don't force it; check its orientation and make sure it is being inserted the correct way. You may have to push the orange plastic retaining latch to one side to allow the battery to slip all the way into its slot; the latch will then anchor the battery in place, as shown in Figure 1-2.

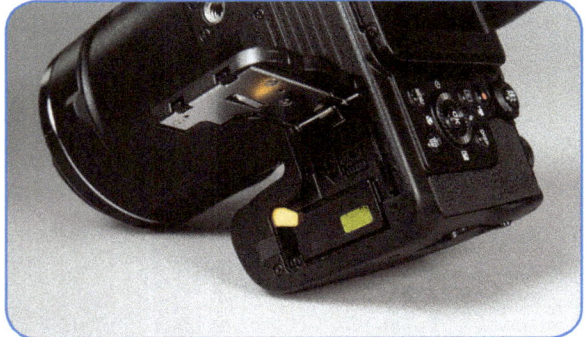

Figure 1-2. Battery Secured by Latch

With the battery inserted into the camera, plug the small end of the USB cable into the USB port under the flap marked HDMI and with a USB symbol on the right side of the camera, as shown in Figure 1-3, and plug the other end of the USB cable into the charging adapter that ships with the camera.

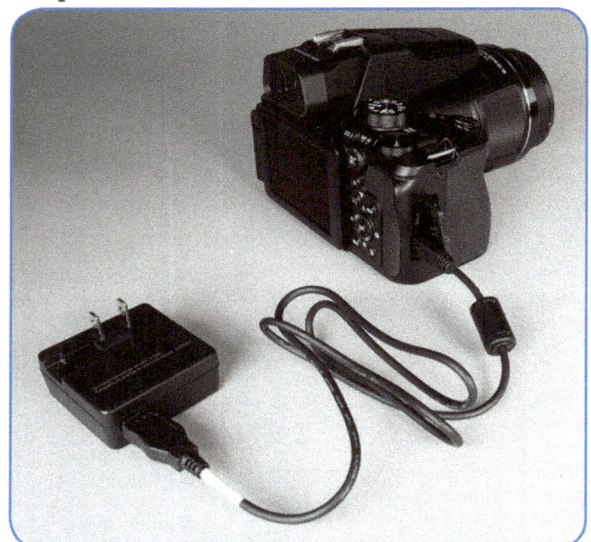

Figure 1-3. Battery Charger Connected to Camera

Then plug the charging adapter into a standard electrical outlet or surge protector. A green light around the power switch on top of the camera will blink about twice per second to show that the battery is charging. When the light goes off, the battery is fully charged. It takes about three hours to charge a fully depleted battery using this system. (This length of time is another factor that makes it a good idea to obtain other batteries and an external charger, as discussed in Appendix A.)

You also can charge the battery in the camera by connecting the USB cable to a compatible USB port on a computer, if the Charge by Computer option is turned on through the camera's menu system. I'll discuss that process in Chapter 7.

Inserting the Memory Card

The Coolpix P950, like most cameras these days, does not ship with a memory card included. If you turn the camera on with no card inserted, you will see the message "No card present" in the center of the screen. With default settings, if you ignore this message and press the shutter button to take a picture, nothing will happen; the camera will not allow you to operate the shutter with no memory card installed.

You can change this behavior using the Slot Empty Release Lock item on the Setup menu. If you set that menu item to Enable Release instead of Release Locked, the shutter will operate and allow you take a few still photos and play them back. However, each of those photos will have "Demo Mode" displayed on it. (If you take more than a few demo images, the camera will delete the earlier ones.) So, in practical terms, in order to use the camera effectively, you need to obtain and insert an appropriate card.

The P950 uses SD cards, which are quite small, about the size of a postage stamp. They come in several varieties, a few of which are shown in Figure 1-4.

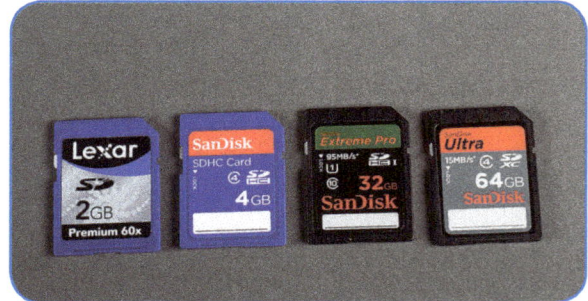

Figure 1-4. Different Types of Memory Card

The standard card, called simply SD, comes in capacities from 8 MB to 2 GB. The next higher-capacity card, SDHC, comes in sizes from 4 GB to 32 GB. The newest, and highest-capacity card, SDXC (for extended capacity), comes in sizes of 48 GB, 64 GB, 128 GB, 256 GB, 512 GB, and 1 TB (terabyte) at this writing; this version of the card can have a capacity up to 2 TB, theoretically. SDXC cards have faster transfer speeds than the smaller-capacity cards.

The P950 also can use micro-SD cards, which are smaller cards, often used in smartphones and other small devices. These cards operate in the same way as SD cards, but you have to use an adapter that is the size of an SD card, as shown in Figure 1-5, to insert this tiny card into the Coolpix P950 camera.

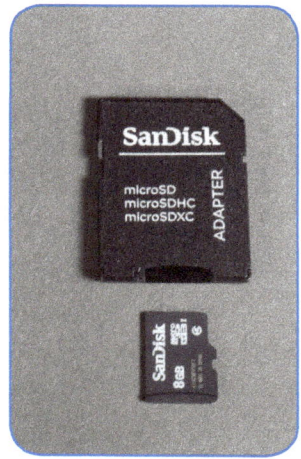

Figure 1-5. Micro-SD Card and Adapter

You might want to use one of these cards so you can transfer images and videos to a smartphone or other device that accepts that size of card.

The type and size of memory card you use depends on your needs and intentions. If you're planning to record a good deal of high-definition (HD) or 4K video or large numbers of high-resolution still photos, you should get a fairly high-capacity card. There are several variables to take into account in computing how many images or videos you can store on a particular size of card, such as which aspect ratio you're using (16:9, 4:3, 3:2, or 1:1), picture size, and quality.

Here are a few examples of how many images (approximately) can be stored on a 32 GB SDHC card: At the highest setting for Image Quality, which is Raw+Fine, a 32 GB card can store about 900 images. At the largest size of 4608 x 3456 pixels and with Fine quality, the card can hold about 3700 still photos; at the next-lower size of 3264 x 2448 pixels and with Fine quality, the same card can hold about 6800 images. At the smaller image sizes, such as 1600 x 1200 pixels, with Fine quality, the card can hold more than 10,000 images. (The number of images that can be stored also varies with factors such as aspect ratio and subject matter of the image, so the numbers stated here are not exact.)

Another consideration is the speed of the card. If you plan to record high-quality video or do a lot of continuous (burst) shooting, you should get a card that is rated in Class 6 or higher for its speed. If you are going to record video using the highest quality setting for 4K (ultra-HD), you should get a card rated in UHS Speed Class 3, or the camera may not be able to record the video successfully. An example of a card in this class is shown in Figure 1-6.

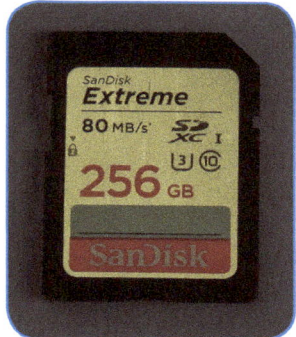

Figure 1-6. SDXC Card Rated in UHS Speed Class 3

As I write this, 64 GB SDXC cards cost about $10 and up, depending on speed. If you don't mind the risk of losing a great many images or videos if you lose the card, you might want to choose an SDXC card with a capacity of 64 GB, or even 128 GB or greater.

I have used cards with capacities of 128 GB, 256 GB, and 512 GB with no problems. However, when I inserted a Lexar Professional 1 TB card, the camera displayed the message, "This card cannot be used." I have used that card successfully in several other cameras, so there evidently is a limit on the capacity of cards recognized by the P950. A capacity of 512 GB is more than enough for most purposes, though. I usually use a high-speed 32 GB or 64 GB SDHC or SDXC card, and I have never had a problem with too little storage space using such cards.

Once you have selected your memory card, open the same door on the bottom of the camera that covers the battery compartment, and slide the card into the card slot until it catches, with the label facing the back of the camera. Once the card has been pushed down until it catches, close the compartment door and push the latch back to the locking position. To remove the card, push down on it until it releases and springs up so you can grab it. Figure 1-7 shows a card being inserted into the P950.

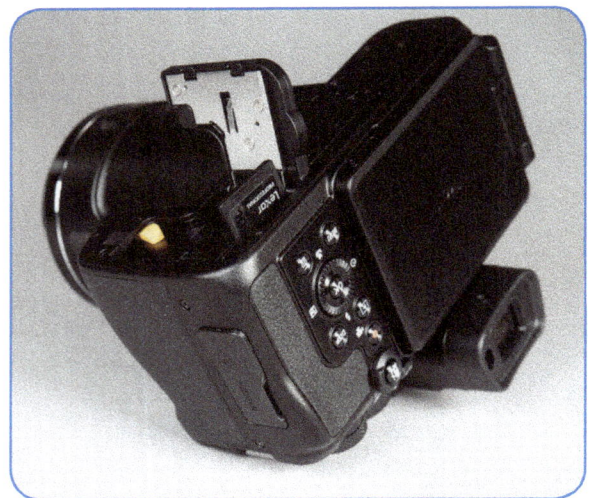

Figure 1-7. Memory Card Going into Camera

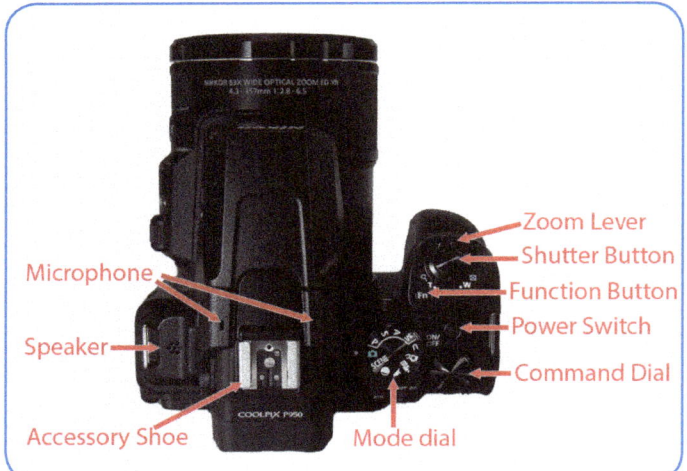

Figure 1-8. Controls on Top of Camera

One note for shooting continuous pictures with the P950: When the camera is writing its image data to the memory card, the camera flashes the numbers in the lower right corner of the display that indicate the number of remaining images or minutes of video. While that display is flashing, it's important not to turn off the camera or otherwise interrupt its functioning, such as by taking out the battery or disconnecting an AC power adapter. You need to let the card complete its recording process before taking further steps.

Introduction to Main Controls

Before I discuss options for setting up the camera to take images and videos, I will introduce the main controls so you'll have a better idea of which button or dial is which as I discuss them in this and other chapters. I will briefly mention the functions of the controls here; I will cover them in more detail in Chapter 5. The following series of images shows the major controls. As I discuss each item, I will describe its position and function; you may want to refer to these images for a reminder about each control.

TOP OF CAMERA

On top of the camera are several important controls and dials, shown in Figure 1-8.

The mode dial is used to select the shooting mode for still images. For basic shooting with the camera making most of the decisions, turn this dial so the green camera icon is next to the white selection marker. The shutter release button is used to take pictures; press it halfway down to lock focus and exposure, and press it all the way down to record the image. In Movie Manual mode, you can use this button to start and stop movie recording. The zoom lever that surrounds the shutter release button is used to zoom the lens between its wide-angle and telephoto focal lengths in shooting mode, and to display index screens or enlarge images in playback mode. The Function button is a versatile control that provides quick access to a single menu option of your choice.

The power switch is used to turn the camera on and off. The microphone picks up sounds when you are recording movies. The command dial is located on top of the camera, but it is most readily accessible by using your thumb from the back of the camera, so it is discussed below, in the section on those controls. The single speaker at the far left of the camera's top emits audio for movies and operational sounds. The accessory shoe is where you can attach an accessory such as an external flash unit, a microphone, or a dot sight, as discussed in Appendix A.

BACK OF CAMERA

The controls on the camera's back are seen in Figure 1-9. The viewfinder is the window you can look through to compose your shots and view recorded images when you have the LCD screen folded in against the camera

Chapter 1: Preliminary Setup

or the viewfinder has been activated through use of the Monitor button or the eye sensor.

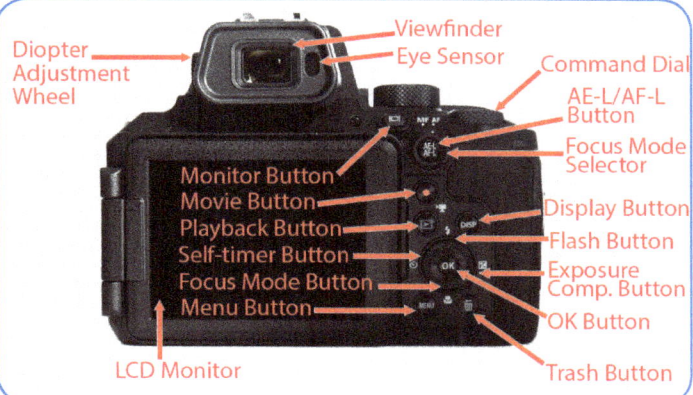

Figure 1-9. Controls on Back of Camera

The eye sensor, to the right of the viewfinder window, senses the presence of your head near the viewfinder and switches the display from the LCD screen to the viewfinder. (That behavior can be changed using the EVF Auto Toggle option on the Setup menu, as discussed in Chapter 7.)

The Monitor button switches between using the LCD screen and the viewfinder. The Display button selects screens for viewing information about shooting settings when images are being recorded and about the images themselves when they are being played back. The red Movie button starts and stops the recording of a video sequence. The Delete button (also called the Trash button) is used to delete recorded images.

The command dial (located on top of the camera but reached most easily from the back) lets you select settings such as shutter speed and flexible program, and has some miscellaneous functions in playback and shooting modes. The AE-L/AF-L button locks either exposure or focus, or both, depending on the setting of the AE/AF Lock Button option on the Setup menu. The focus mode selector, which surrounds the AE-L/AF-L button, lets you switch the camera between using autofocus and using manual focus. The Playback button places the camera into playback mode so you can view recorded images and videos.

The Menu button calls up the camera's system of menu screens with various settings for shooting and other values, such as control functions, audio features, and others. The multi selector dial acts as a wheel for setting values such as aperture and for navigating through menu screens and screens for setting values for various options. In playback mode, you can use it to move through your recorded images and videos.

In addition, each of the dial's four edges acts as a button when you press in on that edge, for selecting items including flash mode, exposure compensation, focus mode, and the self-timer. (Those buttons are called the Up, Down, Left, and Right buttons in this book.) The OK button in the center of the dial is used to confirm selections and for some miscellaneous operations.

FRONT AND SIDES OF CAMERA

The flash pop-up switch, located on the upper part of the left side of the P950, is used to release the camera's built-in flash unit so it can fire if it is needed. The flash unit pops up at an angle, as shown in Figure 1-10.

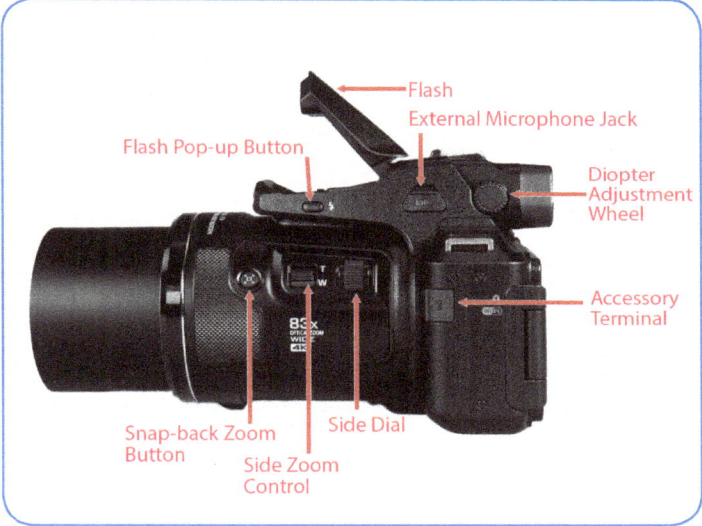

Figure 1-10. Controls on Left Side of Camera

The side zoom control is used to zoom the lens. You can change the speed of zooming for video recording, using the Assign Side Zoom Control option on the Setup menu. The snap-back zoom button is used to move the zoom lens quickly to a wider view while you hold the button down, and back to its zoomed-in position when you release it, to help you locate a distant subject within your field of view. The side dial, located behind the side zoom control, is used to adjust focus when the focus-mode selector is set to manual focus. When autofocus is in effect, this control handles whatever function has been assigned to it using the Assign Side Dial option on the Setup menu, as discussed in Chapter 7.

The diopter adjustment wheel directly to the left of the viewfinder is used to adjust the viewfinder according to your vision.

The ports on the left side of the camera, located under flaps that can be rotated out of the way, as seen in Figure 1-10, are the external microphone jack and the accessory terminal.

The external microphone jack is for connecting an optional microphone to record sound for movies, instead of using the built-in microphone. The accessory terminal is for connecting an optional remote control device, as discussed in Appendix A.

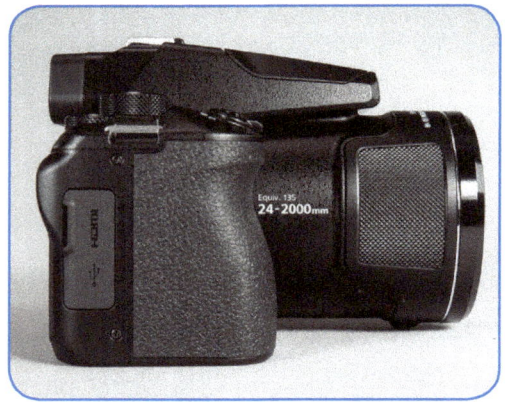

Figure 1-11. Right Side of Camera

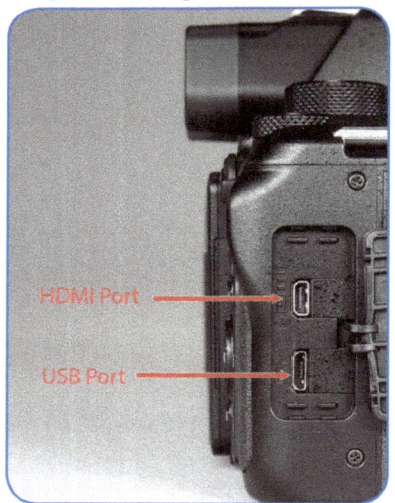

Figure 1-12. Right Side of Camera with Ports Uncovered

The ports on the right side of the camera, located under a single flap, are the HDMI port and the USB port, as shown in Figure 1-11 with the ports covered and 1-12 with the ports uncovered. The HDMI port is for connecting the camera to an HDTV set for playback of images and videos using an optional HDMI cable. It also can be used to output a "clean" HDMI signal to record video to an external recorder. The USB port is for connecting the camera to a computer or charger/power adapter, using the cable provided with the camera.

On the front of the camera is the Self-timer/AF Assist/Red-eye Reduction lamp, shown in Figure 1-13. This lamp illuminates to help the camera use its autofocus technology in dimly lighted areas, and it lights up to indicate the functioning of the self-timer. In addition, when the flash is set to a mode that uses Red-eye Reduction, this bright lamp lights up before the flash fires, to constrict the pupils of a person's eyes, so the flash will not bounce off the retinas to cause the unpleasant "red-eye" effect.

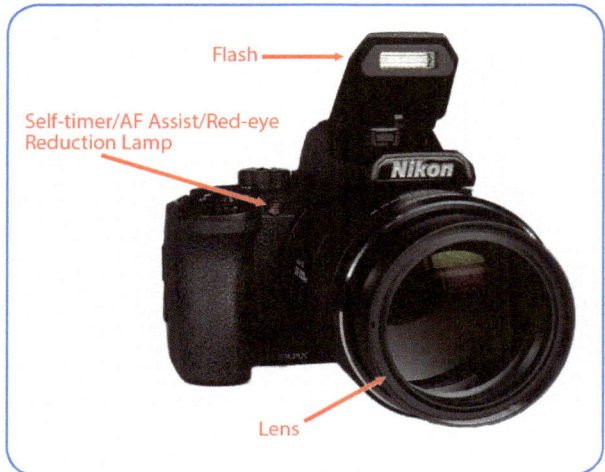

Figure 1-13. Items on Front of Camera

The camera's lens is a variable focal length, or zoom lens, with an optical zoom range from 24mm to 2000mm. It has aperture settings ranging from f/2.8 to f/8.0, as discussed in Chapter 3.

Bottom of Camera

Finally, as shown in Figure 1-14, there are three main items on the bottom of the camera.

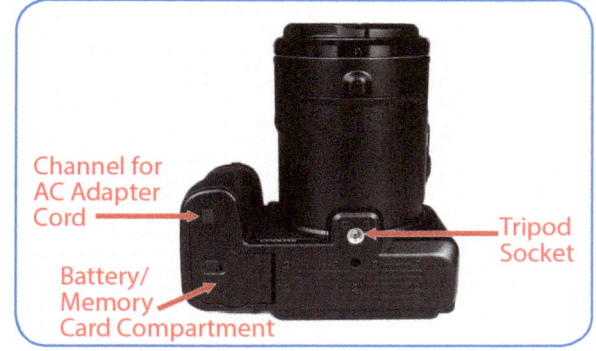

Figure 1-14. Items on Bottom of Camera

Chapter 1: Preliminary Setup | 9

The tripod socket allows the camera to be attached to a tripod with a standard screw. The latching door covers the compartment where the memory card and battery are located. One excellent feature of this camera is that, because the tripod socket is not too close to the battery/memory card compartment, you can get access to the battery and memory card even when the camera is attached to a tripod.

At the outer edge of the battery compartment door is a flap that must be opened up when you install the optional AC adapter in the camera, so the door can close with the cord running through the channel occupied by the flap. I discuss the AC adapter in Appendix A.

Setting the Date, Time, and Language

You need to set the date and time before you start taking pictures, because the camera records that information (sometimes known as "metadata") invisibly with each image, and displays it later if you want. Someday you may be glad to have the date and time correctly recorded with your archives of digital images. If you purchase the camera new, it will prompt you to set the date and time when you first power it on.

If you later need to set the time and date, here is how to do so. Press down on the camera's power switch, marked On/Off, on top of the camera, to turn the camera on. Then press the Menu button to the lower left of the OK button on the camera's back. Next, press the Left button, which is marked with a timer icon.

When you press the Left button, the yellow selection highlight will move to the far left of the screen, to the list of icons, which will have a letter or an icon representing the camera's current mode at the top of the list. If the camera is in shooting mode, the letter or icon will represent that mode, such as, for example, P for Program or an icon for Moon, Bird-watching, or Creative. If the camera is in Auto mode, as it is in Figures 1-15 through 1-19, a camera icon indicating that shooting mode will be at the top of the list.

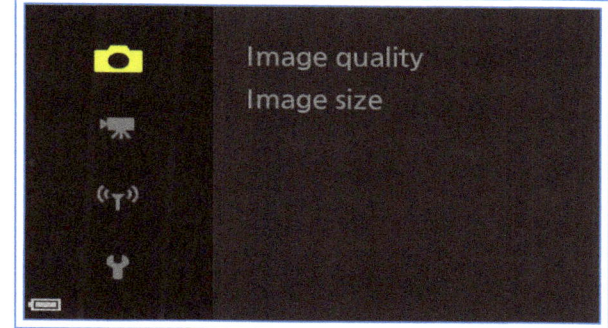

Figure 1-15. Icon for Shooting Mode Highlighted on Menu Screen

Use the Down button, marked with a flower icon, to move the selection highlight down to the wrench icon that represents the Setup menu, as shown in Figure 1-16.

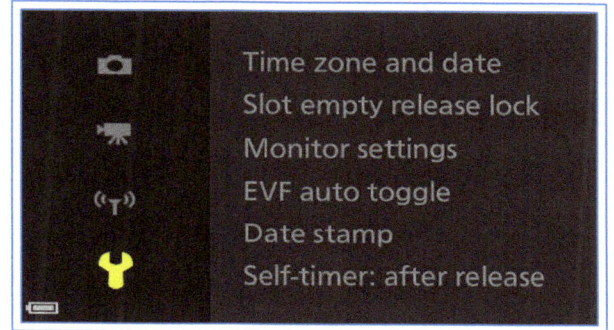

Figure 1-16. Wrench Icon for Setup Menu Highlighted on Screen

Press the Right button, marked with a plus and minus sign, to move the highlight back to the right, where it will become a yellow rectangle highlighting a menu item. Press the Up and Down buttons (or turn the multi selector dial) to move the yellow selection bar to the Time Zone and Date line, as shown in Figure 1-17, and press the OK button to move to a screen with choices of Date and Time, Date Format, and Time Zone, shown in Figure 1-18.

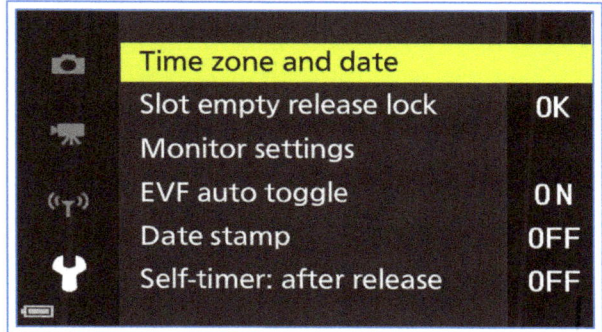

Figure 1-17. Time Zone and Date Item Highlighted on Setup Menu

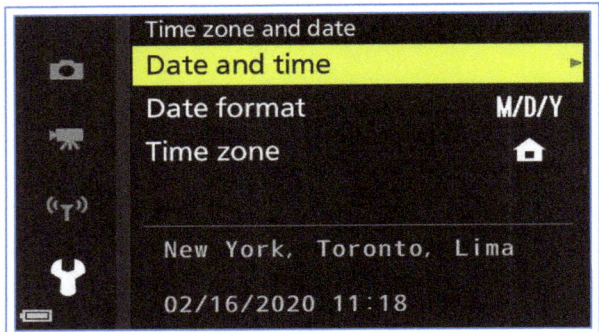

Figure 1-18. Time Zone and Date Menu Options Screen

Highlight Date and Time and press the OK button to move to the settings screen, shown in Figure 1-19.

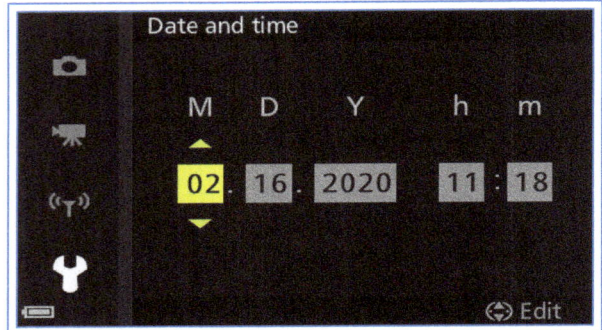

Figure 1-19. Time and Date Settings Screen

You can press the Right button instead of the OK button to move to these menu screens, if you prefer.

On the settings screen, use the Left and Right buttons to move through the date, year, and time settings, and change those settings by pressing the Up and Down buttons. (You also can turn the multi selector dial or the command dial to change the settings.) When everything is set correctly, press the OK button to confirm and press the Menu button to exit the menu system.

If you need to change the language that the camera uses for the menus and other messages, navigate on the Setup menu to the line on the third screen that says Language, and press the OK button or the Right button to select the Language menu item. Then navigate with the Up and Down buttons (or the multi selector dial) to the language of your choice, as shown in Figure 1-20, and press the OK button to select it.

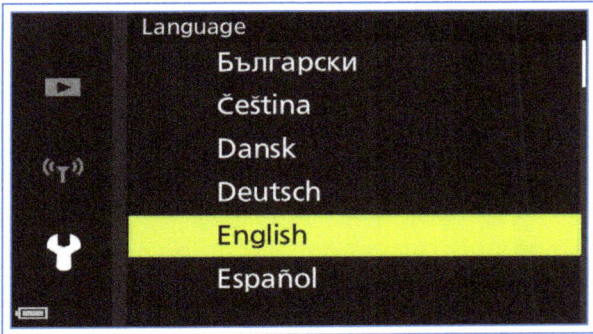

Figure 1-20. Language Selection Screen on Setup Menu

Then press the Menu button to exit from the menu system.

Chapter 2: Basic Operations

Once the Coolpix P950 has the correct time and date set and has a fully charged battery inserted along with a memory card, it is ready for basic picture-taking. For now, I won't discuss all of the available options and why you might choose one over another. I'll just outline a set of steps that will get the camera into action and will record a decent image on your memory card.

Fully Automatic—Auto Mode

Here's a procedure to use if you want to let the camera make (almost) all of the decisions for you. This is a good system to use if you need to grab a quick shot without fiddling with settings, or if you would rather let the camera take control without having to provide much input.

1. Remove the lens cap from the lens and put it in a safe place. (If you forget to remove the cap before turning on the camera, that's okay; Nikon has engineered the P950 to have the lens cap attached to the moving part of the lens, so the cap will not block the motion of the lens in extending out from the camera. But you will notice that the camera's display is black, because the lens cap will be blocking the view.)

2. Press the power switch to turn on the camera. The LCD screen will illuminate to show that the camera has turned on. (If the LCD screen is folded in the closed position, the viewfinder will operate instead of the screen, as discussed in Step 7, below.)

3. Find the mode dial on top of the camera and turn the dial until the green camera icon is next to the white indicator line. This selects Auto shooting mode, as shown in Figure 2-1.

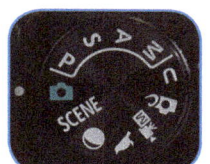

Figure 2-1. Mode Dial at Auto

4. Find the button with AE-L and AF-L marked on it, near the upper right corner of the LCD monitor, then turn the small switch around that button so the white indicator dot points at the AF setting for autofocus, as shown in Figure 2-2.

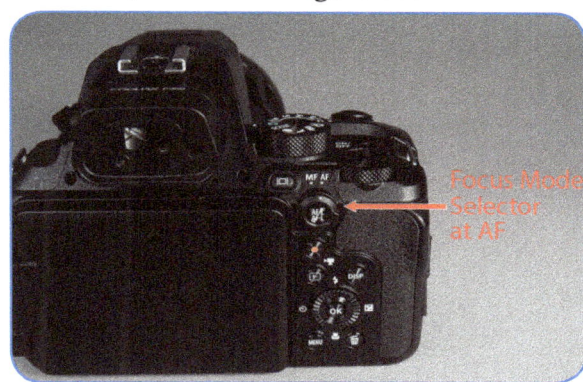

Figure 2-2. Focus Mode Selector at AF

5. Press the Down button on the multi-selector (the button with a flower icon below it), to call up the autofocus mode menu, as shown in Figure 2-3. Navigate to the AF option at the top of the menu, and press the OK button to confirm its selection.

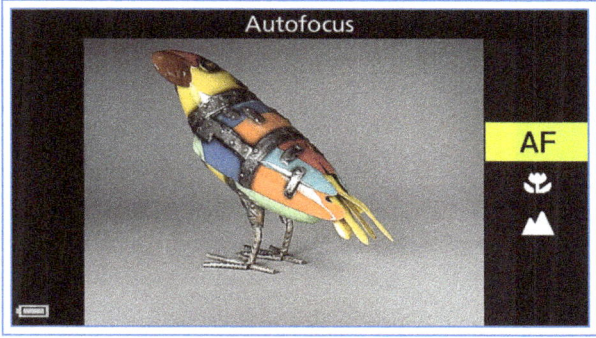

Figure 2-3. Autofocus Mode Menu at AF

6. Press the Menu button at the bottom left of the control area on the back of the camera. Use the direction buttons (four edges of the ridged multi selector dial) to navigate to the entry for Image Quality, select that line with the OK button or the Right button, highlight the Fine setting, and press OK. Then navigate down to the Image Size setting, select it, and choose 4608 x 3456 pixels, the top option, as shown in Figure 2-4. Press the Menu button to return to shooting mode.

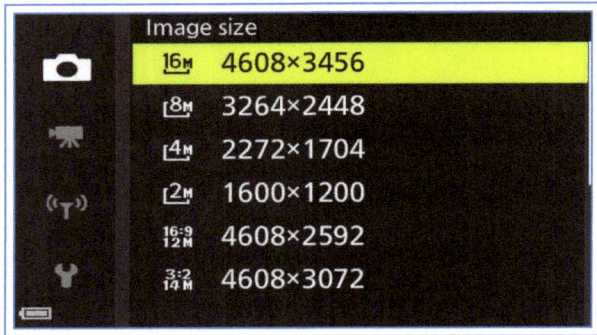

Figure 2-4. Largest Option Highlighted for Image Size

(You can choose other settings for either or both of these options if you wish, but the ones I mentioned provide the highest quality without getting involved with the complications of using Raw files.)

7. If you want to compose your image on the LCD screen on the back of the camera, no action is needed if the LCD screen has its active surface exposed and is turned on. If the screen is folded against the camera, pull it out to the left and swivel it so the screen is visible. If necessary, press the Monitor button to activate it. To use the viewfinder instead, press the Monitor button again.

8. Look at the screen or into the viewfinder to compose the shot and view the camera's settings. You can adjust the viewfinder for your eyesight by turning the diopter adjustment wheel on the left side of the viewfinder's housing. Toggle between the LCD and the viewfinder by pressing the Monitor button. If the EVF Auto Toggle menu option is turned on through the Setup menu, the view will switch from the LCD to the viewfinder when your head approaches the viewfinder. (That option is discussed in Chapter 7.)

9. If you are indoors or otherwise in conditions that might call for the use of flash, press the button on the left side of the camera's built-in flash unit, marked with a lightning bolt, to pop up the flash.

10. If you have popped up the flash, press the Up button on the multi selector, marked with another lightning bolt, to bring up the flash mode menu, shown in Figure 2-5. Make sure the Auto setting, at the top of this menu, is highlighted. (In Chapter 5, I'll discuss the other flash options.)

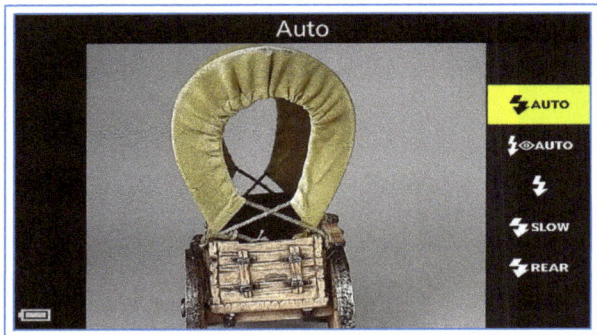

Figure 2-5. Flash Mode Menu

11. Aim the camera toward the subject and look at the LCD screen (or into the viewfinder window, depending on your choice in Step 7) to compose the scene as you want it. Locate the zoom lever on the ring that surrounds the shutter button on the top right at the front of the camera. Push that lever to the left, moving its indicator toward the letter W, to get a wider-angle shot (including more of the scene in the picture), or to the right, moving the indicator toward the letter T, to get a telephoto, zoomed-in shot. Or, if you prefer, use the equivalent zoom switch on the left side of the lens, moving it up for telephoto or down for wide-angle.

12. Once the picture is composed as you want it, press the shutter release button halfway down. You should hear a beep and see one or more green rectangles on the display, meaning the picture is in focus. A flashing red rectangle means the camera is having difficulty achieving focus. In that case, try moving the camera to a different angle before pressing the shutter button halfway again.

13. Press the shutter button all the way down to take the picture.

Other Settings in Auto Mode

With some other camera models, there are very few, if any, settings that can be adjusted when the camera is set to its most automatic shooting mode. With the Coolpix P950, though, there are a few settings that can be adjusted in Auto mode. This section will briefly describe those settings; more details are included in Chapters 4 and 5.

Focus

One option you can control further, even in Auto mode, is focus. Specifically, you can select which of several types of autofocus operation you want the camera to use, if you opt for autofocus, and you can set the camera to use manual focus.

Autofocus Options

As noted earlier, you set the camera to use autofocus by turning the focus mode selector to the AF position. Then, to select a standard autofocus mode, press the Down button (marked by a flower icon). This action puts a small menu with three options on the display, as shown earlier in Figure 2-3. Starting at the top, they are the letters AF, for normal autofocus; the flower icon, for macro (close-up) focus; and the mountain icon, for focus on infinity.

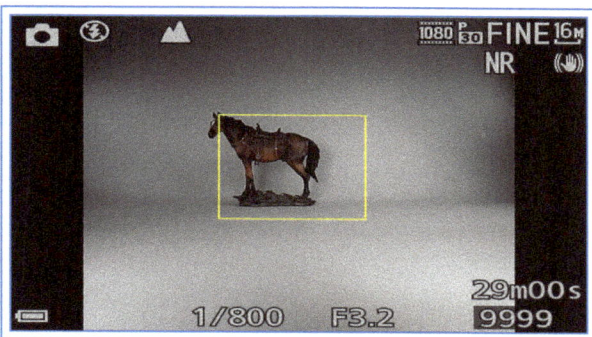

Figure 2-6. Icon for Infinity AF on Shooting Screen

For now, use the direction buttons to select the top icon, for normal autofocus. (You have to be quick; the three choices disappear within a few seconds.) Press the OK button to select and confirm your choice. The letters or icon for your choice will appear at the upper left of the display, as shown in Figure 2-6, unless the choice is AF; if you select AF, those letters will appear for a few seconds and then disappear, because that is the default setting. The icon shown in Figure 2-6 represents the infinity setting.

The AF setting is used for most shooting, where the subject is at least 20 inches (50 cm) away from the camera, when the lens is zoomed back to its wide-angle setting, or at least 16 feet 5 inches (5 meters) at the telephoto setting. The macro setting is used for subjects that are as close to the lens as 0.4 inch (1 cm) at the wide-angle setting or as close as 16 feet 5 inches (5 meters) at the highest zoom settings. The infinity setting is used for distant scenes and landscapes.

For most purposes, you will probably want to leave this setting at AF. However, if you find the camera will not focus on a subject that is fairly close to the lens, set this option to macro, in order to get the autofocus system to focus sharply.

Manual Focus

It can be useful to focus the lens manually in certain situations, such as when you are focusing at very close range, when you need to make sure focus is sharpest on a particular part of a subject, or when you are focusing through a wire fence or glass window. To use manual focus, turn the focus mode selector, which surrounds the AE-L/AF-L button to the top right of the LCD monitor, to the MF position. Then turn the side dial (the ridged dial on the left of the lens housing, just behind the side zoom control) until focus is sharp. Further details about manual focusing are in Chapter 5.

Exposure Compensation

The Coolpix P950's Auto mode is very good at choosing the right exposure. But there are some situations in which you may want to override the camera's automation. For example, consider Figure 2-7, which shows the P950's view of a firefighter figurine. Because the figurine is in front of a white background, the camera's autoexposure system makes the exposure too dark, to account for the large expanse of white.

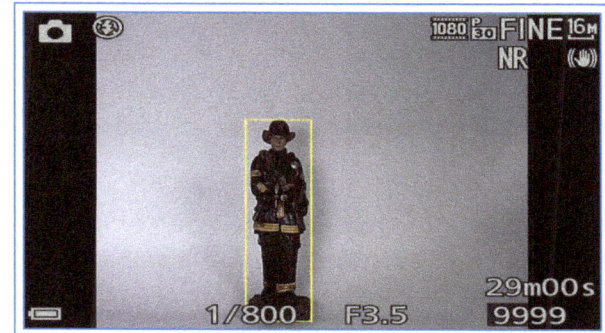

Figure 2-7. Exposure Compensation Example: Before Adjustment

One solution to this problem is to use the camera's exposure compensation control. Look closely at the Right button on the multi selector. That button is labeled with little plus and minus signs, with the plus on a black background and the minus on white. This control activates the exposure compensation system, which will override the automatic exposure as much as you tell it to, within limits. Press the Right button, and a vertical scale will appear on the right side of the display, with a plus sign at the top and a minus sign at the bottom, as shown in Figure 2-8.

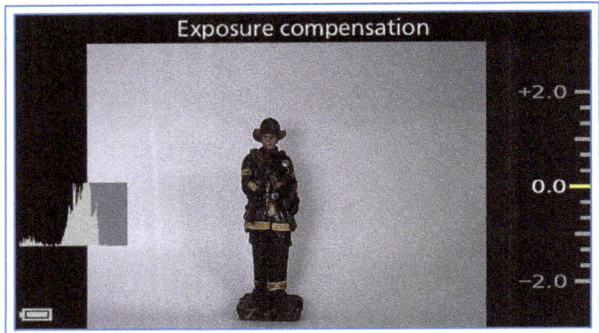

Figure 2-8. Exposure Compensation Scale on Shooting Screen

Once the exposure compensation scale has appeared, press the Up and Down buttons or turn the multi selector dial or the command dial to move the value higher or lower, as indicated by yellow tick marks that appear on the scale to show the value that is being set. If you move the yellow marks all the way to the bottom of the scale, the picture will be considerably darker than the automatic exposure would produce. If you move the yellow tick marks to the top, the picture will be noticeably brighter.

The camera's screen brightens and darkens to show you how the exposure is changing, before you take the picture. The camera also displays a histogram—a chart showing peaks and valleys of brightness values—on the left side of the screen. In this case, you would adjust exposure to be brighter, so the camera will expose for the figurine properly, and let the background show up as a brighter (and more accurate) white than in the first image.

I'll discuss the histogram in more detail in Chapter 6. Basically, brighter values in your image skew the peaks in the chart to the right, and darker ones skew them to the left. In this case, I adjusted exposure upward by 1.7 EV (exposure value), moving the histogram to the right and resulting in a more normally exposed image, as shown in Figure 2-9.

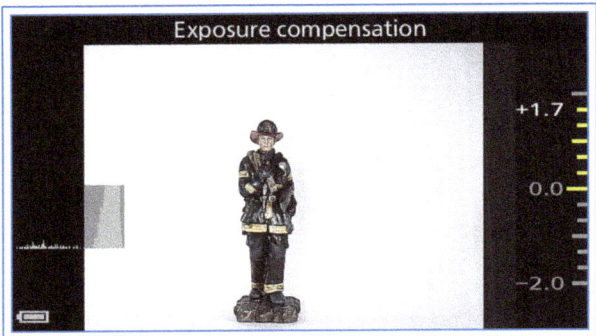

Figure 2-9. Exposure Compensation Example: After Adjustment

If a positive or negative value for exposure compensation is in effect, the camera will display that value, along with the exposure compensation icon, in the lower right corner of the display, as shown in Figure 2-10.

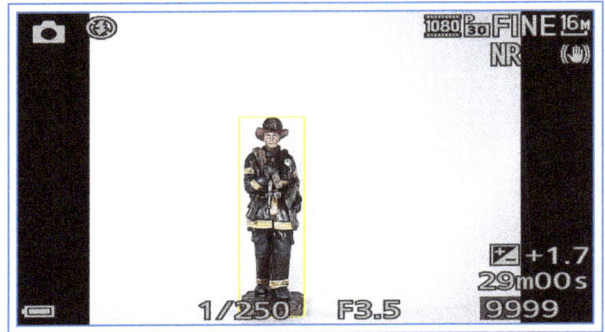

Figure 2-10. Exposure Compensation Value on Shooting Screen

Flash

Another option that is available in Auto mode for controlling exposure is the camera's built-in flash unit. In Chapter 5, I will discuss other options for using the flash, such as the slow sync mode and correcting "red-eye." In Appendix A, I will discuss using other flash units. In this section, I will discuss some basic points for using the flash.

The built-in flash can provide enough illumination to let you take pictures in dark areas and to brighten up areas otherwise lost in shadows, even outdoors on a sunny day.

Pressing the Up button on the multi selector, the one marked with a lightning bolt, gives you access to the various settings for the built-in flash unit on the Coolpix P950, as shown earlier in Figure 2-5.

Before I discuss the details of those settings, it's important to recall one basic fact about this camera: The flash cannot fire unless you first pop it up by pressing

Chapter 2: Basic Operations

the flash pop-up button marked by a lightning bolt on the left side of the flash housing, near the top of the camera. If you think there's any chance the flash may be needed, go ahead and press that button to have the flash ready. (If you're shooting movies, though, you should make sure the flash is down out of the way, because it can't be used and might interfere with your shooting.)

Once you have popped up the flash unit and activated the flash mode menu in Auto mode, you will see five options for flash mode, shown in Figure 2-5. From the top, the icons represent autoflash, autoflash with red-eye reduction, fill-flash, slow sync flash, and rear sync flash. I will discuss the details of these options in Chapter 5. For now, you should be aware of some basic points: If you want the camera to decide whether to use the flash, select autoflash. If you are photographing a person's face, you may want to use autoflash with red-eye reduction to reduce the chance of the unpleasant "red-eye" effect when flash illuminates a person's retinas. If you are photographing a subject outdoors in bright conditions, you might want to choose fill-flash, to reduce harsh shadows on the subject.

Motion Picture Recording

Next, I'll describe steps for recording a video sequence with the P950. In Chapter 8, I'll discuss other options for video, but for now I will stick with the basics.

1. With the camera in Auto mode, make sure the flash unit is pressed down in the off position, because it will not be needed. Once the camera is turned on, press the Menu button and then the Left button to place the yellow selection block in the line of icons at the far left of the screen. Navigate down to the second icon, which looks like a movie camera, then press the Right button to move the selection rectangle back into the list of menu items. You will see six items on this Movie menu screen, as shown in Figure 2-11, which provides the options for recording video footage.

   (If you have an external microphone plugged into the external mic jack on the left side of the camera, you will see one additional menu option on a second screen, for adjusting the sensitivity of the external microphone.)

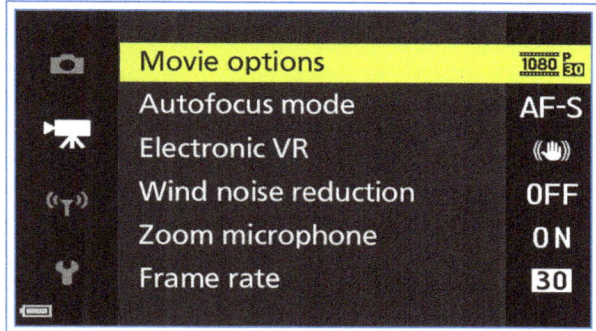

Figure 2-11. Movie Menu Screen

2. Navigate to the last item on the menu screen, called Frame Rate, and press the OK or Right button to move to the screen with the two options for this setting, as shown in Figure 2-12: 30 fps (30p/60p) and 25 fps (25p/50p).

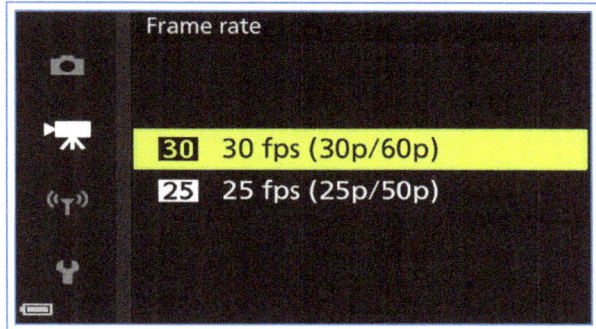

Figure 2-12. Frame Rate Menu Options Screen

This setting determines the frames per second at which the camera will record video in the highest-quality (4K and HD) formats. The 30 fps setting is the standard for the NTSC video system, which is used in the United States, Canada, Mexico, Japan, and some other areas. The 25 fps setting is the standard for the PAL video system, in use in Europe and other locations. If you are in the United States, select the 30 fps option unless you have a specific need to do otherwise. This setting will affect the choices available for the Movie Options item, discussed next.

3. Navigate to the top option on the menu screen, which is Movie Options, press the OK button or the Right button to move to the next screen, and look at the list of options. If you selected 30 fps for Frame Rate, as discussed above, the first five options on this screen will include the number 30 or 60. If you selected 25 fps, the first five options will include the number 25 or 50.

4. You should now choose the second selection for Movie Options, which, if you chose 30 fps for Frame Rate, will be 1080/30p, as shown in Figure 2-13. (If the second item is 1080/25p, that means the Frame Rate menu item is set to 25 fps. Unless you have a reason to make that choice, go back and change it to 30 fps.) This setting provides very high quality for shooting movies with the P950, without getting involved with the highest quality, 4K shooting.

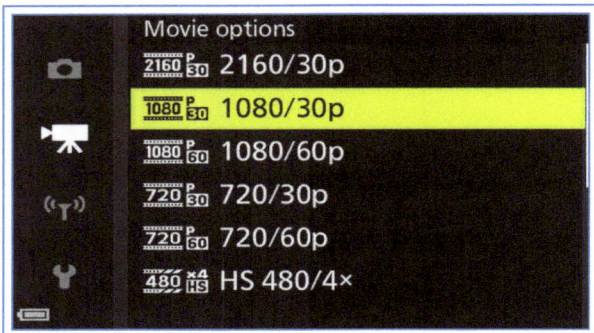

Figure 2-13. 1080/30p Highlighted for Movie Options Item

5. Navigate down to the second option on the Movie menu screen, Autofocus Mode. Move to the next screen by pressing the OK button or the Right button, and select the second option, Full-time AF, as shown in Figure 2-14.

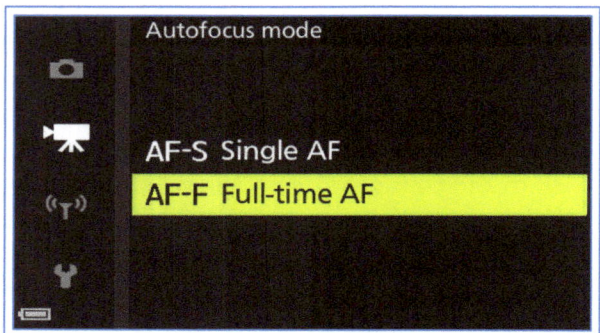

Figure 2-14. Full-time AF Highlighted for Autofocus Mode

6. Press the OK button to confirm this selection. This option will cause the camera to adjust its focus continuously as the distance from the camera to your main subject changes. Then, if you want, make sure Electronic VR and Zoom Microphone are turned on. (If you are using a tripod, turn Electronic VR off.) Exit from the menu system by pressing the Menu button.

7. Now compose the shot the way you want it, and when you're ready, press the red Movie button once.

(That button is near the top of the camera's back, below the AE-L/AF-L button.) You don't need to hold the button down; just press and release it. The camera's display will blank out briefly, then it will show a red REC indicator at the upper left and the minutes and seconds remaining for your recording at the lower right, as shown in Figure 2-15.

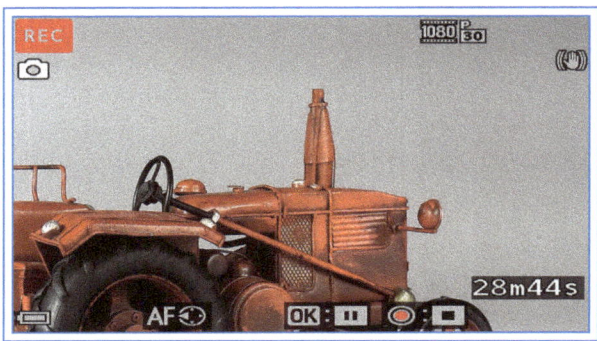

Figure 2-15. Camera's Screen During Video Recording

The camera will keep recording until it reaches a recording limit or until you press the red button again to stop the recording. Don't be concerned about the level of the sound that is being recorded, because you have no control over the audio volume while recording (unless you are using an external microphone, as discussed in Chapter 8).

The camera will automatically adjust the exposure as lighting conditions change. As noted earlier, with the Full-time Autofocus option turned on, the camera will continue to adjust its focus as needed, when the distance to the main subject changes.

One other point that's not specific to the Coolpix P950: Unless you have a good reason to do otherwise, try to hold the camera as steady as possible (use a tripod or monopod if possible), and don't zoom unnecessarily or move the camera except in very smooth, slow motions, such as a pan (side-to-side motion) to take in a wide scene gradually. Video from a jerkily moving camera can be very disconcerting to the viewer.

Viewing Pictures and Movies

Before I delve into more advanced settings for taking still pictures and movies, as well as other matters of interest, I will discuss the basics of viewing your images in the camera.

Chapter 2: Basic Operations

Review While in Shooting Mode

Every time you take a still picture, the recorded image will show up on the screen (or in the viewfinder if it's in use) for a short time, if you have the Setup menu's Monitor Settings option set to turn on the Image Review function. I'll discuss that setting in Chapter 7. By default, your image will stay on the display for about one second after you take a new picture.

Reviewing Images in Playback Mode

To review images that were taken previously, enter playback mode by pressing the Playback button, marked with a small triangle icon, to the right side of the LCD screen. You can then scroll through the recorded images using the Left and Right or Up and Down buttons on the multi selector or by turning the multi selector dial (the dial that surrounds the OK button). You can enlarge any image using the zoom lever on top of the camera, and you can scroll around in the enlarged image using the direction buttons. You can speed through the images by holding down any one of the four direction buttons.

If you have used the continuous-shooting features of the camera, you may see some images labeled with an OK followed by a colon and a triangle at the bottom center, as seen in Figure 2-16.

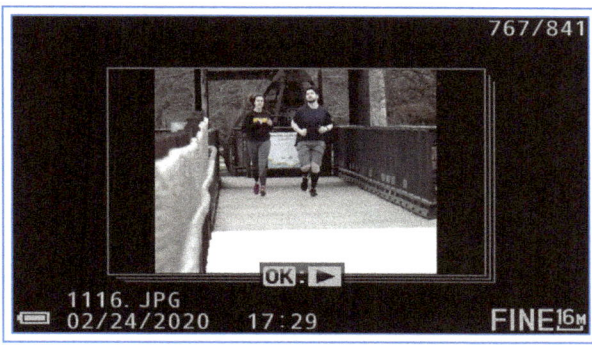

Figure 2-16. Burst of Continuous Shots Displayed as Group

In those cases, you can press the OK button to "open" a series of continuous shots, and use the direction buttons to move among the shots in that series. To return to the main viewing screen so you can see other images and series of images, press the Up button. (I'll discuss playback options in more detail in Chapter 6.)

Playing Movies

To play back motion pictures, move through the recorded images by the methods described above until you find an image with an icon at the lower right of the screen showing a movie format such as 1080p, and a file name that ends in .mp4, as shown in Figure 2-17.

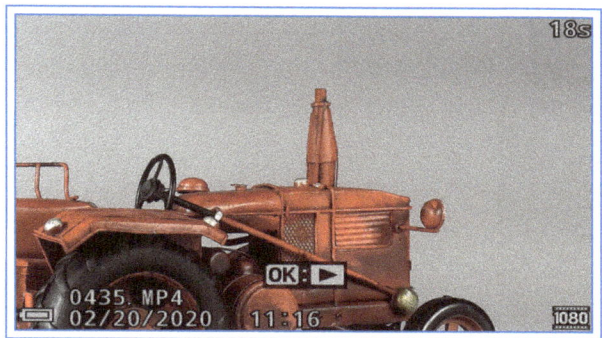

Figure 2-17. Movie Ready to Play in Camera

While the frame from the movie is displayed on the screen, press the OK button and the movie will start playing on the LCD, or in the electronic viewfinder if that display option is active instead of the LCD.

At the bottom left of the display there will be a line of DVR-like controls, as seen in Figure 2-18.

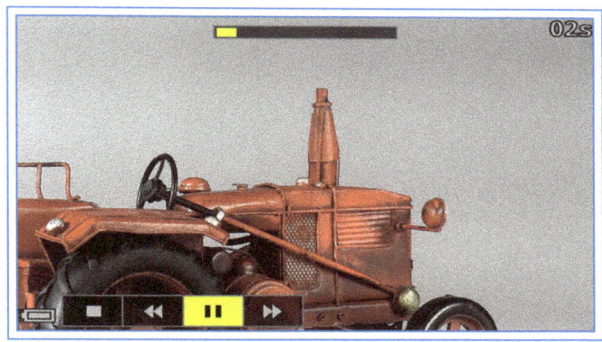

Figure 2-18. Movie Playback Controls on Display

Scroll through the line of controls using the direction buttons on the multi selector and press the OK button to activate one. You also can turn the multi selector dial to the right to fast-forward or to the left to rewind. You can raise or lower the volume of the audio by turning the zoom lever (surrounding the shutter button) toward the T position (louder) or the W position (softer). You will see a little set of volume "waves" increase or decrease next to a speaker icon at the lower right of the screen when you adjust the sound in this way. Note, though, that you cannot adjust the sound with this control if the camera is connected to a TV set; in that case, you must use the TV's volume control to change the sound level.

If you want to play the movies on a computer or edit them with video-editing software, they will import nicely into software such as iMovie for the Macintosh or any other program for Mac or Windows that can deal with video files with the extension .mp4. For some Windows-based video editing software, you may need to convert the P950's movie files to the .avi format before importing them into the software. You can do so with a program such as mp4cam2avi, which can be found on the internet at http://mp4cam2avi.sourceforge.net/. You also can use the ViewNX-Movie Editor software that is available for download from Nikon as part of the ViewNX-i package.

I will discuss more options for playing movies and editing them in the camera in Chapter 8.

Chapter 3: The Shooting Modes

So far, I have discussed setting up the camera for quick shots, relying on Auto mode for taking pictures with settings controlled mostly by the camera's automation. As with other sophisticated digital cameras, though, the Coolpix P950 has a wide range of settings available, particularly for shooting still images. One of the goals of this book is to provide guidance about this range of features. To get started, I will turn my attention to the P950's several shooting modes, which provide you with many options for your photography.

To record still images, you need to select one of the available shooting modes: Auto, Program, Shutter Priority, Aperture Priority, Manual exposure, User Settings, Creative, Bird-watching, Moon, or Scene. So far, I have discussed the use of the Auto mode. Now I will describe the others, after some review of the first. (The Movie Manual mode, used for recording movies, is discussed in Chapter 8.)

Auto Mode

The Auto shooting mode is a good choice if you need to have the camera ready for a quick shot, maybe in an environment with fast-paced events when you won't have much time to fuss with settings.

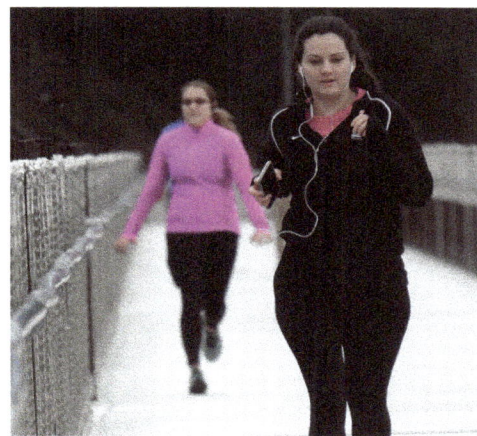

Figure 3-1. Auto Mode Example

For example, in Figure 3-1, I used this mode to grab a quick shot of a pair of runners coming toward me on a pedestrian bridge across the river. In this shooting mode, the camera does not try to figure out what kind of scene it is photographing, though it will detect human faces and focus on them if possible.

To set this mode, turn the mode dial, on top of the camera to the right of the viewfinder, to the green camera icon, as shown in Figure 3-2.

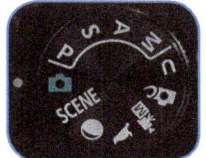

Figure 3-2. Mode Dial at Auto

With this mode, the camera makes several decisions for you and limits your options in some ways. For example, you can't set ISO or white balance to any value other than Auto, and you can't choose the metering method, use exposure bracketing, or use the Picture Control settings to alter the appearance of your images. In addition, you cannot select continuous shooting. The camera will not use its full range of shutter speeds; it is limited to a range between 1/2000 second and one second.

There are still a few settings you can control, however. For instance, you can choose any options for Image Size and Image Quality, including the Raw format for still images; you can use exposure compensation; and you can select any of five available modes for the built-in flash (if you have raised the flash unit). You also can select macro (close-up) autofocus or infinity autofocus as well as normal autofocus; and you can select manual focus. You also can use the self-timer, remote control and smile timer options. My recommendation is to set Image Size to the maximum of 4608 x 3456 pixels and Image Quality to Fine, and use the other available settings (such as exposure compensation and flash mode) as needed.

Program Mode

Choose this option by turning the mode dial to the P slot, as shown in Figure 3-3.

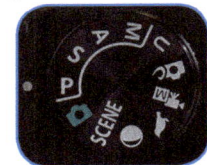

Figure 3-3. Mode Dial at Program

In this mode, the camera evaluates the light and selects both shutter speed and aperture to produce an exposure that the camera's programming considers to be normal. The camera will select an aperture within its full range of f/2.8 to f/8.0, though some aperture values are not available when the lens is zoomed in, as discussed in connection with Aperture Priority mode, later in this chapter.

The camera will select a shutter speed from 30 seconds to 1/2000 second, though the slowest shutter speed available varies with the current ISO setting. For example, when ISO is set to 100, the camera can use a shutter speed of 30 seconds, but at ISO 1600, the slowest shutter speed available in this shooting mode is two seconds.

The Program shooting mode lets you control many of the settings available with the camera, but not shutter speed and aperture. However, even though you can't directly set those two values, you can override the camera's automatic exposure to a fair extent by using exposure compensation, the flexible program feature, and exposure bracketing.

I discussed exposure compensation in Chapter 2, and I'll explain exposure bracketing in Chapter 4. Flexible program is the name Nikon uses for what is sometimes called "Program Shift" for other cameras. This option lets you adjust the values the camera selects in Program mode for shutter speed and aperture. For example, if the camera selects, say, 1/60 second at f/4.5, the flexible program feature will find equivalent combinations that result in the same exposure, such as 1/50 second at f/5.0, 1/40 second at f/5.6, or 1/30 second at f/6.3. To use this feature, when the camera is in Program mode, aim at your subject and turn the command dial (the wheel at the top right corner of the camera's back) to find an equivalent pair of shutter speed and aperture values.

When the camera is using one of these equivalent match-ups of settings rather than the originally chosen settings, it displays an asterisk at the upper right of the letter P that signifies Program mode in the upper left of the display, as seen in Figure 3-4.

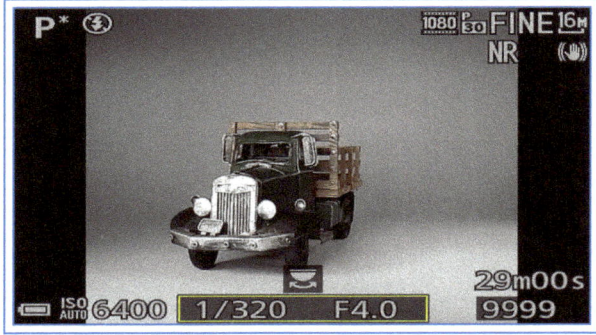

Figure 3-4. Symbol for Flexible Program on Shooting Screen

To cancel flexible program, turn the command dial back to reset the original shutter speed and aperture, select a different shooting mode, or turn off the camera.

The flexible program feature is useful in several situations. For example, you may want to see what the "normal" settings are and then see if you can use a wider aperture to achieve a blurred background, or a faster shutter speed to stop the action or prevent blur from camera motion. And, when you're experimenting with the camera to see what it is capable of, it can be helpful to try various combinations of aperture and shutter speed to see which combinations give you the best results in different situations. With a digital camera, there's no added cost for trying these different approaches, and flexible program is a useful way to experiment.

One way to look at Program mode is that it greatly expands the choices available through the Shooting menu. You will be able to make choices involving white balance, ISO sensitivity, metering method, autofocus mode, continuous shooting, and others. I won't discuss all of those choices here; if you want to explore that topic, go to the discussion of the Shooting menu in Chapter 4 and check out all of the different selections that are available to you.

Shutter Priority Mode

Select Shutter Priority mode by setting the mode dial to the S indicator, as shown in Figure 3-5.

Chapter 3: The Shooting Modes | 21

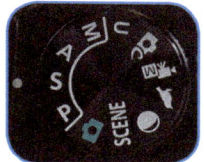

Figure 3-5. Mode Dial at Shutter Priority

In this shooting mode, you set the shutter speed and the camera will set the corresponding aperture in order to achieve a proper exposure. In Shutter Priority mode, you can set the shutter for intervals ranging from 30 seconds to 1/4000 of a second, although the camera has built-in limitations on the use of the fastest and slowest shutter speeds.

For example, if the ISO is set above 3200, the slowest shutter speed available is 15 seconds, and if the aperture is set to f/2.8, the fastest shutter speed available is 1/2000 second. In addition, the zoom range of the lens has a limiting effect on the availability of the fastest shutter speeds. For example, the fastest shutter speed available when the lens is zoomed fully in to the telephoto position is 1/2500 second. The chart in Table 3-1 sets forth some of these limitations.

Table 3-1.	Limits on Shutter Speed Settings in S and M Modes
Slowest Shutter Speed	**ISO Value**
30 seconds	100-3200
15 seconds	6400
Fastest Shutter Speed	**Aperture Value**
1/4000 second	f/6.3 - f/8.0*
1/2500 second	f/8.0**
1/3200 second	f/4.5 - f/5.6*
1/2500 second	f/3.5 – f/4.0
1/2000 second	f/2.8 – f/3.2

* At wide-angle zoom setting

** At telephoto zoom setting

If you are photographing fast action like a baseball swing or a race at a track meet and you want to stop the action with a minimum of blur, you will need a fast shutter speed, such as 1/1000 of a second. In other cases, for creative purposes, you may want to use a slow shutter speed of one second or more to achieve a certain effect, such as leaving the shutter open to capture a trail of automobiles' taillights at night.

Figures 3-6 and 3-7 illustrate the effects of different shutter speeds for two shots of the same subject, a stream of colored beads being poured into a tall pitcher. For Figure 3-6, I set the shutter speed to 1/2000 of a second. In that image, you can see individual beads, as the fast shutter speed froze the action. In Figure 3-7, where I set the shutter speed to 1/30 second, the moving beads are smoothed out into a continuous flow, with no individual beads clearly visible.

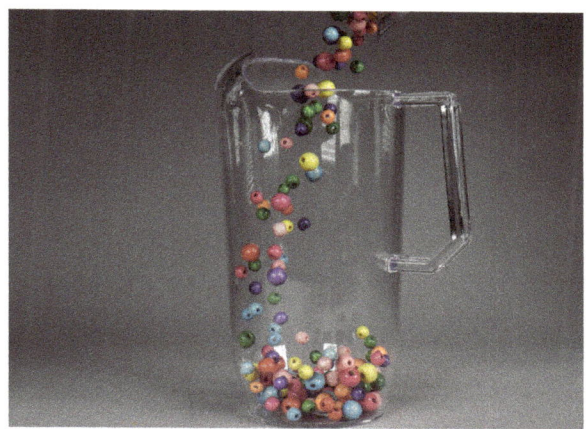

Figure 3-6. Shutter Speed Set to 1/2000 Second

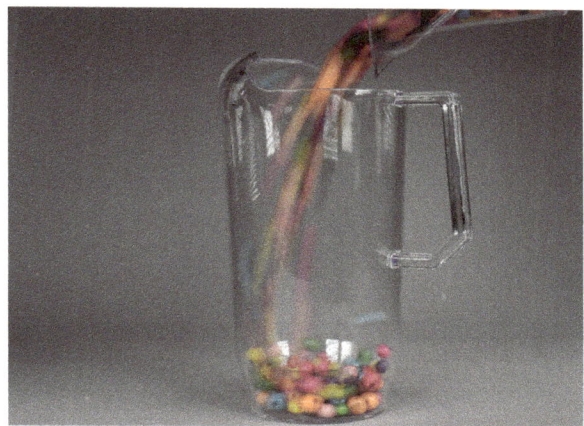

Figure 3-7. Shutter Speed Set to 1/30 Second

To set the shutter speed on the Coolpix P950, turn the command dial—the ridged dial at the top right of the camera's back, behind the power switch. (As discussed in Chapter 7, you can switch this function to the multi selector dial with the Toggle Av/Tv Selection option on the Setup menu.) The LCD (or viewfinder, if selected) will display the selected shutter speed inside a yellow rectangle at the bottom center of the screen, as shown in Figure 3-8.

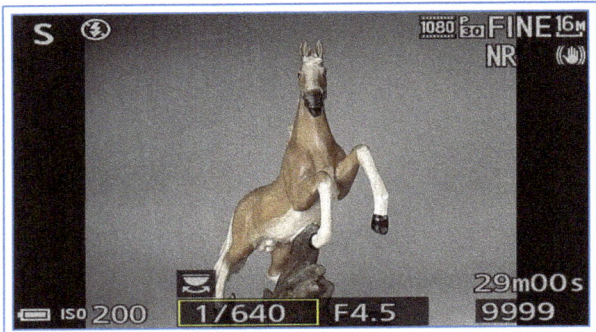

Figure 3-8. Shutter Speed Displayed on Shooting Screen

As you point the camera at scenes with varying lighting, the camera will select and display the appropriate aperture (such as f/4.5 in this example) to achieve a proper exposure.

Once you've pressed the shutter button halfway, watch the aperture number on the screen. If that number blinks, that means proper exposure at that shutter speed is not possible at any available aperture, according to the camera's calculations. For example, with a shutter speed of two seconds in a well-lighted room, the aperture number may begin to blink, indicating that proper exposure is not possible. The camera will still let you take the picture, despite having blinked the number to warn you. The camera is saying, in effect, "Maybe you shouldn't do this, but that's your business. If you want an overly bright picture for some reason, help yourself." (This situation is less likely to take place when the camera is in Aperture Priority mode, because in that mode, there is a wide range of shutter speeds for the camera to choose from—a range from 30 seconds to 1/4000 second in some situations, depending on factors such as ISO, aperture, and continuous-shooting settings.)

When you are setting shutter speed, the fractions of a second are easy to read because they are displayed as standard fractions, such as 1/5 or 1/200. Some of the longer times are a bit harder to read; the camera displays them using quotation marks. So, for example, two seconds is displayed as 2", and 1.3 second is displayed as 1.3."

One feature of the shutter speed display on the Coolpix P950 is a bit confusing, at least to me. Some of the camera's shutter speeds are displayed as fractions whose denominators are decimal numbers, such as 1/1.3. I would have trouble understanding that number without doing some arithmetic, so Table 3-2 provides a brief chart that converts these few values into terms that may be easier to comprehend:

Table 3-2.	Fractional Shutter Speed Equivalents
1/2.5	= 0.4 = 2/5 second
1/1.6	= 0.625 = 5/8 second
1/1.3	= 0.77 = 10/13 second (0.8 sec)

Finally, there is one other limitation on available shutter speeds. When you have selected one of the continuous-shooting options from the Continuous item on the Shooting menu, that setting imposes a restriction on what shutter speeds can be set. For example, if you have selected Continuous H, which causes the camera to shoot in a rapid burst, the slowest shutter speed available is 1/30 second.

Aperture Priority Mode

Aperture Priority mode, represented by the A setting on the mode dial as shown in Figure 3-9, is the inverse of Shutter Priority. In this mode, you select an aperture value and the camera selects a corresponding shutter speed to achieve a proper exposure, within a range of 1/2000 second to 30 seconds, with some limitations involving ISO and other factors. (For example, a shutter speed of 30 seconds is available in this mode only when ISO is set to 100.)

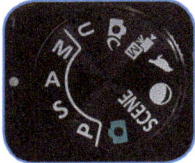

Figure 3-9. Mode Dial at Aperture Priority

The camera's aperture is a measure of the current width of its opening that lets in light to create the image. This width is stated numerically in f-stops. For the Coolpix P950, the range of f-stops is from f/2.8 (wide open) to f/8.0 (most narrow), though this range is limited in some circumstances, as discussed below. The amount of light that is let into the camera to create an image is controlled by the combination of aperture (how wide open the lens is) and shutter speed (how long the shutter remains open to let in the light).

For some purposes, you may want to control the width of the aperture, but let the camera choose the corresponding shutter speed, so you can control the depth of field. Depth of field is a measure of how well a camera is able to keep multiple objects or subjects in focus at different distances. For example, say you have three subjects lined up so you can see all of them, but they are standing at different distances—5, 7, and 9 feet (1.5, 2.1, and 2.7 meters) from the camera. If the camera's depth of field is shallow at a particular focal length, such as five feet (1.5 meters), then, if you focus on the subject at that distance, the other two will be out of focus and blurry. But if the camera's depth of field when focused at five feet is broad, then it may be possible for all subjects to be in sharp focus in your photograph, even if the focus is set for the subject at five feet.

The wider the camera's aperture is, the more shallow its depth of field is at a given focal length. So in the example discussed above, if you have the camera's aperture set to its widest opening, f/2.8, the depth of field will be relatively shallow, and it will be possible to keep fewer items in focus at varying distances from the camera. If the aperture is set to the narrowest, f/8.0, the depth of field will be greater, and it will be possible to have more items in focus at varying distances.

It is hard to illustrate this effect with a camera like the Coolpix P950, for a couple of reasons. First, the image sensor, where the light is gathered to form the image, is relatively small, which results in the depth of field being relatively deep at all apertures. Second, the widest aperture available is f/2.8, whereas some compact cameras have lenses that open as wide as f/2.0, or even f/1.4. With such cameras it is easier to achieve a blurred background, because the depth of field can be quite shallow at such a wide aperture.

With the P950, the widest aperture you can shoot with is f/2.8, and that aperture is available only when the lens is zoomed back to its extreme wide-angle setting, where depth of field is greater. If you zoom the lens in to a telephoto setting, the maximum aperture decreases steadily. At the maximum zoom range, the widest aperture available is only f/6.5, which is not far from the narrowest aperture of f/8.0.

Despite the difficulty of demonstrating the effects of using different apertures, Figures 3-10 and 3-11 illustrate these effects to some extent with two images taken at the same time and in the same location. For both images, the lens was zoomed out to its full wide-angle setting of 24mm. The first image was taken at an aperture setting of f/2.8, the widest possible setting; the second one was taken at f/8.0, the narrowest aperture setting. In both cases, I focused on the mannequin in the foreground.

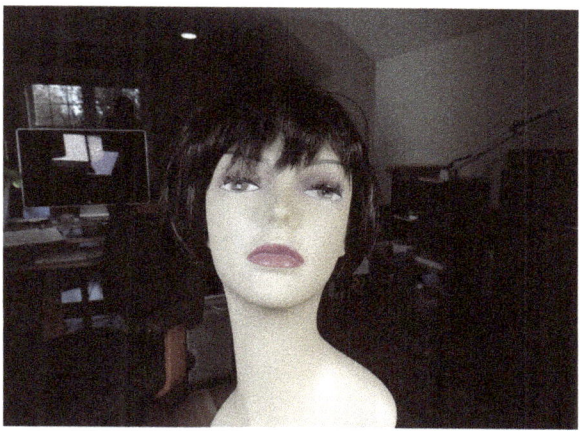

Figure 3-10. Aperture Set to f/2.8

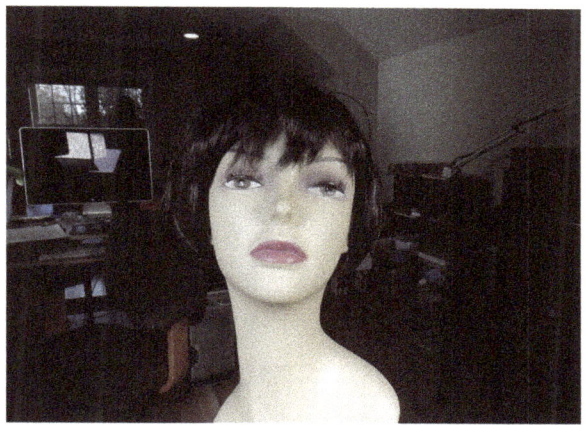

Figure 3-11. Aperture Set to f/8.0

As you should be able to see by looking at the window in the background, in Figure 3-10, with the wider aperture, the background is somewhat blurred because the depth of field is relatively shallow at that setting. In Figure 3-11, on the other hand, the background is in sharper focus because the depth of field is greater at the narrower aperture setting.

If you want to capture the sharpest image possible, especially when you have subjects at varying distances from the lens and you want them all to be in focus, you may want to control the aperture and make sure it is set to the highest number (narrowest opening) possible. It also helps to have the lens zoomed back toward its wide-angle setting and to be somewhat distant from the subject.

On the other hand, there are times when photographers prize a shallow depth of field. This situation arises often in the case of outdoor portraits. For example, you may want to take a photo of a person standing outdoors with a background of trees and bushes, and possibly some other, more distracting objects, such as a swing set or a tool shed. If you can achieve a narrow depth of field, you can have the person's face in sharp focus, but leave the background quite blurry and indistinct. This effect is sometimes called "bokeh," a Japanese term describing an aesthetically pleasing blurriness of the background.

To achieve the greatest blurring of the background, you should try to use a wide aperture, zoom the lens in as much as possible, and get as close to the subject as possible. It also is helpful to have as much distance as possible between the main subject and the background.

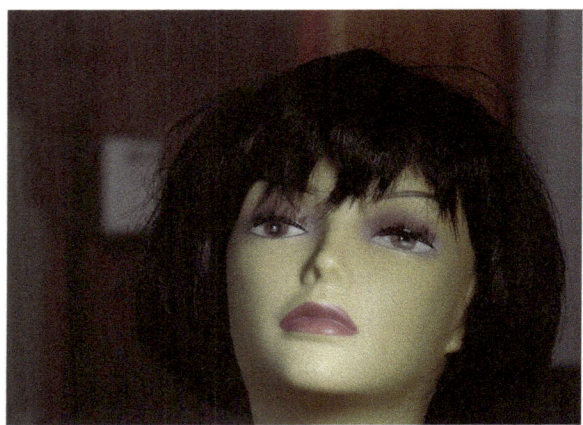

Figure 3-12. Background Blur from Long Zoom Setting

Figure 3-12 is an example using this effect. The blurriness of the background can reduce the distraction factor from unwanted objects and highlight the sharply focused image of your subject.

To set the aperture, once you have moved the mode dial to the A setting, aim the camera at your subject and turn the multi selector dial to change the aperture. The number of the f-stop will appear inside a yellow rectangle at the bottom center of the screen. The shutter speed chosen by the camera will show up also, to the left of the aperture, as seen in Figure 3-13. When you press the shutter button halfway, the camera will lock in the selected shutter speed.

As I noted above, not all apertures are available at all times. In particular, the widest aperture, f/2.8, is available only when the lens is zoomed out to its wide-angle setting (zoom lever moved toward the W). At the highest zoom levels, the widest aperture available is f/6.5. To see an illustration of this point, here is a quick test. Zoom the lens out by moving the zoom lever all the way to the left, toward the W. Then select Aperture Priority mode and choose an aperture of f/2.8 by turning the multi selector dial all the way to the left. Now zoom the lens in by moving the zoom lever to the right, toward the T. When you release the lever, the aperture displayed at the bottom of the screen will change to f/6.5. If you try to reset the aperture to f/2.8 after the zoom action is done, you will see that the lowest aperture number you can set is f/6.5, because that is the widest aperture available on the P950 at the telephoto zoom level. (The aperture will change back to f/2.8 if you move the zoom back to the wide-angle setting.)

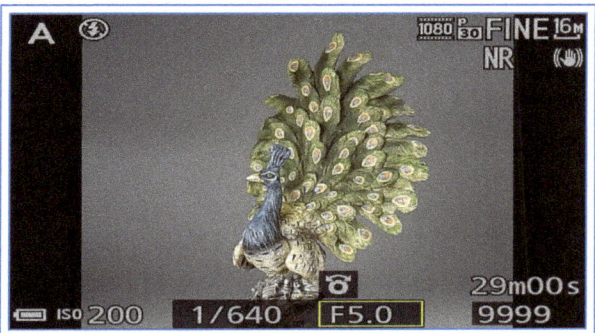

Figure 3-13. Aperture Value Displayed on Shooting Screen

Manual Exposure Mode

The Coolpix P950 has a fully manual mode for control of aperture and shutter speed, which helps you enjoy creative control over exposure decisions.

This mode is useful when you want to use settings that result in an unusual effect, such as an abnormally dark image. For example, I used Manual exposure mode for Figure 3-14 to photograph a bust of Cleopatra against a bright background. I experimented with various Manual mode settings to find the exposure that resulted in this image, which was shot at f/4.5 for 1/8 second, with ISO set to 100.

I also often use Manual mode to take a series of photos at different exposures to create HDR (high dynamic range) images using special software. I will discuss that process later in this chapter, in the discussion of the Backlighting/HDR setting of Scene mode.

Chapter 3: The Shooting Modes | 25

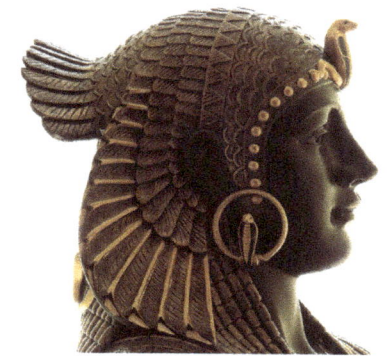

Figure 3-14. Manual Exposure Example

To use Manual exposure mode, set the mode dial to the M indicator, as shown in Figure 3-15. You now have to control both shutter speed and aperture by setting them yourself.

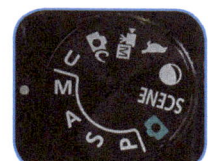

Figure 3-15. Mode Dial at Manual

To set these values, first look at the camera's display and find where the shutter speed (such as 1/800) and aperture (such as F5.0) are displayed at the bottom of the screen, as shown in Figure 3-16.

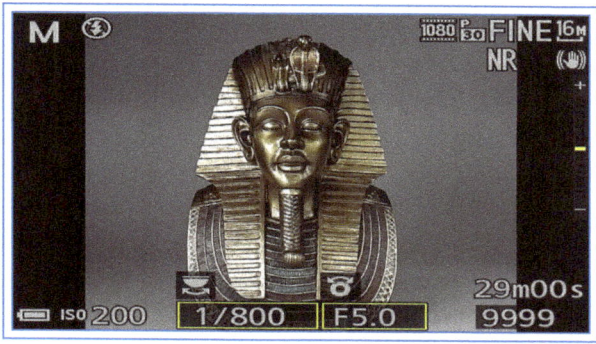

Figure 3-16. Shooting Screen in Manual Exposure Mode

At the bottom of the display is the shutter speed on the left, inside a yellow rectangle. Above that value is a curved arrow beneath an icon that represents the command dial. These icons mean that the shutter speed value is controlled by the command dial (the wheel at the top of the camera's back, behind the power switch). To the right of that value is the value for the aperture, or f-stop, inside another rectangle. Above that value is an icon showing a dial that is oriented vertically; that icon represents the multi selector dial, on the back of the camera surrounding the OK button.

To adjust the settings, turn the command dial until you have selected the shutter speed you want, and turn the multi selector dial to set your desired aperture. As you adjust these values, watch the vertical scale that appears at the right of the screen, as shown in Figure 3-16.

You will see the tick marks turn yellow, either above or below the scale's center point, as the values change. When the exposure is set as the camera judges to be normal, there will be a lone tick mark in the center of the scale, as shown in Figure 3-16.

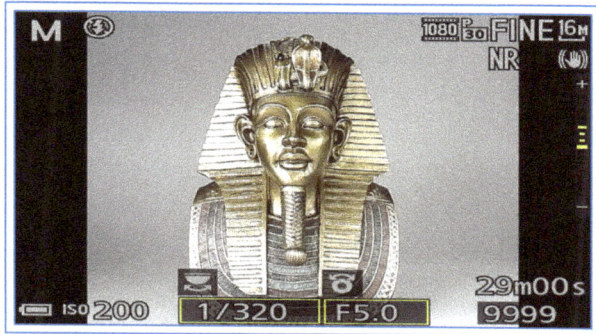

Figure 3-17. Manual Mode with Exposure Too Bright

If the marks above the center of the scale turn yellow, as in Figure 3-17, the exposure is too bright; if they turn yellow below the center, it is too dark. If the setting becomes more extreme than the scale can indicate, a yellow triangle appears at the top or bottom of the scale, indicating that the scale's limit has been exceeded, as shown in Figure 3-18.

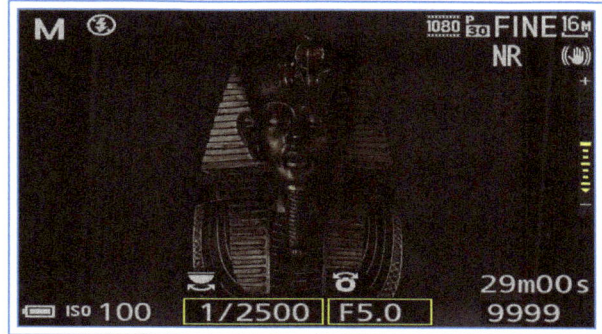

Figure 3-18. Manual Mode with Exposure too Dark

If you are shooting in dim light, such as indoors or in a shadowed area, you may find it impossible to center the yellow tick mark on the exposure scale by adjusting the shutter speed and aperture unless you use a very slow shutter speed, such as one second or longer. If you are handholding the camera, you won't be able to hold it steady for more than about 1/30 second, so it will be difficult to get a clear exposure.

In that situation, you can adjust exposure by changing the ISO setting. I will discuss ISO in more detail in Chapter 4, because it is an option found on the Shooting menu. Briefly, ISO is a setting that controls the sensitivity of the camera's digital sensor. The higher the ISO value, the more sensitive the sensor is to light. With higher ISO values, you can achieve a normal exposure with narrower apertures and faster shutter speeds.

With the advanced shooting modes, including Manual, you can use the Auto ISO settings, which cause the camera to set the ISO value as needed to reach a good exposure level, within a specified range of ISO values. If you use an Auto ISO setting in Manual mode, you can choose the aperture and shutter speed you want, and still have the camera achieve an automatic exposure setting by varying the ISO value, if possible under current lighting conditions.

You also can use the ISO Sensitivity menu item to select a specific value such as ISO 400, 800, or even higher, as shown in Figure 3-19.

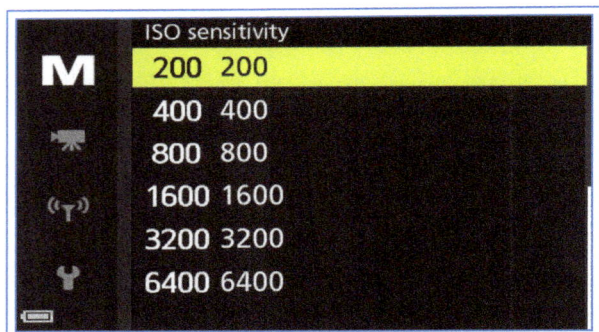

Figure 3-19. ISO Sensitivity Menu

Of course, you don't have to adjust ISO or other values in an effort to center the indicator on the exposure scale; that scale is there only to give you an idea of how the camera would meter the scene. You may want parts of the scene (or the whole image) to be darker or lighter than the metering system would indicate to be "correct." In Manual mode, the settings for aperture and shutter speed are independent of each other. When you change one, the other one stays unchanged until you change it manually. The camera is leaving the creative decision about exposure entirely up to you, even if the resulting photograph would be washed out by excessive exposure or underexposed to the point of near-blackness.

As with Aperture Priority mode, the range of available apertures in Manual exposure mode varies as the lens is zoomed to various focal lengths. Also, the range of shutter speeds has certain limits, as listed earlier in Table 3-1 in the discussion of Shutter Priority mode. For example, the slowest shutter speed available at ISO 6400 is 15 seconds; at ISO 3200, the slowest is 30 seconds.

However, there are longer exposures possible in this shooting mode, even with the ISO set as high as 1600. In Manual mode, the shutter speed settings of Time and Bulb are available, when ISO is set to 1600 or lower. With the Time setting, the shutter opens when you fully press and release the shutter button, and it closes when you fully press and release the shutter button a second time. With the Bulb setting, the shutter opens when you press the shutter button down, and it stays open until you release. The maximum exposure with either of these settings is 60 seconds. Neither setting is available when continuous shooting is activated.

The Auto Flash and Slow Sync flash modes are not available with Manual exposure mode.

Scene Modes

The Coolpix P950 offers several of what I will call scene modes. The terminology can be a bit confusing, because the camera's menus and documentation use the word "scene" in several similar and overlapping contexts. First, there are two modes that occupy slots marked by icons on the mode dial: Bird-watching and Moon. Next, there is another slot on the mode dial marked SCENE. When you select that setting, you can press the Menu button to the lower left of the multi selector and scroll through a list of 19 specific scene settings: Portrait, Landscape, Sports, Night Portrait, Party/Indoor, Beach, Snow, Sunset, Dusk/Dawn, Night Landscape, Close-up, Food, Fireworks Show, Backlighting, Easy Panorama, Pet Portrait, Selective Color, Multiple Exposure Lighten, and Time-lapse Movie. I will discuss all of these scene settings individually, but first I will provide some general remarks about these shooting mode options.

Scene modes are different from the other shooting modes I have discussed up to this point. These modes do not have a single defining feature, such as permitting control over one or more aspects of exposure. Instead, when you select a scene shooting mode, you are in effect telling the camera what sort of environment the picture is being taken in, and what type of image you are looking for, and you are letting the camera decide what settings to use to produce that result.

Some photographers may not like scene modes because they take some creative decisions away from you and limit your options in some ways. For example, you will find that the Shooting menu options are sharply limited when the mode dial is turned to the SCENE setting or either of the scene modes with slots on the mode dial, such as Bird-watching. For example, you cannot set the white balance, but must rely on the camera's Auto White Balance setting, which may not always properly evaluate the existing light source. In most cases, you cannot select features such as continuous shooting, and you can't choose a metering mode or an ISO setting.

Despite the limitations, though, I find the scene settings useful in certain situations. You don't have to use these settings only for their labeled purposes; you may find that some of them are well-suited for shooting scenarios you are regularly faced with. For example, you may find the Sports setting works well for shots of children at play, or that the Sunset setting, which emphasizes red hues, is great for images in a particular garden that is rich with reddish plants and flowers. The Bird-watching setting can work well for taking images of various sorts of wildlife, not just birds.

You need to know something about each of these options to decide whether it's one you would want to select. In general, a given scene setting carries with it a variety of values, including things like focus mode, flash status, range of shutter speeds, sensitivity to various colors, and others. I will discuss each of the scene settings so you can make informed choices. I will first discuss the settings that have their own slots on the mode dial, followed by the settings that are grouped under the SCENE setting on the dial. I will include sample images for some of the most commonly used options.

Moon Mode

This is the setting indicated by the moon icon on the mode dial next to the SCENE setting, as seen in Figure 3-20.

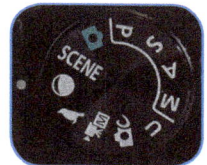

Figure 3-20. Mode Dial at Moon

The Coolpix P950, with its great optical zoom range, is a natural for shooting images of the moon without having to attach the camera to a telescope. With the Moon setting, Nikon has provided a shortcut to using appropriate settings for these shots.

With this option, the camera disables the flash and turns on the self-timer to three seconds so the camera will have time to settle down after you press the shutter button, to avoid camera shake. You can change this setting to ten seconds or turn the self-timer off if you want. You can use exposure compensation, which is useful if the moon appears too bright or too dim because of its phase. If you have the focus mode selector set for autofocus, focus is fixed in the center of the frame, at the infinity setting. You can switch to manual focus using the focus mode selector, if you prefer. You can set Image Quality to Fine or Normal, but not to Raw.

The camera also uses two special settings to help with this type of shot. First, as shown in Figure 3-21, when the lens is zoomed out to its wide-angle setting, the camera places a small rectangle in the center of the focus frame.

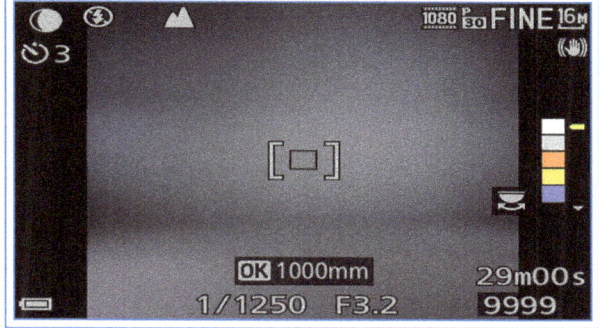

Figure 3-21. Shooting Screen in Moon Mode

By default, that small inner frame represents the viewing angle when the lens is zoomed in to 1000mm. You can place that frame over the moon with the lens zoomed back to its wide-angle setting, then press the OK button to cause the camera to zoom immediately to the 1000mm focal length. In that way, you can easily locate the moon in the sky and zoom in on it with confidence that you will center it in the image.

To select the focal length that the camera will zoom to when you press the OK button in Moon mode, go to the Shooting menu (which is called the Moon menu in this mode), and select either 1000mm or 2000mm for the Focal Length Selection item.

Also, the camera places on the right side of the screen a scale with a variety of hues, as seen in Figure 3-21. This is not a sliding scale, but, instead, is like a set of virtual color filters, which you can move through by turning the command dial. If you select the top option, you will view the moon with no color change. You can try any of the other selections to enhance your view of the moon and its craters. The yellow filter is good for enhancing the overall contrast of the image, while the blue filter can be used to reduce the glare. My suggestion is to switch through all of the options while you are viewing the moon, to see which ones yield better results for the sort of image you are looking for. The hue option you choose for the Moon setting will stay in place even after the camera is turned off and then on again.

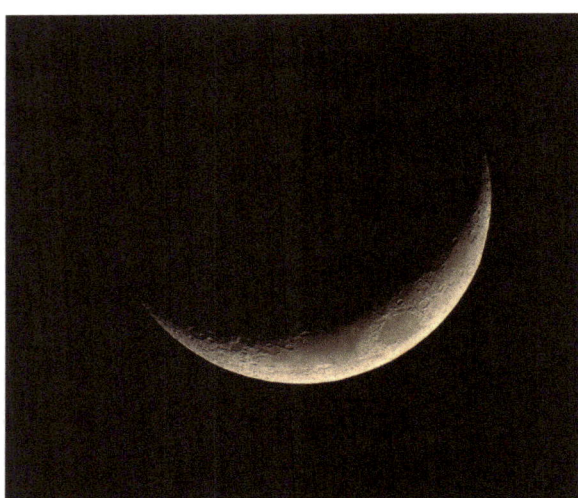

Figure 3-22. Moon, in Moon Mode, 1/30 Sec, f/6.5, ISO 125

In Figure 3-22, I used this setting to capture an image of the moon in its first quarter. I placed the camera on a sturdy tripod and used the self-timer with the three-second setting. The camera used a shutter speed of 1/30 second at f/6.5 and ISO 125.

Bird-watching Mode

The next special scene mode option, Bird-watching, is indicated by the bird icon on the mode dial, as shown in Figure 3-23.

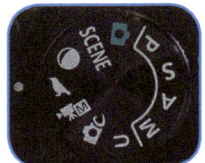

Figure 3-23. Mode Dial at Bird-watching

This setting, like the Moon option, is an important and natural one for the P950. With this mode, the camera disables the flash and turns on normal autofocus, but you can switch to infinity focus, or to manual focus if you want to adjust the focus yourself. You also can use the self-timer or exposure compensation, but you cannot set Image Quality to Raw.

You can turn on continuous shooting, so you can take a burst of shots with one shutter press, increasing the chances of capturing a good image as a bird moves around. To do that, press the Menu button and select the Bird-watching menu, represented by the bird icon at the top of the list of menu icons, as shown in Figure 3-24.

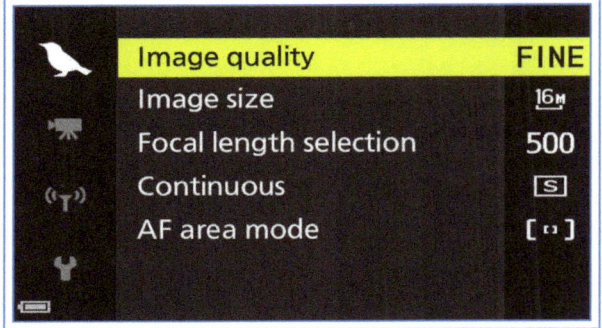

Figure 3-24. Bird-watching Menu

Press the OK or Right button to move to the next screen and select Continuous from that screen, as shown in Figure 3-25. Then, when you press the shutter button and hold it down, the camera will shoot a continuous burst of about ten shots at a rate of up to about seven frames per second.

Just as with the Moon option, when you are using a wide-angle setting, the camera places a special frame in the center of the screen to indicate the angle of view at a higher zoom setting. In this case, by default the frame shows the area that would be in view with the lens zoomed in to the 500mm point, rather than the 1000mm used by default with the Moon setting.

So, when you are trying to capture a closeup shot of a distant bird, you can start with a wide-angle view so it is easy to find the bird, and center the subject in the small frame. Then, press the OK button and the camera will automatically zoom the lens to the 500mm point, with the bird centered in the image. If you then need to zoom back to a wide-angle view, just press the zoom lever to the left to zoom out. If you want to zoom in beyond the 500mm point, you can use the zoom lever to do that, also.

Figure 3-25. Menu Options Screen for Bird-watching Mode

Also, as with the Moon mode, you can use the Focal Length Selection item on the Shooting menu in Bird-watching mode to choose a different focal length setting for the special frame: 500mm, 800mm, 1000mm, 1400mm, or 2000mm. The camera sets AF Area Mode to Manual and places a focus frame in the center the display. You can select Spot, Normal, or Wide for the size of that frame, using the AF Area Mode option on the Shooting menu in this mode. The camera silences the normal beeps and sounds made by the shutter and other operations, such as autofocus.

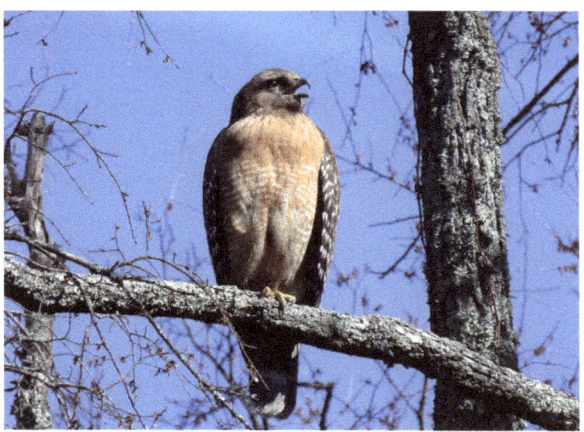

Figure 3-26. Bird-watching Example at 2000mm

In Figure 3-26, I used this setting to fire off several quick bursts of shots when this hawk settled into a perch on a tree within range of the camera, which I used with a tripod hand-held from my front yard, zooming the lens to 2000mm.

The SCENE Setting on the Mode Dial

Turning the mode dial to SCENE, as in Figure 3-27, gives you access to 19 choices of settings.

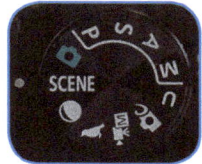

Figure 3-27. Mode Dial at Scene

You can select any one of these choices by pressing the Menu button and selecting a scene type from the menu that appears. The first screen of the Scene mode menu is shown in Figure 3-28.

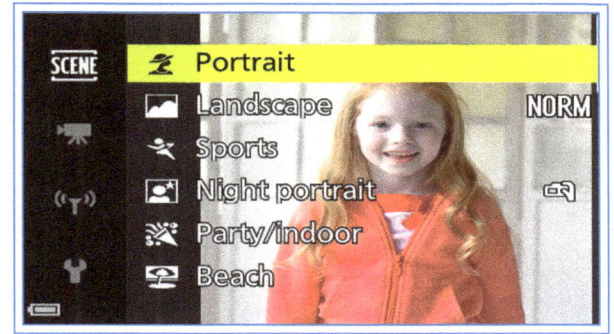

Figure 3-28. First Screen of Scene Menu

Scroll through the four screens of choices using the multi selector dial or the Up and Down buttons.

When you select any of the 19 Scene mode settings, the menu offers few other choices; that is, when you make a selection such as Sunset from the Scene menu, you cannot make any other choices except Image Size and Image Quality, with a few exceptions. The camera will make other settings as it deems appropriate for that selection. These Scene mode settings are convenient if you are faced with a certain type of photographic situation and you want the camera to make reasonable choices for that situation, but you have little control over the camera's other settings. Following are details about each of the types. I will include sample images for several of the selections.

Portrait

With the Portrait setting, the camera automatically sets itself for face detection, which means it looks for human faces and focuses on the one closest to the camera. In addition, the camera automatically applies skin softening to any faces it detects. You can pop up the flash and select any flash mode. You cannot make any changes to the autofocus mode (though, as with any shooting mode, you can choose manual focus), but you can use the self-timer or smile timer, as well as exposure compensation.

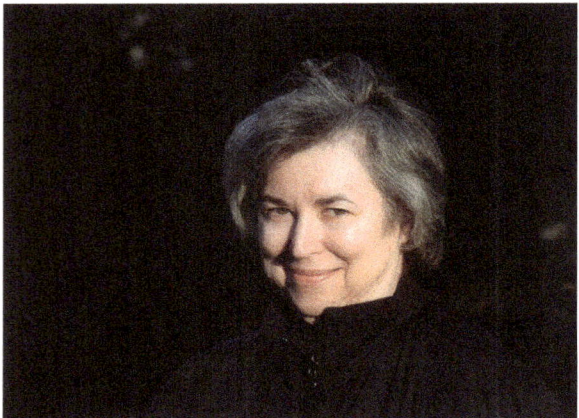

Figure 3-29. Portrait Example

Figure 3-29 is an example of an image I took with the camera on a tripod, with no flash. I zoomed the lens in to 550mm from a fair distance away, to fill the frame and blur the background.

Landscape

I use the Landscape setting often, because it is useful for views of scenery, buildings, and the like. When you first select this setting from the Scene menu, the menu displays the Landscape item, with two options: Noise Reduction Burst or Single Shot, as seen in Figure 3-30.

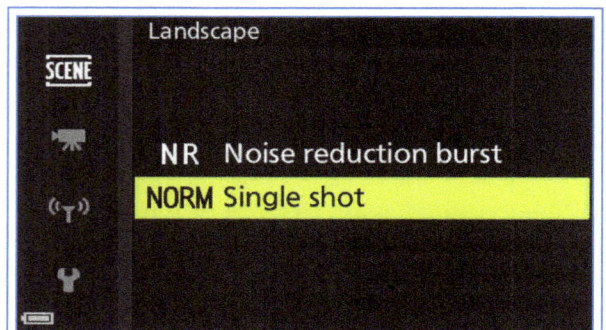

Figure 3-30. Menu Options Screen for Landscape Scene Setting

If you select Noise Reduction Burst, the camera will take a rapid series of shots at a relatively high ISO setting and merge them in the camera into a final image. The camera's internal processing will combine the individual shots so as to reduce the visual "noise" that results from using higher ISO settings. The final image will be cropped slightly because of this processing, so less of the scene will be included in the image. This setting is useful when you are taking photographs in subdued light, to reduce the noise effects caused by a higher ISO setting.

If, instead, you select the Single Shot option, the camera will operate as you would expect for a normal Landscape setting—it will take just one shot at a lower ISO setting, which likely will result in a sharper picture than one taken with the Noise Reduction Burst setting. The example in Figure 3-31 was taken using the Single Shot setting on a normally bright day.

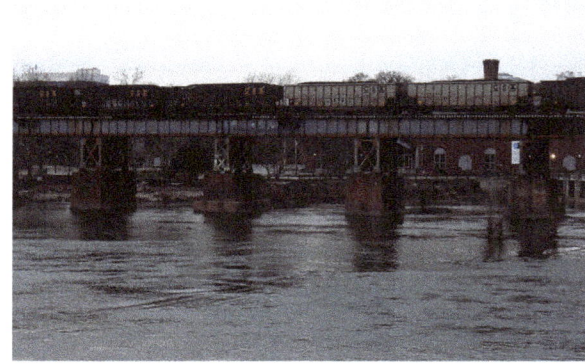

Figure 3-31. Landscape Example

Sports

The Sports setting is intended for fast-moving subjects. The camera sets itself for continuous shooting and takes a series of as many as ten images at a rate of up to seven frames per second when you hold down the shutter button, depending on conditions. The flash is forced off and focus and exposure are locked when the first image is taken, to increase the speed of the sequence of shots. You can use exposure compensation, but you cannot use the self-timer. The Sports setting is useful when you need to stop action in relatively bright lighting conditions.

For Figure 3-32, I used the Sports setting to capture an image of a person rolling through a riverfront park on a scooter on a chilly day in February. I took a burst of several shots to catch this image at a clear angle.

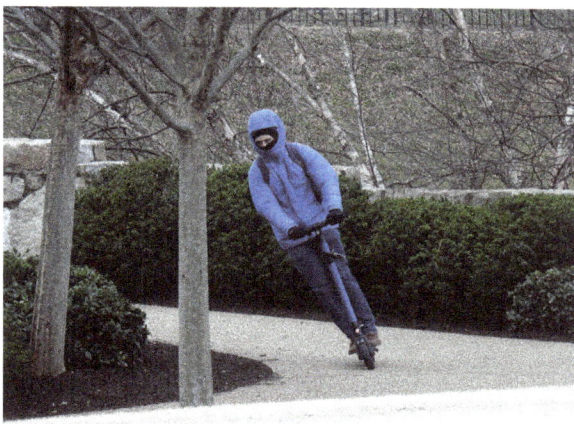

Figure 3-32. Sports Example

Night Portrait

With this setting, the camera will always use the built-in flash. The subject presumably will be close to the camera and, unlike a landscape scene, can be illuminated by the flash. If you haven't popped up the flash unit (or attached a compatible external flash to the hot shoe), the camera will display an error message until you do. The flash mode icon will show Auto with Red-eye Reduction, but the camera will choose a slow shutter speed if possible, as it does with the Slow Sync setting.

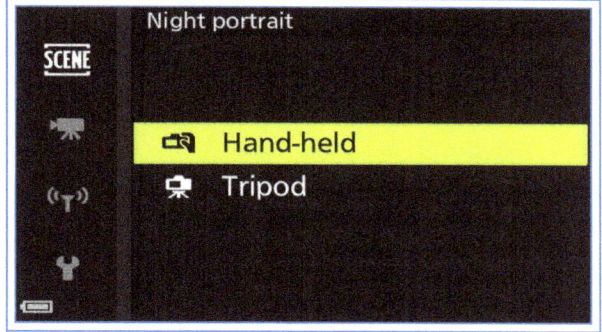

Figure 3-33. Menu Options Screen for Night Portrait Scene Setting

When you first select this option from the Scene menu, you are presented with menu choices of Hand-held or Tripod, as shown in Figure 3-33. If you select Hand-held, the camera may use a faster shutter speed than with the Tripod setting, to counteract camera shake. You can use the self-timer (or the smile timer) or exposure compensation, but you cannot change the autofocus method. If you choose Tripod, the camera will likely use a slower shutter speed. It still will use the flash.

The camera uses its face detection circuitry and attempts to find a face to focus on. If it finds a face, it automatically applies skin softening, which smooths out wrinkles and other harsh features on the skin. However, you cannot control the amount of skin softening or turn it off.

Party/Indoor

This setting is meant for indoor photos of people and rooms. In many cases, you may want to pop up the flash or attach an external flash. The flash mode is initially set to Auto with Red-eye Reduction, but you can change to another flash mode if you want to. If you don't want to use flash, you can leave the flash unit retracted, in which case the P950 will try to use a relatively slow shutter speed. In that situation, you should hold the camera very steady or place it on a tripod. (Realistically, though, you probably are not going to be setting up a tripod for candid or impromptu pictures at a party.) The camera will focus on the subject at the center of the frame.

With the Party/Indoor setting, you can use exposure compensation or the self-timer, but you cannot change the autofocus method.

Beach

With this selection, the camera optimizes its settings for an area with bright sunlight reflected from the ground. In this environment, the camera will have a tendency to underexpose the subject because the exposure meter will be measuring the brightness of the beach. If you pop up the flash, the camera will set the flash mode to Auto in order to light the subject sufficiently, and it is quite likely the flash will fire in order to enhance the brightness of the subject so it will be clearly visible against the glare of the background. You can change the flash mode if you want to. However, you do not have to pop up the flash when using the Beach setting. You can use either macro focus or normal autofocus, but you cannot select infinity autofocus. You can use the self-timer and exposure compensation.

Snow

The Snow setting is similar to Beach. The camera may use flash to compensate for the brightness of the snowy background, if you have chosen to pop up the flash unit or turned on an external unit attached to the hot shoe. The camera appears to use a greater amount of reddish hue than with the beach setting, as a balance against the bluish color temperature of a snowy scene. Other settings are similar to those for the Beach setting.

I took a few test shots of general scenes, not shown here, using both the Beach and the Snow settings. I found that the Beach setting resulted in slightly darker images, but otherwise the results were very similar.

Sunset

With this setting, the P950 disables the flash, but you can use the self-timer and exposure compensation. You cannot change the autofocus mode from infinity autofocus. The camera processes the shot to emphasize reddish tones in the rays of the late afternoon or early morning sun. Of course, you don't have to limit the use of this (or any other) scene setting by its label. If you are photographing autumn leaves, red-brick buildings, or other subjects with reds you want to emphasize, consider this setting as a tool that may be of use. For Figure 3-34, I used this setting to capture the sky over the river on a cloudy day a few minutes before sunset.

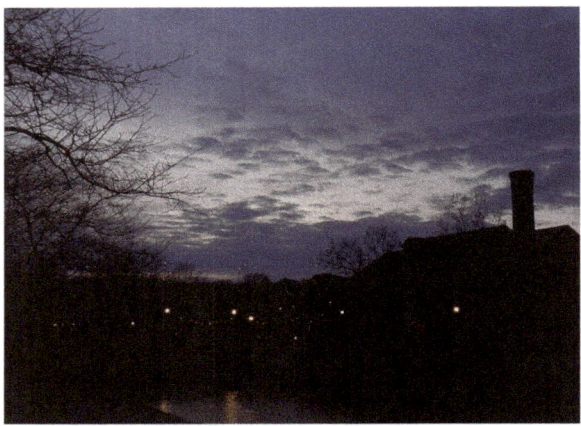

Figure 3-34. Sunset Example

Dusk/Dawn

If you take pictures before sunrise or after sunset, this is a setting to consider. The camera turns off the flash and intensifies colors to add interest to images that otherwise might be flat or washed out because of dim light. You cannot adjust most settings, though you can use exposure compensation and the self-timer. This option emphasizes the purplish or bluish tones that may be present in the twilight or early morning hours.

In Figure 3-35, I used this setting to capture the same view as in Figure 3-34, to show the differences between these two settings.

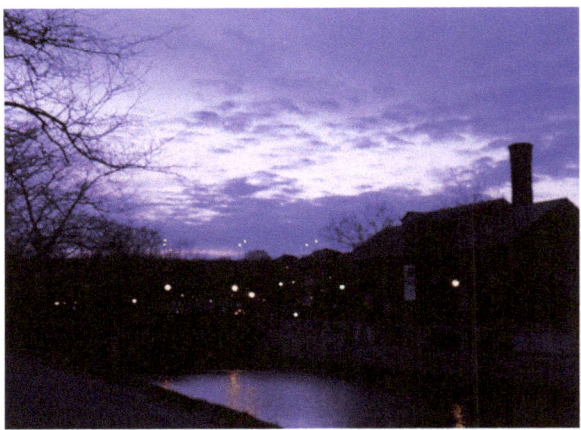

Figure 3-35. Dusk/Dawn Example

Night Landscape

This option is for use without flash at night in areas that are not brightly lighted. When you select this setting, the Shooting menu displays an option called Night Landscape, with two sub-options, as with Night Portrait: Hand-held and Tripod.

With Hand-held, the camera will take a continuous group of pictures and combine them in the camera into a single image, to overcome the effects of the high ISO setting the camera uses to take a good exposure in dim light without flash. A single image could be degraded from the visual "noise" that results from the use of high ISO values; by combining several images, the camera can create a single image using the best aspects of each, and can digitally smooth away the noise. You should try to hold the camera as steady as possible when shooting, but it will use a relatively fast shutter speed if possible, to avoid blur from camera shake.

If you choose the Tripod option from the menu, the camera will use a slower shutter speed and a lower ISO setting, to minimize noise. The use of the tripod will avoid the effects of camera shake. Of course, this setting is useful only if you actually attach the camera firmly to a tripod.

With the Night Landscape setting, the flash is forced off, but you can use exposure compensation and the self-timer. The autofocus mode is set to infinity, if you are using autofocus.

I took the image in Figure 3-36 about 20 minutes after sunset, with the camera on a tripod. The camera exposed the image for 0.6 second at ISO 100 and f/4.0.

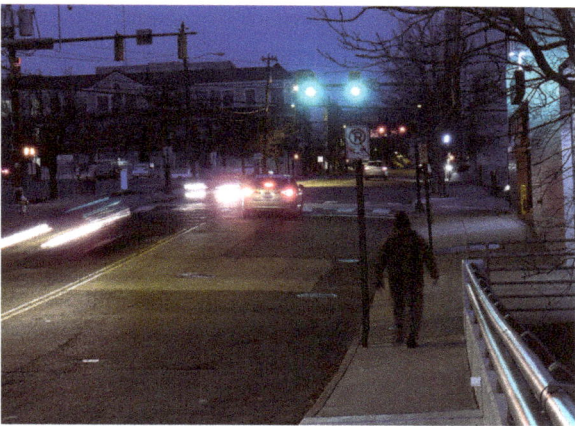

Figure 3-36. Night Landscape Example

Close-up

With this setting, the camera switches into macro autofocus mode to capture images of items close to the lens. If the lens is zoomed in to a telephoto position, when you select the Close-up setting the lens will automatically zoom back out to a position that allows the camera to focus on close subjects. (You can, however, zoom the lens back in if you want to.) You can use the self-timer or exposure compensation; you cannot, naturally enough, change the autofocus mode, which is set on macro. As with all shooting modes, though, you can choose manual focus with the focus mode selector.

The camera also sets AF Area Mode to Manual (Spot). This means you can control exactly where the focus point is placed. To do this, press the OK button in the center of the multi selector, then press the direction buttons to move the focus area around the screen so it covers the point where you want the camera to focus. You also can turn the multi selector dial to move the frame around the screen; it will move up and down as it reaches the right or left edge of the display.

If you need to use one of the direction buttons for its other function (self-timer, flash, or exposure compensation), press the OK button again, and those functions will be available. Press the OK button once more if you need to move the focus area another time. The camera also uses continuous autofocus with this setting, so it continues to adjust the focus until you press the shutter button halfway down to lock in the focus.

As with several other scene types, with Close-up the Shooting menu gives you the option of choosing Noise Reduction Burst or Single Shot. With Noise Reduction Burst, the camera takes a rapid set of shots to counter the effects of high ISO noise and forces the flash off. With the Single Shot setting, the camera takes just one image and lets you pop up the flash (or use an external flash unit) and select any flash mode. The camera also uses processing to sharpen the image's outline with added contrast.

You could, if you want, use another shooting mode, such as Program or Auto, and select macro focusing using the focus button (Down button). But, if you want to quickly set up the camera for closeup shooting, it can be convenient to have this scene setting available. You should hold the camera very steady to avoid blurring the image. Use of a tripod or monopod is the best practice, but of course that is often impractical.

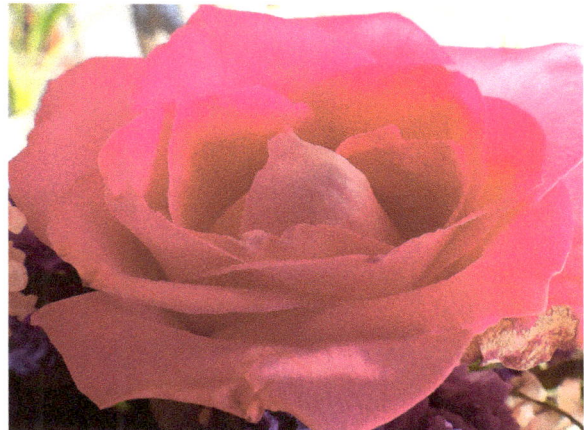

Figure 3-37. Close-up Example

In Figure 3-37, I hand-held the camera and used the Close-up setting to get a detailed view of a rose.

Food

This setting is similar to the Close-up setting, discussed above, though it does not offer Noise Reduction Burst mode; only single shots are available. The camera switches to macro focus mode and zooms the lens back to a wide-angle view so it can focus on a nearby subject. It turns on Manual (Spot) for the AF Area Mode, so you can move the focus point around, and it uses continuous autofocus. The flash is disabled, but you can use exposure compensation and the self-timer.

The one major difference from Close-up mode (apart from the lack of a burst option) is that, in Food mode, the camera places a color scale at the right side of the screen, similar to the scale shown for Moon mode in Figure 3-21, though with more colors available, and allows you to adjust the hues of your images by moving the pointer up and down along the scale using the command dial. Move the pointer toward the top for more reddish hues, and toward the bottom for more bluish ones.

This setting is suited for people who are in the habit of documenting their meals through food blogs or photographic diaries of their dining experiences. With the hue slider, you can experiment until you achieve the desired effect of emphasizing the colors of meats, vegetables, or other aspects of the meal. In Figure 3-38, I used this setting for an image of a bowl of artificial fruit.

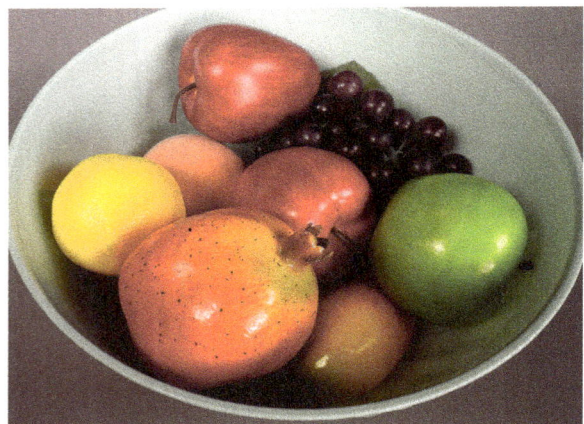

Figure 3-38. Food Example

Unless you want to leave a hue adjustment permanently in place, be sure to return the hue slider to the neutral position when you're done shooting, because the adjustments you make will remain in place the next time you choose the Food setting, even if the camera has been turned off in the meantime.

Fireworks Show

With this setting, the camera sets the focus to infinity and uses a shutter speed of four seconds so you can capture a long burst of color from a fireworks display. (You may notice that the camera uses a mathematical infinity symbol on the display for this focus mode. The camera has two focus modes called "infinity," oddly enough. It appears that this "infinity" focus mode causes the camera to focus at its farthest distance, while the other "infinity" mode, symbolized by a mountain icon, causes it to focus "near infinity.") Actually, Nikon recommends that you use manual focus with the Fireworks Show setting, so you may want to experiment with the focus options.

The camera also uses a low ISO setting to maximize image quality. The flash is forced off and you cannot use exposure compensation or the self-timer. You should set the camera on a tripod if possible, or hold it firmly on a fence post or other solid object as an alternative.

Another way to shoot images of fireworks is to use the Multiple Exposure Lighten setting, discussed later in this chapter.

Backlighting/HDR

This mode is designed for difficult lighting situations—in particular, when there is bright light present, but it is behind the subject. Nikon calls this mode simply "Backlighting," but its single sub-mode is HDR, which, as discussed below, is an important feature for modern cameras, so I have added HDR to the heading here for easier identification.

With this mode, you have two sub-options selectable by pressing the OK button when this option is highlighted on the Shooting menu: HDR Off, or HDR On.

If you choose the default value, HDR Off, the camera requires that you raise the flash or attach an external flash, and it forces the flash to fire to overcome the shadows caused by your subject's being lighted from behind or by contrasting areas of light and dark.

If you choose HDR On, the camera uses a different approach. With this setting, the camera internally performs its own version of HDR, or high dynamic range, processing.

In case you haven't encountered this topic before, HDR photography uses special techniques to deal with scenes that include areas of extreme contrast between light and dark. For example, if a building is partly in sunshine and partly in deep shadow, the contrast is likely to be so great that a photograph cannot depict both parts of the building with normal exposure. Either one area of the image will be much too bright, so highlights are blown out, or one area will be much too dark, so details are swallowed in the shadows.

In the past, HDR was carried out in post-processing, using software such as Photoshop or special programs such as PhotoAcute or Photomatix Pro. The photographer takes multiple images of the scene at different brightness levels, some exposing dark parts of the scene properly and some exposing bright parts properly. When combined in HDR software, the images can produce a composite image with all parts of the scene nicely exposed. These HDR composite images often have an unnatural or surrealistic appearance, because it is obvious that a "normal" photograph could not include such a wide range of well-exposed areas.

With many modern cameras, including the Coolpix P950, the manufacturer includes programming that lets you take multiple photographs that are combined inside the camera to result in an HDR-like image.

When you use the HDR setting on the P950, you should hold the camera very steady, or, ideally, place it on a tripod. When you press the shutter button, you will hear multiple clicks as the camera takes several exposures. It will then create and save two final images. The first will be taken with the Active D-Lighting feature turned on, to brighten shadowy areas of the image to bring out details. (Active D-Lighting is discussed in Chapter 4.) The second will be an HDR composite that contains the best-exposed parts of multiple images, thereby expanding the dynamic range of the final photograph.

To illustrate the effects of this setting, I took several shots of two watering cans in an area partly shaded and party in sunlight.

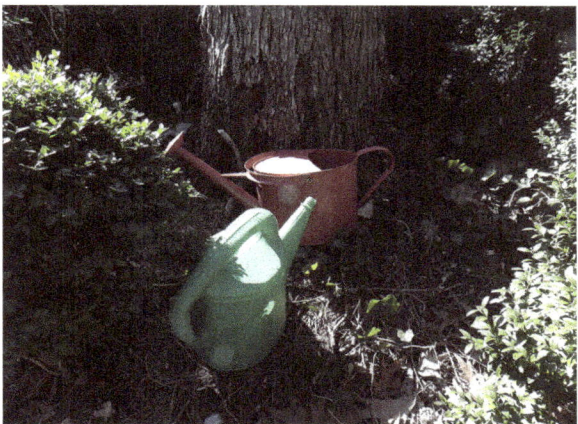

Figure 3-39. HDR Series: No HDR Settings in Use

The first shot, Figure 3-39, was taken in Program mode with no special settings, to show the contrast between the bright and shadowed areas.

Figure 3-40 was taken in Backlighting mode, with HDR turned off. In this mode, the camera always uses flash.

Figure 3-41 was taken with the HDR setting turned on. This is the composite shot created in the camera from multiple exposures. As noted above, with this setting the camera also saves one image with HDR turned off.

Finally, Figure 3-42 is a composite image created in Photoshop, using the Merge to HDR function. I took several images at different settings in Manual exposure mode to use as the basis for this composite.

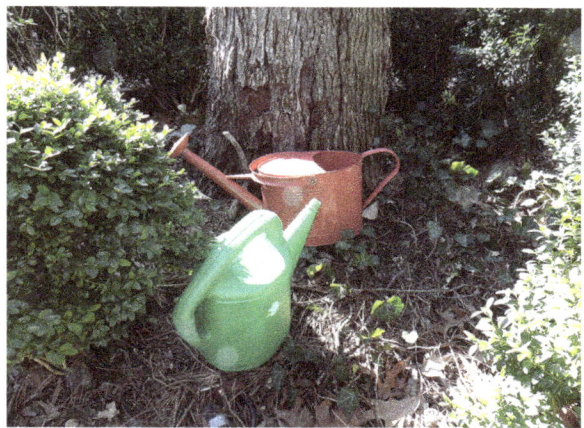

Figure 3-40. HDR Series: Backlighting Setting, HDR Turned Off

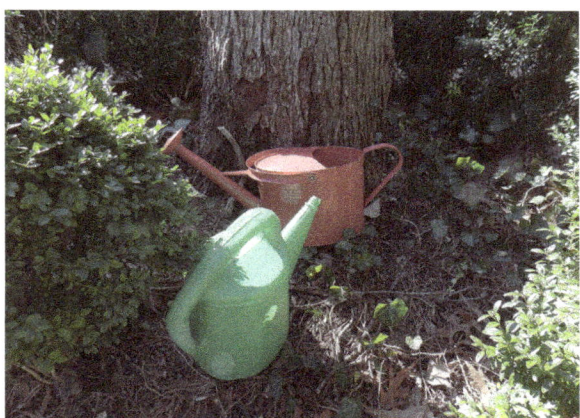

Figure 3-41. HDR Series: Backlighting Setting, HDR Turned On

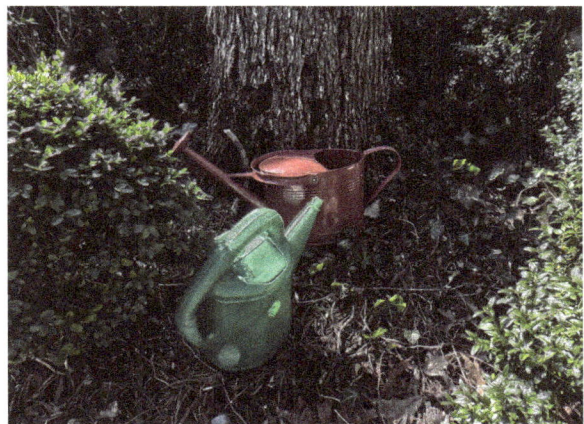

Figure 3-42. HDR Series: Composite HDR Image from Photoshop

The P950's in-camera processing did a good job of reducing the contrast between light and dark areas, producing a final result that looks almost as evenly exposed as that from Photoshop.

Another option for taking shots to create an HDR image is the exposure bracketing feature, discussed in Chapter 4. With that option, the camera takes a series of three shots at different exposure levels; you can combine those shots using HDR software to create a composite.

The HDR setting is an excellent tool, because it is not always practical to take multiple shots to be combined using HDR software. If you take pictures in an area that is partly shaded and partly sunny, or otherwise has contrasting lighting, you can take advantage of this setting to improve the overall appearance of the image.

With either the HDR On or HDR Off setting for Backlighting, you can use exposure compensation or the self-timer. The autofocus area is fixed in the center of the display.

Easy Panorama

When you select this option from the Scene menu, a sub-menu gives you two options—Normal (180°) or Wide (360°).You cannot select Image Quality or Image Size from the menu. If you select Normal, the final panorama will be 4800 x 920 pixels if shot horizontally, or 1536 x 4800 if shot vertically. If you select wide, the dimension with 4800 pixels is doubled to 9600 pixels. After you make your selection, the camera will display a message telling you to press the shutter button and start moving the camera. You should then move it smoothly through a long arc in the direction or your choice, either side to side or up and down.

Aim the camera at the first part of the panoramic scene. For example, if you are shooting a panorama of a wide mountain range, you may want to aim at the far left side of the range.

Press the shutter button halfway down to lock in focus and exposure; the camera will automatically zoom back to the wide-angle position and will not let you zoom in. In addition, the flash is disabled. You can use exposure compensation, but not the self-timer. The autofocus area is fixed in the center of the image. When you are satisfied with the initial view, press the shutter button all the way down and release it; you don't need to hold it down while the panorama shooting proceeds.

Hold the camera steady and level as you sweep it in the direction of your shot—in this case, from left to right—until you have covered the entire scene. The camera will detect the direction you are moving in, and it will automatically stop shooting when it detects the end point of the 180- or 360-degree shot. It will display a yellow progress bar at the top of the screen. You should take about 15 seconds to complete a 180-degree arc.

You can shoot the panorama moving either left to right or right to left, or you can shoot it vertically, moving from low to high or vice-versa. If you select the Wide option, you can move the camera through a complete circle to cover an entire scene. In that case, you should take about 30 seconds to complete the circuit.

When shooting panoramas, try to avoid including moving people, vehicles, or other objects, because they may end up appearing in multiple positions in the panorama.

When you are done, you can view the whole panorama on the screen in a small size by pressing the Playback button. To see the panorama scroll by on the screen in a larger size, press the OK button, and it will scroll in the same direction in which it was taken.

The panorama shown in Figure 3-43 was shot using the Easy Panorama setting with the Coolpix P950 handheld, panning from left to right.

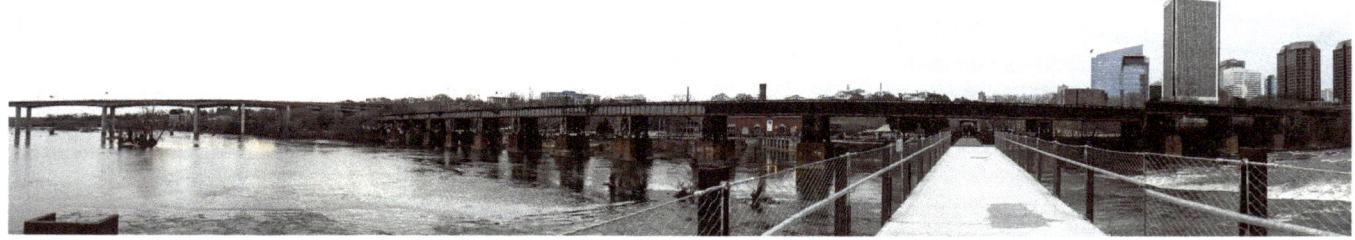

Figure 3-43. Panorama: James River at T. Tyler Potterfield Memorial Pedestrian Bridge, Richmond, Virginia

Pet Portrait

This setting is designed for shooting pictures of the family dog or cat. With this option, the camera turns on continuous shooting and activates a feature called "Pet Portrait Auto Release." With this feature, by default, if the camera detects the face of a pet, it automatically takes three quick pictures. If the camera does not display the yellow frame that indicates face detection, you can press the shutter button to take the image when you're ready. For Figure 3-44, I used this setting to capture an image of my family's dog, when she settled down enough to have her portrait taken.

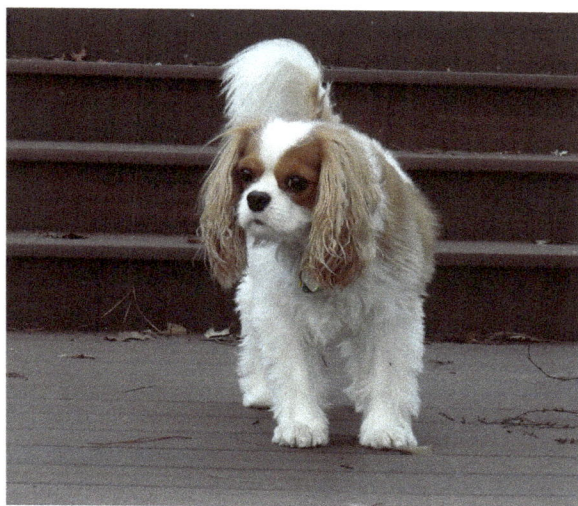

Figure 3-44. Pet Portrait Example

You can change to single shooting from the Shooting menu by pressing the OK button when the Pet Portrait option is highlighted on the menu, and selecting Single on the next screen. You also can change the Pet Portrait Auto Release setting, which is turned on by default. To turn it off, press the self-timer button (Left button), and select the Off setting, rather than the icon of a pet's face. If you turn this setting off but leave continuous shooting turned on, the camera will take up to three shots when you press and hold the shutter button.

With the Pet Portrait setting, the flash is disabled and the camera's beeps are muted. You can use exposure compensation, but not the self-timer. You can select normal autofocus or macro focus, if autofocus is in effect; or you can select manual focus. After the camera has taken five automatic bursts using Pet Portrait Auto Release, the feature turns itself off.

Selective Color

When you choose this option from the menu screen, the camera displays a yellow indicator beside a vertical spectrum of 12 colors plus one entry for no color, as shown in Figure 3-45.

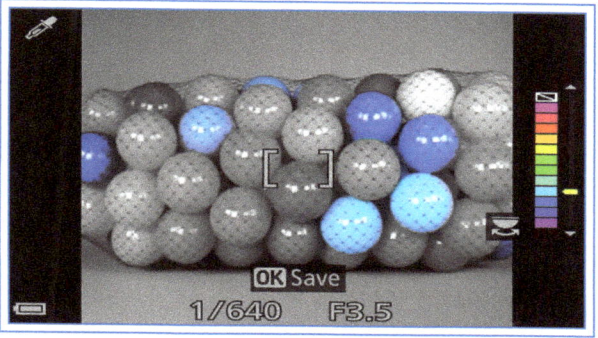

Figure 3-45. Selective Color Shooting Screen

Use the command dial to move the indicator to the block in the spectrum for the single color you want to retain in the image. The topmost block in the spectrum has a negative symbol in it; if you select that block, the camera retains all colors and does not use the Selective Color function. The result in that case is an ordinary image with no special processing at all. It will look as if you took the image using Program or Auto mode.

Once you have selected the color to retain, press the OK button to save it, as indicated by the OK Save prompt seen in Figure 3-45. If you have already selected a color and want to change to a different one, press the OK button again to bring the color-selection display back on the screen.

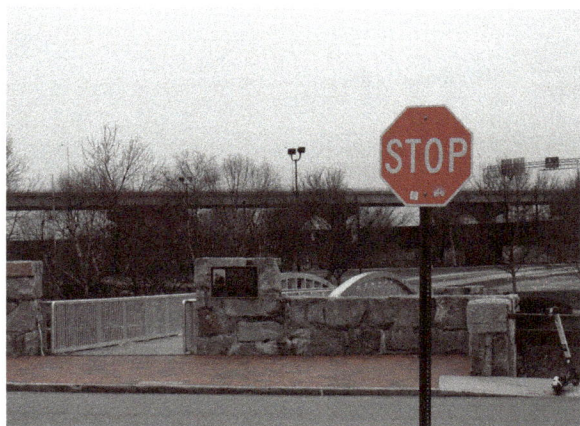

Figure 3-46. Selective Color Example

Figure 3-46 shows the image that resulted from setting the color to red for a shot I took with a stop sign outside a downtown park.

With this setting, you can select a flash mode and autofocus mode, and you can use the self-timer and exposure compensation.

Multiple Exposure Lighten

This setting is designed for taking multiple shots in three particular situations: capturing a trail of automobile headlights and taillights at night, capturing star trails in the night sky, or capturing fireworks displays. After pressing the OK button when this option is displayed on the Shooting menu, select either Nightscape+Light Trails, Star Trails, or Fireworks, as shown in Figure 3-47.

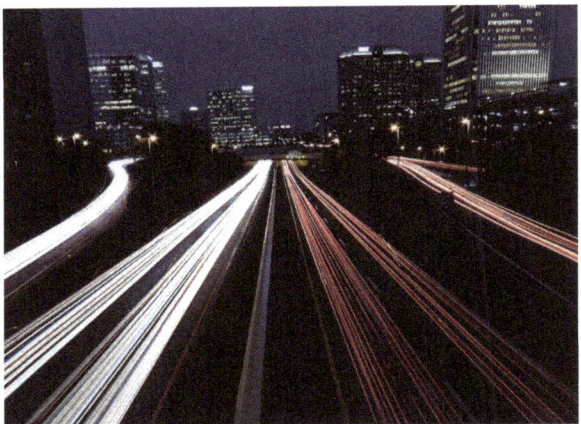

Figure 3-48. Multiple Exposure Lighten Example

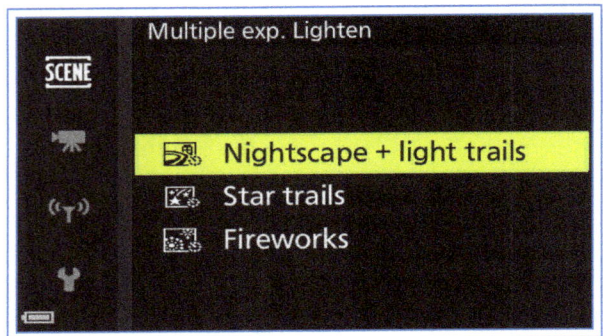

Figure 3-47. Multiple Exposure Lighten Menu Options Screen

If you choose the Nightscape+Light Trails setting, you can turn the command dial to set the shutter speed to one, two, four, or eight seconds. Then, with the camera set firmly on a tripod or equivalent support, press the shutter button to begin the sequence of shots. The camera will automatically capture 50 images in a sequence, using the shutter speed you set, which will also act as the interval between shots.

For example, with the shutter speed set to four seconds, the camera will take 50 shots, one every four seconds, with a shutter speed of four seconds. The camera will save five images out of the 50, and each of those five images will be a composite that includes the brightest areas in 10 of the images. In this way, there is increased likelihood of ending up with several images that include a dramatic series of light trails.

Figure 3-48 is an example of the results I got when I set the shutter speed to one second and positioned the camera on a tripod after dark on an overpass over a busy highway. The image filled up rapidly with light trails, and I ended up pressing the OK button to stop the process, so the image would not be overwhelmed with excessive streaks of light.

If you choose the Star Trails option, there are no further settings to make. Once you press the shutter button, the camera will take a series of 300 shots at 30-second intervals, using a shutter speed of 25 seconds for each shot. The camera will save 10 composite images, each one including the bright areas from 30 of the shots taken.

If you choose the Fireworks option, you can use the command dial to set an interval of one, two, four, or eight seconds. You also can use the multi selector dial to set the aperture. When you press the shutter button, the camera will take 30 shots, and save all of them.

For any of these settings, you can interrupt the shooting sequence by pressing the OK button. Once you see that you have captured the views you were looking for, you should interrupt the sequence in this way, so the images are not washed out by adding excessive bright areas to the composite shots.

Time-lapse Movie

This next selection for Scene mode gives you a way to shoot a time-lapse sequence, in which the camera takes a series of images at a set interval. With this option, for example, you might capture a series of 300 images of a sunset taken at 10-second intervals. The result would show the progress of the sunset over a period of 3000 seconds, or 50 minutes. At the standard playback rate of 30 frames per second (in the United States), this sequence of 300 images would play back in 10 seconds, producing a dramatically speeded-up view of the sunset.

You can achieve a similar effect using the interval timer setting under the Continuous menu option on the Shooting menu, as discussed in Chapter 4. However, the shortest interval available with that option is 30 seconds. In addition, the Time-lapse Movie option provides you with several preset options for typical time-lapse subjects, so you do not have to choose the interval and number of shots, or make other settings; you can just choose the subject matter and let the camera make the appropriate settings.

The five available subjects, along with the elapsed time for each shooting sequence, are: Cityscape (10 minutes); Landscape (25 minutes); Sunset (50 minutes); Night Sky (150 minutes); and Star Trails (150 minutes). In each case, the resulting time-lapse movie is about 10 seconds long, when played back at 30 frames per second.

You can use exposure compensation with all settings except the last two, and you can use the self-timer. Flash is disabled and the autofocus area is fixed in the center.

To use this option, with the mode dial at the SCENE setting, press the Menu button and select Time-lapse Movie from the menu. When you press the OK or Right button, you will see a screen listing the five options for the subject matter.

Highlight the one you want, and press the OK or Right button to move to a screen where you can select either AE-L On or AE-L Off.

With the AE-L On setting, the camera will lock exposure with the first image, so the exposure will not be adjusted as the lighting conditions change. With the AE-L Off setting, the camera will automatically adjust exposure as appropriate. (The AE-L settings are not available with the Night Sky or Star Trails options.)

The choice of the AE-L setting depends on your preference. If you select AE-L Off, the exposure adjustments as clouds pass over the sun can be distracting. Also, for a sunset, the exposure adjustments are likely to make the scene appear somewhat unnatural, with the sky staying relatively uniform in brightness even as the sun sets. I generally prefer the AE-L Off setting to achieve a more natural effect, but the choice depends on the particular circumstances.

You should set the camera on a sturdy tripod and be careful not to touch it or disturb it while the sequence is being recorded. The camera does not record sound with the images. You can stop the sequence at any time by pressing the OK button. When the sequence has been recorded, it will appear as a movie file, with the file extension .mp4.

To play it, press the OK button as with any other movie. You will see a greatly speeded-up version of the subject matter.

Creative Mode

Several notches around the mode dial from the SCENE mode is the slot indicated by a white camera icon with a stylized letter C, indicating the Creative shooting mode. This shooting mode provides you with interesting ways to alter the appearance of your images. These settings operate in a manner similar to the scene settings, but there are some differences. The Creative settings are not designed for particular types of subjects, such as portraits, landscapes, or fireworks, as the scene settings are. Instead, the Creative mode settings offer manipulations to change how an image looks, regardless of the subject.

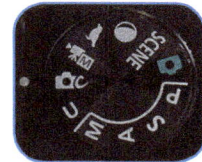

Figure 3-49. Mode Dial at Creative

To select one of these settings, turn the mode dial to the Creative position, as shown in Figure 3-49, then press the OK button to go to a screen like that shown in Figure 3-50.

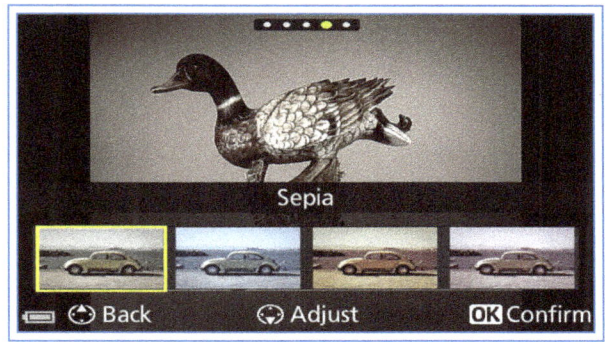

Figure 3-50. Creative Mode Shooting Screen

This screen has five dots at the top, which represent the five overall effect groups for this mode, from left to right: Light, Depth, Memories, Classic, and Noir. To move among those groups, turn the command dial. Each time you turn that dial to select a different group, the thumbnail images at the bottom of the screen change, to show the four individual effects that are available within the currently selected group. To move among the individual effects within a group, you turn the multi selector dial or press the Left and Right buttons.

For example, if you start from the screen shown in Figure 3-50, above, and turn the command dial three times to the left, you will move from the Classic group to the Light group. If you then turn the multi selector dial to the right (or press the Left and Right buttons), you will move through the four individual effects within the Light group: Dream, Morning, Pop, and Sunday. If you keep turning the multi selector dial beyond the last (or first) setting within the current group, you will move to the first (or last) setting of the next group, either after or before the current group.

Once you have highlighted an individual setting you want to use, such as Sepia, you can press the OK button to select it without further adjustment. If you want to make some adjustments, press the Down button, which takes you to the screen shown in Figure 3-51. On this screen, you can turn the multi selector dial or press the Left and Right buttons to highlight Amount, Exposure Compensation, Contrast, Hue, Saturation, Filter, or Peripheral Illumination.

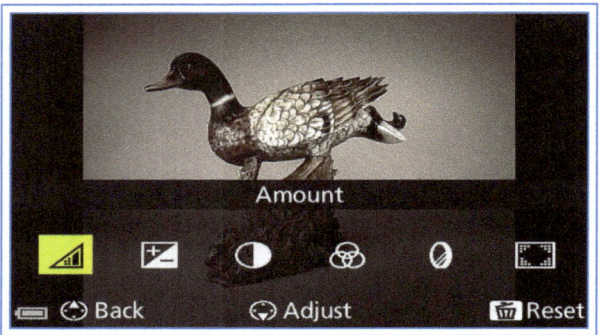

Figure 3-51. Main Adjustments Screen for Sepia Setting

The available parameters vary according to the setting that is in use. The Hue parameter is available only with the Light group settings, for example. The Filter parameter, which is available only for settings in the Classic and Noir groups, lets you simulate the addition of a yellow, orange, red, or green filter on the lens. The Peripheral Illumination parameter controls the amount of vignetting, or darkening of the corners, for an effect.

When you have highlighted the parameter you want to adjust, such as Contrast or Peripheral Illumination, press the Down button to move to the adjustment screen for that parameter, as shown in Figure 3-52, the screen for Contrast.

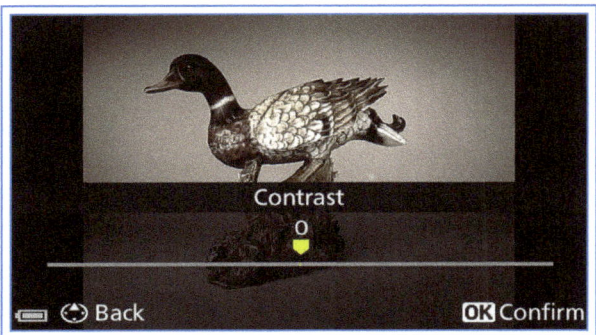

Figure 3-52. Adjustments Screen for Contrast Setting

On that screen, use the Left and Right buttons or the multi selector dial to set the amount of the adjustment for the selected parameter and press the OK button to confirm. For example, with Peripheral Illumination, to increase the darkening, adjust the scale downward, to the left. To brighten the corners and reduce the vignetting, adjust the scale upward, to the right. To reset the adjustments for an effect, press the Trash/Delete button, and the camera will ask you to confirm that operation. Select Yes, and the options will be reset to the default settings.

When you have finished adjusting all of the parameters you want to alter, press the Up button to select the effect, as adjusted. Or, just press the shutter button halfway to return to the shooting screen. You can then proceed to capture still images or videos with the chosen effect.

The camera's display will change according to the setting you have chosen. For example, if you select the Binary effect within the Noir group, the display will be in black and white and will appear grainy, with harsh contrast.

There are no other options available on the Shooting menu when you are using Creative mode, apart from Image Quality and Image Size. You cannot select any Raw options for Image Quality. However, you can use the buttons on the multi selector to choose exposure compensation, the self-timer, or an autofocus mode (normal autofocus or macro autofocus only). As with all shooting modes, you can select manual focus using the focus mode selector. You can choose a flash mode, if the flash unit is popped up or an external flash is attached and turned on.

You also can use the menu system to select an effect group and an effect within the group, by pressing the menu button when Creative mode is in effect. However, in order to make adjustments to a setting, you still need to press the OK button to call up the options screen, and then press the Down button to make adjustments.

I will list the groups and their individual settings below, along with two charts, in Figures 3-53 and 3-54, with sample images that use all 20 of the settings for the same subject, to give a general idea of the effect that each setting produces. The settings are used here with no adjustments.

Light: Dream, Morning, Pop, Sunday

Depth: Somber, Dramatic, Silence, Bleached

Memories: Melancholic, Pure, Denim, Toy

Classic: Sepia, Blue, Red, Pink

Noir: Charcoal, Graphite, Binary, Carbon

Figure 3-53. Creative Mode Chart, Part 1

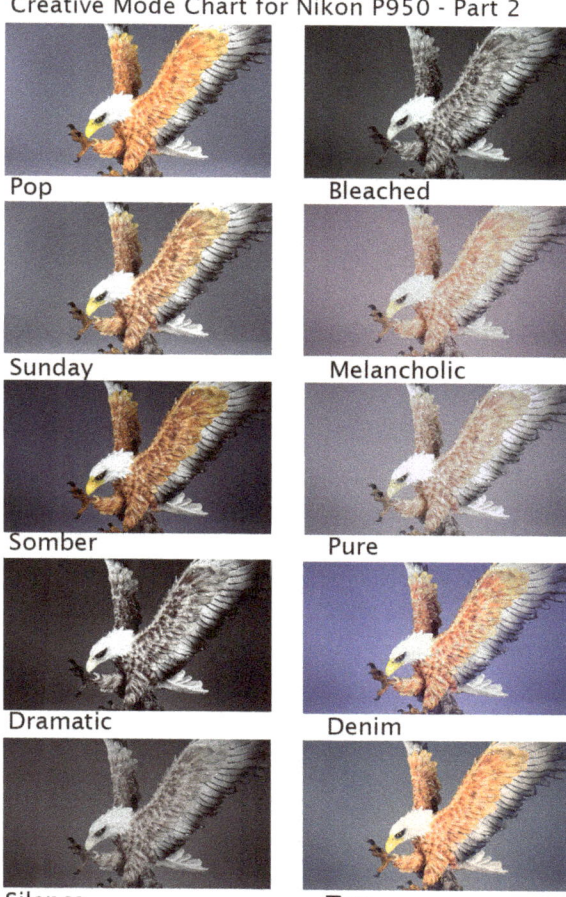

Figure 3-54. Creative Mode Chart, Part 2

User Settings Mode

The last slot on the mode dial to be discussed in this chapter is the U setting, as shown in Figure 3-55, which allows you, the user, to store a full set of your favorite or most often-needed settings for immediate recall.

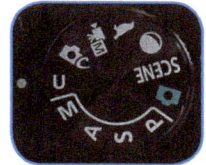

Figure 3-55. Mode Dial at User Settings

When you turn the mode dial to the U position, you take advantage of a powerful feature of the Coolpix P950. You can set up the camera exactly as you want it, with a shooting mode, zoom amount, white balance, ISO, and other settings, and then recall all of those settings instantly just by turning the mode dial to the letter U. The only shooting modes that you can save settings for are Program, Aperture Priority, Shutter

Priority, and Manual; you cannot save them for the Auto, Scene (including Bird-watching and Moon), or Creative modes.

Here is how this works. First, set up the camera with the settings you will want to recall. For example, suppose you are doing street photography. You may want to shoot with a fast shutter speed, say 1/250 second, at ISO 1600 in black-and-white, using continuous shooting, at the 16:9 aspect ratio with a large image size and Fine quality.

First, make all of these settings. Turn the mode dial to S for Shutter Priority, and use the command dial to set a shutter speed of 1/250 second. Then press the Menu button and choose Fine for Image Quality on the Shooting menu. For Image Size, select 4608 x 2592 pixels, which, as indicated to the left of those numbers, translates to a 16:9 aspect ratio with an image size of 12 megapixels.

Then navigate in the menu to Picture Control and select Monochrome. Set the ISO Sensitivity menu option to 1600. Next, select the Continuous item on the Shooting menu and navigate to the next screen; on that screen, go down to the second option, Continuous H, marked with an H on a stack of frames, for high-speed shots. You also may want to push the zoom lever all the way to the left, for wide-angle shooting.

Once all of these settings are made, press the Menu button to call up the Shooting menu, and scroll down (or scroll up and wrap around to the bottom) to select the Save User Settings item, shown in Figure 3-56, and then press the OK button or the Right button; you will see a confirming message saying Done.

Be sure you have all the settings the way you want them before you press OK or the Right button, because the camera does not ask you to confirm your choices; it just says "Done." I was a bit taken aback the first couple of times I used this feature, because in most other cases there's a chance to back out before you make your choices final; not here.

Now, to check how this option worked, try making some very different settings, such as Manual exposure with continuous shooting turned off, a shutter speed of one second, Picture Control set to Standard, the zoom lever moved all the way to the T for telephoto, ISO set to 200, and Image Size set to the maximum, 4608 x 3456 pixels. Then turn the mode dial to the U setting, and you will see that all of the custom settings you made earlier have come back, including the zoom position, shutter speed, black-and-white shooting at ISO 1600, and everything else. This is really a wonderful feature, and more powerful than similar features on some other cameras, which can save menu settings but not settings such as shutter speed and zoom position.

The lone flaw I find with this mode is that there is only one slot for it on the mode dial, and therefore only one group of settings that can be saved at a time. But it's much better than nothing. I suggest you experiment to find one group of custom settings that is the most useful to you, and save it to the U mode for instant recall. Of course, you can change the settings that are stored as often as you like. You may want to jot down in a notebook some of your favorite groups of settings for various situations, so you can program the most appropriate set into the U slot when you're setting out for a particular type of shooting session.

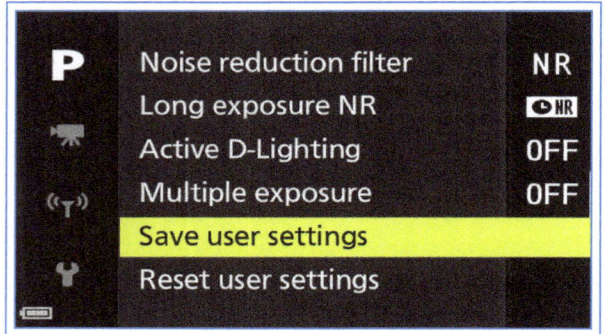

Figure 3-56. Save User Settings Option Highlighted on Shooting Menu

Chapter 4: The Shooting Menu

Much of the power of the Nikon Coolpix P950 comes from the options included in the Shooting menu, which helps you control the appearance of images and how they are captured. Depending on your preferences, you may not have to use this menu often. You may prefer to use the various scene settings or Creative mode selections, which choose many options for you, or you may prefer, at least on occasion, to use Auto mode, in which the camera makes its own choices. However, it's good to have this degree of control available if you want it, and it is useful to understand what items you can control.

As I discussed earlier, the menu options change depending on the setting of the mode dial on top of the camera. For example, if the mode dial is set to the green camera icon, for Auto mode, the Shooting menu options are limited, because Auto mode is for a user who wants the camera to make many decisions without input from him or her. If you have chosen one of the dedicated scene types with its own slot on the mode dial (Bird-watching or Moon), the Shooting menu is custom-tailored for that mode.

For example, if you select the Moon mode from the mode dial and then press the Menu button, the menu that appears on the display, as shown in Figure 4-1, is labeled Moon, rather than Shooting. (The Moon label at the top of the menu appears for only a few seconds when you highlight the Moon icon at the left, then disappears.)

These menus, as in Auto mode, are abbreviated versions of the Shooting menu; they include only a few items from the normal Shooting menu, usually Image Quality and Image Size. In addition, they may include a specific menu item for the mode that is in effect. In this case, with the Moon menu, there is a Focal Length Selection menu item, which lets you set the focal length for the automatic zooming feature in Moon mode.

When the mode dial is turned to the SCENE setting, pressing the Menu button brings up another version of the Shooting menu, called the Scene menu. This menu provides a way to select any one of 19 specific scene types (Portrait, Landscape, Sports, Sunset, etc.).

In addition, at the very bottom of the Scene menu, just after the entries for Selective Color, Multiple Exposure Lighten, and Time-lapse Movie, are the options for Image Quality and Image Size, as shown in Figure 4-2. (The Image Quality and Image Size menu options are dimmed and unavailable for selection when Easy Panorama or Time-lapse Movie is selected for the scene type.)

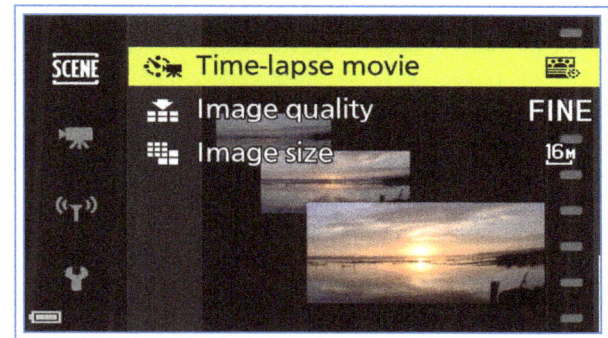

Figure 4-2. Image Quality and Image Size Options on Scene Menu

When the Creative option on the mode dial is selected, the menu becomes the Creative mode menu, which lets you choose an effect, along with Image Quality and Image Size.

Although the Shooting menu (or its equivalent, such as the Scene or other specialty menu) presents you

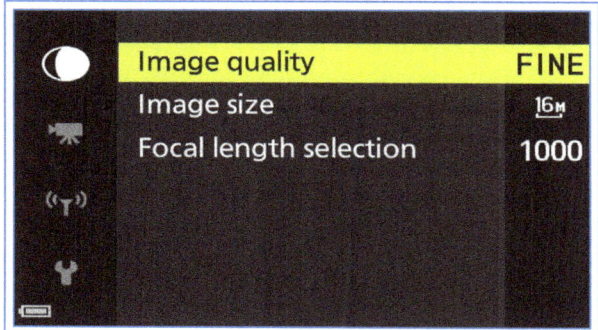

Figure 4-1. Moon Mode Menu

with some choices in all shooting modes, in the more automatic modes, including Auto and the various Scene mode types, there are only a few options, apart from options specific to a given mode, such as choosing a scene type. It is only when the mode dial is set to the P, S, A, or M setting for the Program, Shutter Priority, Aperture Priority, or Manual exposure mode, that the wide variety of Shooting menu options is available.

For the following discussion, I'm assuming you have the camera set to Program mode (mode dial turned to the P setting), because with that setting you potentially have access to all of the power of the Shooting menu. (Though some menu options will be unavailable in certain situations.)

After you turn the mode dial to P for Program mode, enter the menu system by pressing the Menu button. In the menu system, when the camera is in shooting mode, besides the Shooting menu (or Scene or Creative menu), there are the Movie menu, designated by a movie camera icon in the column at the left of the menu, the Network menu, marked by a wireless network icon, and the Setup menu, marked by a wrench icon. These icons are shown in Figure 4-3.

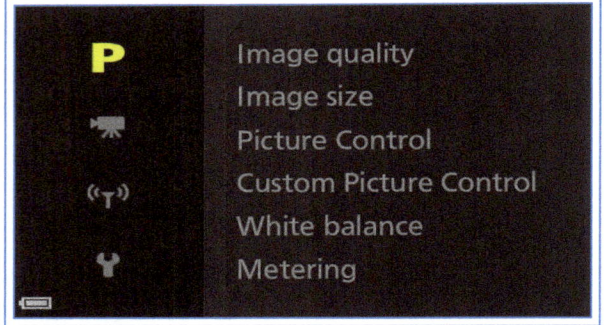

Figure 4-3. Menu Icons Displayed at Left of Menu Screen

When the camera is in playback mode, there are only three choices: the Playback, Network, and Setup menus. For now, I will discuss only the Shooting menu, which is designated by a capital letter or icon at the left standing for the current shooting mode: P, S, A, or M, or an icon for one of the more automatic modes.

On the Shooting menu (in Program mode), you'll see a fairly long list of options. Each option (such as Picture Control) occupies one line, with its name on the left and its current setting (such as the Standard icon) on the right.

You have to scroll through four screens to see all of the options. If you find it tedious to scroll using the Up and Down buttons, you can rotate the multi selector dial on the camera's back, which may help you speed through the menus a bit more quickly. Also, depending on which menu option you are trying to reach, you may be able to get there more quickly by reversing direction with the buttons or multi selector dial, and wrapping around to reach the option you want. In other words, if you're on the top line of the first screen of the menu, you can scroll up to reach the bottom option on the last screen. Or, if the highlight is already near the bottom option, you can scroll down to go back to the options at the top of the menu.

Once you have highlighted the menu item you want, you can make any sub-selections by pressing either the OK button or the Right button, which will take you to the next screen (if one exists) for that menu item. To go back to a previous menu screen, press the Left button; to exit the menu system, press the Menu button. It is important to press the OK button to confirm your choice of a particular menu item selection; just highlighting it and then exiting from the menu screen will not activate that item.

On occasion you will find you are unable to select a certain menu option. That is, although an option will appear on the menu screen, you will not be able to navigate to it and select it. This situation occurs when there is an option in effect that is not compatible with the menu option you are trying to select. For example, if you have selected Raw for the Image Quality menu option, the Image Size setting is dimmed on the menu screen, because Raw images are always at the largest image size, so Image Size cannot be selected on the menu, as shown in Figure 4-4.

Or, if you have selected the option to shoot in monochrome from the Picture Control menu setting, you will not be able to get access to the White Balance menu option.

With the mode dial set to P you should have access to just about every option on the Shooting menu. If you find you can't select certain options, check to make sure you have set other options to compatible settings. For example, make sure the Continuous option on the Shooting menu is set for single-shot exposures rather than a continuous setting, and set Image Quality to Fine.

Chapter 4: The Shooting Menu | 45

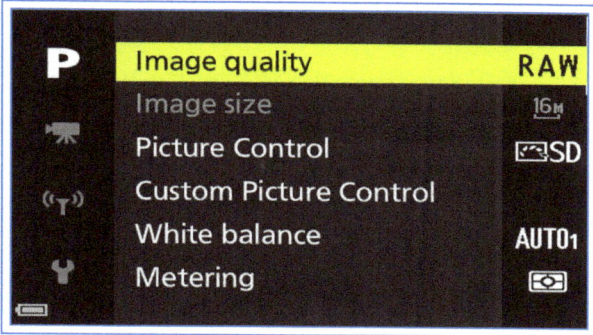

Figure 4-4. Image Quality Option Dimmed on Menu Screen

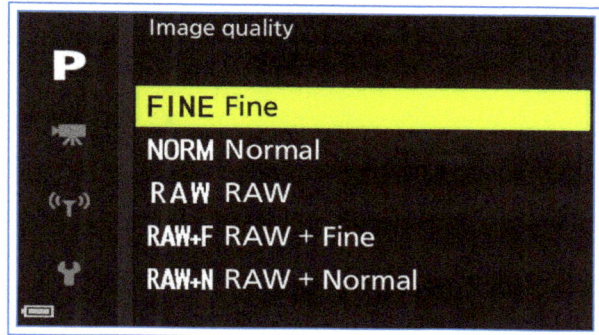

Figure 4-6. Image Quality Menu Options Screen

If you have trouble getting to some menu options and can't figure out what setting is causing the problem, you can go to the Setup menu (marked at the left of the screen by the wrench icon) and scroll down (or scroll up and wrap around) to the Reset All option, the third-to-last option on the menu. That action will reset all of the camera's basic shooting functions to their default values. In this way, you will undo whatever setting is causing a conflict with the setting you are trying to make. (You also will undo any custom settings you have made, so be sure you don't mind taking that step.)

Starting at the top line of the Shooting menu, I will discuss each option on the menu's four screens. The first menu screen is shown in Figure 4-5.

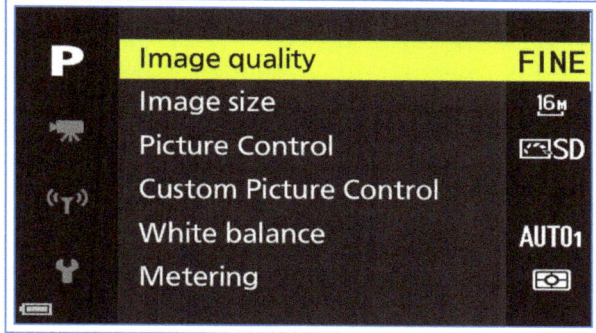

Figure 4-5. Screen 1 of Shooting Menu

Image Quality

The Image Quality setting is one of the most important Shooting menu options for still images. The choices are Fine, Normal, Raw, Raw+Fine, and Raw+Normal, as shown in Figure 4-6.

The term "quality" in this context concerns the way in which digital images are processed. In particular, JPEG (Fine or Normal, and not Raw) images are digitally "compressed" to reduce their file size without losing too much information or detail from the picture. However, the more an image is compressed, the greater the loss of detail and clarity in the image.

Raw files, which are in a class by themselves, are the least compressed of all and have the greatest level of quality, though they come with some complications, as discussed below. All other (non-Raw) formats for still images used by the Coolpix P950 (as with many similar cameras) are classified as JPEG. The JPEG files, in turn, come in two varieties on the P950: Fine and Normal. The Fine setting provides the least compression. Images captured with the Normal setting undergo more compression, resulting in smaller files with somewhat reduced quality.

Here are some guidelines for using these settings. First, you need to choose between Raw and JPEG images. Raw files are larger than other files, so they take up more space on your memory card, and on your computer, than JPEG files. But Raw files offer advantages over JPEG files. When you shoot in the Raw format, the camera records as much information as it can about the image and preserves that information in the file it saves to the memory card. When you open the Raw file later on your computer, your software can process that information in various ways. For example, you can change the exposure or white balance of the image when you edit it on the computer, just as if you had changed your settings while shooting. In effect, the Raw format gives you what almost amounts to a chance to travel back in time to improve some of the settings that you didn't get quite right when you pressed the shutter button.

For example, Figure 4-7 is an image I took with the P950 using the Raw format, with the exposure purposely set too dark and the white balance set to Incandescent, even though I took the picture outdoors during daylight hours.

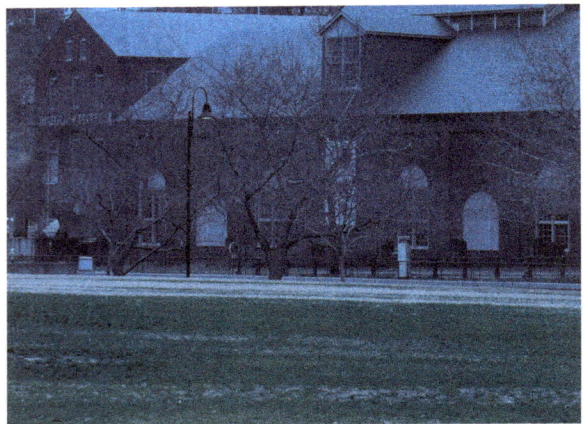

Figure 4-7. Raw Image Captured with Abnormal Settings

Figure 4-8 shows the same image after I opened it in Adobe Camera Raw software and adjusted the settings to correct the exposure and white balance. The result is an image that looks just as it would if I had used the correct settings when I shot it.

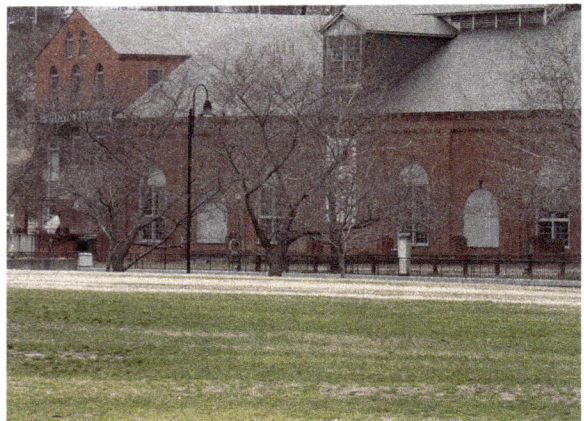

Figure 4-8. Raw Image After Settings Adjusted in Software

Raw is not a cure-all; you cannot fix bad focus or excessive exposure problems. But you can improve some exposure-related issues and white balance with Raw-processing software. You can use Nikon's Capture NX-D software to view or edit Raw files from the P950, and you also can use other programs, such as Adobe Camera Raw, that have been updated to handle Raw files from this camera.

Using Raw can have disadvantages, also. The files take up a lot of storage space; Raw images taken with the P950 are about 25 MB in size, while Large JPEG images I have taken are between about 5 and 7 MB, depending on the settings used. Also, Raw files have to be processed on a computer; you can't take a Raw image and immediately share it through social media or print it; you first have to use software to convert it to JPEG, TIFF, or some other standard format for manipulating digital photographs. If you are pressed for time, you may not want to take that extra step. Finally, some features of the P950 are not available when you are using the Raw format, such as the Scene mode and Creative mode settings, the Continuous settings of Pre-shooting Cache, Continuous H:120 fps and Continuous H:60 fps, and the Multiple Exposure, Date Stamp, and digital zoom options.

If you're undecided as to whether to use Raw or JPEG, you have the option of selecting Raw+Fine or Raw+Normal, the fourth and fifth choices for the Image Quality menu item. With either of those settings, the camera records both a Raw and a JPEG image of the designated quality (Fine or Normal) when you press the shutter button.

The advantage with that approach is that you have a Raw image with maximum quality and the ability to do extensive post-processing, and you also have a JPEG image that you can use for viewing, sharing, printing, and the like. Of course, this setting consumes storage space more quickly than saving your images in just Raw or JPEG format, and it can take the camera longer to store the images, so there may be a slowdown in the rate of continuous shooting, if you are using that option. You also cannot use some menu options that conflict with the Raw setting.

When you choose Raw+Fine or Raw+Normal, you can select an Image Size setting that will apply only to the JPEG image; the Raw image, as noted earlier, is always at the maximum size. There are only a few Image Size settings available in this context, not the full range of those options.

The best way to preserve the quality of your images and your options for post-processing and fixing exposure mistakes later is to choose Raw files. However, if you want to use features such as scene modes and Creative mode, which are not available with Raw files, then choose Fine or Normal, depending on your needs for using a small file size. If you do choose JPEG, I strongly recommend that you choose the Fine quality and the largest image size, unless you have an urgent need to conserve storage space on your memory card or on your computer. If you want Raw quality and are not concerned about storage space or speed of shooting, choose Raw+Fine. However, you will still not be able to use settings that conflict with the Raw format.

Image Size

The next option on the Shooting menu, Image Size, works together with Image Quality to determine the overall quality of your JPEG (Fine and Normal) images. (For Raw images, Image Size is always at the largest size and at the 4:3 aspect ratio.) With the Coolpix P950, Image Size actually has two components, which can be selected separately on some other cameras: resolution and aspect ratio. On the P950, these two components are not named, but their numerical values are listed on the Image Size menu. (The aspect ratio values are listed on the menu only for the settings that deviate from the normal aspect ratio of 4:3.)

The resolution of the image is the number of pixels it contains, given in a formula with the horizontal pixel count followed by the vertical pixel count. For example, the largest Image Size setting available on the P950 is 4608 x 3456, as shown in Figure 4-9, meaning the image has 4608 pixels horizontally and 3456 vertically.

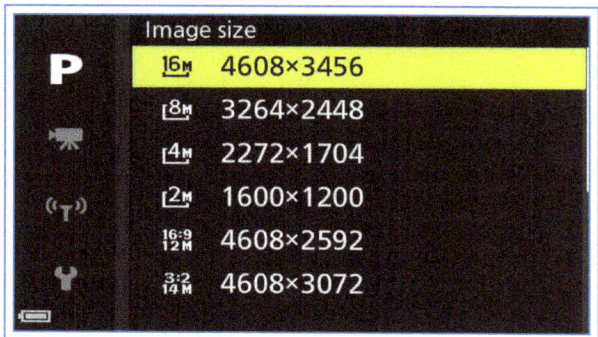

Figure 4-9. Largest Image Size Setting Highlighted on Menu

When you multiply these two numbers together, the result is about 16 million pixels, also written as 16 megapixels or 16M. So, as in Figure 4-10, you will see the figure 16M on the menu screen when you have selected this largest value for Image Size.

You can also determine the aspect ratio of the image from the Image Size setting. For example, the 4608 x 3456 setting yields an image four units wide for every three units tall, for a 4:3 aspect ratio. Most of the Image Size settings for the P950 are in that ratio, which is a standard one for digital images, being the same shape as the camera's LCD display. However, if you scroll down through the lines of the Image Size menu, you will see a few entries that note a different aspect ratio.

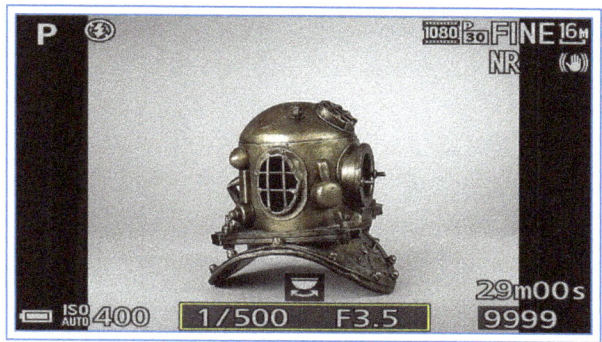

Figure 4-10. Shooting Screen with Largest Image Size Selected

Specifically, just below the setting for 2M (1600 x 1200), there is the entry for 4608 x 2592 pixels, as shown in Figure 4-9. At the far left on the line for this entry, above the number of megapixels, 12M, the menu shows the notation 16:9, meaning this Image Size setting is in a 16:9 aspect ratio: 16 units wide for every nine units tall. This aspect ratio is another fairly common one, which corresponds to the shape of a widescreen HDTV set, and therefore often is called "widescreen."

Below that entry, another setting, 4608 x 3072, is labeled as 3:2, meaning its aspect ratio has three horizontal units for every two vertical ones. This is a common aspect ratio, which corresponds to the standard print size in the United States of six by four inches (15 by 10 cm).

Finally, the last entry on the Image size menu, 3456 x 3456 pixels, on screen 2 of the Image Size menu, is in an aspect ratio of 1:1, resulting in a square image. Some photographers like to use this aspect ratio because of its symmetry, or because it suits a particular composition. (There are a few other possible Image Size settings, labeled as 1M, VGA, and 16:9 2M, for smaller images that result when you set Continuous to Pre-shooting Cache, Continuous H:120, or Continuous H:60. However, the camera makes those settings automatically; you cannot select them from the Image Size menu.)

With the Image Size menu setting, you have two choices to make. First, you can choose your images' resolution, or number of pixels (megapixels). The larger the number of pixels, the larger you can make high-quality prints on paper, and the more options you have for cropping the image to highlight particular details from the exposure. Second, although most of the choices on the menu are in the standard 4:3 aspect ratio, you have the option of selecting an aspect ratio of 3:2, 16:9, or 1:1 if you want.

Of course, you can always just shoot with the maximum image size of 4608 x 3456 and then crop the image down in software later; in that way, you can use any aspect ratio you want, including those listed here or any other. But, if you want to use a 1:1 aspect ratio for creative reasons, or you want your landscape photo to have the 16:9 widescreen look and you don't want to be bothered with changing the aspect ratio in software, you can select an Image Size setting that corresponds to your desired aspect ratio, so the final result will come straight out of the camera. In addition, you will have the advantage of seeing how the final image will be composed as you set it up on the camera's display screen or in the viewfinder.

If you choose Raw+Fine or Raw+Normal for Image Quality, you cannot choose an aspect ratio other than 4:3 for the Fine or Normal JPG image that will be taken when you press the shutter button. The Image Size settings for those aspect ratios will be dimmed and unavailable for selection. However, you can choose any of the first four options for Image Size.

Figures 4-11 through 4-14 were all taken at the same time and place; the only differences are that they were taken with different Image Size settings, resulting in different aspect ratios, as indicated in the captions.

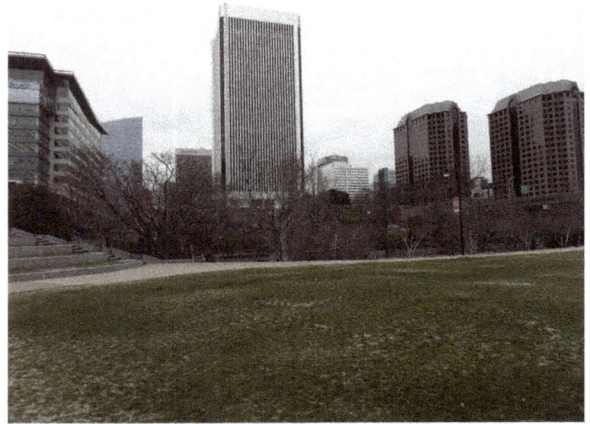

Figure 4-11. Aspect Ratio 4:3

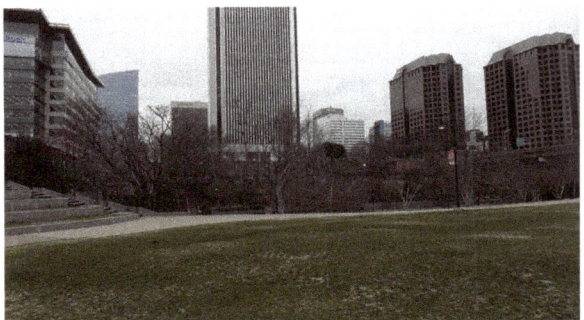

Figure 4-12. Aspect Ratio 16:9

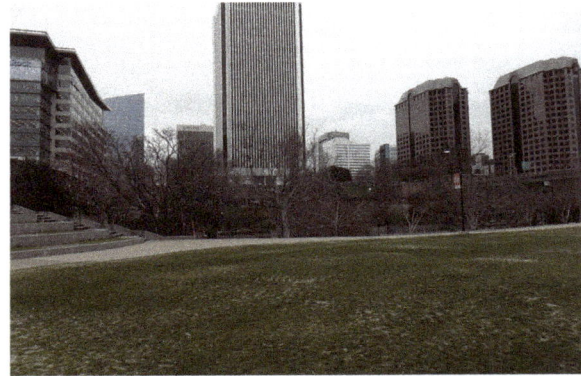

Figure 4-13. Aspect Ratio 3:2

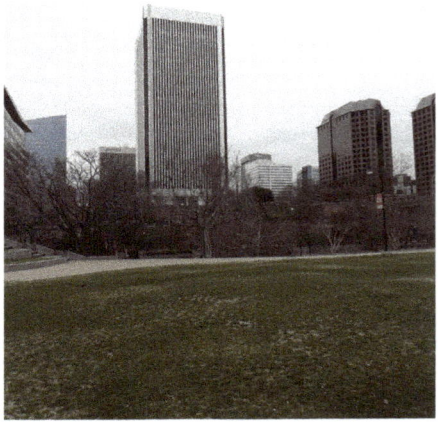

Figure 4-14. Aspect Ratio 1:1

Figure 4-11 was taken with the largest image size, which uses the 4:3 aspect ratio. With this setting, the camera captures the maximum number of pixels, and the resulting image includes all of the pixels included with the other aspect ratios, as well as some that are cut off with other settings.

Figure 4-12, taken with the 16:9, widescreen aspect ratio, includes all of the horizontal reach of the 4:3 image, but cuts off pixels at both the top and bottom of the image, as shown here.

Figure 4-13, taken with the 3:2 aspect ratio, also includes all of the horizontal reach of the 4:3 setting, but cuts off some pixels at the top and bottom of the image.

Finally, Figure 4-14 illustrates the use of the 1:1 aspect ratio, with which the camera cuts off pixels at the left and right sides of the image to achieve a square shape.

Picture Control

This option provides you with four choices for the appearance of your images through in-camera processing: Standard, Neutral, Vivid, and Monochrome, as shown in Figure 4-15.

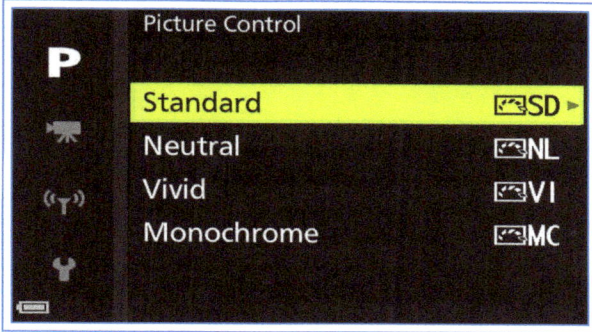

Figure 4-15. Picture Control Menu Options Screen

With these options, the camera provides varying degrees of adjustment to three basic parameters: sharpening, contrast, and saturation.

This setting affects images taken with Image Quality set to Raw as well as JPEG (non-Raw) images. However, the setting may not be effective when the Raw image is viewed with certain software. For example, when I took a Raw image using the Monochrome setting, the image appeared in color in Adobe Camera Raw software. So, in order to use the Picture Control settings effectively with Raw images, you may need to process the images using Nikon's ViewNX-i software, which does apply the Picture Control effects.

Following are descriptions of the settings, with a sample photo for each one showing the same mannequin head, for comparison. Although the differences among the four settings are not all that dramatic (except for Monochrome), you should be able to see the general characteristics of each selection.

STANDARD

This setting, seen in Figure 4-16, provides normal colors, with no emphasis on any particular aspect.

The camera does some internal processing of the captured image to make it appear suitably sharp and contrasty for ordinary purposes. This is the setting you should use for everyday shooting when you have no interest in producing a specific effect.

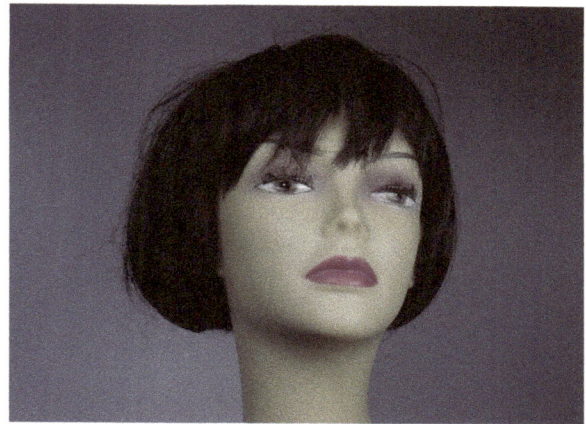

Figure 4-16. Picture Control Standard

NEUTRAL

With the Neutral setting, illustrated in Figure 4-17, the camera does minimal internal processing of the image.

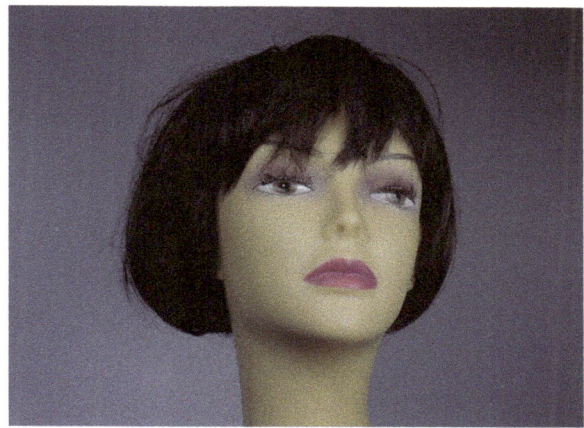

Figure 4-17. Picture Control Neutral

Therefore, the image may appear less sharp and contrasty, and have less color intensity, than you would like. The intent with this setting is for you to process the image after the fact in software such as Photoshop. With minimal processing, the camera is leaving the fine-tuning of the image up to you.

Vivid

Use this setting to increase the saturation, or intensity, of the colors in the image, as seen in Figure 4-18. The Vivid setting also provides some increase in sharpening and contrast, with the result that the image may "jump" off the page or screen with increased impact.

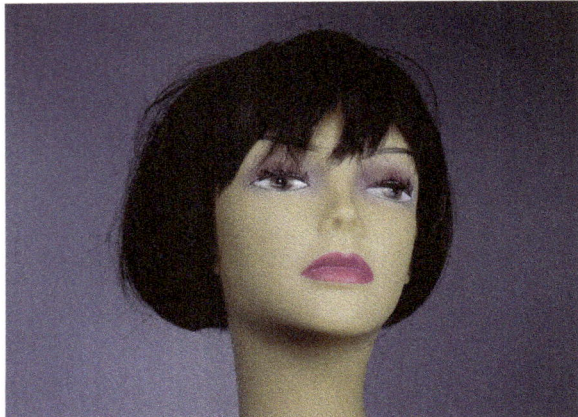

Figure 4-18. Picture Control Vivid

Monochrome

The Monochrome setting gives you a quick way to set the camera to take black-and-white images.

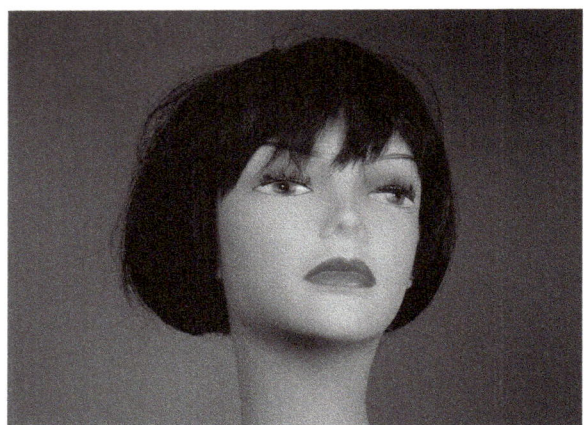

Figure 4-19. Picture Control Monochrome

Of course, as with many aspects of digital photography, you can always convert color images to monochrome using software such as Photoshop or Photoshop Elements, but it is convenient to be able to view your images in black-and-white on the camera's display before pressing the shutter button, and you may not want to devote your time and effort to converting images on the computer. The Monochrome setting is illustrated in Figure 4-19.

Adjustments to Picture Control Settings

Once you have selected Standard or Vivid from the Picture Control menu, the camera will display a secondary menu screen with four lines: Quick Adjust, Image sharpening, Contrast, and Saturation, as shown in Figure 4-20.

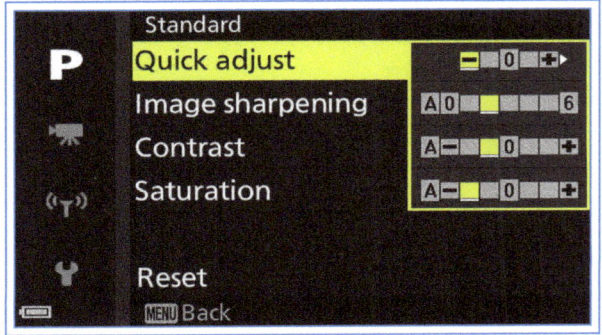

Figure 4-20. Picture Control Adjustment Screen for Standard Setting

You can highlight any one of those four lines using the Up and Down buttons. When the line is highlighted, use the multi selector dial, the command dial, or the Left and Right buttons to change the settings. If you change the Quick Adjust value, you will see that the three values below it—Image sharpening, Contrast, and Saturation—also move, but not all in the same amounts. Nikon has programmed the Quick Adjust feature to move the other three values in what Nikon considers to be "balanced" amounts, so that sharpening, contrast, and saturation may be adjusted upward or downward in amounts that work well with the adjustments to the other values.

If, instead of using the Quick Adjust option, you move the highlight down to the specific line for Image sharpening, Contrast, or Saturation, you can adjust any one of those values individually. For example, suppose you especially like the punchy, aggressive look of images taken with the Vivid setting, but you don't want to have the colors quite so intense. You can set Picture Control to Vivid, and then, on the secondary screen, adjust the Saturation value to a lower level, to reduce the intensity of the colors.

Note, though, that the Contrast adjustment is unavailable if Active D-Lighting (discussed later in this chapter) is turned on in the Shooting menu.

If you select Neutral from the Picture Control menu, the secondary screen does not include the Quick Adjust option, but it does let you adjust Image sharpening, Contrast, and Saturation individually.

If you select Monochrome from the Picture Control menu, the secondary adjustment screen, seen in Figure 4-21, is even more different from the screens for the previous settings, all of which include saturation processing that affects colors.

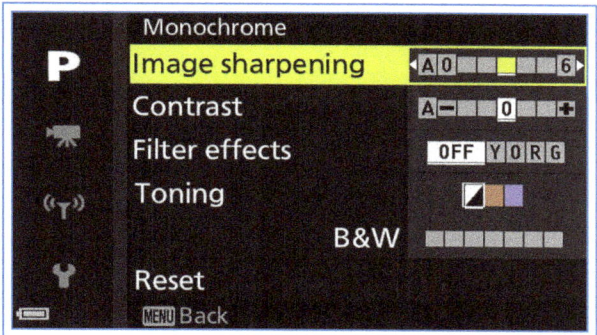

Figure 4-21. Picture Control Adjustment Screen for Monochrome Setting

With the Monochrome setting, adjustments are available for Image sharpening and Contrast, but not for Saturation, and there is no Quick Adjust option. However, the Monochrome setting includes two other options: Filter Effects and Toning. Image sharpening and Contrast work just the same as with the other Picture Control settings, as discussed above.

The third sub-option, Filter Effects, is a simulation of the use of a filter over the lens. If you select Filter Effects, you have four choices on the adjustment screen: Off, Y, O, R, and G, for yellow, orange, red, and green. These settings are intended to mimic the effects of colored filters, which can be used with film cameras when taking photographs with monochrome films. The yellow, orange, and red filters provide increasing levels of contrast that may darken the sky and enhance the appearance of a landscape scene. The green filter setting is intended to soften skin tones for use with portraits.

The Toning options let you add a color cast to your monochrome shots. The three Toning choices on the Monochrome menu are B&W (none), Sepia (brown), and Cyanotype (blue). With Toning highlighted, use the Left and Right buttons, multi selector dial, or command dial to select one of the three options. If you select either Sepia or Cyanotype and then press the Down button, the cursor will move to a scale below the three options that includes gradations of intensity for the selected color tone. Using the direction buttons, the multi selector dial, or the command dial, move the cursor right for more intensity, or left for less. (The normal setting is level 4.) Then press the OK button to lock in the setting.

Custom Picture Control

The Custom Picture Control option lets you take one of the four available Picture Control settings (Standard, Neutral, Vivid, or Monochrome) and tweak the available parameters (Image sharpening, Contrast, Saturation, Filter Effects, and Toning) to create a new setting that is crafted to your individual taste and that can be saved for later recall as an added selection for the Picture Control menu option.

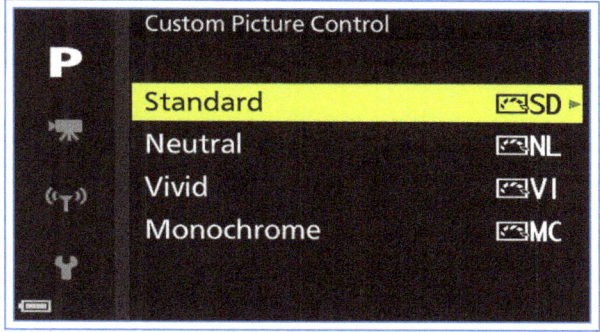

Figure 4-22. Custom Picture Control Main Options Screen

To use this feature, select Custom Picture Control from the Shooting menu, then press the OK button or the Right button. You will first see a screen with the choices of Edit and Save or Delete. Select Edit and Save and press the OK or Right button again to bring up the menu with the four choices, as shown in Figure 4-22, and select one of them by pressing the OK button or the Right button.

When the adjustment screen appears, adjust the parameters, which are the same as for the Picture Control item, discussed above. As noted before, the options are different for some of the settings: Monochrome, for example, has no Saturation adjustment, but does have Filter Effects and Toning adjustments.

For example, suppose you have found a group of adjustments to the Neutral setting that produces an appearance you want to be able to use whenever you take photographs of a certain waterfall. Go to the Custom Picture Control menu item, press OK or the Right button, and, on the next screen, select Edit and Save. You then are taken to a screen with the four basic Picture Control settings. Select Neutral, and, on the next screen, make your adjustments to Image sharpening, Contrast, and Saturation. When you are done, press OK, and you are taken to a screen that lets you save this setting to the Custom 1 or Custom 2 slot, as shown in Figure 4-23.

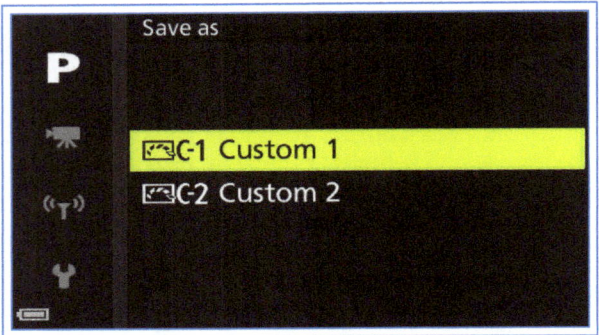

Figure 4-23. Screen to Save Custom Picture Control Setting

Highlight one of those options and press the OK button to confirm that selection. The camera will display a Done message. Then, whenever you want to recall that setting, go to the Picture Control menu item, where Custom 1 (or Custom 2) will now appear as an option below Monochrome, as shown in Figure 4-24.

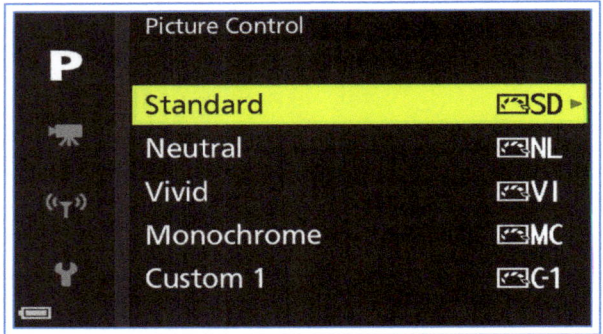

Figure 4-24. Custom Setting Added to Picture Control Menu

If you later want to delete the Custom 1 or 2 option, use the Custom Picture Control item and select Delete instead of Edit and Save.

White Balance

One issue that arises in photography is that film, or a digital camera's sensor, reacts differently to colors than the human eye does. When you or I see a scene in daylight or indoors under various types of artificial lighting, we generally do not notice a difference in the hues of the things we see depending on the light source. However, the camera's image sensor does not have this auto-correcting ability. The sensor "sees" colors differently depending on the "color temperature" of the light that illuminates the object or scene in question.

The color temperature of light is a numerical value expressed in a unit known as kelvins (K). A light source with a lower kelvin rating produces a "warmer" or more reddish light. A light source with a higher kelvin rating produces a "cooler" or more bluish light. For example, candlelight is rated at about 1,800 K; indoor tungsten light (ordinary light bulb) is rated at about 3,000 K; outdoor sunlight and electronic flash are rated at about 5,500 K; and outdoor shade is rated at about 7,000 K.

If you are using a film camera, you may need a colored filter in front of the lens or light source to "correct" for the color temperature of the light source. Any given color film is rated to reproduce colors accurately at a particular color temperature (or, to put it another way, with a particular light source). So if you are using color film rated for daylight use, you can use it outdoors without a filter. But if you happen to be using that film indoors, you will need a color filter to correct the color temperature; otherwise, the resulting picture will look excessively reddish because of the imbalance between the film and the color temperature of the light source.

With a modern digital camera you do not need to worry about filters, because the camera can adjust its electronic circuitry to correct the "white balance," which is the term used in the context of digital photography for balancing color temperature. The Coolpix P950, like most digital cameras, has a setting for white balance, which lets you choose the proper color correction to account for any given light source. Here is how to make this setting through the Shooting menu.

After you highlight the white balance setting, which is the fifth item down on the first screen of the Shooting menu, press the OK button or the Right button to bring up the list of the following choices for the white balance setting, each of them represented by an icon or a word or abbreviation: Auto (normal) [AUTO1]; Auto (warm lighting) [AUTO2]; Preset Manual [PRE]; Daylight [sun]; Incandescent [round light bulb]; Fluorescent [rectangular light bulb]; Cloudy [cloud]; Flash [lightning bolt]; and Choose Color Temperature [K]. The first six of these are shown in Figure 4-25.

The labels for these settings are self-explanatory. To select a setting, highlight it and press the OK button to confirm. If you select either Auto setting, you are done; there are no further adjustments available. With each of the other selections, though, you can fine-tune the setting, as described below.

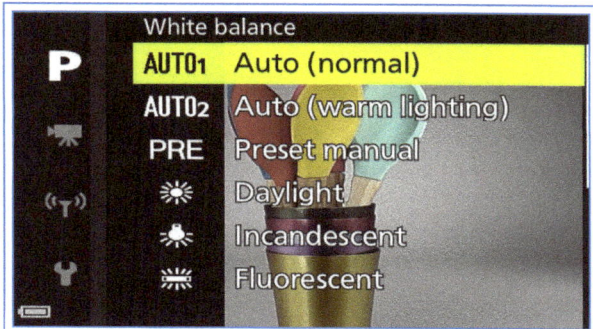

Figure 4-25. First Screen of White Balance Menu Options

If you highlight Daylight, Incandescent, Cloudy, or Flash, you can then press the Right button to bring up a screen with a scale at the left going from -3 at the bottom to +3 at the top, as shown in Figure 4-26.

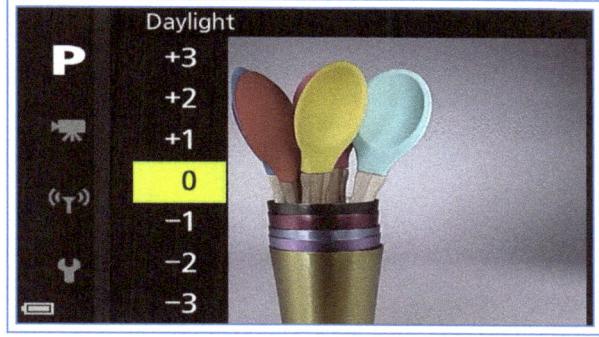

Figure 4-26. Scale to Adjust White Balance Daylight Setting

You can use the Up and Down buttons or the multi selector dial to move the yellow selection block up and down this scale to select a value. If the value is positive, the white balance is biased toward a bluish tint, and if it is negative, it is biased toward a reddish tint.

If you highlight the Fluorescent option, pressing the Right button brings up the further choices of 1, 2, or 3. These three sub-varieties of Fluorescent range from white to neutral to daylight. There are no other adjustments available with this setting.

With any of these settings that have an adjustment scale (Daylight, Incandescent, Fluorescent, Cloudy, or Flash), you need to press the OK button to confirm the setting once you have highlighted an adjustment amount, even if it is zero. The new white balance setting will not be effective until you have done that.

Finally, if you select Preset Manual, you can set the white balance manually. Use this option when you are faced with mixed light sources, or a reddish or otherwise unusual light source. To make this setting, highlight Preset Manual, then press the OK button or the Right button. The next screen will present the options to Cancel or Measure, as shown in Figure 4-27.

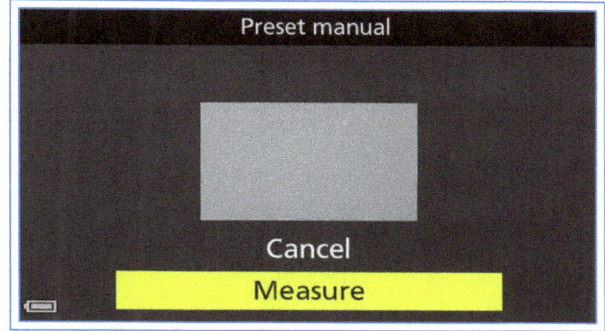

Figure 4-27. Screen to Measure Preset Manual White Balance

Highlight Measure and aim the square in the middle of the screen so it will be filled by a white or gray surface that is illuminated by the light source you will be using. Then press the OK button, and the camera will measure the white balance and store the setting. To use this setting now or in the future, turn back to the Preset Manual option at any time, even after the camera has been turned off and back on.

You can take advantage of the Preset Manual setting to add a color tint to a scene for creative effect if you want. For example, you can set the white balance manually using a red or orange surface for the measurement, which will result in a pronounced blue tint for any pictures taken under the same light source that you used when setting that white balance value. Just be careful to turn the white balance setting back to Auto or another more normal setting when you don't want that special effect for your images.

The other choice for the white balance menu option is Choose Color Temperature, the last item on the second screen of this menu item. Highlight this option, then press the OK button or the Right button to bring up the screen shown in Figure 4-28, with a scale of values at the left ranging from 2500 K to 10,000 K.

You can use this scale to set the numerical kelvin reading of your light source if you know it. You can determine this number using a color temperature meter, but, if you don't have a meter, you can still use the Choose Color Temperature option if you rely on guesswork or your sense of color. For example, if you have lighting from incandescent bulbs, you can use 3,000 K as a starting point, then change the value and watch the camera's display to see how natural the colors look. As you lower the color temperature setting on the menu, the image will become more "cool," or bluish; as you raise it, the image will appear more "warm," or reddish. Once you find the best setting, leave it in place and take your shots.

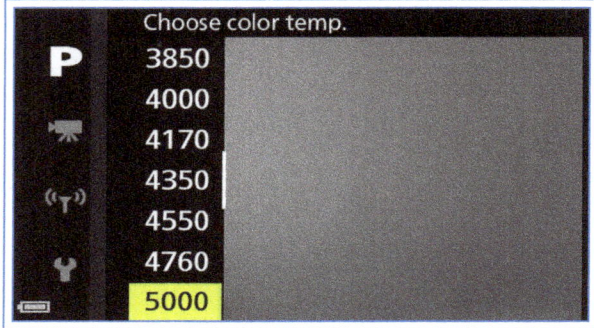

Figure 4-28. Screen for Setting White Balance by Color Temperature

Before I leave this topic, I am providing a chart of images showing how the various white balance settings on the P950 affect the colors of your shots. All of these images, shown in Figure 4-29, were taken under the same indoor lighting, which was balanced for daylight; the only thing that changed from shot to shot was the camera's white balance setting, as indicated.

In my opinion, Auto 1, Preset Manual, Daylight, Fluorescent 2, Flash, and Choose Color Temperature (using a value of 5000) all resulted in good color balance. Auto 2, Fluorescent 3, and Cloudy would be acceptable. However, even the results of those settings could be improved if you were to make further adjustments to tweak them for more or less bluish and reddish tints. The only settings that probably would not be usable in this situation were Incandescent and Fluorescent 1. In practice, I usually leave white balance set to Auto 1, but it is good to know that you have the option to make more individually crafted settings when the occasion calls for it.

Also, it is worthwhile to note that, if you use the Raw setting for Image Quality, you can adjust the white balance setting for your images after the fact, when you are using post-processing software. However, it is best to capture images using the correct settings if possible.

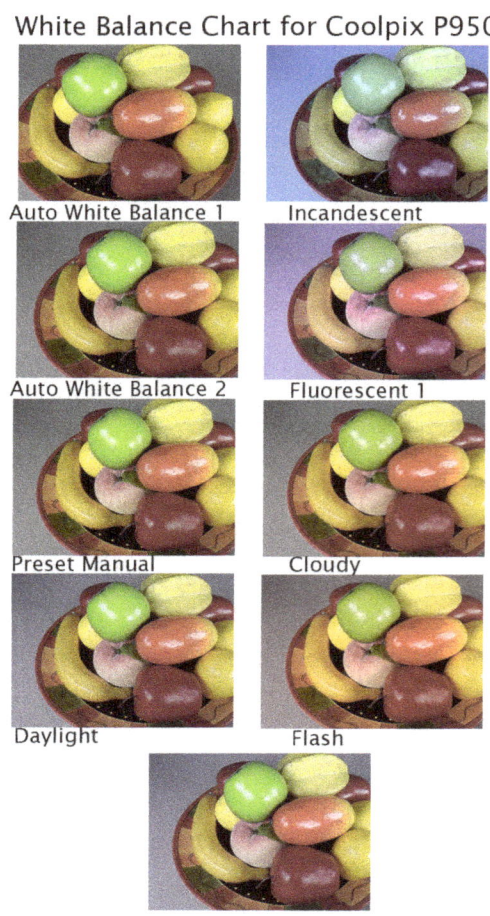

Figure 4-29. White Balance Comparison Chart

Metering

This next option on the Shooting menu lets you choose one of the three patterns of exposure metering offered by the Coolpix P950: Matrix, Center-weighted, or Spot. The menu selection screen is shown in Figure 4-30.

This setting tells the camera's automatic exposure system what part of the scene it should evaluate when deciding how to set the exposure. If you choose Matrix, the default option, the camera uses the entire scene that is visible on the display and bases its exposure setting on the overall average brightness of the scene. For example, if the camera is aimed at a landscape scene with trees, grass, buildings, sky, and people, the camera will measure the light being reflected from all of those parts of the scene and set the exposure accordingly. The resulting image is likely to look properly exposed.

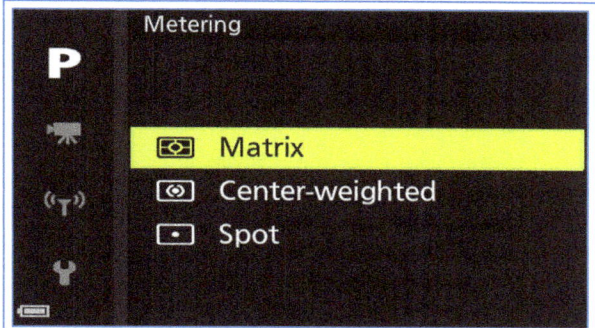

Figure 4-30. Metering Menu Options Screen

If, instead of a standard landscape scene, the camera is aimed at a small, dark object in front of a large, white wall, the camera will take into account the large expanse of white and likely will set the exposure to be too dark to show the dark object properly. In that case, the Matrix metering mode probably will not work well. You can use exposure compensation or Spot metering to achieve a better exposure measurement.

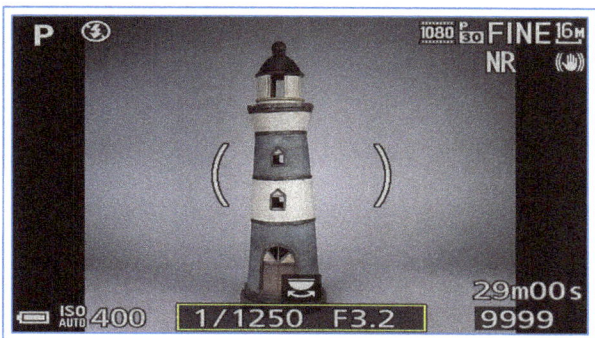

Figure 4-31. Shooting Screen with Center-weighted Metering

If you choose Center-weighted for metering, as shown in Figure 4-31, the camera still considers all of the light from the scene, but it gives additional weight to the center portion of the image, on the theory that your main subject is in or near the center. The camera displays two large arcs to mark the area that is being emphasized. This is a good metering method to use when you have a subject in the center of the scene that is the most important item in your composition—for example, the subject of a portrait, or an antique that you are photographing for an auction.

With Spot, as illustrated in Figure 4-32, the camera considers only the light in the area covered by the small circle that appears in the center of the screen.

When you set the metering method to Spot, you can see the effects of the exposure system quite dramatically by setting the camera to the Program exposure mode and aiming the small circle at various points, some bright and some dark, and seeing how dramatically the brightness of the scene changes on the camera's display. If you try a similar experiment by moving the camera around to aim at differently lit areas in Matrix mode, you may still see changes, but more subtle and gradual ones.

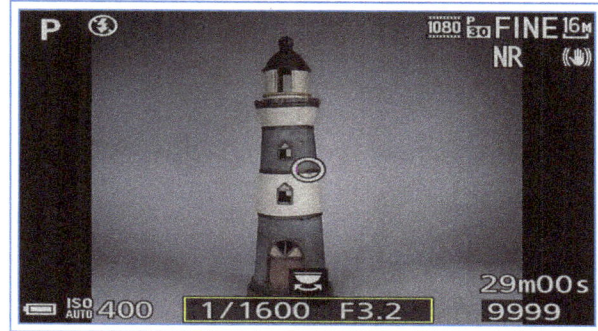

Figure 4-32. Shooting Screen with Spot Metering

The Spot setting is appropriate when you have a small subject for which proper exposure is particularly important, such as a collectible item that you are photographing for a catalog or online auction.

My preference is to use Matrix metering for outdoor shots with even lighting, such as landscapes, groups of people, and views of buildings, monuments, and the like. I use Spot metering on occasion, primarily when I am photographing an object whose brightness level contrasts sharply with the background. For example, if I am photographing a black camera against a white background, I may use Spot metering on the camera in order to avoid confusing the metering system because of the expanse of bright white in the scene. The Center-weighted method is useful when taking portraits and other images with one central subject that is of primary importance to the scene.

With all of the metering settings, including Center-weighted and Spot, the autofocus mode has no effect on metering. So, even if you set AF Area Mode to Manual and move the focus frame away from the center of the screen, the camera will meter the area outlined by the

Center-weighted arcs, the Spot circle, or the overall scene, depending on the metering setting.

The Metering menu option is dimmed and unavailable if Active D-Lighting is turned on at any level; in that case, the camera sets the metering mode to Matrix.

Next, I will discuss the items on screen 2 of the Shooting menu, shown in Figure 4-33, starting with Continuous.

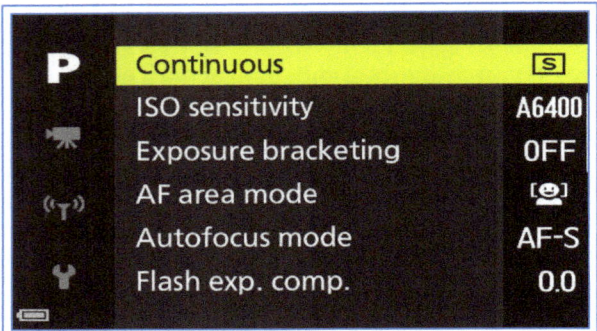

Figure 4-33. Screen 2 of Shooting Menu

Continuous

With some cameras, there is a button you can use to turn on continuous (or "burst") shooting. With the P950, the numerous options for continuous shooting are located on the Shooting menu, under the item called "Continuous." However, as discussed in Chapter 5, the Function button on top of the camera can be assigned to call up the Continuous option, so you can use a physical control for this purpose if you want to.

Regardless of whether you reach the continuous-shooting options through the menu system or by pressing the Function button, when the camera is set to a shooting mode in which burst shooting is available, the continuous options provide an impressive array of features.

The usefulness of rapid bursts of exposures is clearer in some contexts than in others. For example, when you're shooting sports, you can fire off a swift sequence of shots to catch the instant when a baseball player tags a runner, or to catch a soccer ball as it bounces off a player's head. But continuous shooting also can be helpful for more ordinary subjects, such as children at play. You have a better chance of capturing a fleeting smile or gesture if you keep the exposures rolling. Even if your subject is not moving, it can be useful to take multiple shots. When you're taking a portrait there may be subtle changes in the subject's expression, or in the way sunlight falls on a cheek. Taking a series of shots gives you some assurance that you won't come away from the photo session with no winning images.

In Figure 4-34, I used the Pre-shooting Cache option to capture an image of a bird spreading its wings as it flew away from a backyard bird feeder.

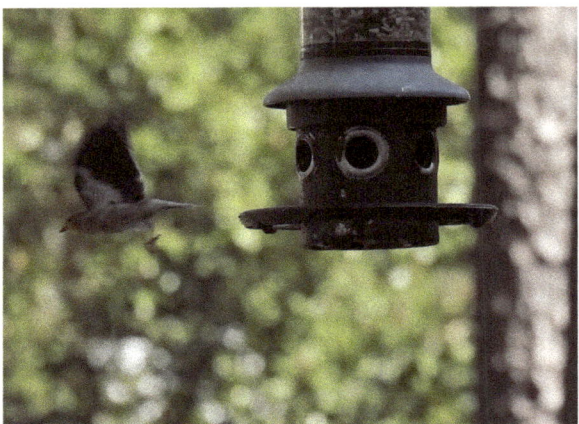

Figure 4-34. Continuous Shooting Example

To get access to the continuous options, the camera has to be in the Program, Aperture Priority, Shutter Priority, or Manual exposure mode, with a few exceptions. (With the Bird-watching mode and the Pet Portrait setting of Scene mode, you can select continuous shooting. With the Sports setting of Scene mode, continuous shooting is turned on by the camera and cannot be turned off.)

To use this feature, select the Continuous menu item, press the Right button or the OK button, and the next screen will display the first six of the seven available settings, as shown in Figure 4-35. (Or, as noted above, press the Function button if it is assigned to call up the Continuous menu option.)

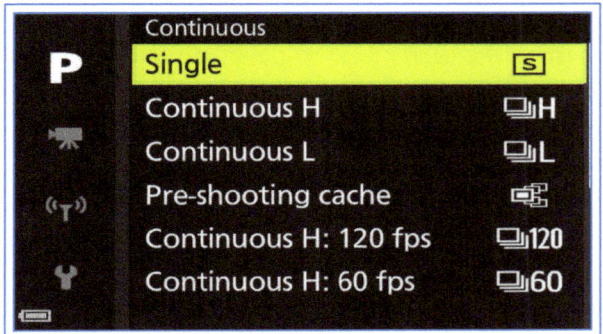

Figure 4-35. First Screen of Options for Continuous Shooting

These settings (except the first, for single shots, and the last, for intervals) offer various ways to take multiple shots while you hold down the shutter button. In each case, the exposure and focus settings are fixed when the first image is taken, and they will not vary for later shots, even if conditions would require different settings. The white balance is setting is fixed after the first shot for all multiple-shot options except Continuous L and Interval Timer. You cannot use flash for any of the multiple-shot settings except for the last one, the interval timer option.

You can activate the self-timer when continuous shooting is turned on and it will work, but, with several settings (Continuous H, Continuous L, and Pre-shooting Cache), when the timer triggers the shutter only one image will be taken. (With Continuous H and Continuous L, the camera will continue to shoot if you keep holding down the shutter button, but that defeats the purpose of using the self-timer.)

So there is no point in turning on continuous shooting and the self-timer at the same time, with those settings. However, with the Continuous H: 120 fps and Continuous H: 60 fps settings, the camera will take the full 60 shots when the self-timer triggers the shutter. Also, the self-timer can be used to start a sequence using the interval timer setting.

There are limitations on the shutter speeds the camera can use or that you can set when any of the continuous options is in effect, other than the interval timer. The slowest speed you can set is 1/30 second, 1/60 second, or 1/125 second, depending on what setting is selected.

As I discuss in Chapter 6, playing back continuous shots in this camera can be confusing. In playback mode, you will see the first image of a continuous series displayed on what looks like a stack of frames, indicating that this is the first of a continuous set, or, using Nikon's terminology, the "key" image of a "sequence."

There also will be a pair of icons at the bottom of the screen indicating that you have to press the OK button to display the full set of images, as shown in Figure 4-36.

After you press the OK button, you can move through the images in this group of continuous shots using the Left and Right buttons or the multi selector dial. To return to the main playback screen, press the Up button. You can then keep navigating through the other individual shots and sequences on the memory card.

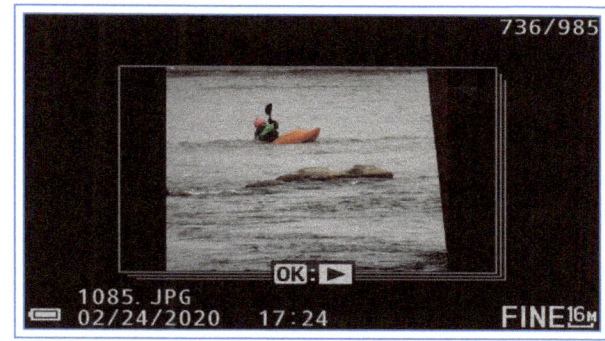

Figure 4-36. Burst of Images Displayed as Group

Following are details about the choices for continuous shooting with the Coolpix P950, as shown in Figure 4-35. The first option at the top of the Continuous menu screen is an icon with an S, for single shots. This is the default option. In effect, choosing this first option turns off continuous shooting.

The second option on the menu is the first selection for multiple shots. It is marked by an icon that looks like a stack of rectangular frames with the letter H inside, representing high-speed continuous shooting. With this option, the camera shoots up to ten shots at a speed of up to seven frames per second, depending on factors such as image size, image quality, lighting conditions, and the like. You can use any settings for the image quality and size, including the maximum quality, Raw+Fine, at 4608 x 3456 pixels.

The next icon, marked by an L for low-speed shooting, provides a capability similar to that for high-speed shooting, except that there is a trade-off of increased capacity versus slower speed. That is, you can take up to 200 images, but at a speed of no more than about one frame per second. With this setting, the camera will adjust white balance as needed for any given exposure.

The next icon on the list looks like a stack of frames branching out in two directions. Selecting this icon activates an interesting feature called Pre-shooting Cache. With this option, the camera actually captures several images before you press the shutter button to take pictures.

In practice, this option has its limitations, though it is still a welcome innovation. When you press the shutter button halfway to evaluate exposure and focus, the camera will capture up to ten images before you press the button the rest of the way down, and up to 30 more as you hold the button down to take the images. The Pre-shooting Cache icon on the display turns green while images are being recorded to the cache; once you press the shutter button all the way down, the last ten of those cached images are saved to the memory card, along with up to 30 shots taken while the shutter is pressed all the way down. The maximum rate is a speedy 15 frames per second, but the catch is that the images are fixed at a small size of one megapixel, or 1280 x 960 pixels, and at Normal quality.

Pre-shooting Cache is a tool to use when you are monitoring a scene and waiting for just the right moment to catch a particular action or expression that may come up very quickly, and possibly will fade away quickly as well. When it looks as if the action is about to happen, you can press the shutter button halfway down to get ready, and, if the action comes up faster than expected, you won't miss it because of slow reactions. You can then press the shutter button all the way down to capture the rest of the sequence. If you don't mind a reduction in the resolution of your images, this is an interesting option to have available.

As noted earlier, I used this option to capture the image in Figure 4-34. I used this approach because it is hard to predict when a bird will take off from the feeder, and some birds linger there for quite a while, so it made sense to rely on the Pre-shooting Cache option to make it easier to capture the bird in mid-flight.

Be sure to note one possible pitfall here: If you press the shutter button down halfway but never press it all the way to take any pictures, the contents of the pre-shooting cache will be discarded and no pictures at all will be recorded. You have to press the shutter button down all the way at some point in order to "lock in" the pre-shooting images. Note also that, when you have finished shooting, you may see circulating-block icons on the screen, indicating that the camera needs time to process the contents of the cache as well as the contents of the other images you have taken.

The next choice on the menu, Continuous H: 120 fps, is indicated by the number 120, representing the extremely rapid rate of 120 frames per second. With this setting, the camera emphasizes both speed and quantity, giving you 60 images at this super pace, but at a drastic reduction in quality down to 640 x 480 pixels

(VGA), which is the resolution of an old-fashioned computer monitor. Images shot using this option may look fine on your computer, but they will be quite grainy and will not be suitable for any degree of enlargement. Still, if you need to analyze a golf swing or otherwise shoot a sequence of many pictures over a period of about one-half second, this may be the choice for you. Here again, you will almost certainly see the time-delay icons after shooting, as the camera processes the large quantity of image information that it sucked in like a vacuum cleaner.

The next option, Continuous H: 60 fps, is similar to the previous one, except that the camera takes 60 shots at a somewhat higher resolution of two megapixels, or 1920 x 1080 pixels, and at the slower speed of 60 frames per second. Use this option if you need a very speedy sequence of shots, but need a bit better quality or prefer the 16:9 widescreen aspect ratio of this setting.

The last entry on the continuous-shooting menu is interval timer shooting, which gives the Coolpix P950 a capability for time-lapse shooting. When you select this option and move to the next screen, the camera displays two blocks, as shown in Figure 4-37—one for minutes and one for seconds.

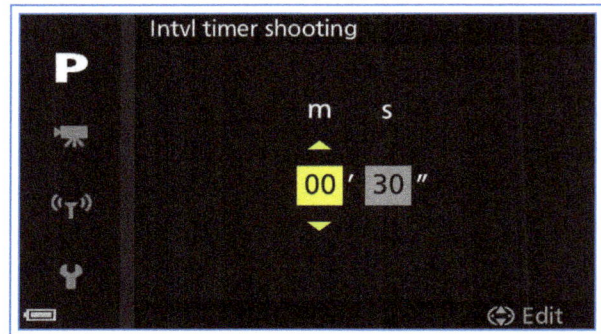

Figure 4-37. Screen to set Interval for Interval Timer Option

You can select a value for the interval from 0 to 60 minutes plus either 0 or 30 seconds, up to a maximum time of 60 minutes overall. The shortest interval available is 30 seconds; the next is one minute; then one minute 30 seconds, and so on.

There is no setting for the number of shots; the camera will keep taking shots at the specified interval until (1) the memory card is filled up, (2) you stop the process by pressing the shutter button, or (3) the camera has captured 9999 shots in the sequence. You can use any settings for Image Quality and Image Size, including the highest quality, Raw+Fine.

When you press the shutter button all the way, the camera takes the first image, then blanks out the display. The green light around the power button will blink slowly while interval shooting is active. Shortly before each interval elapses, the display will turn back on, and at the specified time the camera will take the next shot. To interrupt the sequence of shots before it is complete, you can press the shutter button and the sequence will end. The camera adjusts its focus and exposure for each shot, if its current settings for focus and exposure permit those adjustments, but it does not allow you to zoom the lens in or out, so be sure to have the focal length adjusted as you want it before beginning a sequence.

The resulting images are stored on your memory card in specially designated folders with the letters INTVL in their names. For example, a folder with shots from one shooting session might be labeled as 102INTVL, and the images inside it might be labeled DSCN001.jpg, DSCN002.jpg, and so on. The camera does not assemble the images into a time-lapse movie; you have to do that yourself using the Nikon software or another photo-processing program.

The interval timer option gives you excellent opportunities for creative photography. For example, you can aim the camera at a construction site and record all work that is done over a period of time, then play back the images as a time-lapse movie using software such as Adobe Premiere Elements or iMovie. If you set the camera to shoot one image every minute for 24 hours, you would end up with 1440 images. If you play them back at the standard video rate (in the United States) of 30 frames per second, the video showing 24 hours of action would play back in just 48 seconds. You may have seen sequences of this sort on television showing weather patterns unfolding at rapid speeds or speeded-up views of crowds gathering for events.

Also, interval shooting can be used to operate the camera remotely, as when you place it on a pole or other location that is out of your reach, to record images from a high or otherwise inaccessible vantage point. If you are able to attach the P950 to a remote-controlled aerial drone, you could turn on interval shooting to capture images from the air.

When you use interval shooting on the ground, you need to set the camera on a sturdy, steady tripod; the slightest motion of the camera will be obvious when the sequence is played back. Also, you need to be able to keep the camera powered on continuously. The camera turns off its display between shots, so its battery power is conserved to some extent.

However, if you are shooting a sequence that lasts several hours or more, you should use the Nikon AC adapter designated for this camera, which is discussed in Appendix A. Finally, it's generally a good idea, if it is practical under the circumstances, to use Manual exposure mode and to set the white balance and ISO Sensitivity options to definite settings rather than to Auto settings, so there is no distracting flickering among the images when the camera adjusts these settings automatically.

Note that the Coolpix P950 offers a similar feature called Time-lapse Movie as one of the scene types for Scene mode, as discussed in Chapter 3. With that option, you select a preset type of time-lapse subject, such as Sunset or Cityscape, and the camera makes all of the necessary settings for you. Three of those settings, Cityscape, Landscape, and Sunset, use intervals shorter than 30 seconds, so you would not be able to duplicate those settings using the interval timer feature.

On the other hand, the interval timer option can take as many as 9999 shots, whereas the Time-lapse Movie option will only take 250 or 300 shots, depending on the setting for Frame Rate on the Movie menu. And, of course, with interval timer, you can make many settings on the Shooting menu, but you cannot do so with the Time-lapse Movie option. So, with interval timer and Time-lapse Movie, you have two different features available with different capabilities.

ISO Sensitivity

ISO is a measure of the light sensitivity of photographic film or digital sensors. The higher the ISO rating, the more sensitive the film or sensor is to light. Therefore, if you shoot an image or video using a high ISO value, you will not need as much light to achieve a normal exposure as you would with a lower value. One result is that you can use a faster shutter speed, narrower aperture, or possibly both, than with a lower ISO.

The trade-off is that, with higher ISO values, the sensor is likely to produce visual "noise" that affects the image with an appearance of graininess. Camera makers have made considerable strides in creating sensors that can use high ISO values without too much noise, but there still is some drop-off in quality, especially at the highest ISO values.

Generally speaking, you should shoot your images with the camera set to the lowest ISO possible that will allow the image to be exposed properly. (One exception to this rule is if you want, for creative purposes, the grainy look that comes from shooting at a high ISO value.) For example, if you are shooting indoors in low light, you may need to set the ISO to a high value (say, ISO 800) so you can expose the image with a reasonably fast shutter speed. Otherwise, if the camera uses a slow shutter speed, the resulting image would likely be blurry and possibly unusable.

To summarize: Shoot with low ISO settings (such as 100 with the P950) when possible; shoot with high ISO settings (400 or higher, up to 1600 or even 3200 or 6400) when necessary to allow a fast shutter speed to stop action and avoid blurriness, or when desired to achieve a creative effect with graininess.

With that background, here is how to set ISO on this camera. Press the Menu button and move to the ISO Sensitivity line on the second screen of the Shooting menu, then press the Right button to get to the screen that lets you select either ISO Sensitivity or Minimum Shutter Speed, as shown in Figure 4-38.

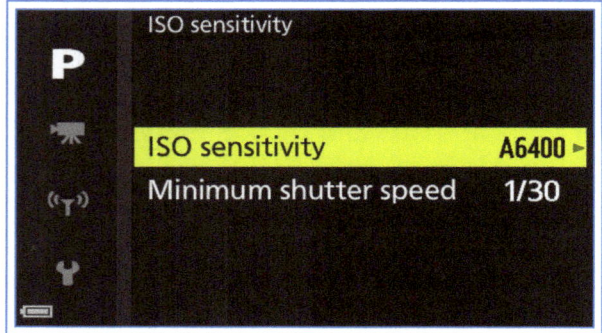

Figure 4-38. ISO Sensitivity Main Options Screen

For now, select ISO Sensitivity and press the Right button again to get to the ISO Sensitivity options. This first of the two ISO setting screens is shown in Figure 4-39. (As an alternative, you can assign the Function button to call up a menu with the ISO settings, as discussed in Chapter 5.)

With many other cameras in this class, the available ISO settings include one called Auto ISO as well as a list of specific values, ranging from a low value such as ISO 100 to a high value of ISO 3200 or higher. With the Coolpix P950, however, there is not a single Auto ISO selection. Instead, the first several selections on the ISO menu, each of which begins with the letter "A," are all Auto ISO options, with specific ranges of values.

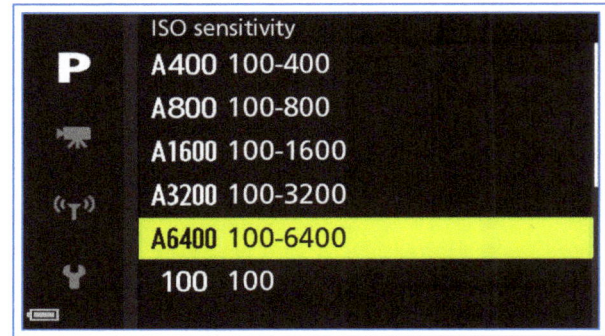

Figure 4-39. Screen to Select ISO Sensitivity Setting

For example, as seen in Figure 4-39, the first option is shown as A400 100-400. If you select this option, the camera will automatically select an ISO value within the range of ISO 100 to ISO 400, depending on the existing lighting conditions, the settings for aperture and shutter speed, and the setting you have made for Minimum Shutter Speed, discussed later in this section. If you choose the final option for Auto ISO, shown as A6400 100-6400, the camera will automatically select an ISO value within the range of 100 to 6400.

So, in effect, if you want to use a traditional Auto ISO option, select A6400, and the camera will select an ISO value from its full range of possibilities. If you want to limit the range of options, so the camera does not choose a high value that may introduce unwanted noise into your images, select one of the lower Auto ranges, or set a specific value from the list of values that follows the listing of Auto settings, as seen in Figure 4-40, which shows the second screen of the ISO Sensitivity menu option. The choices are 100, 200, 400, 800, 1600, 3200, and 6400.

Chapter 4: The Shooting Menu

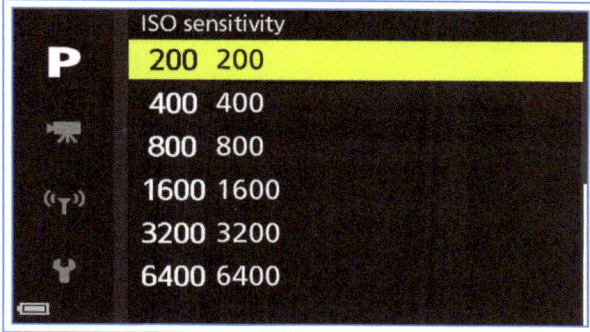

Figure 4-40. Second Screen of ISO Sensitivity Settings

I usually leave the ISO setting at A6400 for everyday shooting. However, in some cases, I will choose a specific numerical value. When I am using a tripod and want to have the best possible quality, I will set the ISO to 100. Because of the tripod, I am not concerned about image blur from camera motion if a slow shutter speed is needed. However, if I am shooting fast action such as sports or shooting in dim light, I often will set the ISO to a high value, such as 800 or 1600, so the camera can use a fast shutter speed to stop the action or to make a bright enough exposure.

I rarely set ISO as high as 3200 or 6400, because of the negative effect of such a setting on image quality. Figures 4-41 and 4-42 are segments of two shots I took of a doll, the first one shot at ISO 100, and the second one at ISO 6400, to illustrate the difference in quality that often results from using such a high ISO value.

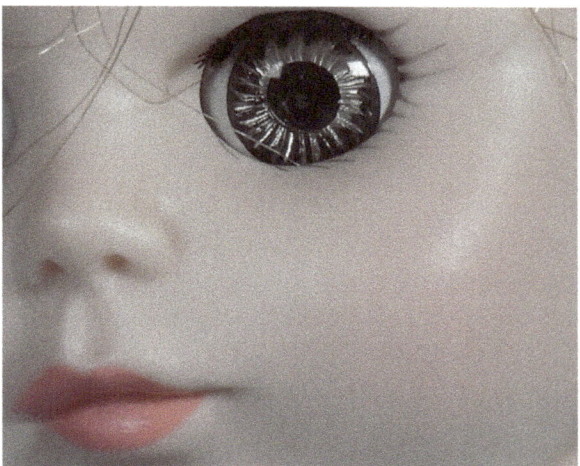

Figure 4-41. ISO Set to 100

As you can see, Figure 4-42, taken with the high ISO setting, shows considerable graininess and distortion of the picture of the doll. That image would not be usable for many purposes. Figure 4-41, taken at ISO 100, is a higher-quality image that depicts the subject clearly.

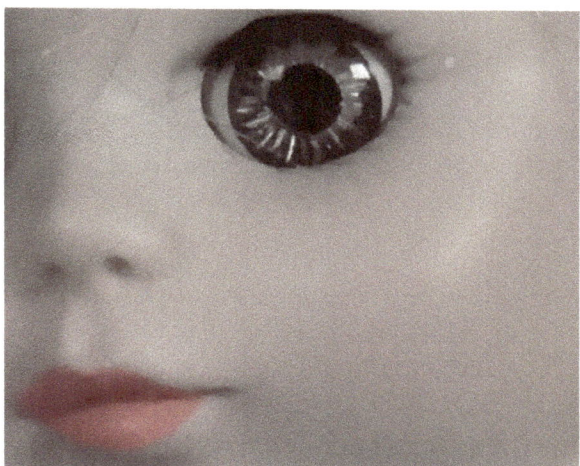

Figure 4-42. ISO Set to 6400

Minimum Shutter Speed

Going back to the first branch on the ISO menu screens, you can use the Minimum Shutter Speed setting to specify the slowest shutter speed the camera will use when it is set to the Program or Aperture Priority mode and any of the Auto ISO settings (A400 to A6400) is in effect, before it starts to increase the ISO sensitivity.

To understand this setting, it's helpful to consider an example. Set the camera to Program mode. Press the Menu button, use the multi selector dial or the Up and Down buttons to highlight ISO Sensitivity on the display, and press the Right button to get to the next screen. Set the ISO Sensitivity option to A6400. Then go back to the main ISO Sensitivity menu, highlight Minimum Shutter Speed, press the Right button, and select 1/30 second from the list of values on the screen, as shown in Figure 4-43. Press the OK button to confirm.

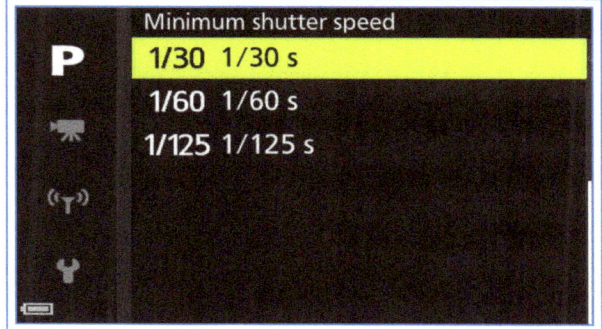

Figure 4-43. Minimum Shutter Speed Options Screen

With those settings, the camera will attempt to expose the image properly using a shutter speed no slower than 1/30 second, your Minimum Shutter Speed setting. If the A6400 setting increases to its maximum limit of ISO 6400 and the image is still too dark, then the camera will drop to a slower shutter speed in order to achieve a good exposure. So, in effect, this setting forces the camera to try to keep the shutter speed at 1/30 second or faster, but if that's not possible, the camera will change to a slower shutter speed.

You may want to use this setting to avoid using slow shutter speeds that are likely to result in blurred photos because of camera motion, or to capture images of moving subjects, such as children playing. If you use a setting such as 1/125 second (the fastest setting possible) for Minimum Shutter Speed, along with an ISO setting such as A1600, which allows the ISO to go as high as 1600, you are likely to be able to take all of your exposures using the 1/125 second shutter speed (if the light is bright enough), preserving your ability to avoid camera shake and to capture ordinary action.

In Auto mode and with all of the scene settings, Auto ISO is automatically set and you cannot adjust the ISO setting. The same is true of the Creative, Moon, Bird-watching, and Scene modes. With several continuous-shooting options (Pre-Shooting Cache, Continuous H:120 fps, and Continuous H:60 fps), ISO is automatically set to A1600. In Movie Manual mode with an HS (high-speed) option in effect, ISO is set to A1600.

Exposure Bracketing

Exposure bracketing is a feature that lets you take three pictures with one press of the shutter button, with three different exposure settings, giving you an added chance of getting one good, usable image. In addition, exposure bracketing is a good way to take three pictures that can be merged in software to produce an HDR (high dynamic range) composite, which shows clear details in both the highlights and the shadows throughout the image by combining the best-exposed parts of each shot.

To use exposure bracketing, the camera must be set to the Program, Aperture Priority, or Shutter Priority mode. Navigate to the third line on screen 2 of the Shooting menu and press the OK or Right button to go to the next screen, which lists four choices: ±0.3, ±0.7, ±1.0, and Off, as shown in Figure 4-44.

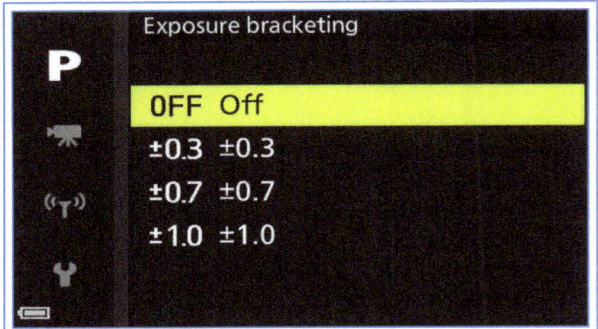

Figure 4-44. Exposure Bracketing Menu Options Screen

Use the multi selector dial or direction buttons to highlight your choice, then make the selection by pressing the OK button. When you exit to shooting mode, the camera's display will include a notation such as BKT±0.7, as shown in Figure 4-45, unless you left bracketing turned off. (Press the Display button, if necessary, to show this detail on the screen.)

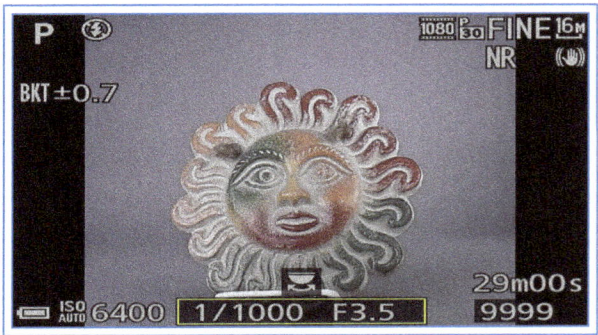

Figure 4-45. BKT Icon on Shooting Screen

This notation means the camera will take three exposures separated by the indicated amount of exposure value (EV, a standard measure of brightness). Adding a single unit of EV, +1.0, has the same effect as opening the aperture by one full f-stop.

When you are ready to shoot, press and release the shutter button and hold the camera steady (or use a tripod) while it takes the three exposures. The first picture taken is always at the metered level, or 0 change in exposure value (EV); the second is at the lower EV (darker), and the third is at the higher EV (brighter). If you have added exposure compensation, the bracketed exposures are taken at three levels relative to the adjusted exposure.

The flash cannot be used when bracketing is in effect. If you press the Flash button (Up button) when bracketing is turned on, nothing will happen. If the

Chapter 4: The Shooting Menu

flash was previously set to forced on (Fill Flash) or any other mode in which the flash might fire, the camera will turn the flash off when bracketing is selected. Exposure bracketing also cannot be used with continuous shooting, Multiple Exposure, the self-timer, the smile timer, or when Picture Control is set to Monochrome.

Be sure to cancel exposure bracketing when you are done using this feature; otherwise, it will stay in effect even after you turn the camera off and back on again.

AF Area Mode

This next option on the second screen of the Shooting menu gives you several options for controlling how the autofocus frame is set up when the camera is in autofocus mode.

Once this menu option is highlighted, press the OK button or the Right button to display the next menu screen, and then use the multi selector dial or the Up and Down buttons to select one of the six options shown in Figure 4-46, as follows:

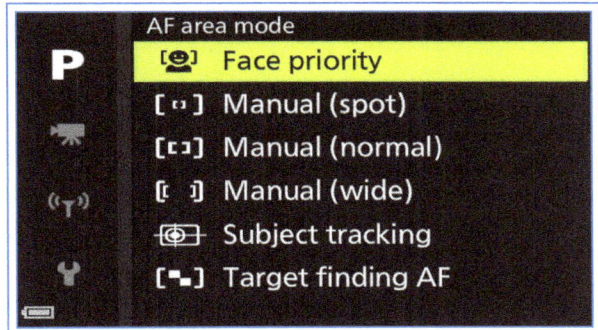

Figure 4-46. AF Area Mode Menu Options Screen

Face Priority

With this option, the camera looks for human faces. If it detects one or more faces, it puts a yellow, double-bordered frame on the closest face, and single-bordered frames on other faces, as shown in Figure 4-47. When you press the shutter button halfway, the camera will focus on the main face and place a double-bordered green frame on it.

If no faces are detected with this setting in effect, the camera selects the closest subject it can focus on.

This is a good option to choose when you're at a picnic or other group function and you need to take a quick snapshot with focus fixed on people's faces rather than on trees, buildings, or other objects. In other situations, you may want to take more time and select the focus point and other options yourself.

The camera also uses face detection with the Portrait and Night Portrait settings for Scene mode, and when the smile timer is in use.

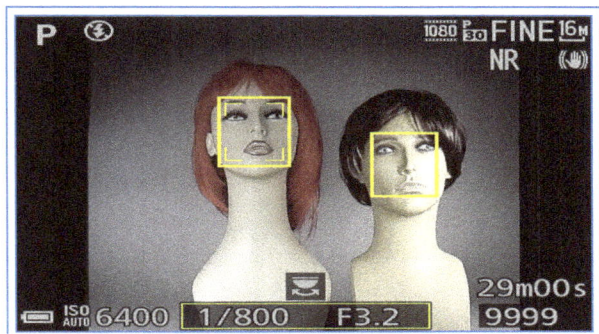

Figure 4-47. Faces Detected by Camera

Manual (Spot, Normal or Wide)

The next three options for AF Area Mode are variations of the Manual setting. The only differences are the sizes of the focus frames used—Spot, Normal, or Wide. The illustrations here all use the Normal size.

If you select one of the three Manual settings for AF Area Mode, the camera displays a focus frame of the chosen size in the center of the screen, with arrows pointing in each direction outside the frame. You can now press the four direction buttons or turn the multi selector dial to move the focus frame to any of 99 possible locations around the screen, as shown in Figure 4-48. (There are only 81 locations available if you are using the 1:1 aspect ratio, with Image Size set to 3456 x 3456, and there are only 63 or 49 positions when AF Area Mode is set to Manual-Wide.)

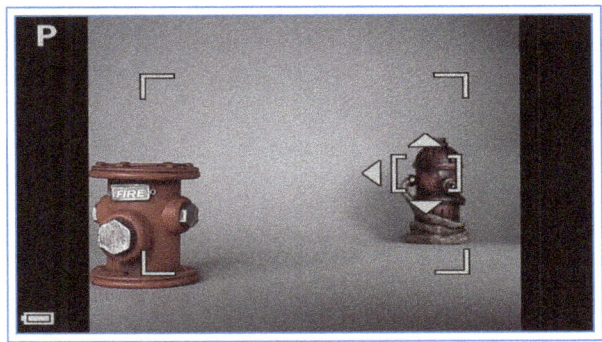

Figure 4-48. Movable Focus Frame with Manual Setting

This is a good option if you are shooting a scene with items at varying distances from the camera and you want to focus on an item that is not in the center of the scene. Of course, this option is useful only if you have time to select it and move the focus frame to the location where you want it. If you don't have time, it may be easier just to place the center of the frame over the item you want to focus on, press the shutter button halfway to lock focus, and then move the camera back to compose the image as you want it. That method is also the best way to proceed when you are using Center-weighted or Spot for the Metering option and you want to lock both focus and exposure for a subject that is not in the center of the scene. If you use the Manual setting for AF Area Mode in that situation, the focus will be set on the off-center subject, but the exposure will be based on the subject in the center of the screen.

If you do have the time to use the Manual option for AF Area Mode, here is how to use it. Once you have located the focus frame where you want it using the buttons or dial, press the shutter button to lock focus and then take the picture. The focus frame will stay in this location even after the camera is powered off and back on, so be sure to reset it to the center when you no longer need it in an off-center position. When the frame is in the center of the screen, a dot will appear in the center of the frame while it is movable.

If you need to use one of the four direction buttons for another purpose while using Manual AF Area Mode, press the OK button to return the buttons to their other functions (flash mode, focus mode, self-timer, and exposure compensation); then, after using a button for another function, press OK again to return the buttons to controlling the location of the focus frame.

Subject Tracking

This next AF Area Mode option is designed for situations in which you need to track a moving subject, such as a sports competitor, a pet, or a child at play. Once you have selected this mode, you will see a small, white, square-shaped bracket in the center of the screen, with the words OK Start below it, as shown in Figure 4-49.

Aim this square bracket at the subject you want to track and press the OK button. The frame will change to a double set of yellow brackets, as shown in Figure 4-50, which the camera will try to keep centered over the subject, even as the subject (or the camera) moves.

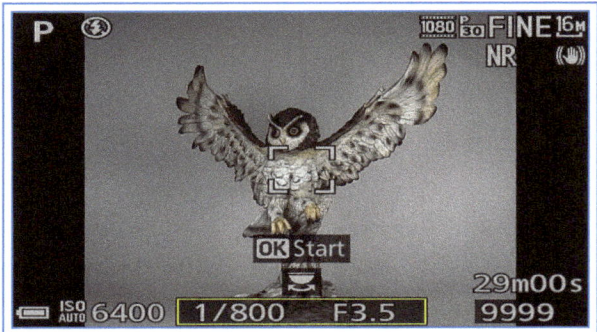

Figure 4-49. Subject Tracking Option Ready to Activate

When you press the shutter button halfway to check exposure, the frame turns green to confirm exposure, and tracking stops. To start tracking again, release the shutter button. To end tracking without taking a picture, press the OK button. Press the shutter button all the way down when you are ready to take the picture.

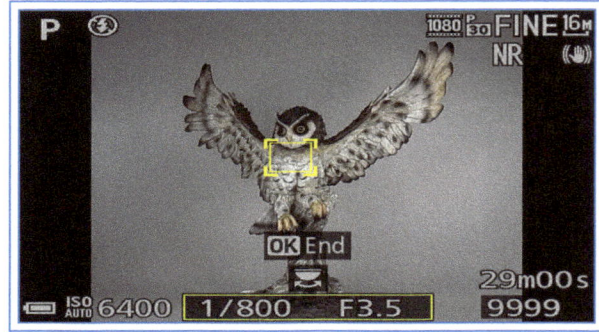

Figure 4-50. Subject Tracking AF Frame in Use

Target Finding AF

The final option for AF Area Mode, Target Finding AF, is the default setting and the one the camera uses when it is set to the Auto or Creative shooting mode. With this option, the P950 uses its programming to try to select the main focus point(s) in the scene it is aimed at. The camera does not have any focus frame on its display screen at first. As you aim the camera at a scene, though, the camera may display yellow frames of varying sizes and shapes on the screen, as shown in Figure 4-51, as it tries to detect the subject to focus on.

When you press the shutter button halfway to lock focus, the camera will try to select the "main" subject. It will first look for a human face, then for a subject that matches programmed factors, such as size, position, and color. If it has not found a main subject, it will focus on the items closest to the camera within nine focus blocks in the central part of the display. It will display one or more green rectangles on the screen to show the point(s) it chose for focusing, as shown in Figure 4-52.

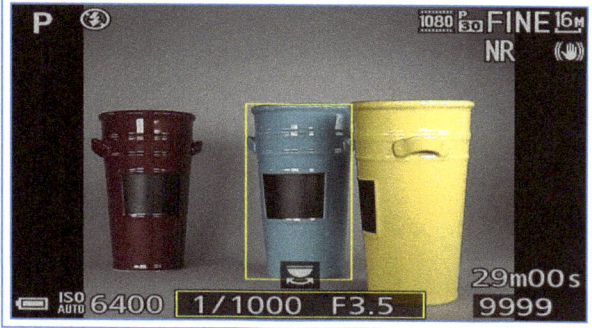

Figure 4-51. Target Finding AF Option in Use Before Focusing

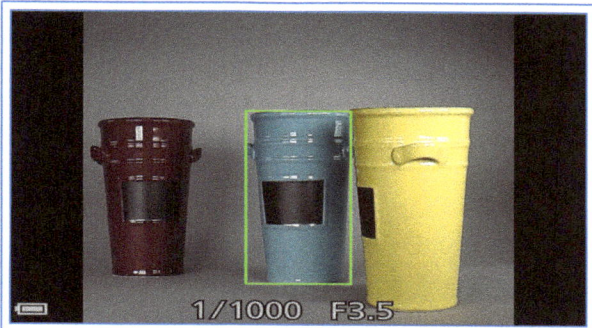

Figure 4-52. Target Finding AF in Use After Focusing

This focusing mode is good for shots of general scenes when you don't have time to choose a focus point yourself or when there is not much doubt about where the camera will set its focus. For example, if you are taking a snapshot of a person in front of a scenic view, you can safely assume that the camera will focus on the person. If the scene includes multiple objects fairly close to the camera, you might be better off using one of the Manual settings to make sure the subject you want to focus on is inside the focus frame.

Autofocus Mode

This feature, whose menu screen is shown in Figure 4-53, lets you decide whether the camera will focus just once, when you press the shutter button halfway, or will focus continuously before you press the button halfway. This setting is available only when the focus mode selector is set to the AF position, for autofocus.

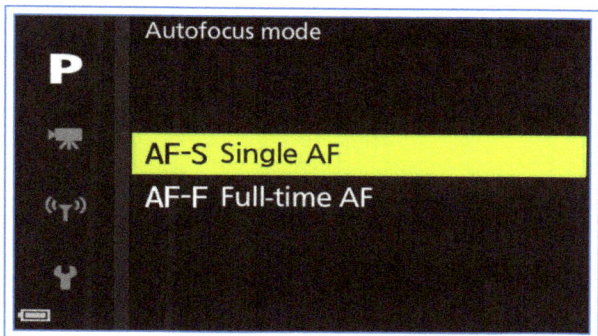

Figure 4-53. Autofocus Mode Menu Options Screen

Choose Single AF if you want to conserve the battery and wait until you are ready to take the picture before the camera uses its autofocus mechanism; choose Full-time AF if you want the camera to focus continuously. Although the Full-time option will use up your battery more quickly, it has the advantage of keeping the image in focus as you move the camera or your subject moves around; in that way, when you are ready to capture the image, the camera can make the final focusing adjustments quickly when you press the shutter button.

This option does not apply for shooting movies; you need to select an autofocus mode from the Movie menu for that situation. With the infinity focus mode, the camera uses Single AF for Autofocus Mode, regardless of the setting for this option. When the smile timer is active, the camera uses Single AF in all cases.

Flash Exposure Compensation

This option works in similar fashion to standard exposure compensation, discussed in Chapter 2. It is available only in the Program, Aperture Priority, Shutter Priority, and Manual exposure modes. You can dial in an amount of positive or negative flash exposure compensation up to two EV units in either direction, in increments of 1/3 EV. When you do that, the camera will increase or decrease the output of the flash, unless it was already using its maximum or minimum power. This option also works when a compatible flash unit, such as Nikon Speedlight SB-500, is attached to the camera's accessory shoe and powered on.

I find this setting of most use when I'm taking a portrait with flash. I like to use some negative flash exposure compensation to make sure the flash does not wash out the image with excessive brightness.

To use this setting, go to its entry on the second screen of the Shooting menu and press the OK button or the Right button to get to the adjustment screen. At that screen, turn the multi selector dial or use the Up and Down buttons to dial in up to +2.0 EV or -2.0 EV, as shown in Figure 4-54.

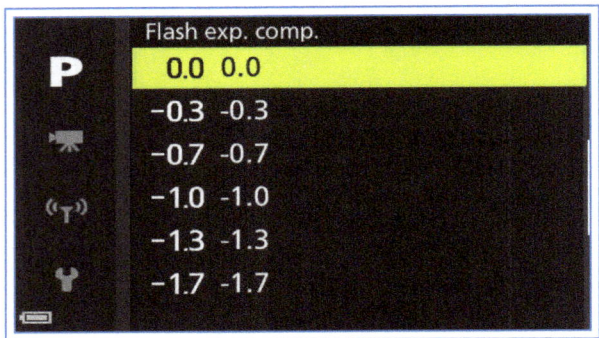

Figure 4-54. Flash Exposure Compensation Setting Screen

Press the OK button to confirm your selection when the value you want to choose is highlighted in the yellow bar. When you have activated a positive or negative amount of flash exposure compensation, that value will appear on the camera's display in the lower right-hand corner, but only when the flash is popped up or an external flash is attached and turned on. That value will remain in effect even after the camera has been powered off and back on, so be sure to cancel it when you no longer need the compensation.

The third screen of the Shooting menu is shown in Figure 4-55.

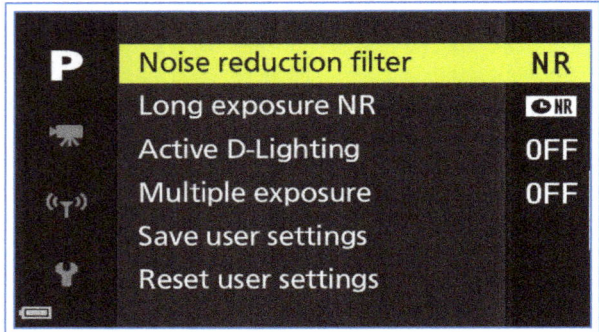

Figure 4-55. Screen 3 of Shooting Menu

Noise Reduction Filter

Noise reduction is an electronic feature built into the P950's programming to compensate for visual noise in your images, which can be caused by long exposures or by the use of high ISO settings. By default, this option is set to Normal, which causes the camera to use a moderate amount of noise reduction. If you want to have larger or smaller amounts of noise reduction applied in every case, you can switch the setting to High or Low, as shown in Figure 4-56. You cannot turn noise reduction completely off.

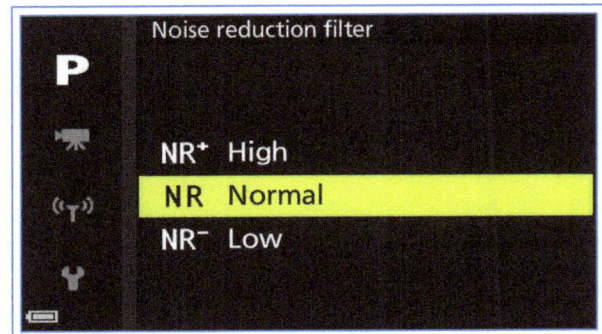

Figure 4-56. Noise Reduction Filter Menu Options Screen

What you do with this setting is a matter of personal preference. If you are going to be using Photoshop, Photoshop Elements, or similar software to process the images on your computer, you may want to leave Noise Reduction Filter set to Low, so you can minimize the amount of processing done in the camera.

Excessive noise reduction can reduce the detail and other positive features of an image. However, if you will be using the shots straight from the camera and you are shooting with long shutter speeds or high ISO settings, you may well want to turn this setting up to High to avoid the graininess that comes from visual noise.

Long Exposure NR

This next setting is similar to the previous one, although this one addresses only the noise that is caused in long exposures (those that last for one-quarter of a second or longer). If this option is set to Auto (the default), the camera processes exposures of that length to reduce noise; if it is turned off, that processing does not take place.

Active D-Lighting

This second entry on screen three of the Shooting menu can help you avoid problems with excessive contrast in your images. Such problems arise because digital cameras cannot easily process a wide range of dark and light areas in the same image—that is, their "dynamic range" is limited. So, if you are taking a picture in an area partly lit by bright sunlight and partly in deep shade, the resulting image is likely to have dark areas in which details are lost in the shadows, or areas in which highlights, or bright areas, are excessively light, or "blown out," so, again, the details of the image are lost. One approach to this problem is to use HDR techniques, with which multiple photographs of the same scene with different exposures are combined into a composite image that is properly exposed throughout the entire scene. I discussed that technique in Chapter 3, in connection with the Backlighting/HDR setting of Scene mode.

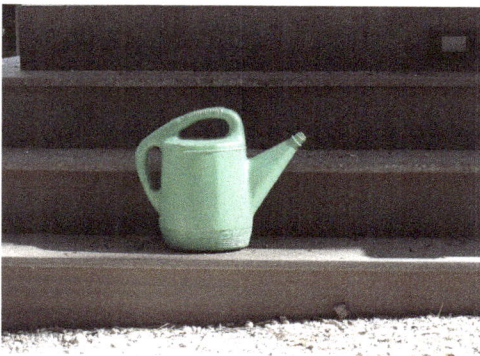

Figure 4-58. Active D-Lighting Turned Off

The Active D-Lighting menu option gives you another way to approach the problem of uneven lighting. This feature uses processing in the camera to boost details in dark areas and reduce overexposure in bright areas, resulting in a single image with better exposure than would be possible otherwise. If you turn this option on, the camera reduces the overall exposure and performs digital processing as it records the image, resulting in some restoration of details in the shadows and in the highlights, to even out the lighting. The Shooting menu, as shown in Figure 4-57, provides three levels of this processing: High, Normal, and Low, as well as Off, the default setting.

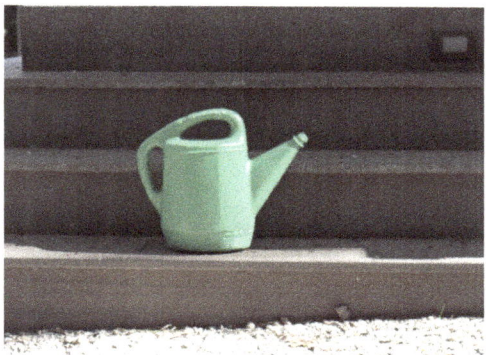

Figure 4-59. Active D-Lighting Set to High

In my opinion, with Active D-Lighting set to High, the camera noticeably reduced the overexposure in the brighter part of the image. It also brought some details out of the shadowed areas. My recommendation is to turn on Active D-Lighting when you are shooting a subject that is partly in the sun and partly in the shade. In those cases, if you have time, I would try setting this menu option to its various levels to see how the results compare. You also might want to use exposure bracketing, discussed earlier in this chapter, and merge those three exposures using HDR software, as discussed in Chapter 3. Or, you can use the Backlighting/HDR setting of Scene mode, also discussed in Chapter 3.

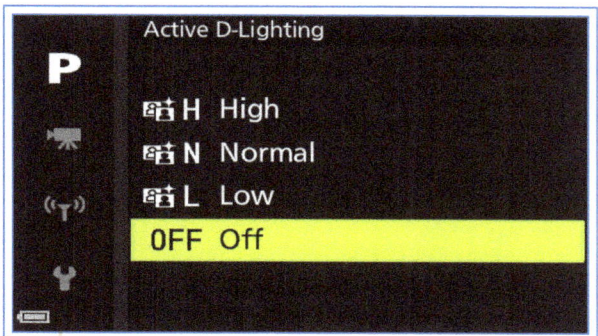

Figure 4-57. Active D-Lighting Menu Options Screen

To illustrate the effects of this setting, I took a pair of photographs of a watering can sitting on stairs in partial shade on a sunny day. For the first sample image, Figure 4-58, Active D-Lighting was turned off; for Figure 4-59, it was turned on to the High setting.

The Metering option is not available on the Shooting menu when Active D-Lighting is turned on to any level; in that case, the camera uses the Matrix setting for metering. Also, when Active D-Lighting is in effect, you cannot adjust the Contrast parameter for the Picture Control settings.

The Coolpix P950 has a related feature called simply D-Lighting, which is used in playback mode for images that have already been taken. I'll discuss that option in Chapter 6.

Multiple Exposure

This menu option lets you shoot multiple exposures in the camera. You can shoot either two or three images on the same digital frame. When you highlight this option and press the OK button or the Right button, the camera displays the options screen, shown in Figure 4-60. (If you cannot select this option, check for an incompatible setting, such as Raw for Image Quality, or having exposure bracketing or continuous shooting turned on.)

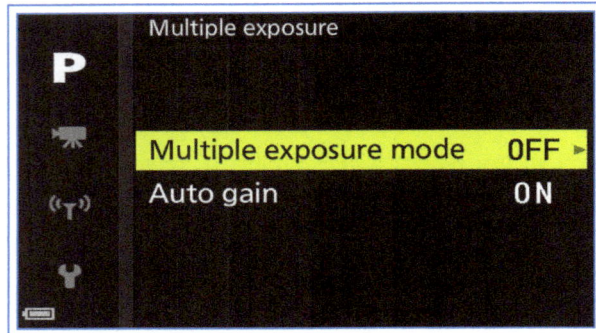

Figure 4-60. Multiple Exposure Menu Options Screen

To shoot multiple exposures, set the Multiple Exposure Mode option to On. You can set the Auto Gain option to On, which is the default setting, or turn it off. If it is turned on, the camera will use its programming to adjust the relative brightness of the multiple images as it sees fit. If you turn this option off, then the images will be recorded without adjustment. In my experience, this feature produces better results with Auto Gain turned on, though certain situations may yield better results with it turned off.

After you turn Multiple Exposure on, aim at your first subject. If you will be shooting the second subject to appear beside the first one, then be sure to plan ahead, leaving space where the second subject will appear. Plan for a third subject also, if you will be shooting three items. If the positioning of the subjects will be critical, you should use a tripod to keep the composition precise.

Press the shutter button to take the first picture. After some processing time, the camera will display the first image on the screen in a translucent mode, so you can continue to view the first image while you compose the next one. Now, line up the second image while viewing the first one, as illustrated in Figure 4-61.

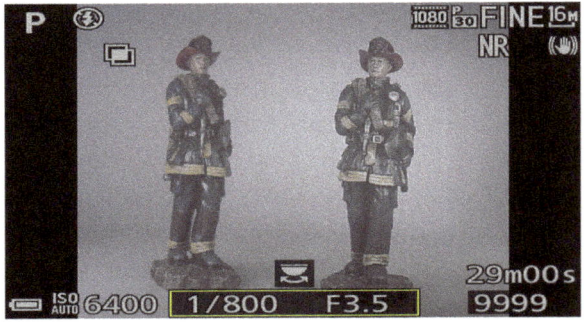

Figure 4-61. Multiple Exposure Screen After First Shot

When this composition looks right, press the shutter button to take the second image. The camera will take even longer to process this exposure. When it has finished processing, the double exposure will be displayed on the screen. It will still appear translucent, because you now have the option of taking one more picture to add to the composition. If you want to do that, go ahead and line up the third shot and press the shutter button. After the camera finishes processing the third image, it will return to the shooting screen. To view the final composition with three exposures, press the Playback button and you will see the finished product. The camera also saves each individual image you take for the multiple exposure composite.

If you want to use only two exposures, then, after you take the second one, go to the Menu system and turn off the Multiple Exposure Mode option, or just turn the mode dial to a shooting mode that does not provide access to this menu item, such as Auto, Scene, or Creative.

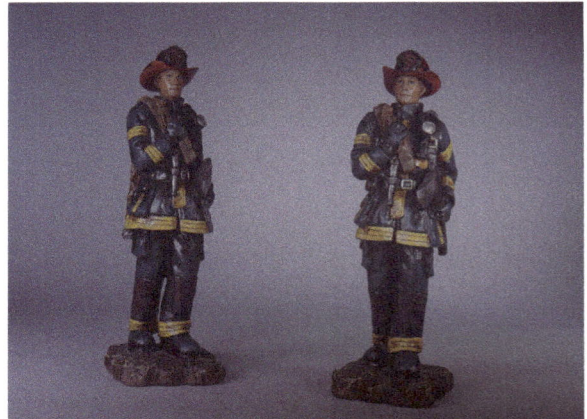

Figure 4-62. Final Image Taken Using Multiple Exposure Option

Figure 4-62 shows the finished image from two shots of a firefighter figurine. I had Auto Gain turned on and I added some contrast and sharpening to the final image

Chapter 4: The Shooting Menu | 69

in Photoshop, because it looked a bit faded as it came out of the camera.

Save User Settings

I discussed this feature in Chapter 3 in connection with the User Settings shooting mode, marked by the letter U on the mode dial. To save your current shooting settings for instant recall with the U slot on the dial, navigate to the Save User Settings option on the Shooting menu, as shown in Figure 4-63, and press the Right button or the OK button to save the settings.

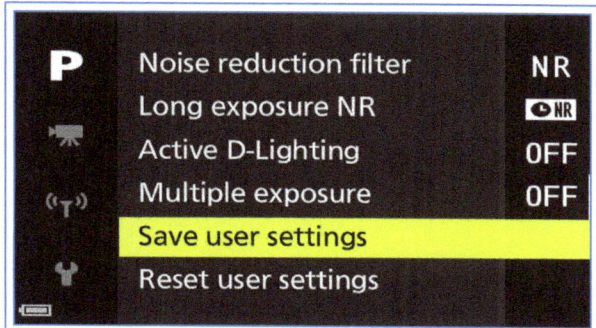

Figure 4-63. Save User Settings Option Highlighted on Menu

Be sure the settings are as you want before you press the button, because the camera does not ask you to confirm your choice; it just displays a "Done" message once you press the button.

Reset User Settings

This option, shown in Figure 4-64, resets all settings that were saved to the User Settings mode.

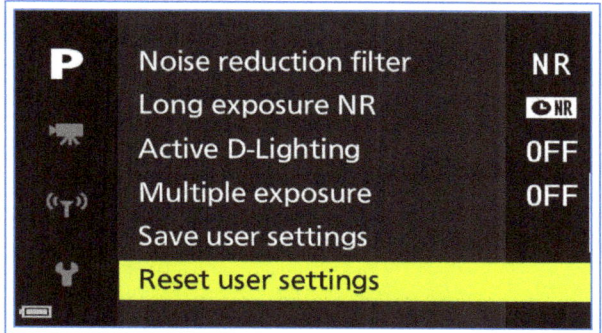

Figure 4-64. Reset User Settings Option Highlighted on Menu

When you select this option, the camera resets all of those items to their default values without your having to adjust each one in the menu screens. For example, choosing this option sets the shooting mode to Program, the flash mode to Auto, exposure compensation to 0.0, the zoom lens to its wide-angle position, and all items on the Shooting menu to their default settings.

Note that this option affects only the settings saved for the User Settings shooting mode; if you want to reset all settings for the camera for all modes, you have to use the Reset All menu option, which is found on the Setup menu, as discussed in Chapter 7.

Screen 4 of the Shooting menu is shown in Figure 4-65.

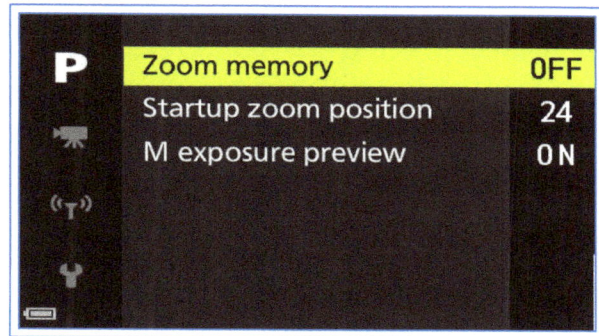

Figure 4-65. Screen 4 of Shooting Menu

Zoom Memory and Startup Zoom Position

The next two items on the Shooting menu are closely related, so I will discuss them together. The first of these, the first option on screen 4 of the menu, is zoom memory. This feature lets you control whether the zoom lever zooms the lens in continuous increments or in distinct, separate steps. By default this option is turned off, so you can zoom continuously in any amount, zooming either in or out.

If you turn the zoom memory setting on using this menu option, the camera displays a list of focal lengths, from full wide-angle to full telephoto: 24mm, 28mm, 35mm, 50mm, 85mm, 105mm, 135mm, 200mm, 300mm, 400mm, 500mm, 600mm, 800mm, 1000mm, 1200mm, 1400mm, 1600mm, 1800mm, and 2000mm, the maximum range of the optical zoom. It takes four menu screens to include all of these values; the first screen is shown in Figure 4-66.

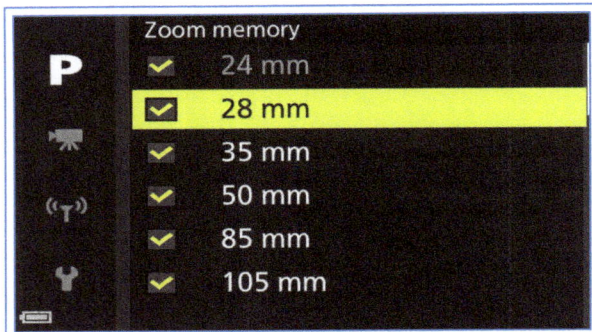

Figure 4-66. First Screen of Zoom Memory Options

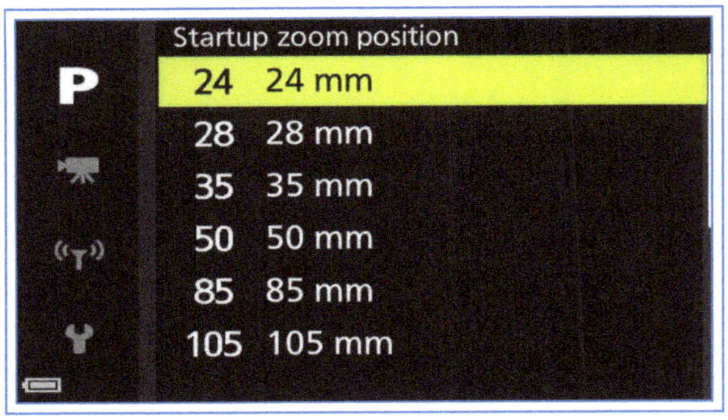

Figure 4-67. Startup Zoom Position Menu Options Screen

Each value has a check box to its left. Move the selection bar through the list using the Up and Down buttons or the multi selector dial. As each value is highlighted, you can press the OK button to check or un-check its box. If the box is checked, the camera includes that focal length in the zoom memory.

When you have finished checking the boxes for the focal lengths you want to include in the zoom memory, exit from the menu screen by pressing the Menu button or by half-pressing the shutter button. Now, when you press the zoom lever, each press will take the lens to the next focal length that was checked for zoom memory.

For example, suppose you turned on the zoom memory option and checked the boxes for 50mm, 200mm, and 1000mm. Then, if you are starting from the full wide-angle position of 24mm, when you press the zoom lever to the right, the lens will zoom in to 50mm. If you press it again, the lens will zoom to 200mm, and one more press will take it all the way to 1000mm. You will not be able to zoom the lens to any other positions. The same will be true when you zoom back out by pressing the zoom lever in the other direction. It does not matter if you use a very quick press of the lever or hold the lever in position; it will zoom only to the next level that has its box checked on the zoom memory menu screen.

As I noted above, zoom memory is closely related to the startup zoom position option, the second item on screen 4 of the Shooting menu. With that option, whose settings screen is shown in Figure 4-67, you select the focal length to use when you first turn the camera on.

In this case, the choices are more limited: 24mm, 28mm, 35mm, 50mm, 85mm, 105mm, or 135mm. You select this menu option, then move to the next screen and position the yellow selection bar on the focal length you want to choose. Press the OK button to confirm. Then, when you turn the camera on the next time, the lens will automatically zoom to that focal length.

Here is how these two settings are related. When you select a focal length for startup zoom position, you will see that that value is automatically checked on the screen for zoom memory, and its menu item is dimmed, meaning you cannot alter it. In other words, you cannot un-check the box for that focal length, because the camera is going to start up at that focal length.

For example, suppose you select 50mm for startup zoom position, and 35mm, 200mm, and 1000mm for zoom memory. The next time you turn on the camera, the lens will zoom to the 50mm position. If you press the zoom lever to zoom out, the lens will move to 35 mm. If you then press the lever to zoom in, the lens will zoom back to 50mm, the startup position. From there, it will zoom to 200mm, then 1000mm.

These two menu options, working together, give a good deal of control over how the lens zooms. Of course, you don't need to have that degree of control; you may be content to use the default settings, using the startup position of 24mm and allowing the lens to zoom to any setting, without using the zoom memory option. However, it can be convenient to be able to zoom quickly to a preset value, if you often use a certain focal length.

The zoom memory option does not control the operation of the side zoom control, the switch on the left side of the camera that can also be used for zoom. So, even if you have turned on the zoom memory menu option, thereby restricting the zoom lever to certain focal lengths, you can still use the side zoom control to zoom the lens continuously.

Manual Exposure Preview

This last item on the Shooting menu has a narrow, specific purpose—to control whether the camera's display reflects the brightness of the image that will result from current settings when the camera is in Manual exposure mode. When you select this item and press the OK button or the Right button to move to the next screen, you will see a screen with options to turn this feature on or off. If you leave it at its default setting of Off, then, when the camera is in Manual exposure mode, the camera's display will show a normally exposed view of the scene, even if the current settings of aperture, shutter speed, and ISO would result in a heavily underexposed or overexposed image.

If you turn this feature on, then, when you adjust the shooting settings in a way that would result in an unusually dark or bright image, the camera's display will become darker or brighter also, so you will have notice that the image may be improperly exposed.

This feature works only in Manual exposure mode, although the menu option is available for selection in Program, Aperture Priority, and Shutter Priority mode. When it operates, it is quite useful in alerting you that a particular set of settings will result in noticeable underexposure or overexposure.

There is one more aspect of this option to point out. As discussed in Chapter 7, you can turn on a shooting-mode histogram using the View/Hide Histograms option of the Monitor Settings item on the Setup menu. If you do that, the camera will display a histogram to help you gauge the exposure level of your shot. However, in Manual exposure mode, this histogram will not be accurate unless you turn on the Manual Exposure Preview menu option. If you leave this option turned off, the histogram will reflect the exposure level seen on the camera's display, which, in most cases, will look normal, even if the exposure settings would result in a heavily underexposed or overexposed image. If you turn the Manual Exposure Preview option on, the histogram will reflect the actual shooting conditions more accurately. (The histogram is not displayed at all in some situations, such as when AF Area is set to Target Finding, or when a movie is being recorded.)

Chapter 5: Physical Controls

The Coolpix P950, like many compact cameras, does not have very many physical controls, relying heavily on its menus for changing settings. But the P950 is an advanced camera, and it has more controls than many cameras. In this chapter, I'll discuss each of these controls and how they can be used to best advantage. I'll start with the controls on the top of the camera, as shown in Figure 5-1.

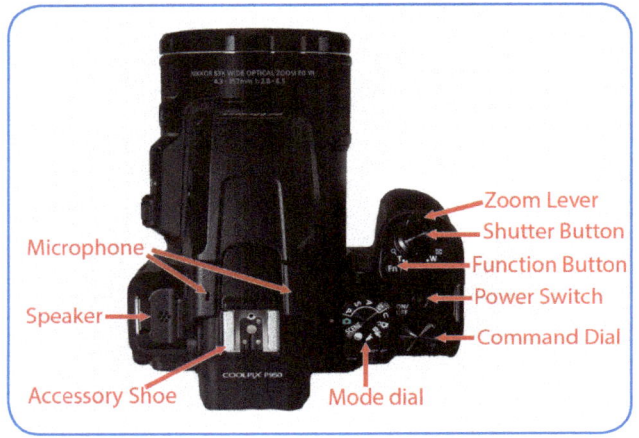

Figure 5-1. Controls on Top of Camera

Power Switch

The power switch, at the right side of the camera's top, has only one function—to turn the camera on and off. When the camera is turned on, the green light around this button illuminates. When the camera enters standby mode to save power, the green light starts to blink, and does so for about three minutes. During that time, you can press the power switch, the Playback button, the shutter release button, or the Movie button, to cancel standby mode and restore the camera to full power. After the three minutes, the camera turns itself off and you have to use the power switch to turn it back on again. When the battery is charging, the light around the switch flashes slowly; it turns off when the battery is fully charged.

Shutter Release Button

The shutter release button (often called simply the shutter button) is the single most important control on the camera. When you press it halfway down, the camera evaluates and adjusts exposure and focus (unless you're using Manual exposure mode and/or manual focus). Once you are satisfied with the settings, you press the button all the way down to record the image.

If you need to set the camera's automatic exposure and focus for a subject that is not in the center of the scene, you can aim the center of the display at that subject, half-press the shutter button to lock exposure and focus, and then move the camera back to the position for taking the picture, with that subject at one side. This procedure is useful when you are using Center-weighted or Spot for the metering mode and Manual for the Autofocus Area mode, with the focus frame set in the center of the screen. In those situations, the camera will lock both focus and exposure on the object away from the center of the scene when you press the shutter button halfway.

When the camera is set for continuous shooting, you hold this button down to make the camera take a burst of images.

You can press this button halfway to switch from playback mode to shooting mode so you can resume taking pictures. You also can press it to exit from a menu screen. Note, though, that you have to press the OK button to confirm your selection on the menu screen before pressing the shutter button; otherwise, your setting on the menu screen will not be saved. You can press the shutter button to re-awaken the camera from standby mode, which it enters after a period of inactivity. You have to press this button (or the Playback button, power switch, or Movie button) while the green light around the power switch is flashing.

Chapter 5: Physical Controls

The shutter release button also can be used to take still images while recording a movie, with some restrictions. There are more details about this option and its limitations in Chapter 8. And, when the camera is in Movie Manual mode, you can use this button, as well as the Movie button, to start and stop a video recording.

Mode Dial

The mode dial, located at the right side of the camera's top, is central to the operation of the camera. Its function is to change from one shooting mode to another. The shooting modes for still images were discussed in Chapter 3; the Movie Manual mode will be discussed in Chapter 8.

Zoom Lever

The zoom lever is a small ring with a handle, surrounding the shutter release button. The lever's main function is to change the focal length of the lens to various settings between its wide-angle setting of 24mm and its full telephoto setting of 2000mm. If you have the camera set for digital zoom, the lever will boost the focal length to a maximum of 8000mm. (That impressive-sounding zoom amount is illusory, though, because the quality will be degraded by the electronic enlargement of the image.) If you move the lever sharply to either side, the zoom range will adjust quickly; if you move it more gradually, the range will change more slowly.

When you turn the camera on, the lens moves to whatever position has been selected with the Startup Zoom Position option on the Shooting menu, as discussed in Chapter 4. And, the behavior of the zoom lever will change depending on the settings for the Zoom Memory menu option, also discussed in that chapter. As a brief reminder, if Zoom Memory is turned on, pressing the zoom lever will move the lens to the next zoom level that was selected through the Zoom Memory menu option. If that feature is turned off, pressing the lever will zoom the lens continuously through its full range of focal lengths.

In playback mode, moving the zoom lever to the left (pointing to the W setting) produces index screens with increasing numbers of images, and moving the lever to the right enlarges the current image. These functions are discussed in Chapter 6.

Function Button

One very useful control is the Function button—the small button marked with the Fn designation, behind the shutter release button.

As discussed in Chapter 4, many of the most important settings on the Coolpix P950 are located in the Shooting menu, including Image Size, ISO, White Balance, Continuous, and others. It can be inconvenient to change these settings when you have to press the Menu button, navigate to the Shooting menu, and move to the proper line on the menu before you can make a change.

With this small button, you can assign any one of 16 settings to a physical control. The options available for choice are Image Quality, Image Size, Picture Control, White Balance, Metering, Continuous, ISO, AF Area Mode, Autofocus mode, Vibration Reduction, Digital Zoom, Toggle Av/Tv Selection, Peaking, Virtual Horizon, Assign Side Zoom Control, and AE/AF Lock Button. When you press the Function button, a menu for the item that is assigned to the button pops up on the screen, as shown in Figure 5-2, letting you quickly change the setting (in this case, continuous shooting).

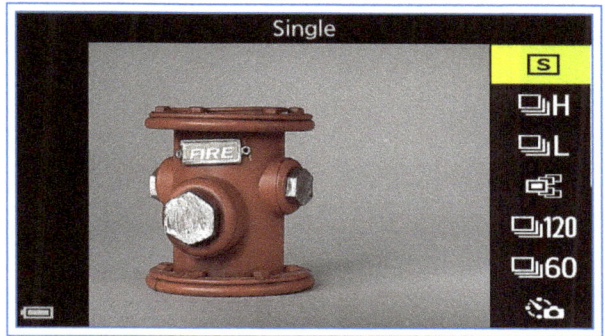

Figure 5-2. Function Button Menu for Continuous Shooting

You can move through that menu using the Up and Down buttons or by turning either the command dial or the multi selector dial; you have to press the OK button to confirm your selection once it is highlighted.

The default choice, as shown here, is Continuous, for continuous shooting, which I tend to prefer as the item assigned to this button. If I want to fire off a burst of shots, it is convenient to press the Function button and switch to one of the burst modes for a short time. When that situation has passed, I can just as quickly press the button again and reset the camera to single-shot mode. However, it also can be useful to be able to adjust ISO quickly. Of course, the value you choose to assign to this button will depend on your own particular circumstances. If you like to experiment with various image-processing settings, you might want to program Picture Control as the setting. In any event, it is great to have this option available.

To change the feature assigned to the Function button, use the same menu that pops up when you press the button. The last item, on the second screen of the menu, is the Fn item.

After you press the Function button, the easiest way to reach this menu item is to press the Up button and wrap around to the bottom of the menu, to the Fn item.

Then, press the Right button or the OK button, and the camera will display a menu of the options available for assignment to the Function button, with a yellow frame marking the one that is currently assigned, as shown in Figure 5-3.

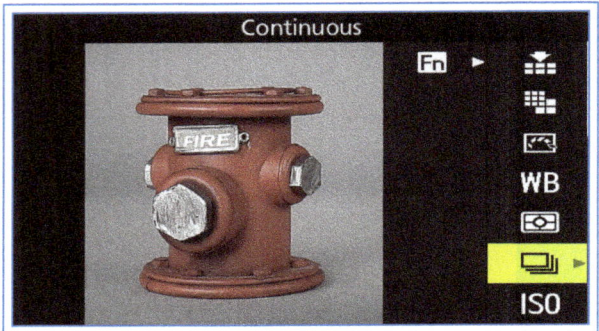

Figure 5-3. Function Button Menu of Options for Fn Button

Using the Up and Down buttons, the multi selector dial, or the command dial, scroll through the choices until the one you want to select is highlighted by the yellow selection block, and then press the OK button. The next time you press the Function button, the menu for the newly selected item will appear on the display.

The Function button operates only when the camera is in shooting mode and the mode dial is set to the Program, Aperture Priority, Shutter Priority, Manual exposure, or User Settings mode.

Microphone and Speaker

The two small openings on top of the camera, just in front of the accessory shoe, are where the camera receives sounds to record audio for movies. If you plug in an external microphone, the external device takes priority and disables the built-in microphone. The small holes on the left side of the camera's top are where the speaker emits sound for videos.

Next, I'll discuss the controls on the left side of the camera, as shown in Figure 5-4.

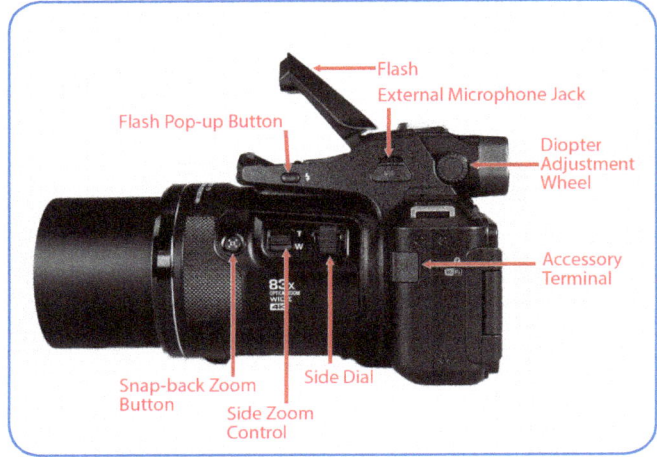

Figure 5-4. Controls on Left Side of Camera

Flash Pop-up Button

This small button on the left side of the flash housing has one simple purpose—to release the built-in flash unit so it will pop up and be available for use. If you expect you will be using the flash, you need to press this button to make the unit available; if you don't press the button, the flash will not pop up and cannot fire. If you select a setting that requires use of the flash, such as the Night Portrait setting of Scene mode, the camera will display a message prompting you to raise the flash. When you have finished with the flash unit, press it gently back down until it clicks into place.

The requirement that you press this button to pop up the flash has one clear advantage: When you are in a museum or other location where photography is permitted but the use of flash is prohibited, you can just leave the flash unit stowed away and you can be sure it will never pop up by itself and send out a flash that proves to be embarrassing. (With some compact cameras, the flash is always available to fire, and you have to remember to set the flash mode properly to avoid having it go off unexpectedly.)

Side Zoom Control

A useful feature of the P950 is this second zoom switch, located on the left side of the lens barrel as you hold the camera in shooting position. Press the switch toward to the T label for zooming in toward the telephoto position, or toward the W for zooming out toward the wide-angle position.

One reason for having this alternative control available is to free up your right hand to hold the camera firmly, rather than having to reach up to the standard zoom lever on top of the camera. With the super-powerful zoom range of the P950, you need to hold the camera as steady as possible when zooming in to the longer ranges.

The functioning of the side zoom control is not governed by the zoom memory setting on the Shooting menu. That is, when zoom memory is turned on, restricting the operation of the zoom lever to certain focal lengths, the side zoom control can still be used to zoom the lens continuously to any focal length.

You can change the behavior of this control in one way, using the Assign Side Zoom Control option on screen 2 of the Setup menu. With that option, you can set the speed of zooming, for movie recording only, to High, Mid, or Low. Using this setting, you can cause the camera to perform a smooth zoom in or out while you are recording a movie, at the speed you prefer.

Snap-back Zoom Button

The button marked with a square with arrows coming out of its corners, next to the side zoom control, operates a function that Nikon calls "snap-back zoom." When you have zoomed the lens in to a powerful telephoto setting, you can press and hold the snap-back zoom button to "snap" the focal length back to a wider view in a preset amount. Continue to hold down the button while you frame the subject, using the inset frame that is displayed on the screen. While holding down the button, you can widen the view further by pressing the zoom lever toward the W position. When you have finished locating and framing the subject, release the snap-back button and the lens will zoom back in to its original position.

With the snap-back button, when you have the camera zoomed in for a magnified, telephoto view, you can experiment with different telephoto settings. You can "snap" the lens back out, which can help you get a sense of your ultimate subject by seeing a wider view. Afterwards, you can snap the camera back to its original telephoto setting without having to use trial and error; that setting has been preserved precisely for you in the camera's "snap-back" memory.

To control the amount that the zoom position snaps back, use the Snap-back Zoom item on screen 2 of the Setup menu, and choose Long, Medium, or Short for this amount, as discussed in Chapter 7.

When I am trying to photograph a bird at a long distance using the superzoom lens, I find this feature very useful. When the lens is zoomed all the way in, it can be hard to locate the bird. I can quickly snap the lens back to a wider view until I find the bird in my field of view. Once I have the bird centered again, I can release the snap-back zoom button to snap the zoom back to the full-power telephoto view. This function is available for shooting still images only, not for movies.

Side Dial

The side dial, located directly behind the side zoom control switch, is used to adjust manual focus when the focus mode selector switch is set to MF, for manual focus. Just turn the dial as needed to adjust focus until it is sharp, as discussed later in this chapter in connection with the discussion of the focus mode selector switch.

When the focus mode selector switch is set to autofocus, the side dial can handle one function that has been assigned to it using the Assign Side Dial option on the Setup menu. The possible assignments for this button using that menu option are exposure compensation (the default setting); ISO; White Balance; shutter speed; aperture; or none. Of course, shutter speed or aperture can be adjusted with this control only when the camera is set to a shooting mode in which that value can be adjusted, such as Shutter Priority mode, Manual mode, or Movie Manual mode.

External Microphone Jack

Near the top of the left side of the camera is a microphone jack, covered by a triangular flap. In that jack, you can connect a microphone with a standard

3.5mm stereo plug. This jack can provide power to a microphone that needs it.

Accessory Terminal

This rectangular port, located on the front part of the grip on the left side of the camera, is where you can plug in certain compatible Nikon accessories, such as remote control devices, as discussed in Appendix A.

The next controls to be discussed are those located on the camera's back, most of them to the right side of the LCD screen, as shown in Figure 5-5.

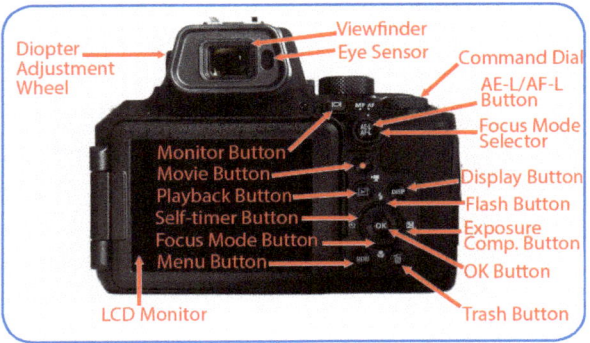

Figure 5-5. Controls on Back of Camera

Viewfinder, Eye Sensor, and Monitor Button

The viewfinder window, recessed within an eyepiece in the center at the top of the camera's back, is where you can view the scene being recorded by the camera, images and videos that were previously recorded, and menu screens. The P950 has a large, bright viewfinder window, with a display providing about 2.4 million dots of resolution. The button with a monitor icon, directly to the right of the viewfinder, is used to switch the view of shooting, playback, and menu screens between the LCD screen and the viewfinder. Press the button to toggle those views. This button can switch the views only when the LCD screen is unfolded and visible; when it is folded in against the camera in its protective position, the viewfinder is activated and the Monitor button will not change the view.

If you want the camera to switch automatically between the viewfinder and the LCD screen, use the EVF Auto Toggle option on the first screen of the Setup menu. When that option is turned on, the view will switch from the LCD screen to the viewfinder when your head (or another object) approaches the eye sensor, the small opening in the right side of the viewfinder eyepiece. When that menu option is active, you can still switch the view with the Monitor button or by folding in the LCD screen.

Diopter Adjustment Wheel

The small wheel on the left side of the viewfinder is used to dial in optical correction to the viewfinder, so you can see a sharply focused image in the viewfinder window. As discussed above, when you fold the LCD screen in the closed position, press the Monitor button, or (depending on a menu setting) move your head near the eye sensor, the viewfinder is activated. You can then turn this little wheel in either direction until the image in the viewfinder is at its clearest for your eyesight. If you wear glasses, you may be able to dial in enough of an adjustment that you can take your glasses off and still see the image clearly through the viewfinder.

AE-L/AF-L Button

This button, located directly below the mode dial at the top of the camera's back, is labeled AE-L/AF-L. When you press this button, the camera locks its autoexposure or autofocus setting, or both, depending on how a menu option is set. That option, called AE/AF Lock Button, is the first item on the third screen of the Setup menu. The choices are AE/AF Lock, AE Lock Only, AE Lock (Hold), or AF Lock Only. I will discuss those options in Chapter 7.

Focus Mode Selector

The focus mode selector is the small switch that surrounds the AE-L/AF-L button at the top of the camera's back. You use this switch to set the camera for autofocus or manual focus. Turn it so the white dot points to MF for manual focus or to AF for autofocus.

Autofocus

When the focus mode selector switch is set to AF, for autofocus, you can press the Down button on the multi selector to select normal, macro, or infinity for the autofocus mode, as discussed later in this chapter. You also can use menu options such as AF Area Mode and Autofocus Mode on the Shooting menu, if the camera

Manual Focus

When the focus mode selector switch is set to MF, for manual focus, you adjust the focus yourself, using the side dial on the left side of the lens.

Many photographers like the amount of control that comes from being able to set the focus exactly how they want it. And, in some situations, such as focusing in dark areas or areas behind glass or wire fences, taking extreme closeups, or cases where there are objects at various distances from the camera, it may be useful to control exactly where the point of sharpest focus lies.

To use manual focus, turn the focus mode selector to the MF position. When the camera is first set to manual focus mode, the screen is displayed at its normal magnification, or at two or four times its normal magnification.

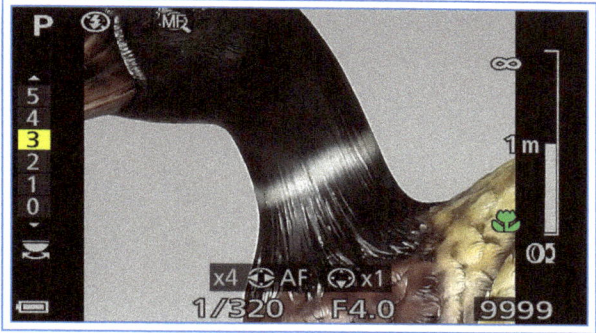

Figure 5-6. Shooting Screen for Manual Focus

The system Nikon uses to display the magnification options is a bit confusing, so I will take some time to discuss those options. Figure 5-6 shows the shooting screen as it is displayed when the focus mode selector is turned to the MF position for manual focus. The icons that are displayed just above the shutter speed and aperture values at the bottom of the screen indicate what buttons you can press to change the magnification of the screen.

In this example, the x4 indicator is next to the icon for the Left button. This means that you can press the Left button to change the magnification to x4, or times four. The letters AF are next to the icon for the right button. This means that you can press the Right button to cause the camera to use autofocus. The x1 indicator is next to the icon for the Down button. This means that you can press the Down button to return the image on the screen to normal size, with no magnification.

What I find confusing about this system of notation is that it does not tell you what the current magnification is. You have to "decode" the current setting, based on the options for changing the magnification. Here is the way to decode it:

If you see the number 4 in the left-most position, as here, that means 2x magnification is in effect, and you can press the Left button to switch to 4x magnification. If you see the number 2, that means 1x magnification is in effect, and you can press the Left button to switch to 2x magnification. If you see the number 1, that means 4x magnification is in effect, and you can press the Left button to switch to 1x magnification.

The amount of magnification that is used when manual focus is selected is saved from the last time manual focus was used. So, when you turn the focus mode selector to the MF position, the magnification amount will vary depending on the setting you last used previously.

Once the camera is in manual focus mode, start turning the side dial (the ridged dial on the left side of the camera, closest to the lens) to adjust the focus. Look at the focusing scale on the right side of the screen and turn the dial until the focus appears as sharp as possible. As shown by the prompts in the lower left corner of the screen and as discussed above, you can press the Left button to switch the magnification amount or the Down button to set the screen to normal size (shown as x1 on the display) with focus locked at the current setting. After you have returned the screen to its normal magnification using the Down button, you can press the Down button again to go to the magnified screen to continue adjusting focus.

As you move the focus point using the side dial, you will see a white bar go up and down inside the focus scale. (The bar turns green when focus is in the macro, or closeup range.) Continue adjusting until the focus is as sharp as you can get it, and then take the picture.

If you want the camera to assist you with its autofocus capability, press the Right button, as prompted on the display, and the camera will autofocus on the subject in the center of the screen. You can then continue adjusting focus manually using the side dial.

If the Peaking feature is turned on through the last screen of the Setup menu, you can turn the command dial to change the intensity of the Peaking effect on the scale numbered from 0 to 5 at the left of the display. This feature displays an increasing number of white pixels at the areas of sharp focus as the focus gets sharper. I'll discuss that option in Chapter 7.

Movie Button

The red Movie button, at the top of the camera's back just below the mode dial, has one major purpose: to start and stop recording of your videos. Press it once and release it to start recording; press it again to stop recording. I will discuss movie recording options in Chapter 8. You also can press this button to cancel standby mode when the monitor turns off in connection with the camera's power-saving function.

Playback Button

This button, marked with a triangle, is used to put the camera into playback mode, which allows you to view your images on the LCD (or in the viewfinder) and lets you get access to the Playback menu by pressing the Menu button. You also can press and hold the Playback button instead of the power switch to turn the camera on, placing it immediately into playback mode. You might want to do this if you're only going to view your recorded images and won't be using shooting mode.

If you turn the camera on using the Playback button, pressing it again will not turn the camera off; it will just switch the camera into shooting mode. When the camera is in playback mode, you can always press the shutter button down halfway to change into shooting mode.

When the camera enters power saving mode and the light around the power button starts to blink, you can press the Playback button, among others, to stop the camera from powering off. If you do that, the camera will then be in playback mode.

Display Button

The button marked DISP, to the right of the Playback button, switches among the various displays of information on the camera's LCD or viewfinder, in both shooting and playback modes. In shooting mode, there are three displays available that are called up by successive presses of the Display button.

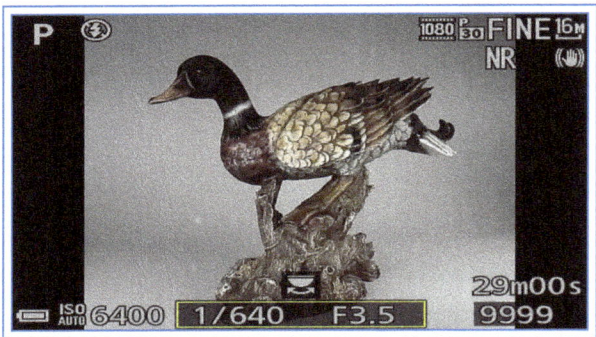

Figure 5-7. Shooting Display Screen: Basic Information

The display screen that I use most, seen in Figure 5-7, shows the live view overlaid with icons for shooting mode, flash mode, shutter speed, aperture, image size and quality, images remaining, and a few other items.

Another press of the Display button produces a similar screen, illustrated in Figure 5-8, which includes the same shooting information with a frame overlaid that shows the area of the image that would be used for shooting a movie, based on the current setting for movie format.

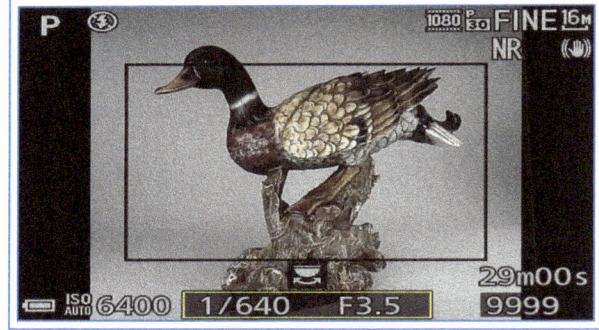

Figure 5-8. Shooting Display Screen: Movie Frame

One more press of the button produces a view of the image alone, with no information.

Through the Monitor Settings item on the Setup menu, as discussed in Chapter 7, you can add a histogram and a framing grid to the shooting information display. The grid, if activated, will appear on all three shooting screens described above, including the screen with no shooting information. In addition, the camera will add a fourth screen with no information and no grid.

This grid can be useful in framing your composition with straight lines and for arranging a composition according to the Rule of Thirds, which states a preference for having the subject located at a point one-third of the way from an edge of the frame.

Similarly, the histogram, if activated, will appear only on the three screens described above, but the camera will add a fourth screen with no information and no histogram. The histogram is discussed in Chapter 6, in connection with the histogram that displays in playback mode. Figure 5-9 shows the shooting screen with both the framing grid and the histogram in use.

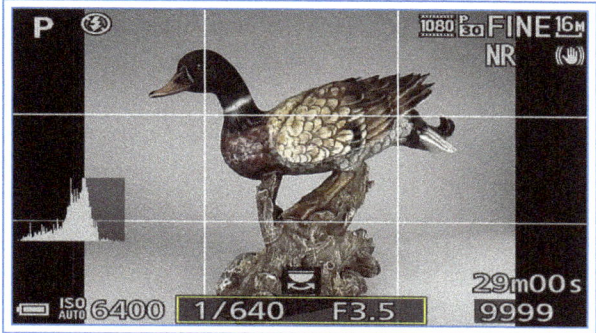

Figure 5-9. Shooting Display Screen: Framing Grid and Histogram

In playback mode, there are four screens available through presses of the Display button. The first option provides photo information, which shows the recorded image overlaid with icons and figures showing the date and time the picture was taken, its identification number, image quality and size, and which image is being shown out of how many total images. The battery status icon also is shown. The second view is a detailed display of shooting information, including a thumbnail image and a histogram that shows the brightness values in the image along with details about shutter speed, aperture, exposure compensation, ISO value, white balance, Picture Control setting, and image number. The third view adds comment and copyright information, and the final view is of the image only, with no information added. I will provide information about the playback displays in Chapter 6.

Command Dial

This wheel, sticking out near where your right thumb is likely to grip the camera at the top of the right side of the camera, has several functions. It is used to adjust shutter speed in the Shutter Priority and Manual exposure modes. In the Program exposure mode, this dial is used to activate the flexible program function, which causes the camera to choose an alternative pair of shutter speed and aperture values. If you use the Toggle Av/Tv Selection option on the Setup menu, these functions of the command dial are switched with those of the multi selector dial, so the command dial controls aperture rather than shutter speed, and the command dial no longer controls the flexible program feature.

In playback mode, you can turn the command dial to magnify and shrink an image once you have pressed the zoom lever to begin enlarging it.

Also, the command dial can be used to adjust values in the on-screen menus after you have pressed one of the direction buttons to bring up a menu on the display. That is, the command dial can be used to adjust exposure compensation after the Right button has been pressed to put that scale on the display; it can be used to select a focus mode after the Down button has been pressed to put the focus mode menu on the display; it can be used to set the mode for the self-timer after the Left button is pressed; and it can be used to select a flash mode after the Up button is pressed. This dial also can be used to select an item from the menu that appears on the screen when the Function button is pressed.

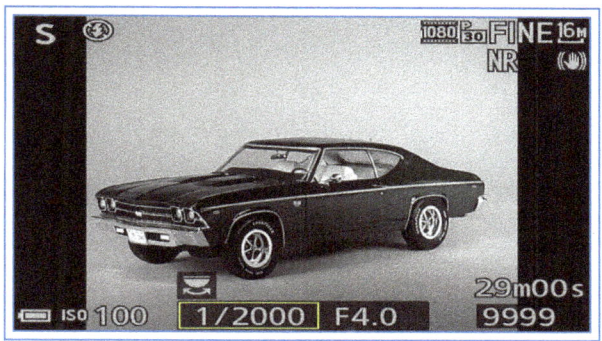

Figure 5-10. Icon for Command Dial on Shooting Screen

One nice feature of the Coolpix P950 is that it puts an icon on the screen representing the command dial when there is a value that can be adjusted by turning the dial. For example, as shown in Figure 5-10, in Shutter Priority mode, the icon, which looks like a white half-disk with a curved arrow below it, is positioned above the value for shutter speed. This means you can turn the command dial to adjust that setting.

Menu Button

The Menu button, to the lower left of the multi selector, has one main function. Press it to enter the menu system, and press it once more to return to whatever mode the camera was in previously (shooting mode or playback mode). There are several different menus available, depending on the shooting mode. The main menu systems are for Shooting, Playback, Network, and Setup, but there also are specific menus for various shooting modes, including Scene, Creative, Moon and Bird-watching, as well as a menu for Movie mode. I discuss the menu systems in Chapters 4, 6, 7, 8, and 9.

In playback mode, you can press the Menu button when an image is enlarged, to save a cropped portion of the image as a separate file.

Delete/Trash Button

To the right of the Menu button is the Delete button, which can also be called the Trash button. The main function of this control is to delete images and videos. When the camera is in playback mode, press the Trash button and the camera will display a short menu of choices: Current Image, Erase Selected Images, or All Images, as shown in Figure 5-11.

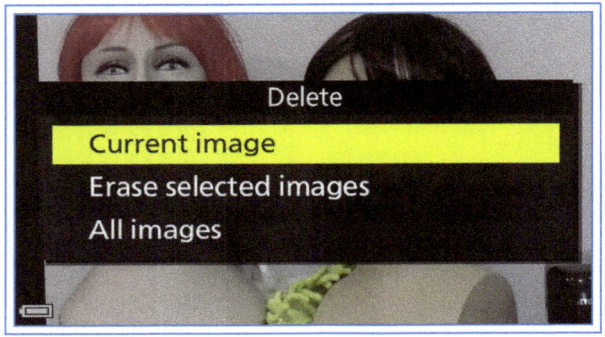

Figure 5-11. Options Screen from Pressing Trash Button

Use the multi selector dial or the Up and Down buttons to highlight your choice. If you select Current Image and press the OK button, the camera will display a message asking you to confirm. You can cancel out of this (or any) deletion message by pressing the Menu button. When you are using the Trash button to delete images in this way, if the image displayed is the key image for a sequence of continuous shots (see discussion of continuous shooting in Chapter 4), choosing Current Image will delete all images in the sequence. If the images in the sequence are displayed individually, only one image at a time will be deleted.

If you choose Erase Selected Images and press OK, the camera displays an index screen showing thumbnail versions of all recorded images and movies. Navigate through them with the Left and Right buttons or the multi selector dial, and press either the Up or Down button to mark (or unmark) any image you want to delete. Trash can icons will appear below images marked for deletion. You can enlarge any of the thumbnails to get a better view of an image by turning the zoom lever toward the telephoto position; turn it back the other way to reduce the image back to the thumbnail size. When all selected images have been marked, press the OK button and the camera will ask you for one final confirmation before deleting the selected images.

If you choose All Images, the camera will delete all images and movies that are not protected using the Protect function, as discussed in Chapter 6.

When the camera is in shooting mode, if you press this button, the camera will ask if you want to delete one image. If you select Yes, the last image to be saved will be deleted and the camera will return to shooting mode. With this option, you will not get a chance to preview the image (or movie) fully before deletion (though it will be displayed behind the message), so be careful when using it. I recommend switching the camera to playback mode before deleting images.

This button also can be used to reset a Creative mode setting to its default state after adjustments have been made to that setting.

Multi Selector and its Buttons and Dial

The most prominent set of controls on the back of the camera is contained within the perimeter of the multi selector, the circular area with raised edges, also known as buttons, that function as the four direction buttons. Each of these four buttons also has another purpose designated by an icon next to the button. In the center of the multi selector is the OK button, and the round, ridged wheel functions as a rotating dial. I will discuss each of these controls in turn.

Multi Selector Dial

The ridged wheel that surrounds the OK button, known as the multi selector dial, is easy to operate, because you can catch it on your thumbnail or engage it with the flesh of your thumb or finger and spin it freely. One of its duties is to control the aperture setting when you are shooting in Aperture Priority mode or Manual exposure mode. If you turn on the Toggle Av/Tv Selection option on the Setup menu, the functions of this dial and the command dial are reversed, and the multi selector dial controls shutter speed for Shutter Priority mode and Manual exposure mode. In addition, if that menu option is activated, the multi selector dial controls the flexible program feature, which ordinarily is controlled by the command dial.

When you are navigating in the menu systems, this dial moves up and down the lists of menu options, and it can be used to highlight an item from the pop-up menu that appears on the screen when the Function button or one of the direction buttons is pressed. When the camera is in playback mode, the dial navigates through your individual images and fast-forwards or rewinds through movies. It also moves through screens of images when index screens are displayed. As with the command dial, the camera displays an icon representing the multi selector dial when the dial controls a given function, such as aperture.

OK Button

This button in the center of the multi selector serves as a selection, confirmation, or "set" button when you choose certain options. For example, after you highlight a desired menu option, you press the OK button to confirm and set your selection. Similarly, when you press the focus mode button (Down button) and then highlight a focus mode on the pop-up menu (normal autofocus, macro focus, or infinity focus), you press the OK button to confirm that choice. You also can use this button to get access to sub-menus. For example, after you highlight Image Quality on the Shooting menu, you can press the OK button to bring up the sub-menu with the list of choices: Fine, Normal, Raw, and others. Then, you can press the OK button again to confirm the selection after you highlight it.

When AF Area Mode is set to Manual, pressing the OK button in shooting mode activates the movable focus frame so it can be moved, or locks it in place once its position is chosen. The OK button also can be used to pause and resume video recording. In Moon or Bird-watching mode, you press the OK button to zoom the lens in for a magnified view, after finding the subject in the small frame that appears on the display.

In playback mode, when the first frame of a movie is displayed on the screen, the OK button is used to start the movie playing. The button also is used to select any one of the playback controls that appear at the bottom of the screen during movie playback. (You use the direction buttons to highlight one of these controls, such as play, stop, or rewind, and then press OK to choose that function.) You can press this button to start a panorama scrolling across the display screen at a larger size. The button is also used to "open up" a sequence of continuous shots so you can view them individually. Pressing this button returns an enlarged image to normal size in playback mode.

Direction Buttons

Each edge—Up, Down, Left, and Right—of the multi selector dial is a "button" you can press to get access to a setting or operation. This may not be immediately obvious, and sometimes it can be tricky to press the dial in exactly the right spot, but these four direction buttons are important to your control of the camera. You use them to navigate through menus and screens for settings, whether moving left and right or up and down.

When you are navigating in the menu system, you can use the Left button to move back one screen in the system. When you are on the main screen of a given menu system (Shooting, Playback, Scene, etc.), pressing the Left button moves the yellow selection highlight to the left column of the screen, which contains the icons that identify the currently available menus. You can navigate up and down through these icons to select the symbol for the menu you want to use. You can then press the OK button to select that menu.

The Right button can be used to move to the sub-menu screens within the menu system. In most cases, you can press either the OK button or the Right button to move to the sub-menu screen that contains further options for a given menu item.

You use the direction buttons in playback mode to move through your images and, when you have enlarged an image using the zoom lever, to scroll around within the magnified image.

The Up button also has a non-obvious extra function. When you are viewing a "sequence" of continuous shots as individual images, as discussed in Chapters 4 and 6, pressing the Up button returns the camera to normal playback mode, in which you view only the "key" image from the continuous set (assuming the Sequence Display setting on the Playback menu is set to show key images rather than individual images from sequences).

Finally, each of the four direction buttons has its own separate identity, as indicated by the icon that appears next to each of the buttons, as discussed below.

Up Button: Flash Mode

When the camera is in shooting mode with the flash unit popped up or an external flash attached and turned on, pressing the Up button displays a small menu showing the options for setting the behavior of the flash unit, as shown in Figure 5-12.

If the flash unit is not popped up and no other flash is active, the camera will display a message telling you to raise the flash. Depending on the shooting mode, these options may include Auto, Auto with Red-eye Reduction, Red-eye Reduction, Fill Flash/Standard Flash, Slow Sync, and Rear-curtain Sync, or in some cases only three or four options. In other cases, such as when you have selected Night Landscape, Landscape, or Night Portrait for the Scene mode setting, pressing the Up button will not bring up any menu, even if the flash unit is popped up. The camera makes all flash decisions for you in those modes.

Once the menu with options has appeared, you need to press the Up and Down buttons or turn the command dial or multi selector dial to highlight your choice, and press the OK button to select it. With this menu, as with all four of the menus that are summoned by the direction buttons, you have to make your selection quickly, because the menu disappears in about five seconds if you don't take some action with a control button or dial.

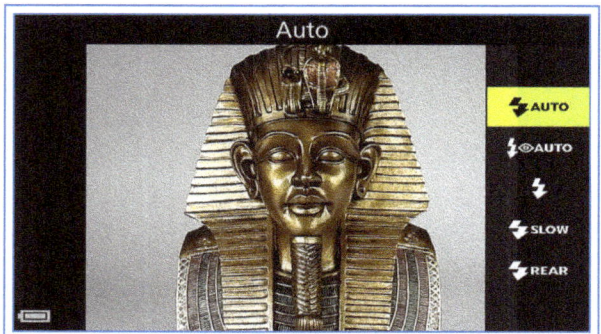

Figure 5-12. Flash Mode Menu

Before I discuss details of those settings, it's important to recall one basic fact: The built-in flash cannot fire unless you first pop it up by pressing the flash pop-up button marked by a lightning bolt on the left side of the flash housing, near the top of the camera. If you think there's any chance the flash may be needed, go ahead and press that button to have the flash ready. (If you're shooting movies, though, you should make sure the flash is down out of the way, because it can't be used and might interfere with your shooting.)

The next point to note about the use of flash with the P950 is that a lot depends on the shooting mode you have set on the mode dial. If that dial is set to Auto or Creative, you will have access to five possible settings for the flash. Other shooting modes place various limits on your flash choices. For example, with the Program, Aperture Priority, Shutter Priority, and Manual exposure modes, Auto Flash is not available. With Shutter Priority and Manual exposure modes, Slow Sync is not available.

With the Night Landscape and Landscape settings of Scene mode, the flash is forced off and cannot fire. With other settings available in Scene mode, the behavior of the flash varies according to the particular characteristics of the setting. For example, the flash has five possible settings if Portrait is selected for the scene type. In a few cases, such as with the Night Portrait and Party/Indoor settings for Scene mode, the camera may select another combination of settings, such as Slow Sync with Red-eye Reduction.

Apart from the shooting mode, there are other factors that affect how the P950 uses flash. So, if you have the camera set to Program mode, in which you normally would have four flash modes available, there are some conditions that will disable the flash. For example, you cannot use the flash if you have set focus to infinity, turned on exposure bracketing, or activated any continuous-shooting option other than interval shooting. If you believe the flash should fire but you are unable to turn it on using the flash mode menu, check to see if one of the settings mentioned above is in use.

Once you have set the camera to a mode that permits the choice of some of the possible flash settings, such as Auto mode or the Portrait setting of Scene mode, you have to decide whether to choose Auto Flash, Auto with Red-eye Reduction, Red-eye Reduction, Fill Flash/Standard Flash, Slow Sync, or Rear-curtain Sync.

Auto Flash is a setting I discussed earlier—the camera's automatic exposure system will fire the flash if it's needed to achieve a good exposure. This setting is available only when the mode dial is set to Auto, certain Scene mode settings, or Creative mode.

Auto with Red-eye Reduction is a special flash mode that operates to prevent or minimize the effects of "red-eye," the unpleasant reddish glow that can appear in people's eyes when the light from the on-camera flash bounces off their retinas and picks up the red from blood vessels. When this mode is selected, the camera lights up the bright reddish lamp on the front of the camera for a second or two before the flash fires, so as to cause the pupils of a person's eyes to narrow. In that way, there should be less chance of light from the flash reaching the retinas.

The next option, the Fill Flash/Standard Flash setting, forces the flash to fire, whether or not the conditions are dark enough for the camera to fire the flash on its own. This setting is useful when there is enough backlighting that the camera's exposure controls could be fooled into thinking the flash isn't needed. If, in your judgment, the subject will be too dark for that reason, you may want to force the flash to fire. Another such situation could be an outdoor portrait for which you need fill-in flash to highlight your subject's face adequately.

This setting, as indicated above, has different names with different shooting modes. If the camera is set to Auto, Scene, or Creative mode, this flash mode is called Fill Flash. With the Program, Aperture Priority, Shutter Priority, and Manual exposure shooting modes, this flash mode is called Standard Flash. There is no significant difference between Fill Flash and Standard Flash. With either setting, the flash fires whenever the shutter button is pressed, and the exposure metering system takes it into account. If you want to vary the intensity of the flash yourself, you can use the Flash Exposure Compensation item on screen 2 of the Shooting menu.

In Figures 5-13 and 5-14, I took two shots of a mannequin's head in an outdoor setting during daylight hours to illustrate the effect of Fill Flash. For Figure 5-13, with no flash, the image was exposed normally, with no special settings. For Figure 5-14, I turned on the flash using the Fill Flash setting. As you can see, there is a definite difference. With the shot on the right, the shadows are evened out and the mannequin's face is considerably more visible.

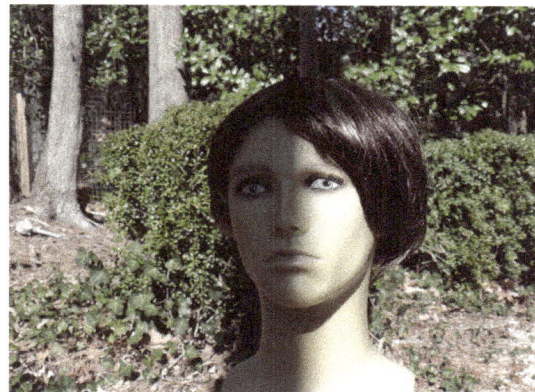

Figure 5-13. Flash Turned Off

Next, the Slow Sync setting is useful when you are taking a portrait in a dark environment. If you use a normal flash setting such as Auto Flash or Fill Flash, the camera will use a fairly fast shutter speed and let the flash illuminate only the portrait subject. Because the exposure time is short, the surrounding scene and background may be black.

If you use the Slow Sync setting, the camera will attempt to take the picture with a considerably slower shutter speed so that the ambient (natural) lighting will have time to register on the image and illuminate the background also. For example, Figures 5-15 and 5-16 were taken at the same time and in the same conditions.

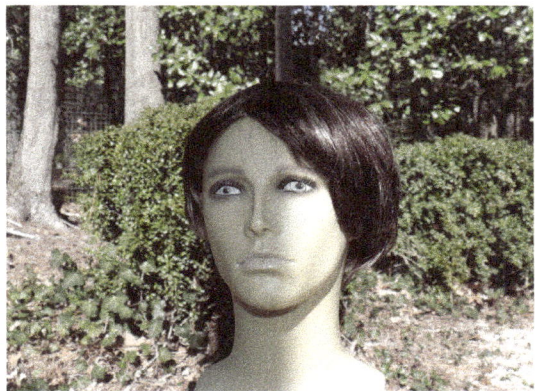

Figure 5-14. Fill-flash Used

The only difference is that Figure 5-15 was taken with the shutter speed set at 1/60 second in Standard Flash mode, while Figure 5-16 was taken in Slow Sync mode with a shutter speed of 0.5 second, which allowed the ambient lighting to light up the area behind the subject.

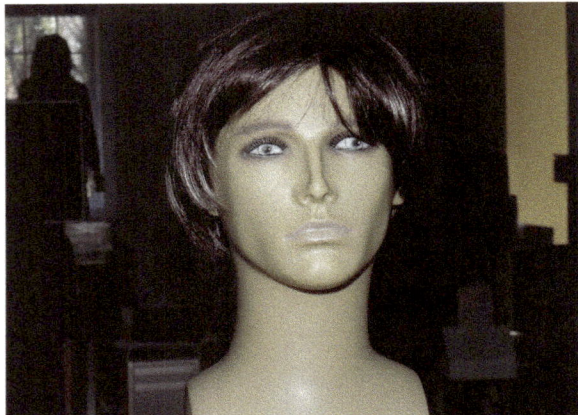

Figure 5-15. Normal Flash at 1/60 Second

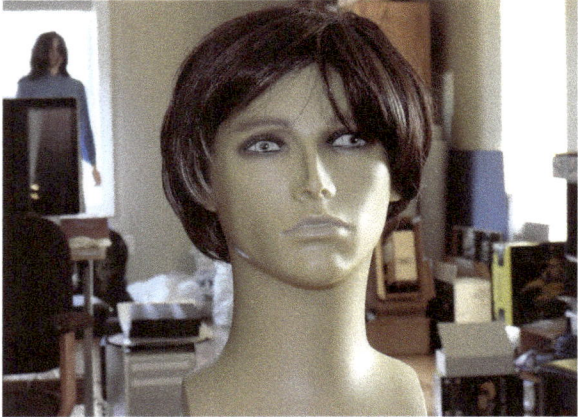

Figure 5-16. Slow Sync Flash at 0.5 Second

The last setting on the flash mode menu is Rear-curtain Sync. This option is one you may not have a lot of use for unless you encounter the particular situation it is designed for. If you don't activate this setting, the camera uses the unnamed default setting, which could be called Front-curtain Sync. In that mode, the flash fires very soon after the shutter opens to expose the image. If you choose the Rear-curtain setting instead, the flash fires later, just before the shutter closes.

The reason for using Rear-curtain Sync is to help you avoid a strange-looking result in some situations. This issue arises, for example, with a relatively long exposure, say one-half second, of a subject with lights, such as a car or motorcycle at night, moving across your field of view. With normal (Front-curtain) sync, the flash will fire early in the process, freezing the vehicle in a clear image. However, as the shutter remains open while the vehicle keeps going, the camera will capture the moving lights in a stream extending in front of, or superimposed over, the vehicle.

If, instead, you use Rear-curtain Sync, the initial part of the exposure will capture the lights in a trail that appears behind the vehicle, while the vehicle itself is not frozen by the flash until later in the exposure. With Rear-curtain sync in this particular situation, if the lights in question are taillights that look more natural behind the vehicle, the final image is likely to look more natural than with the Front-curtain (default) setting.

Figures 5-17 and 5-18 illustrate this concept using a flashlight. Both pictures were shot using an exposure of 0.5 second in Manual exposure mode. For both images, I was moving the flashlight from right to left across the scene.

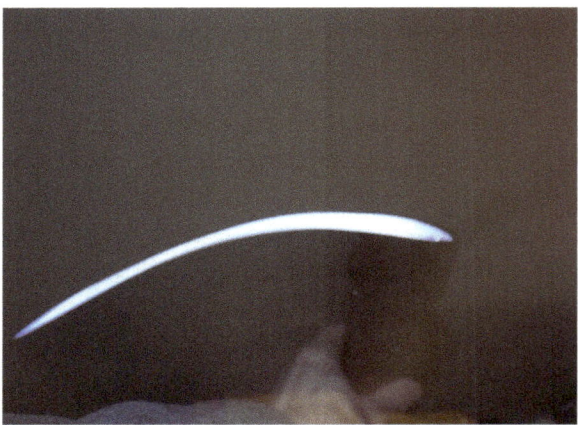

Figure 5-17. Normal Flash

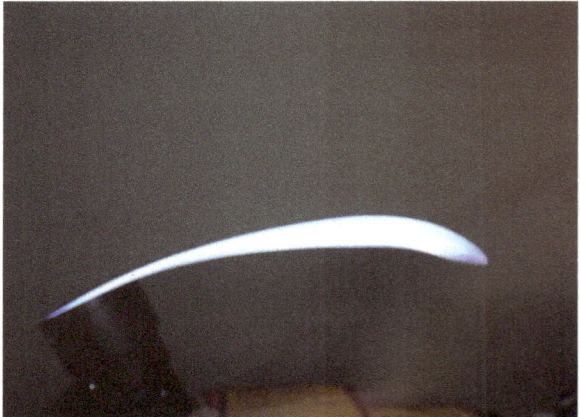

Figure 5-18. Rear Sync Flash

In Figure 5-17, using the normal Front-curtain setting, the flash fired early in the exposure, making an image of the flashlight, while the light beam continued on to the left during the long exposure, to make the trail of light in front of the flashlight. In Figure 5-18, using Rear-curtain Sync, the flash did not fire until the flashlight had traveled to the left, overtaking the place where the light beam had traced its trail.

A good general rule is not to use Rear-curtain sync unless you have a definite need for it. Using the Rear-curtain setting makes it harder to compose and set up the shot, because you have to anticipate where the main subject will be located when the flash finally fires late in the exposure process.

One other setting you should keep in mind is flash exposure compensation, which is available through the Shooting menu when the camera is set to the more advanced shooting modes. This setting reduces the intensity of the flash, even when the camera is automatically setting the exposure. Just as with normal exposure compensation, when using flash you can adjust this setting if your test shots appear too bright or too dark. Just go into this menu item and set the value to a positive number to brighten the image or to a negative number to darken it, as discussed in Chapter 4. Be sure to set it to zero when you no longer need the adjustment.

Right Button: Exposure Compensation

When not acting as the Right button, this control serves as the exposure compensation button. As I discussed in Chapter 2, you press this button to bring up an EV scale on the screen, as shown in Figure 5-19, and then press the Up and Down buttons on the multi selector or turn the command dial or multi selector dial to adjust the value.

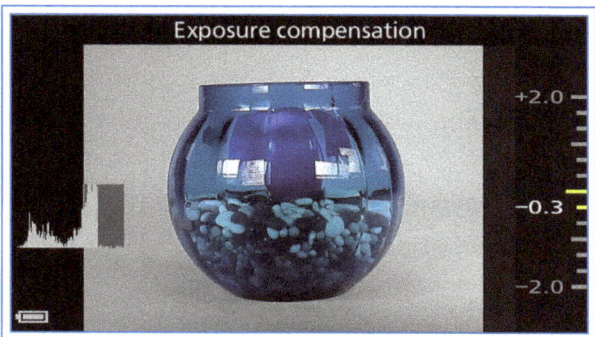

Figure 5-19. Exposure Compensation Scale on Screen

You do not need to press the OK button to select the value; just let the pop-up menu disappear and the setting will take effect. This adjustment is available in all shooting modes except for Manual exposure mode; the Manual Exposure Mode setting in Movie Manual Mode; and the Fireworks Show, Multiple Exposure Lighten, and Time-lapse Movie setting (Night Sky or Star Trails options) of Scene mode. Any adjustment to exposure compensation will be retained in the camera's memory if it is adjusted in Program, Aperture Priority, or Shutter Priority mode; however, it will not be retained in memory in other modes. Therefore, if you are shooting in P, A, or S mode, be sure to adjust exposure compensation back to zero when you have finished using it, or else the adjusted value will be in effect the next time you turn the camera on in that mode.

When you are using manual focus, you can press the Right button to force the camera to use its autofocus mechanism on the subject in the center of the screen. You can then adjust the focus further manually by turning the side dial.

When you are recording a video, the Right button can be used to lock exposure when the AE-L/AF-L Button menu option is set to AF Lock Only, as discussed in Chapter 8.

Down Button: Focus Mode

In shooting mode, press this button to bring up the menu of options for the camera's focus mode when using autofocus: normal autofocus, macro focus, and infinity focus, as shown in Figure 5-20. This button brings up this menu only when the focus mode selector is at the AF position, for autofocus.

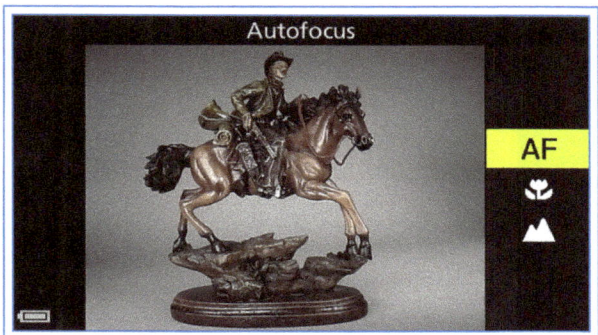

Figure 5-20. Focus Mode Menu

You have limited choices for focus mode in some of the shooting modes. For example, in Moon mode the setting is fixed at infinity, and in Bird-watching mode you can choose normal autofocus or infinity, but not macro. With most of the settings of Scene mode, the choice of focus modes is limited to one or two options. In Creative mode, you can choose only normal autofocus or macro. You can make the full range of choices in the Auto, Program, Aperture Priority, Shutter Priority, Manual, and Movie Manual modes.

After you press the Down button, use the Up and Down buttons or the multi selector dial or command dial to navigate to the icon for your desired mode, then press the OK button to confirm.

For most purposes, the normal autofocus setting works well. Use the infinity setting when you want to force the camera to focus in the distance. Note that the flash is disabled when infinity is selected for the focus mode. Note, also, that there is another infinity setting, symbolized by a mathematical infinity sign, that is automatically selected in Scene mode with the following settings: Fireworks Show, the Star Trails setting of Multiple Exposure Lighten, and the Night Sky and Star Trails settings of Time-lapse Movie. With the Fireworks setting for Multiple Exposure Lighten, you can select either type of infinity setting for autofocus.

Macro photography using the macro autofocus mode is discussed in Chapter 9.

In manual focus mode, pressing the Down button toggles the display between the screen for adjusting focus, at either normal magnification or an enlarged view, and the screen with the focus locked, at the normal magnification.

Left Button: Self-timer; Smile Timer; Pet Portrait Release

If you press the Left button when the camera is in shooting mode, the camera displays the menu of available choices for setting the self-timer and the smile timer, as shown in Figure 5-21 with the camera set to Program mode.

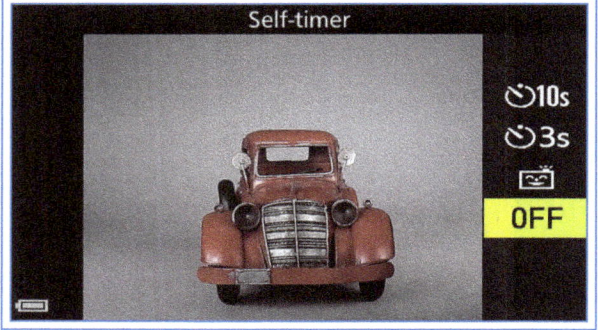

Figure 5-21. Self-timer/Smile Timer Menu

In this shooting mode, as with several other modes, the choices are, from top to bottom: ten-second self-timer; three-second self-timer; smile timer; and Off.

With most of the scene modes and all Creative mode settings, the same list of choices is available, except that the smile timer is not included. (The smile timer is available with the Portrait and Night Portrait settings, but not with the other Scene mode settings.) With the Pet Portrait setting of Scene mode, the only option available is Pet Portrait Release, as discussed later in this section. Neither the self-timer nor the smile timer is available with the Sports, Fireworks Show, or Easy Panorama scene setting.

If you set a self-timer delay of either ten seconds or three seconds, the camera will delay the specified amount of time before taking the picture, after you press the shutter button. Choose ten seconds if you need a substantial delay so you can get into a group picture after pressing the shutter button; choose three seconds if you just need to avoid touching the camera during the exposure, to minimize the camera shake that can accompany a shutter press.

You might need to use the three-second delay when you're taking extreme closeups, because any camera motion could be magnified by the closeness to the subject. Also, the three-second delay can help when you're shooting in dim light and a slow shutter speed is needed, because any camera motion during the long exposure could blur the image.

When you turn on continuous shooting through the Shooting menu, the self-timer is available to a certain extent, though it is not useful with the higher-quality continuous settings.

As I noted in Chapter 4, with the Continuous H and Continuous L settings, when the self-timer triggers the shutter, only one image will be taken, unless you continue to hold down the shutter button. With Pre-shooting Cache, no continuous shooting will take place, even if you hold down the shutter button. However, with the Continuous H: 120 fps and Continuous H: 60 fps settings, the camera will take the full 60 shots when the self-timer triggers the shutter, even if you don't hold down the shutter button. The self-timer can also be used to start a sequence using the interval timer setting.

You can use the self-timer with movie recording, so you can turn on a delay with the self-timer and then press the red Movie button to start a movie recording after the specified delay.

When the camera is set to the Auto, Program, Aperture Priority, Shutter Priority, or Manual exposure mode, or to the Portrait or Night Portrait Scene mode setting, the smile timer is added to the options on the self-timer menu.

The smile timer is a special feature that fires the shutter automatically when the camera detects a smile. This function works together with the camera's face detection system, which is automatically turned on when the smile timer is selected. The smile timer operates only when the focus mode selector is set to the autofocus position; it cannot function when manual focus is in use. It also does not work if AF Area Mode is set to Subject Tracking.

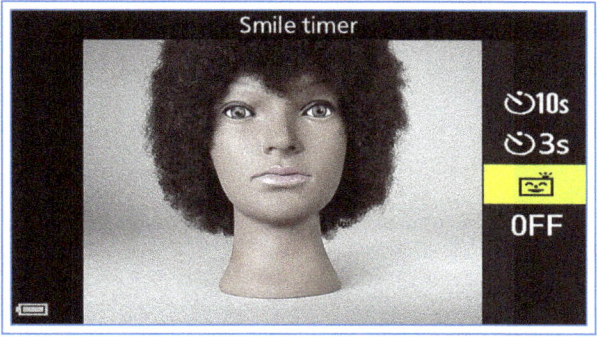

Figure 5-22. Smile Timer Icon Highlighted on Menu

Activate the smile timer by selecting its icon on the self-timer menu, as shown in Figure 5-22. Once the smile timer is turned on, the camera places the smile timer icon in the upper left corner of the screen. Then, whenever the camera detects one or more faces, it focuses on the face that appears to be the primary one and places a yellow double border around that face, as shown in Figure 5-23. The self-timer lamp on the front of the camera will start to blink, to indicate that a face has been detected.

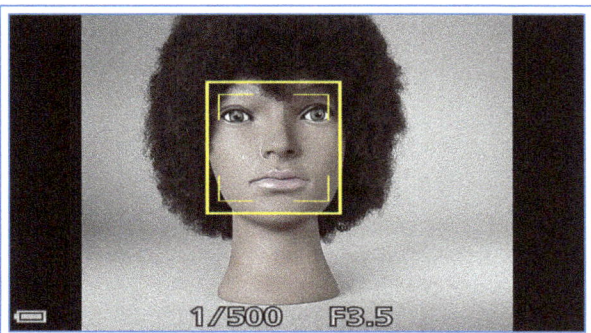

Figure 5-23. Double Border on Face for Smile Timer

The smile timer icon is no longer displayed once a face has been detected. The shutter is triggered automatically if the face inside the double border smiles. Once that happens, the lamp on the front of the camera will blink quickly a few times to indicate that a picture of a smiling face has been taken.

This feature is more of a novelty than a particularly useful function in my opinion, though it may be of use in some situations, such as when you need to encourage a child to smile by telling him or her that a smile will automatically trigger the camera. Also, the smile timer acts as a sort of remote control for the camera; each time the subject smiles, the camera is triggered again. So, if you are taking self-portraits, you can stand in front of your P950 on its tripod, and control the camera's operation with your smile as it takes repeated portraits.

In the Pet Portrait setting of Scene mode, the Left button has a special function of turning on or off the Pet Portrait Auto Release function. As was discussed in Chapter 3, when that feature is turned on, the shutter is automatically triggered when the camera detects the face of a cat or dog. With the Pet Portrait setting, the self-timer and smile timer settings are not available.

When the camera is using manual focus, pressing the Left button toggles between views that are normal size or enlarged two times or four times.

When you are recording a video with the Autofocus Mode option on the Movie menu set to AF-S, you can press the Left button to cause the camera to refocus on the subject. When that option is set to AF-F, you can press the Left button to lock focus in some situations, as discussed in Chapter 8.

There are a few other controls that are located on the front and right side of the camera, as described below.

Self-timer/AF Assist/Red-eye Reduction Lamp

The small lamp on the front of the camera, shown in Figure 5-24, has multiple functions. Its reddish light blinks to signal the operation of the self-timer and face/smile detection when the smile timer is used, and it also turns on in dark environments to assist with autofocusing. In addition, when the flash mode is set to a mode that uses red-eye reduction, this lamp lights up for a second or two before the flash fires, in an effort to cause a human subject's pupils to narrow. In that way, there should be less chance of the flash's light bouncing off of the person's retinas to cause the unsightly "red-eye" effect.

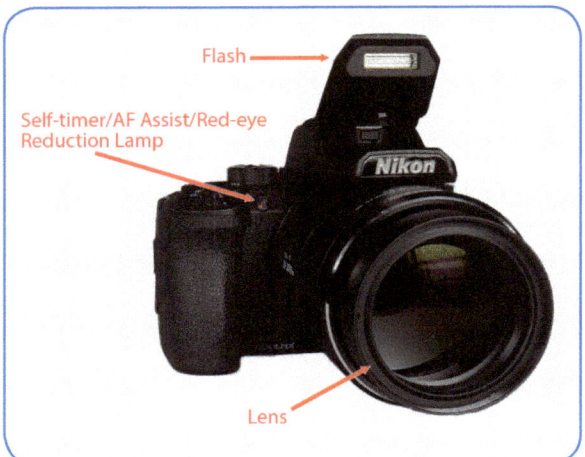

Figure 5-24. Items on Front of Camera

You can control the use of the lamp for autofocusing with the AF Assist item on screen 2 of the Setup menu, as discussed in Chapter 7. You might want to disable it when taking pictures during a religious ceremony or in another environment where this rather bright light could be distracting. Even if you disable it for purposes of autofocus, though, the lamp will still light up to indicate the functioning of the self-timer and smile timer, and it will still function as the Red-eye Reduction Lamp if the flash mode is set to use the lamp for that purpose.

USB Port and HDMI Port

The USB port and HDMI port are small openings under a flap on the right side of the camera, shown in Figure 5-25. These two ports have several functions. The one at the bottom, the USB port, is where you plug in the charging cable when you charge the battery inside the camera or operate the camera by power from the charger. It also is where you connect the camera to a computer to transfer your photos and movies using the supplied USB cable.

The upper port is where you plug in an HDMI cable (which you need to purchase as a separate option) to view photos or videos on an HDTV set or to send a "clean" HDMI signal to an external monitor or video recorder, as discussed in Chapter 8. The end going into this port is a micro-HDMI connector; the end going to the HDTV should be a standard HDMI connector. These cables are available through various sellers, including Amazon.com.

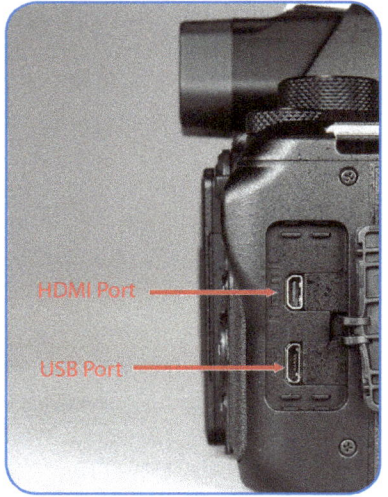

Figure 5-25. Ports on Right Side of Camera

Tilting and Swiveling LCD Screen

The last item to be discussed in this chapter is not really a "control," but it does allow physical adjustment, so I will discuss it here. This is the articulated LCD display on the back of the camera. This screen, even without its tilting and swiveling ability, is a notable feature of the camera. It has a diagonal span of 3.2 inches (8.1 cm) and provides a resolution of 921,000 dots, giving a clear view of your images and videos before and after you capture them, as well as clear views of camera settings and menu screens.

With its ability to pivot both horizontally and vertically, the monitor gives you a considerable amount of added flexibility for your shooting. If, as shown in Figure 5-26, you pull it out to the left and then rotate the screen so it aims downward, you can hold the camera high above your head and view the scene as if you were an arm's-length taller, or were standing on a small ladder.

If you attach the camera to a monopod or other support and hold it up in the air, you can extend the camera's height even farther and still see the LCD quite well. You can activate the self-timer before raising the camera up to take the photo, or you can turn on interval timer shooting with the Continuous option on the shooting menu, and have the camera take a series of shots while it is elevated. You also can use the P950's Wi-Fi capability, discussed in Chapter 9, or an optional remote control, discussed in Appendix A, to trigger the camera remotely.

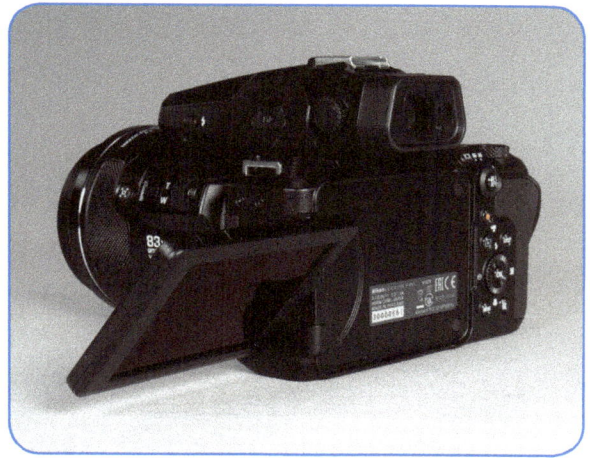

Figure 5-26. LCD Screen Tilted Down for Overhead Shots

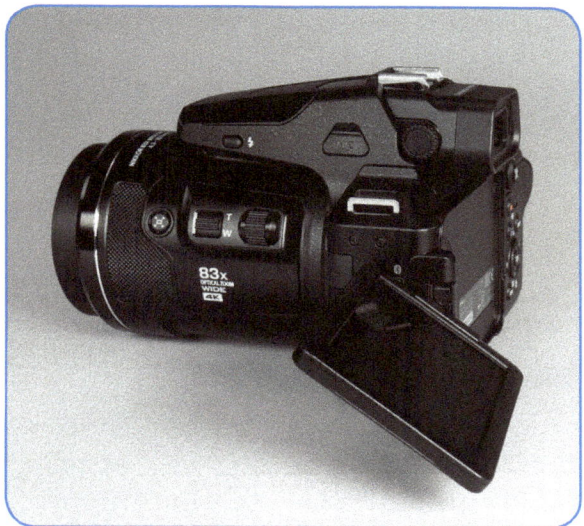

Figure 5-27. LCD Tilted Up for Low-angle Shots

On the other hand, if you need to take images from a low vantage point near ground level, you can rotate the screen so it tilts upward toward your eye, as shown in Figure 5-27, and hold the camera down as far as you need to get a mole's-eye view of the world. Also, as I discuss further in Chapter 9, this angle is useful for street photography, because you can look down at the camera while taking long-zoom photos of people on the street without drawing attention to yourself.

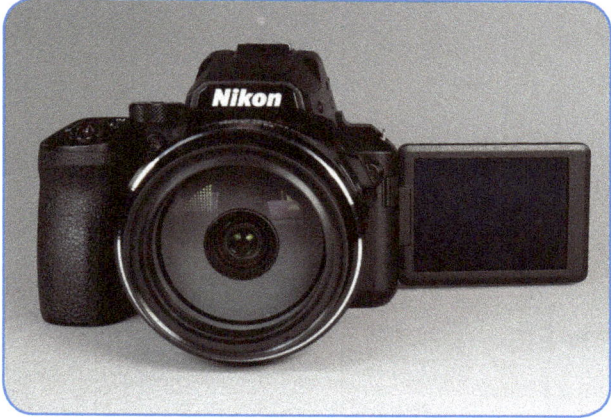

Figure 5-28. LCD Screen Rotated Forward for Self-portraits

If you fold the screen out so that its viewing area faces in the same direction as the lens, as shown in Figure 5-28, you can take a self-portrait while observing your image on the display.

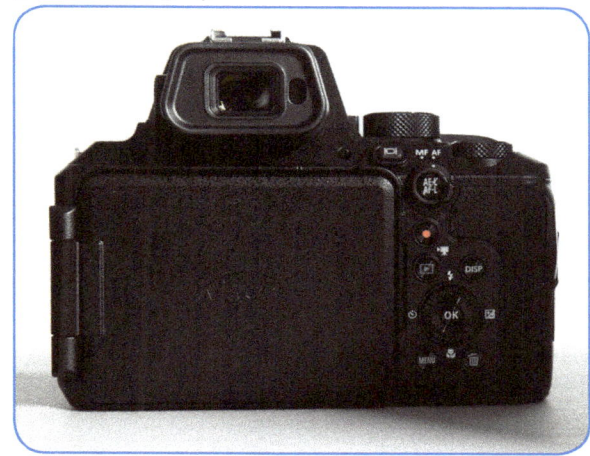

Figure 5-29. LCD Screen Folded in Against Camera

Finally, the screen can be folded in so its viewing surface is hidden. In this configuration, shown in Figure 5-29, the LCD display is protected against damage, and the camera automatically switches to using the viewfinder.

Chapter 6: Playback

Normal Playback

When you take a new photo, by default, the recorded image stays on the screen for about one second for review. If your major concern with viewing images in the camera is to check them right after they are taken, this feature is helpful, but the review time is very brief and there is no way to adjust its duration. You can turn this feature off using the Monitor Settings/Image Review item on screen 1 of the Setup menu, as discussed in Chapter 7. If you want to view your images in more detail, you need to use the features that are available in playback mode.

For ordinary image review in playback mode, the process is simple. Press the Playback button, marked by a right-facing triangle, to the right of the LCD screen on the camera's back. Once you press that button, the camera is in playback mode and you will see the most recent image or video saved to the memory card that is in the camera. To move back through older images, press either the Left button or the Up button or turn the multi selector dial (the dial that surrounds the OK button on the camera's back) to the left. To move through the increasingly more recent images, use the Right button or the Down button, or turn the multi selector dial to the right. To scroll through your images rapidly, hold down the Left or Right (or Up or Down) button. To delete images, press the Trash button and follow the prompts on the screen, as discussed in Chapter 5.

Index Views, Calendar View, and Enlarging Images

In playback mode, you can press the zoom lever on top of the camera to view an index screen of images or to enlarge an image. When you are viewing an image, press the zoom lever once to the left (toward the W setting), and you will see a screen showing four images, one of which is outlined by a yellow frame, as shown in Figure 6-1.

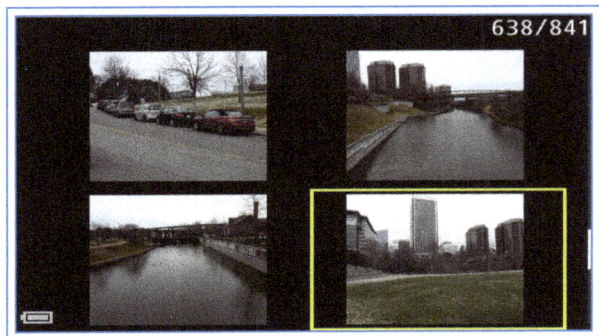

Figure 6-1. Index Screen with Four Images

You can then press the OK button to bring up the outlined image as the single image on the screen, or you can move through your images with the four-image index screen by pressing the four direction buttons or by turning the multi selector dial.

If you move the zoom lever to the W mark once more, the camera will show an index screen of nine images; another press brings 16 images; and another press brings a 72-image screen, as seen in Figure 6-2 (assuming in each case that you have that many images; if not, there will be blank spaces on the screen).

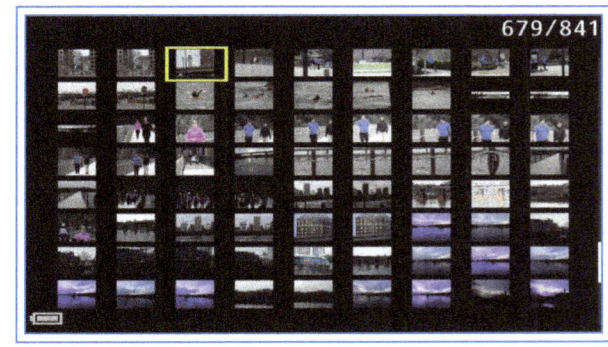

Figure 6-2. Index Screen with 72 Images

If you press the lever in the same direction one more time, the camera displays a calendar screen with a thumbnail image on each date for which images exist, as shown in Figure 6-3.

Chapter 6: Playback

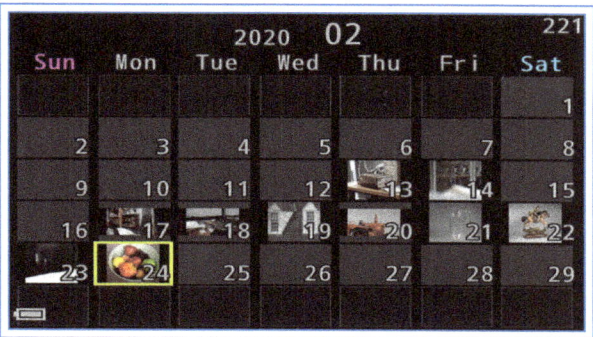

Figure 6-3. Calendar Index Screen

You can maneuver through any of the index screens to select a single image for viewing. If you want to reduce the number of images per screen, press the zoom lever to the right (toward the T position) repeatedly to reverse the progression of index screens. On the calendar screen, highlight a date and press the OK button to display images and videos from that date.

When you are viewing a single image, a press of the zoom lever to the right enlarges that image, as seen in Figure 6-4.

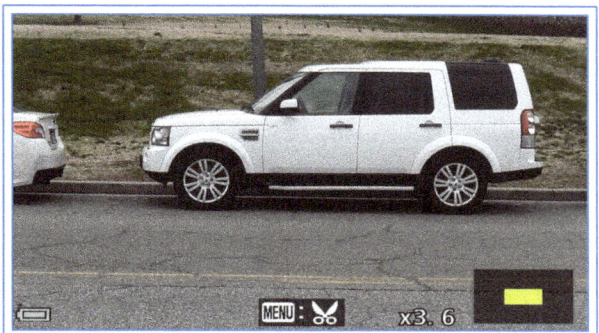

Figure 6-4. Enlarged Image in Playback Mode

You will see a display in the lower right corner with an inset yellow block that represents the portion of the image that is now filling the screen in enlarged view. The display with the inset block appears only if you are viewing the screen with basic information or the screen with comment and copyright information. With the screen that includes no information and the screen with detailed information with a histogram, the image will be enlarged, but without the inset block. If an image was captured using face detection or pet detection, the camera will zoom in on the detected face. (This function does not work if the image was captured using continuous shooting or exposure bracketing.)

If you press the zoom lever to the right repeatedly, the image will be enlarged up to a maximum of about ten times normal. While the image is magnified, you can scroll around within it using the four direction buttons; you will see the inset yellow block move around within the larger rectangle that represents the whole image. To reduce the image size again, press the zoom lever to the left as many times as necessary. You can also increase or decrease the zoom level by turning the command dial right or left, once the enlargement has been started with the zoom lever. Press the OK button to restore the image to its original size immediately.

While the image is enlarged, the word MENU appears on the screen with a scissors icon, as shown in Figure 6-4. (If you don't see these items, return the image to normal size and press the Display button to reach the more detailed view.) When you see the scissors icon, you can press the Menu button to save the enlarged area as a separate file. This feature gives you a rough-and-ready way to crop your images in the camera.

For example, if you want to crop a group photo to save just the face of one person, you can enlarge the image and scroll it around using the direction buttons until just that face is visible. Then press the Menu button to save a separate file with that face as the only subject. This process is no match for editing with a computer, but it could come in handy when no computer is available and you need a particular part of an image for a special purpose, such as a business presentation. This feature does not work with Raw images or images taken using the Easy Panorama setting of Scene mode.

Various Playback Screens

When you are viewing an individual image in playback mode, pressing the Display button repeatedly cycles through four screens. (The screens are different for sequences of continuous shots, as discussed later in this chapter.)

These are the full image with no added information except movie format for movies (not shown here); full image with basic information, including date and time it was taken, file name, image number, image size and quality (Figure 6-5); reduced-size image with detailed recording information, including shooting mode, aperture, shutter speed, ISO, exposure compensation, and other data, plus a histogram (Figure 6-6); and image with black box superimposed, including information in Comment, Artist, and Copyright categories (Figure 6-7). That information can be entered using the Image Comment and Copyright Information items on the Setup menu.

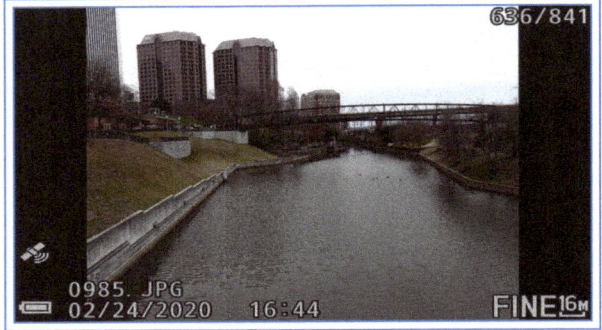

Figure 6-5. Playback Display Screen: Basic Information

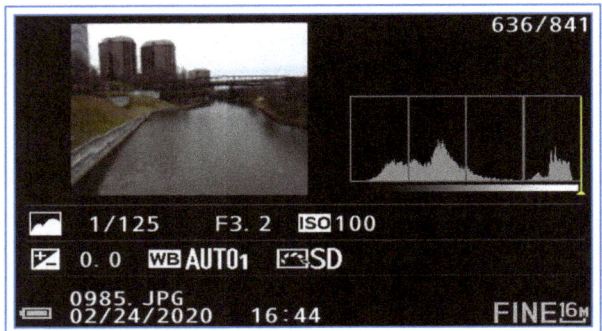

Figure 6-6. Playback Display Screen: Histogram

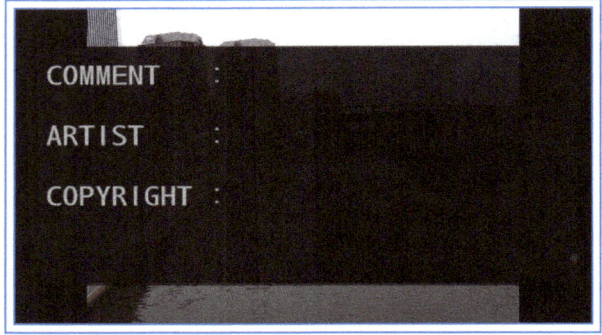

Figure 6-7. Playback Display Screen: Comment/Copyright

These four screens are available for still images. For movies there are only three screens; the screen with the histogram is not available.

The detailed display screen, as noted above, includes a histogram. The histogram is a graph, or chart, representing the distribution of dark and bright areas in the image displayed on the screen. The darkest blacks are represented by vertical bars on the left, and the brightest whites by vertical bars on the right, with continuous gradations in between.

If you have a histogram in which the pattern looks like a tall ski slope coming from the left of the screen down to ground level in the middle of the screen, that means there is an excessive amount of black and dark areas (high points on the left side of the histogram), and very few bright and white areas (no high points on the right), as shown in Figure 6-8.

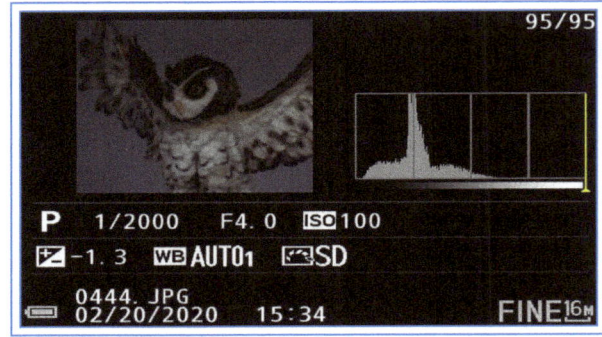

Figure 6-8. Histogram for Underexposed Image

A ski slope moving from the middle of the screen up to the top of the right side of the screen would mean just the opposite—too many bright and white areas, as illustrated in Figure 6-9.

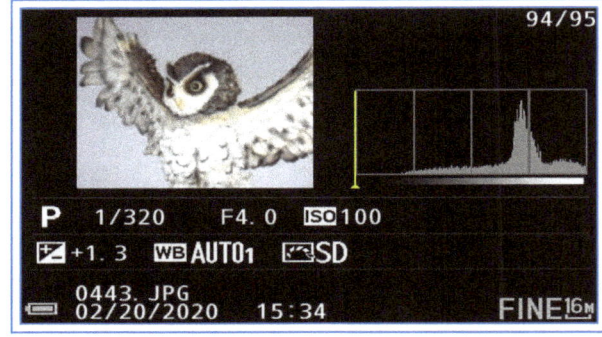

Figure 6-9. Histogram for Overexposed Image

A histogram that is "just right" would be one that starts low on the left, gradually rises to a medium peak in the middle of the screen, then moves gradually back down to ground level at the right. That pattern indicates a good balance of whites, blacks, and medium tones. Figure 6-10 shows a histogram of that sort.

The histogram is an approximation, and should not be relied on too heavily. It is useful to give some feedback on how evenly exposed your image is likely to be.

When the histogram is displayed in playback mode, you can see information about the tone levels in the image. To do this, look closely at the histogram, to the right of the thumbnail image, and you will see a vertical yellow line. If you press the Left and Right buttons or turn the multi selector dial, you can move that yellow line across the histogram. As you do this, you will see different parts of the image flash. With this screen, the camera gives you a way to select which parts of the tone map to check. As you move the line over the chart, corresponding parts of the image will flash to show where in the image there are tones at that level.

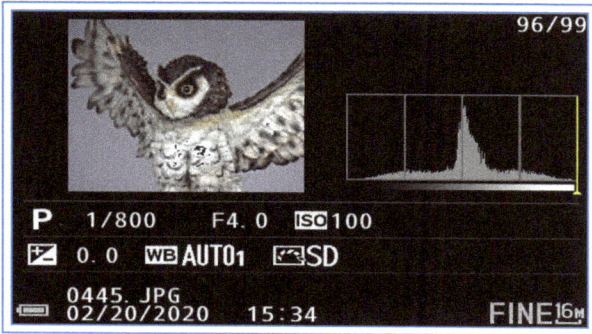

Figure 6-10. Histogram for Normally Exposed Image

For example, as you start with the line at the extreme right of the histogram, the brightest areas of the image will flash, and, as you move the line to the left, progressively darker areas of the image will flash. Using this tool, you may be able to gather some information about what parts of the image are too dark or too bright, so you can take another image that avoids having details swallowed up by blown highlights or excessively dark shadows.

When the histogram screen is displayed, you cannot use the Right and Left buttons or the multi selector dial to move through your images, because those buttons and the dial move through the tone level information. You can use the Up and Down buttons to navigate through the images in that situation.

Viewing Shots Taken in a Sequence

When you take photos with the Coolpix P950 in certain shooting modes or with certain functions, the images become part of what Nikon calls a "sequence." When you enter playback mode to view those images, you ordinarily will see only the "key" image of the sequence, usually the first one of the group that was taken. To see the rest of the images in the sequence, you have to take other steps. I'll discuss this process in some detail, because it can be a bit confusing at first.

For example, suppose you have placed the camera in Program mode by turning the mode dial to P, and then selected continuous high-speed shooting by selecting Continuous H from the Continuous item on the Shooting menu. Now, when you aim the camera at your subject and hold down the shutter button for a second or two, you will hear the sounds of the camera operating. The LCD screen (or viewfinder) will display the last captured image for about one second and then return to the view of the live scene.

When the camera settles back to the live view, you can press the Playback button to start viewing your images. If everything worked as expected, there will be as many as ten new images to view, because that is the longest burst the camera can take using the Continuous H setting. However, when you press the Playback button, you will see only one image from this sequence. If you press any of the direction buttons or turn the multi selector dial, you will move to an entirely different image, assuming one exists; you will not see the other images from this sequence.

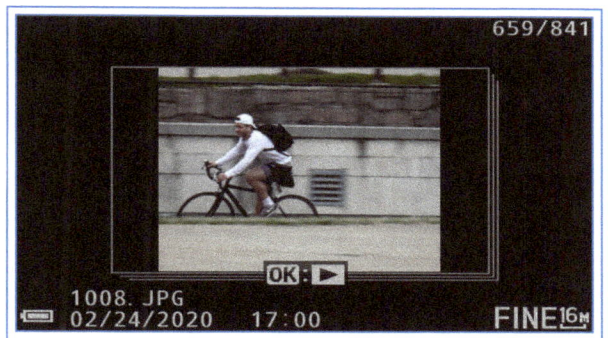

Figure 6-11. Burst of Images Displayed as Group

Look at the display on the screen, as shown in Figure 6-11, which has a few unusual aspects. (If you see a display with no information, press the Display button to show the screen with basic information.) If you press the Display button, the basic image information will appear or disappear, but you cannot produce the histogram display, because you are viewing the "key" image of a sequence rather than an individual picture.

Also, you will see the notation OK at the bottom of the screen with a triangle, indicating the Play function, to its right. This means that, to view the other images in this sequence, you need to press the OK button.

If you now press the OK button, you will see the same image as before, but with a different appearance, as shown in Figure 6-12.

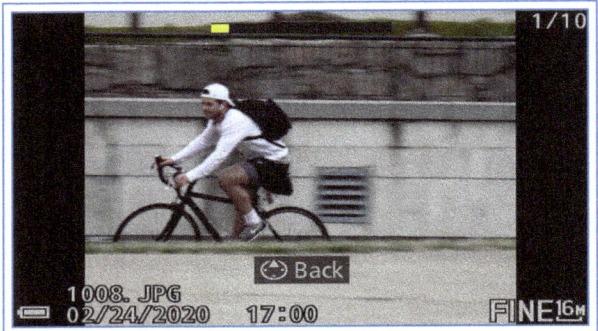

Figure 6-12. Burst of Images Displayed Individually

Now, pressing the Display button will cycle through the three possible views of each image, including the histogram view and the comment/copyright view, because you are viewing this photo as an individual image, not as the key image for a sequence.

You will no longer see the OK notation; instead, you will see a yellow bar at the top center of the display, and the number 1 with a slash followed by the total number of images at the upper right. In Figure 6-12, the numbers are 1/10, because the sequence includes ten images. The yellow bar will progress across the top of the screen as you navigate through the images in the sequence using the Left and Right (but not Up and Down) buttons or the multi selector dial, and the numbers will increase from 1/10 up to 10/10 as you move to the most recent images in the sequence. If you have captured a group of 60 or 120 images, you may want to speed through them in playback mode using the multi selector dial, rather than pressing the Left and Right buttons repeatedly.

You can magnify each individual image by moving the zoom lever toward the T position, but (naturally enough) you cannot call up an index screen by pressing the zoom lever in the other direction, because only the images in this sequence are available for viewing at this point.

Once you have "entered" the sequence by pressing OK, you will be "stuck" inside it—you can keep navigating through these images, but you will continue to navigate through the same set of images, over and over, until you exit from the sequence and go back to viewing the key image. If you are viewing the display screen with basic information, as seen in Figure 6-12, there is a prompt on the screen that tells you how to do this: an icon highlighting the Up button with the notation Back, meaning you have to press the Up button to go back to the key-image view. That is, when you want to stop viewing these individual images and return to the key image so you can navigate through the rest of the images on your memory card, you have to press the Up button.

If you would rather not have the camera display your continuous-mode shots in sequences, but would prefer to have them displayed as individual shots at all times, you can select that option using the Sequence Display item on the Playback menu, as discussed later in this chapter. However, if you take many sequences using a feature such as Continuous H: 120 fps, which takes 60 shots at a time, you may appreciate the ability to display just the key frame from the sequence when you browse through your images in playback mode.

The Playback Menu

Several useful playback functions are controlled by the options on the two screens of the Playback menu. To get access to this menu, you must put the camera into playback mode by pressing the Playback button (right-facing triangle). Then press the Menu button and, if necessary, move the yellow block on the screen to the left column and navigate to the triangle icon to select the Playback menu, as shown in Figure 6-13.

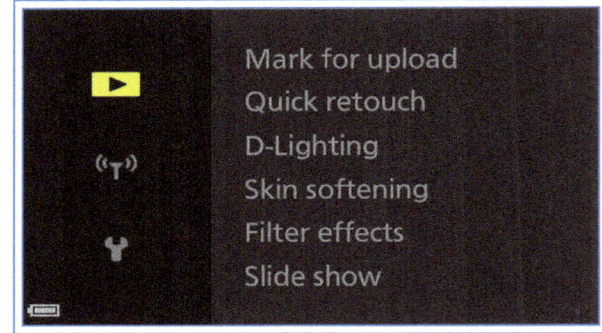

Figure 6-13. Icon for Playback Menu Highlighted at Left

Then move the yellow block back to the right to highlight the various entries in the menu, whose first screen is shown in Figure 6-14. I'll discuss the options on the Playback menu one by one.

Chapter 6: Playback

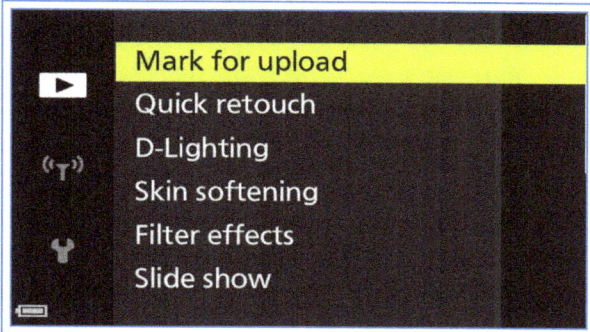

Figure 6-14. Screen 1 of Playback Menu

Mark for Upload

This first Playback menu option lets you mark images for later upload to a smartphone or tablet using the P950's built-in wireless network capability. To do this, highlight this option and press the OK or Right button to move to the next screen. The camera will display a screen with six thumbnail images. Scroll through those images with the Left and Right buttons or the multi selector dial. When you have highlighted an image you want to upload, press the Up or Down button to mark it; the camera will place a jagged, two-headed arrow below the thumbnail to indicate that that image is now marked for upload, as shown in Figure 6-15.

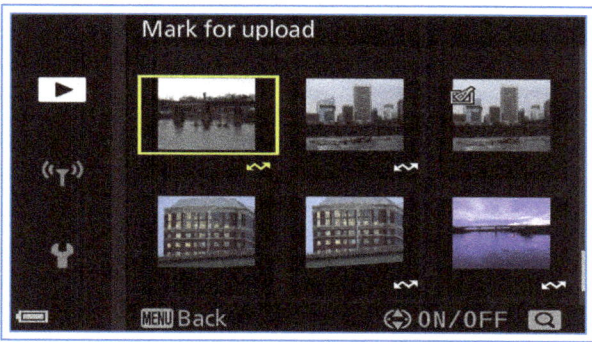

Figure 6-15. Images Marked for Upload

If you change your mind about an image, press the Up or Down button again, and the image will be unmarked. When you have finished, press the OK button to confirm your selections. Only JPEG images will be displayed for marking with this option, because videos and Raw images cannot be uploaded using this process. In Chapter 9, I will discuss the procedure for uploading the marked images, along with other topics involving Wi-Fi and Bluetooth options. Basically, you need to select the Auto Link option in the SnapBridge app, and then select the sub-option for Auto Download under that option.

Quick Retouch

The Quick Retouch option gives you a way to add some brightness or "punch" to recorded images with in-camera processing. You can apply this enhancement to any individual image. If the image you want to enhance is displayed as part of a sequence, you first have to use the technique described earlier (pressing the OK button) to display the images individually. When the image you have selected is displayed, press the Menu button and choose Quick Retouch from the menu. You can then use the Up and Down buttons or the multi selector dial to choose the desired amount of alteration—Low, Normal, or High, as shown in Figure 6-16.

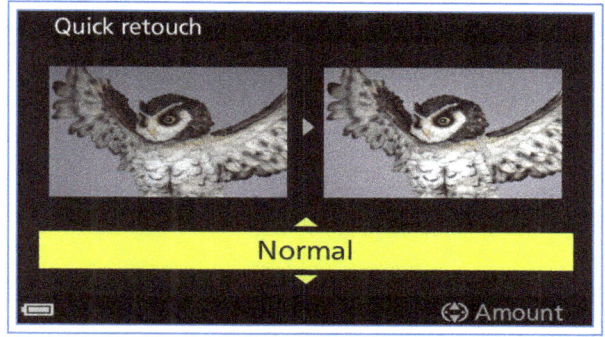

Figure 6-16. Quick Retouch Menu Options Screen

As you change the amount, you will see a preview of the finished product in a thumbnail on the right side of the screen, with the unchanged original on the left, for comparison. When you have selected the amount of change, press the OK button to confirm, and a new image will be saved with the retouched appearance and a new file number. It will have the Quick Retouch icon in the upper left area of the image, as shown in Figure 6-17.

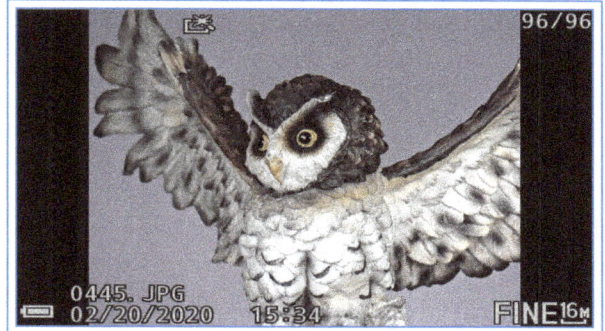

Figure 6-17. Image with Quick Retouch Icon in Upper Left Corner

You cannot make any choices other than the level of the retouching. When it applies this processing, the camera increases the contrast (difference between light and dark areas) and saturation (intensity of the colors).

This is a feature I don't use often, because I prefer to do my processing with software such as Photoshop. But there could be times when you take images at a party to display on a TV set during the party. You could use this function to brighten up some muddy images and make them livelier for the audience.

Raw images and panoramas cannot be modified by this or any other of the editing features on the Playback menu.

D-Lighting

The D-Lighting option works in the same way as the Quick Retouch feature. Select a still image that is being displayed individually (not as the key frame of a sequence), press the Menu button, and select D-Lighting. Then press the OK button or the Right button to move to the next screen, and choose Low, Normal, or High for the degree of enhancement, as shown in Figure 6-18. When the desired level is highlighted, press the OK button, and the camera will record a new image with the desired level of enhancement.

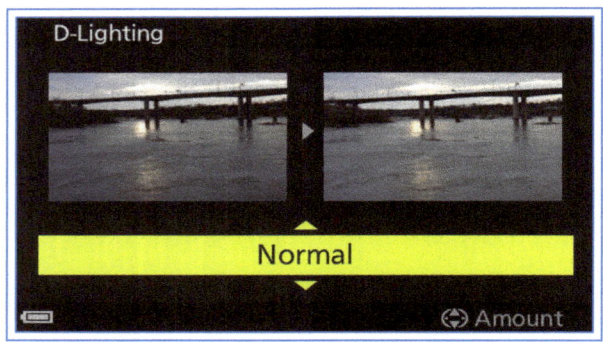

Figure 6-18. D-Lighting Options Screen

In this case, the camera will attempt to add details in both the shadow and highlight areas, as it does when you use the Active D-Lighting option in shooting mode. (I discussed that option in Chapter 4.) This feature can be quite useful, because you can use it to recover details from an image that was taken in conditions with excessive contrast, or even one that was taken with inadequate lighting, at least to some extent.

The new version will be saved to a new file, with a D-Lighting icon in the upper left corner when displayed in the camera. As with the previous option, certain image types cannot be modified with this feature.

Skin Softening

This next entry on the Playback menu gives you another way to modify your recorded images. With this option, you can add a softening effect to the areas in an image that the camera considers to be showing a human face. As with the previous two menu items, you select the image, press the Menu button, and then select how strong the effect should be. One difference with this feature from the other ones is that the camera will decide whether or not there are any faces in the image you have selected.

If the P950 does not detect any faces, it will display an error message saying the image cannot be modified and return you to the menu without doing any processing. If it does detect a face, it will take you to a screen where you select the amount of processing. Once you select the amount and press OK, the camera will show you a larger view of the image with a preview of the effect, as shown in Figure 6-19; you can then press OK to save the processed image, or press Menu to go back and revise your setting.

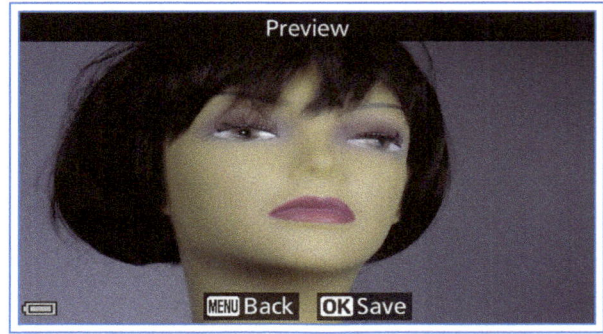

Figure 6-19. Skin Softening Preview Screen

Filter Effects

The Filter Effects menu selection has nine sub-options, the first six of which are shown in Figure 6-20, which the camera can use to make copies of your images with altered aspects. Some of these are similar to settings in the Scene shooting mode. The first entry on the list of effects is called Soft Portrait.

With this option, the camera softens the focus of the image, leaving the center of the image, or a human face if one was detected, in sharp focus, and blurring the focus toward the edges of the image. As with the Skin Softening effect, after you have selected the effect, the camera displays a screen with a preview of the image with the effect applied; you then can press the OK button to apply the effect.

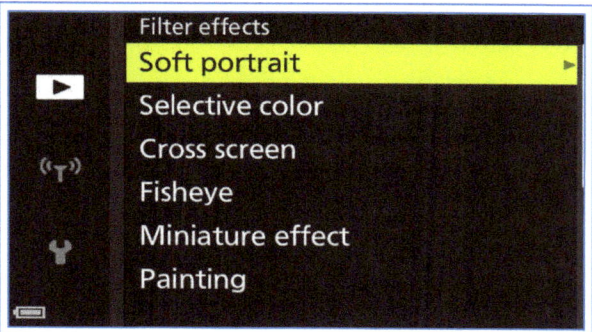

Figure 6-20. Filter Effects Menu Options Screen

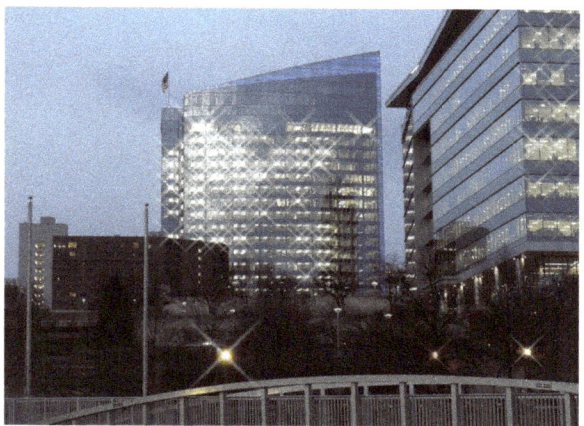

Figure 6-21. Cross Screen Example

Second on the list is the Selective Color effect, similar to the Scene mode setting of that name, discussed in Chapter 3. When you display an image on the screen, the camera places a vertical spectrum of colors to the right of the image, with a pointer that you can move up and down the scale using the multi selector dial or the Up and Down buttons. As you move the pointer next to a color on the scale, the image changes to preserve only the portions that are approximately that color.

If no parts of the image are that color, the image turns completely black-and-white. If you use this effect carefully, you can take an image with one area of bright color, remove all other colors using this effect, and end up with a photo that dramatically highlights the single colored object or area that remains, surrounded by a monochrome environment.

As with earlier effects, the camera presents you with a large preview screen before you decide whether to apply the effect.

The third choice on this menu is Cross Screen. With this option, as with Soft Portrait, there are no adjustments to make; you either save a copy of the image using this processing feature, or you cancel out of the selection. If you choose to go ahead, the camera makes a copy of the selected image with streaks radiating from bright objects such as lights. If there are no bright areas in the image, this option will not produce any changes at all, though the camera will still produce the new image. Figure 6-21 shows an example using this setting, after the camera saved a new copy.

Next on the list is the Fisheye effect, which simulates photographs taken with a fisheye lens, a super wide-angle lens that distorts the image, making it look spherical as if seen through a fishbowl.

The result of using this effect will not look good unless you choose your subject carefully. I find this effect works best with a clearly identifiable subject, like a single building or structure. If you use the Fisheye effect on a busy or cluttered scene, it may be difficult to make out the subject at all, because of the distortion.

The next option is called the Miniature effect. With this feature, the camera adds blurring at the sides of the image to simulate a photograph of a tabletop model or miniature. Such images often appear blurred at the edges, either because of the shallow depth of field of closeup photos, or because of the use of a tilt-and-shift lens, which causes blurring at the edges.

Here, again, you need to choose an appropriate subject. I have found that it works well with something like a street scene or a house, which might actually be reproduced in a tabletop model. For example, if you are able to get a photo from a vantage point above or across from a parking lot or a street with cars parked or driving on it, you can use this processing to make it look as if you had photographed a tabletop display with model cars. Try to keep the main subject in the center of the image. This was the approach I took for Figure 6-22.

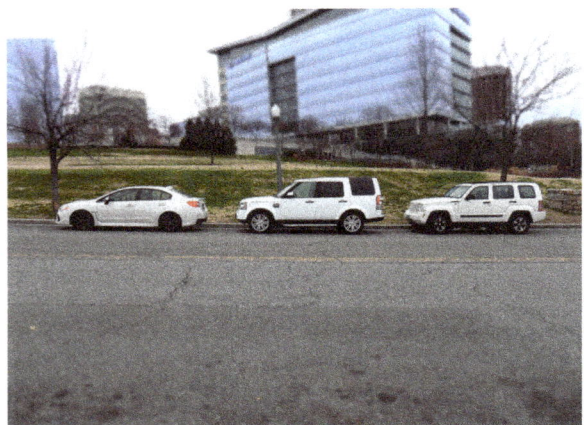

Figure 6-22. Miniature Effect Example

With the next option on the Filter Effects menu, Painting, the camera applies a distinctive form of processing that results in heightened emphasis on colors and imbues the image with a pastel-like look, as shown in Figure 6-23, where I applied this effect to an image taken after dark using the Night Landscape setting.

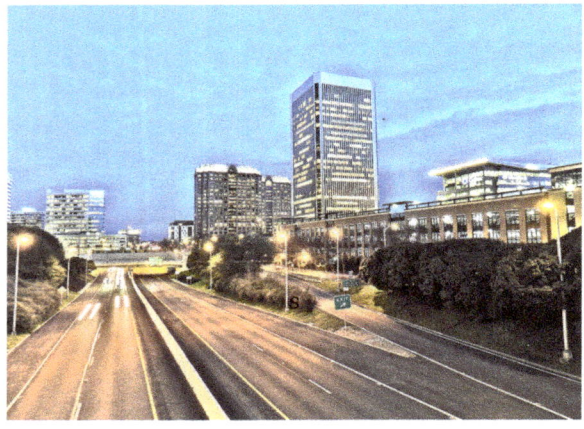

Figure 6-23. Painting Example

This is one of the more dramatic of the Filter Effects settings. The camera increases the intensity of colors and uses processing to give an appearance like that of an HDR image, as discussed in Chapter 3, with shadowed areas brightened. This setting is not appropriate if you are looking for a realistic representation of your subject; it is useful when you want a stylized, vibrant image, possibly for a poster or illustration. I have found that it works best if you start with a somewhat underexposed image.

The next option, Vignette, the first option on the second screen of this menu item, darkens the image toward its edges to create the appearance of an old-fashioned vignette, with the center highlighted but fading out on the edges, and reduces saturation to make the image look faded. An example is shown in Figure 6-24.

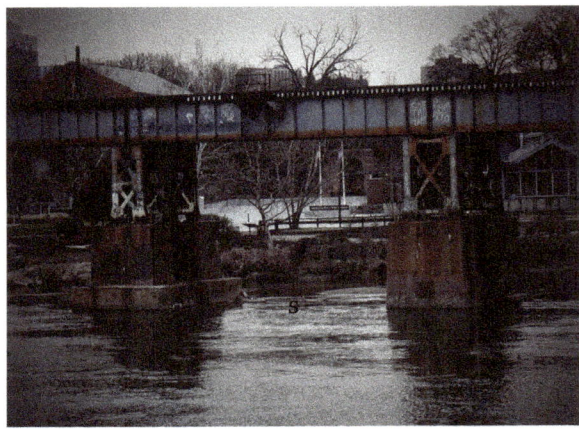

Figure 6-24. Vignette Example

The next option, Photo Illustration, alters the image by darkening the outlines of objects and reducing the number of colors, to make the image appear like a pen-and-ink illustration that has been colored in with poster paints. This option can create a very pleasant effect if used with an appropriate subject. I used it with a view of the city skyline in Figure 6-25.

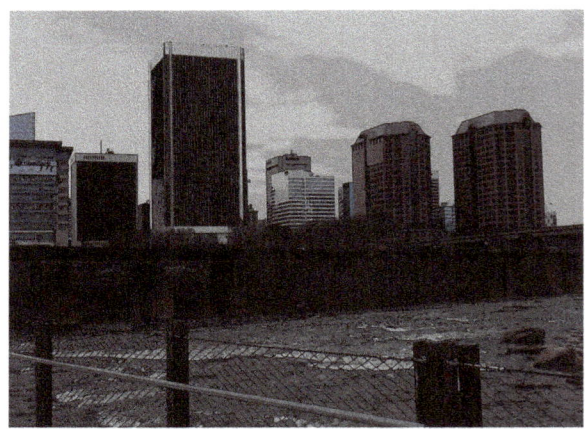

Figure 6-25. Photo Illustration Example

The final choice for the Filter Effects option, Portrait (Color + B&W), is somewhat like the Selective Color option, discussed above, but it is specially designed for images of people. If the camera detects a human face, it will leave the face in color and convert the background to black-and-white, as in Figure 6-26. If the camera does not detect a human subject, it will leave the central part of the image in color and convert the rest of the image to black-and-white. This can be an effective way to highlight a portrait subject and isolate him or her from the background.

Chapter 6: Playback | 99

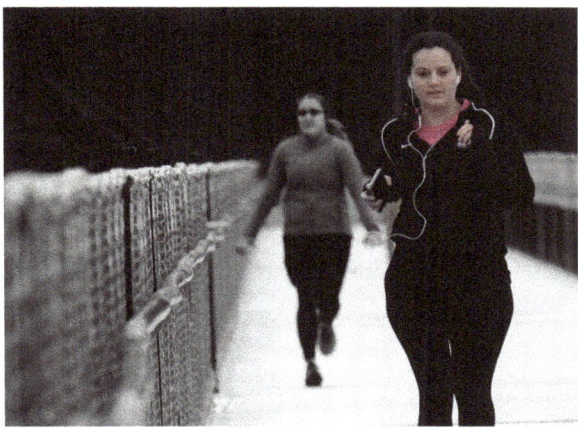

Figure 6-26. Portrait (Color + B&W) Example

SLIDE SHOW

Like most modern digital cameras, the Coolpix P950 can display the images on your memory card in a slide show that plays back on the camera's display or on a connected HDTV. The P950 does not offer options such as music or a variety of transitions; your pictures are played back with straight cuts between them and in silence.

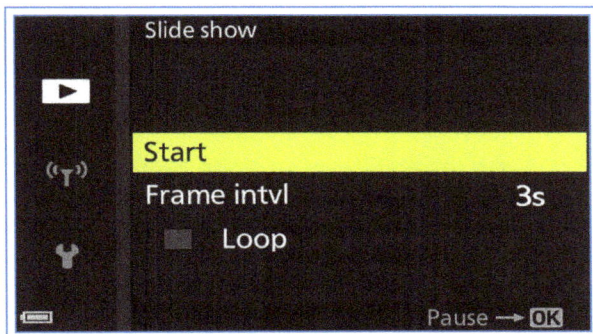

Figure 6-27. Slide Show Menu Options Screen

The only choices you can make from the Slide Show menu option, shown in Figure 6-27, are the length of time between images and whether or not the show should repeat in a loop. (The loop is not endless; the show will repeat for a maximum of 30 minutes.)

To start a slide show, go to the Playback menu and choose Slide Show. You can then navigate to the option for Frame Interval and select 2, 3, 5, or 10 seconds for the time between images. Next, press the Left button to go to the previous screen and press the OK button while the Loop option is highlighted, if you want the show to repeat. After selecting these options, highlight the Start option and press OK to start the show. To pause the show, press OK again. To restart it, highlight the playback triangle that appears on the screen and press the OK button. To stop the show, highlight the square "stop" icon and press the OK button. You also can stop the show at any time by pressing the Playback button. To skip forward or backward to the next image, you can press the Left or Right button at any time; hold either of those buttons down to move more rapidly through the images. You also can turn the multi selector dial to move through the images.

There is no way to select the images that will be played; all images on the memory card will be played. For movies, only the first frame will be played. For sequences of continuous shots, only the key images will be displayed, if the Sequence Display item on the Playback menu is set to Key Picture Only.

The remaining menu options are on screen 2 of the Playback menu, shown in Figure 6-28.

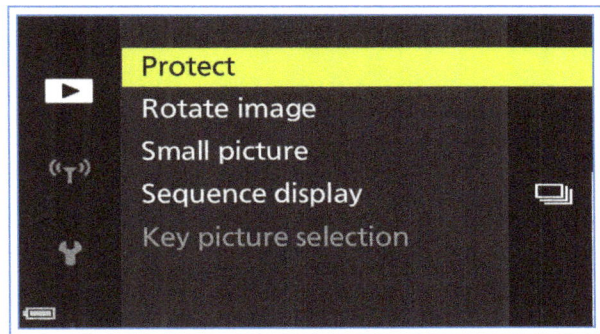

Figure 6-28. Screen 2 of Playback Menu

PROTECT

With the Protect feature, you can "lock" selected images so they cannot be erased with the normal erase functions using the Trash button. However, if you format the memory card using the Format command, all data will be erased, including protected images.

To protect images, after selecting this menu option, navigate through your images using the Left and Right buttons or the multi selector dial, and use the Up and Down buttons to mark or unmark any image you want to protect. You can use the zoom lever to enlarge an image before deciding whether to apply protection to it. A key icon will appear on the thumbnail of each marked image, as shown in Figure 6-29.

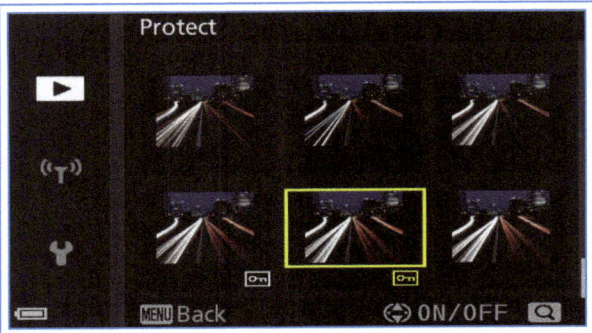

Figure 6-29. Images Marked for Protection

When you have marked all images as you want them, press the OK button to apply the protection. If you mark the key image of a sequence while it is displayed as a sequence, all images within the sequence will be protected. An image that is protected will have a key icon in the upper left corner, as shown in Figure 6-30.

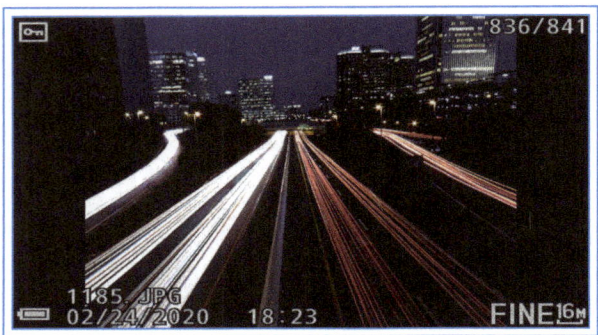

Figure 6-30. Protected Image with Key Icon at Upper Left

That icon will be visible when the image is viewed with the basic information screen; the icon will not appear in the image-only view, in the detailed view with the histogram, or in the comment/copyright view.

Rotate Image

Using this second option on the Playback menu's second screen, you can rotate still photos 90 degrees clockwise or counter-clockwise. You cannot rotate the key image of a sequence when it is displayed in sequence mode; you have to display the pictures from the sequence individually in order to rotate them.

After you select the Rotate Image option from the Playback menu, the camera displays the Select Image screen. Navigate with the multi selector dial or the Left and Right buttons until you have highlighted with a yellow frame the image you want to rotate, then press the OK button to select it.

On the next screen, as shown in Figure 6-31, use the Left or Right button to rotate the image counter-clockwise or clockwise. (You can also do the rotation by turning the multi selector dial.) Press OK when the image is rotated to the orientation you wish, then press the Menu button to exit from the Rotate Image screen. The image will now appear in its rotated orientation; the original view of the image will not be available. (You can rotate the image back to its original orientation using this menu option, if needed.)

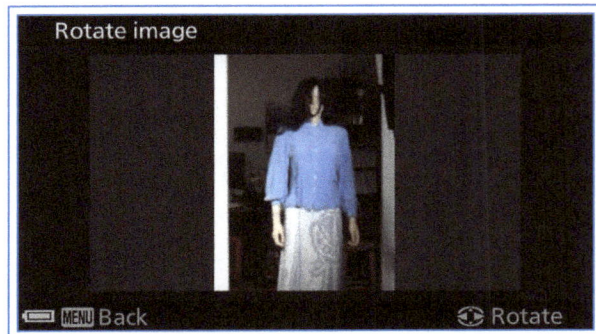

Figure 6-31. Screen for Rotating Image

If an image was taken with the camera turned sideways, so the camera ordinarily has to be turned in order to view the image right-side-up, the camera will let you rotate it as much as 180 degrees; other images can be rotated only 90 degrees.

Before you use this option to rotate images, be aware that it is not necessary for ordinary purposes. If you have taken an image with the camera held sideways so a vertical subject is shown on the horizontal screen, if you just turn the camera sideways in playback mode, the image will display vertically, filling the display screen, as it did when it was captured. So, try just flipping the camera to the side to view images, rather than rotating them, if that approach satisfies your needs.

Small Picture

This option lets you do a simple form of in-camera editing. This feature allows you to take any saved JPEG image that was captured in the aspect ratio of 4:3 or 16:9 and create a new version in a file small enough to send by e-mail or post on the internet. This feature does not work with Raw images, panoramas, or images in the aspect ratio of 3:2 or 1:1.

This function could come in handy if you need to take a quick photo and e-mail it to a friend or colleague. If you don't have software available on your computer to edit the image down to a smaller size, you can let the camera take over this task. Of course, you could take the image in the small size to begin with, but you might want to have a higher-resolution version available for later editing or printing, and be able to create a small version for e-mailing after you have already recorded the original version.

To use this feature, navigate to the image you want to re-size. Once it is displayed, in either full-frame or thumbnail view, press the Menu button, then select the Small Picture option. On the next screen, if the original image was taken with the 4:3 aspect ratio, you can choose from three options: 640 x 480 pixels, 320 x 240 pixels, or 160 x 120 pixels. If the image was taken with the 16:9 aspect ratio, the only option is 640 x 360 pixels. Each of these choices produces a low-resolution image, well under 1 megapixel in size.

If you confirm the operation on the next screen, the camera will copy the selected image at your chosen size and save it to the memory card.

The image will be displayed in the camera with a large, black border area around the image itself, to show that this is a "Small Picture" copy. This border does not become part of the actual image; it displays only in the camera.

SEQUENCE DISPLAY

This menu option controls how the camera displays images taken in one of the continuous-shooting modes such as Continuous H, Continuous L, Pre-shooting Cache, and others, which normally are displayed as "sequences." This option is straightforward: You have just two choices—Individual Pictures or Key Picture Only, as shown in Figure 6-32.

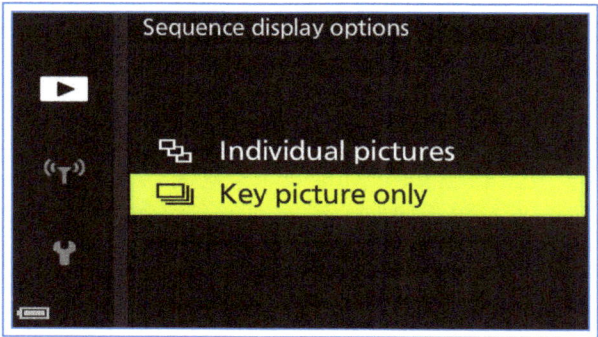

Figure 6-32. Sequence Display Menu Options Screen

If you choose Key Picture Only, then, as you navigate through your images, when you come to a sequence, only the key image will display; it will be displayed in a frame that appears like a stack of images, indicating that it is the key frame of a sequence, and there will be a prompt to press the OK button to view the individual images from the sequence, as seen earlier in Figure 6-11.

You cannot call up the detailed information for the key image with the Display button or use the Playback menu options to manipulate the image; you first have to press the OK button to "enter" the sequence and display the individual images. If you choose the Individual Pictures option, all sequences will automatically be opened up, so all images from the sequences will be displayed as you scroll through your saved images; you will not see any key images or have to "enter" into the sequences.

KEY PICTURE SELECTION

This final option on the Playback menu lets you change the key picture that displays for a sequence. Ordinarily, the first image in a sequence is used as the key picture. If you would prefer to display one of the other images when the shots are displayed in sequence mode, you can use this feature. First, you have to set the previous menu option, Sequence Display, to Key Picture Only. Then display the sequence whose key picture you want to change. Select this menu option and press the OK button or the Right button to activate it.

The camera will display all of the images from the sequence, as shown in Figure 6-33.

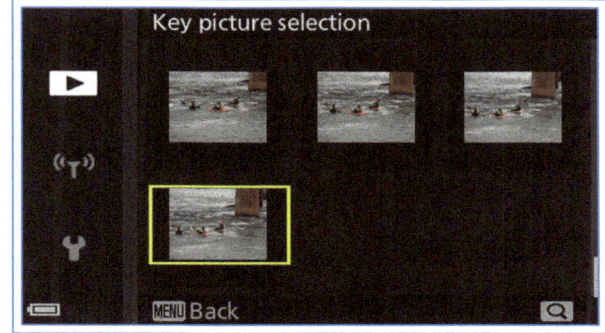

Figure 6-33. Key Picture Selection Screen

Navigate through those images using the multi selector dial or the Left and Right buttons. Press the OK button when the picture you want to use is highlighted. A check mark will appear beneath that image.

Chapter 7: The Setup Menu

The Setup menu gives you options for housekeeping matters such as screen brightness and operational sounds, but it also includes some settings that affect how you take your images, including Vibration Reduction, Peaking, and Digital Zoom. In addition, this menu is where you perform the important task of formatting a memory card.

As a reminder, you enter the menu system by pressing the Menu button. The available menus change depending on whether the camera is set to shooting mode or playback mode, and, in shooting mode, which exposure mode is selected (Program, Auto, or Scene, for example). However, no matter what mode the camera is set to, you can always enter into the Setup menu. After you press the Menu button, use the Left button to move the yellow highlight to the far left column and move the highlight down the line of icons to the wrench icon that indicates the Setup menu, as shown in Figure 7-1.

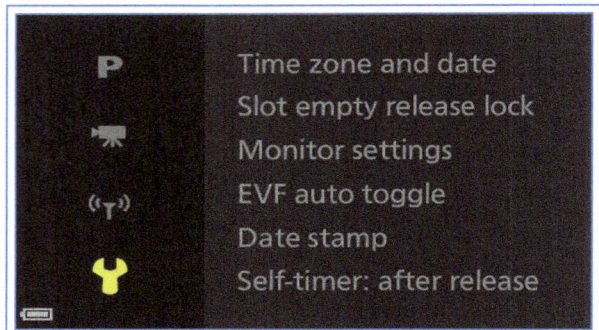

Figure 7-1. Wrench Icon for Setup Menu Highlighted at Left

Once that icon is highlighted, use the Right button to move the selection block back into the list of menu items, and then use the multi selector dial or the Up and Down buttons to navigate through the various options on the menu. The first screen of the Setup menu is shown in Figure 7-2. I'll discuss all of the choices on the menu in the order in which they appear.

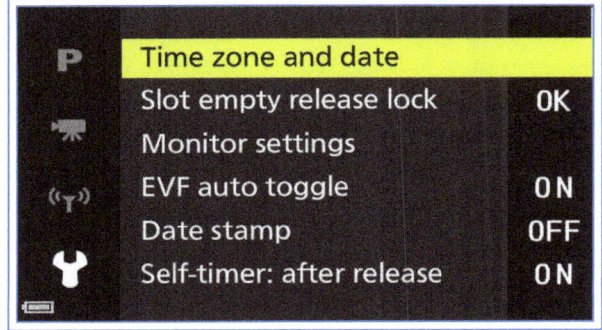

Figure 7-2. Screen 1 of Setup Menu

Time Zone and Date

Chances are you set the date, time, and time zone when you first turned on the camera. If you haven't done so or need to change these settings, use this menu option. First, select Time Zone and Date, and press the Right button or the OK button to move to the Time Zone and Date options screen, shown in Figure 7-3.

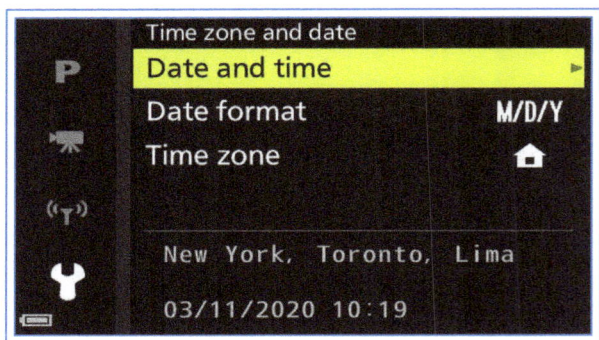

Figure 7-3. Time Zone and Date Menu Options Screen

Select Date and Time and press the Right or OK button to get to the Date and Time Settings screen, shown in Figure 7-4. Navigate through the selections for month, day, year, hours, and minutes using the Left and Right buttons; change the values using the multi selector dial, the command dial, or the Up and Down buttons. If you are in an area where Daylight Saving Time is observed, set the time here to Standard Time; you can activate Daylight Saving Time in a later step.

Chapter 7: The Setup Menu

When you have finished with the minutes setting, press the OK button to confirm all of the settings. You can then return to the Time Zone and Date screen, select Date Format, and choose your preferred order for displaying the month, day, and year.

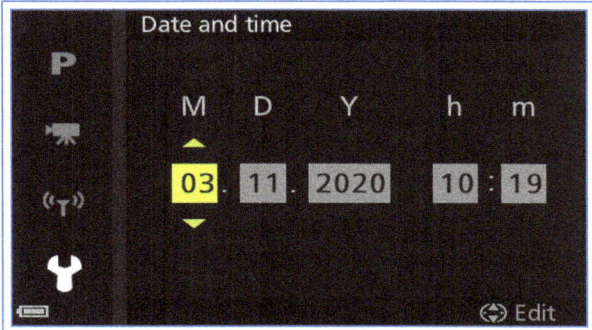

Figure 7-4. Date and Time Settings Screen

Finally, return to the Time Zone and Date page and select Time Zone. For this option, you have two choices—the home time zone and the travel destination, as shown in Figure 7-5.

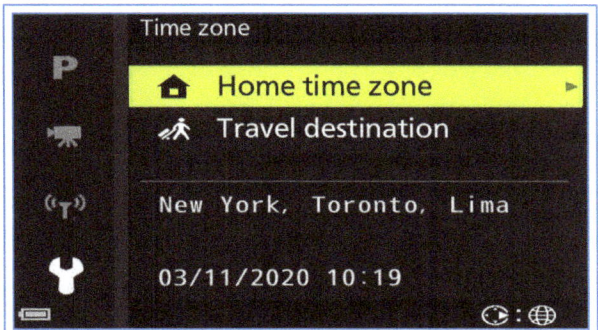

Figure 7-5. Time Zone Selection Screen

First, highlight Home Time Zone, as shown in Figure 7-5, and press the Right button to reach a screen with a world map, as shown in Figure 7-6.

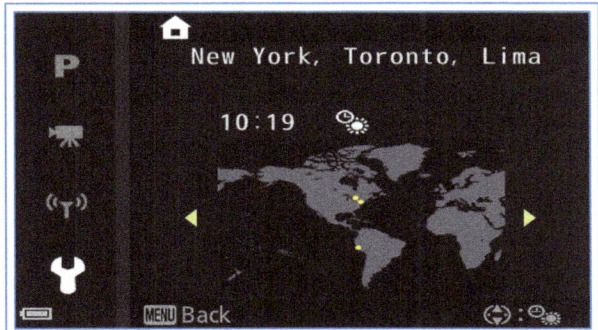

Figure 7-6. Map Screen for Setting Time Zone and Daylight Saving Time

Scroll through that map using the multi selector dial or the Left or Right buttons to set the home zone to the location where you spend most of your time. One or more yellow dots will appear in the area you have selected. Then use the Up and Down buttons to turn the Daylight Saving Time option on or off. If it is turned on, as it is in Figure 7-6, an icon with a clock dial and sun will appear to the right of the time on that screen.

Then, if you want, set the travel zone for an area you are most likely to travel to. Or, you can wait until you travel to set this zone. When you take a trip, select the travel time zone from this menu option and the camera's time and date will change as required, so your images will have the correct dates and times when you take pictures in your destination time zone.

Slot Empty Release Lock

This second option on the Setup menu determines how the camera reacts if you press the shutter button when there is no memory card installed in the camera. It provides two options: Release Locked or Enable Release.

If you choose the default option, Release Locked, the camera will display the message "No card present" and will not let you operate most of the controls, including the shutter button, when no memory card is installed in the camera. You can still use the Menu button, however, to get access to the menu system.

The Release Locked option is the one I prefer, because it ensures that I will not press the shutter button, thinking I am recording images, when there is no card in the camera.

If you choose the second option, Enable Release, then, even when no card is in the camera, you can press the shutter button and an image will appear on the display screen. You can capture one or two large-sized images or about ten small ones and play them back, but they will have the words Demo Mode marked in the lower right corner, and they will not be saved if you turn off the camera. There is no easy way to transfer these images to a computer or other device. These images are meant to be taken only for the purpose of demonstrating how the camera works, such as in a camera store. In a pinch, you could transfer the images to a video capture device using a micro-HDMI cable connected to the camera's HDMI port, but that would not be a good way to proceed normally.

Monitor Settings

With this menu item, whose main screen is shown in Figure 7-7, you can control several aspects of the way your camera's monitor (LCD display screen or viewfinder) displays your images.

First, you can turn the Image Review feature on or off. If it is turned on, a new image shows up on the display for about one second when you first take the picture. If it is turned off, the display immediately goes back to the shooting screen when you take a picture. There is no way to control the length of time the image displays; this feature is either on or off. If you want to view a new image for a longer period of time, press the Playback button and use the normal playback procedures.

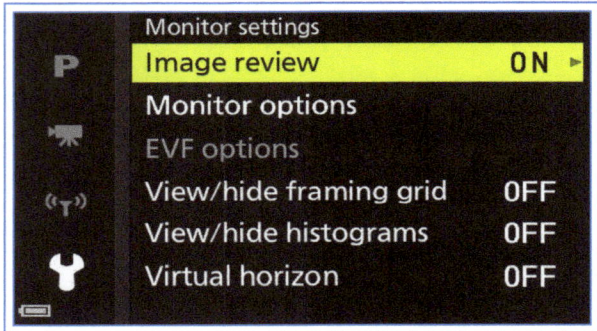

Figure 7-7. Monitor Settings Menu Options Screen

The next option, Monitor Options, lets you select from five levels of brightness for the LCD screen, as shown in Figure 7-8. This option is available only when the LCD screen is active.

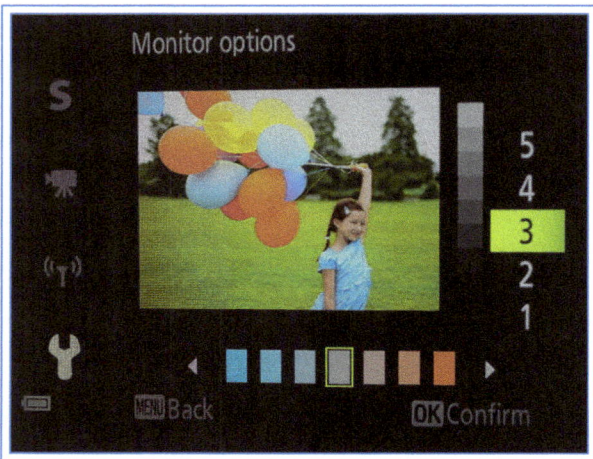

Figure 7-8. Monitor Options Screen

Select the brightness level you want using the Up and Down buttons. The default value is level 3. If you use the higher settings, the camera's battery will run down faster than usual, so take that factor into account when increasing the brightness.

On the same screen, you can also adjust the color of the display on the screen, using the scale at the bottom of the display. Use the Left and Right buttons to change this aspect of the display to be more bluish or reddish in order to calibrate the display for the conditions in which you are shooting. Press the OK button to confirm the settings when you have finished adjusting the monitor's brightness and color.

When you are using the viewfinder instead of the LCD screen, the next menu option, EVF Options, becomes available for selection. With this menu item, you can make similar adjustments to brightness and color that affect only the display in the viewfinder.

Next, the View/Hide Framing Grid option lets you turn on or off a grid of vertical and horizontal lines that divide the screen into nine blocks. The grid itself is shown in Figure 7-9, as it is displayed on the shooting screen.

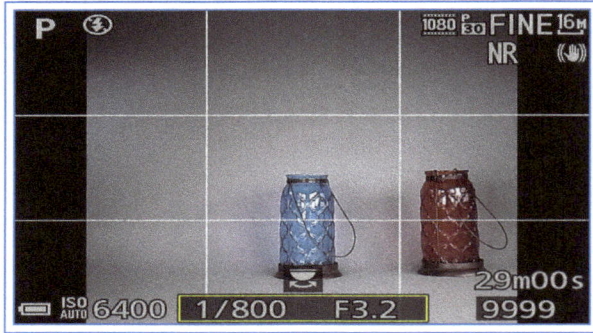

Figure 7-9. Framing Grid on Shooting Screen

You may appreciate having this grid available to help you compose your images according to the Rule of Thirds, which calls for placing the most important subject close to the intersections of these lines, to increase visual interest in the photo.

The grid also may help you keep the horizon or your subject, such as a building, properly horizontal or vertical by lining it up against one of the lines on the screen. If turned on, the grid will appear on all three shooting screens, including the screen with no shooting information. In addition, the camera will add a fourth screen with no information and no grid. The grid does not appear when a video is being recorded. If you don't find the grid useful, just leave it turned off.

The next option under Monitor Settings, View/Hide Histograms, controls whether or not the histogram is displayed when the camera is in shooting mode. If you turn this option on, the histogram appears in the left half of the screen when the camera is set to shooting mode, as shown in Figure 7-10.

Like the framing grid, the histogram displays on all shooting screens except for a fourth screen that the camera adds, with no shooting information and no histogram. The histogram is not displayed when AF Area Mode is set to Target Finding, or when the camera is in Auto or Creative mode, except when the focus mode selector is set to MF and focus has been locked by pressing the Down button. It also is not displayed with the Easy Panorama setting for Scene mode, or when a movie is being recorded.

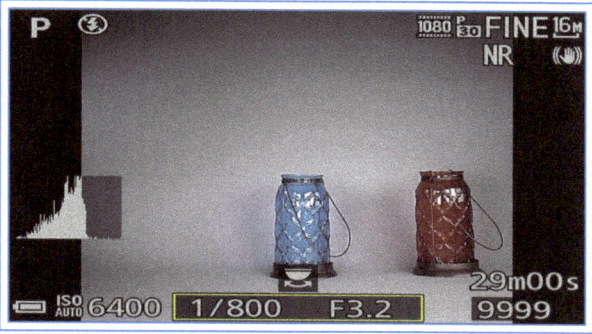

Figure 7-10. Histogram on Shooting Screen

Even when this option is turned on and the histogram is otherwise available, the histogram does not display under certain conditions, including when you are using the enlarged view for manual focus or using the pop-up menu to select focus mode, the self-timer, or flash mode.

If this option is turned off, you can still display the histogram in shooting mode by pressing the exposure compensation button (Right button) to adjust the exposure, when that option is available. The histogram will turn on in that situation to help you gauge how much exposure compensation to apply.

I prefer to display histograms in shooting mode using the exposure compensation control, because I can call up the histogram when I want it and it will disappear quickly after I am finished using it. However, exposure compensation is not available with Manual exposure

mode, so this menu option is the only way to display a histogram when shooting in that mode. If you want to display a reasonably accurate histogram in Manual mode, you need to turn on the Manual Exposure Preview option on the last screen of the Shooting menu; otherwise, the histogram may not reflect the settings you have made for your manual exposure.

The histogram will always display for still images in playback mode when you have selected the histogram display screen by pressing the Display button, as discussed in Chapter 6.

As also discussed in Chapter 6, the histogram is useful for indicating whether your image will be underexposed or overexposed. In most cases, it's a good idea to adjust exposure settings so the histogram looks roughly like a mountain with gradual slopes from left and right to a moderate peak in the center.

The final option for Monitor Settings, Virtual Horizon, causes the camera to add a special display to the shooting screen that helps you orient the image to be completely level with respect to side-to-side movement and front-to-back movement, as shown in Figure 7-11.

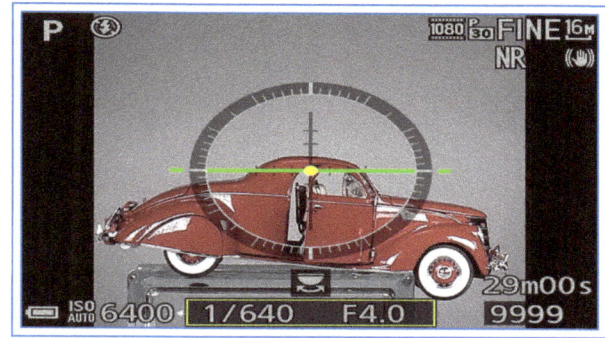

Figure 7-11. Virtual Horizon on Shooting Screen

When the camera is level side-to-side, the line in the center of the display turns green. When it is level front-to-back, the dot in the center of the display turns green.

EVF Auto Toggle

This next option on screen 1 of the Setup menu, if turned on, causes the view of shooting displays and playback displays to switch from the LCD screen to the viewfinder when your head (or another object) gets close to the eye sensor to the right of the viewfinder. If this option is turned off, the view does not switch when an object approaches the eye sensor. In that case, you can use the Monitor switch, directly to the right of the viewfinder, to switch the view. You also can switch the view to the viewfinder by folding the LCD screen in against the camera, with the viewing screen concealed.

I prefer to leave this option turned on most of the time, because it is convenient to have the view of the scene switched to the viewfinder when I lift the camera to my eye. However, if I have the camera on a tripod and am examining the LCD display closely, I may turn this option off so the view does not switch unexpectedly as I get close to the screen to look at the details of the shot.

Date Stamp

With this option, you can control whether the camera places the current date, or date and time, on a still image when it is recorded, as shown in Figure 7-12.

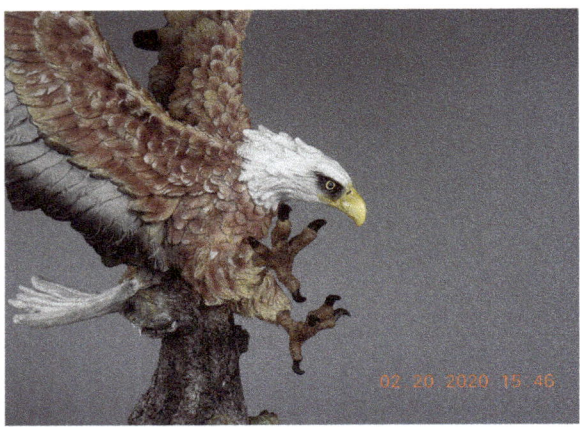

Figure 7-12. Date Stamp in Use on Image

This option places the information permanently on the image, and the information cannot be deleted (unless you use Photoshop or similar software to edit it out). You might want to use this feature if you are taking images as part of a scientific experiment in which you need to record this information as part of your data, but you probably would not want to use it for general picture-taking, because the date (or date and time) information will mar the image. For ordinary images, you can always use editing software to retrieve the date and time information, which is recorded invisibly with the images (assuming the camera is set to the correct date and time).

To use this feature, go to the Date Stamp option on the menu, then select either Date, Date and Time, or turn the option off altogether. This setting does not operate when you have selected Pre-shooting Cache or either of the 60-shot continuous shooting options, or with certain scene types that use continuous shooting or other special processing, such as Bird-watching, Sports, or HDR. It also does not work when Raw, Raw + Fine, or Raw + Normal is selected for Image Quality.

Self-timer: After Release

This option lets you set whether the self-timer continues to operate after being used once. This item can be set to either On or Off. If it is set to On, then, once the self-timer has been used to trigger the camera, it will turn itself off, and will no longer be set. If this item is set to Off, the self-timer will remain set after the camera has been triggered.

For example, if you have set the self-timer to its three-second option, with this option turned on, the self-timer will not be active after it has been used for one shot or video recording. If this option is turned off, the self-timer will remain set to the three-second option for further shots. However, even with this option turned off, when the camera is turned off and back on, the self-timer will not turn back on until you turn it on. Once the self-timer is turned on, though, it will remain set for further shots.

Even if this option is turned on, the self-timer is not canceled in Moon mode, which sets the self-timer to three seconds. Also, the smile timer and pet portrait release options are not canceled with the On setting.

Your setting for this option depends on the situation. If you want to use the self-timer for every shot you take, then set this option to Off. If you only want to use it once or occasionally, set this option to On, so the self-timer will be canceled after each shot.

The options on screen 2 of the Setup menu are shown in Figure 7-13.

Vibration Reduction

This is one of the more important settings for the camera, especially because of the extreme telephoto range of the P950's lens. When you activate Vibration Reduction (VR), the camera uses its lens-shift system to stabilize the image. When you are handholding the camera, there is bound to be a slight amount of camera motion or shake. At slow shutter speeds, this motion

Chapter 7: The Setup Menu | 107

can cause blurring of your images. Any such blurring is magnified at higher telephoto levels, as you can see if you look through the viewfinder or at the LCD screen at a zoomed-in level. The slightest motion can make the image appear to jiggle uncontrollably.

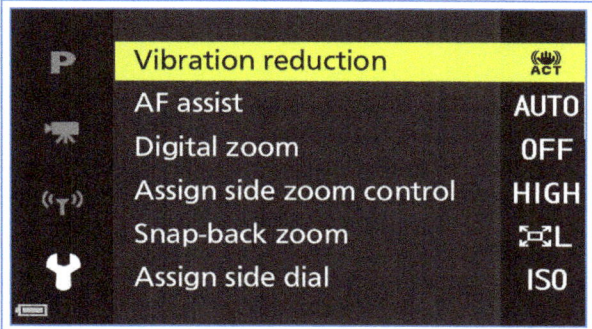

Figure 7-13. Screen 2 of Setup Menu

There are five available settings for the VR system: Normal, Active, Normal (Framing First), Active (Framing First), and Off, as shown in Figure 7-14.

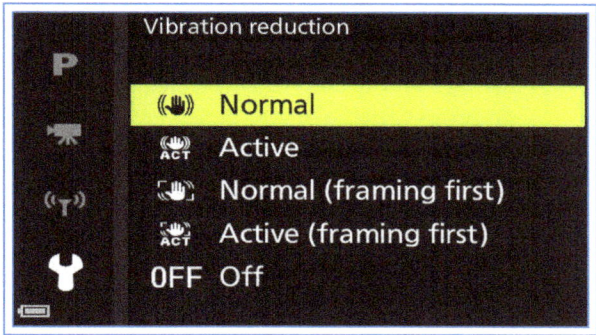

Figure 7-14. Vibration Reduction Menu Options Screen

These settings are applicable when you are shooting either still pictures or movies. When you have the camera on a tripod, you should ordinarily turn off the VR setting, because the camera's circuitry can get confused and attempt to correct for camera shake when there is none, thereby degrading the image. However, if you have zoomed the lens in to a long focal length, such as 1000mm or more, you may want to activate one of the VR options even when using a tripod, if you find that the image is shaky because of the extreme focal length.

The Normal setting is intended to correct relatively mild camera movement, such as when you are handholding the camera and panning it to record a movie (moving side to side smoothly). The camera can detect the smooth horizontal motion, and will correct only for vertical motion caused by the handholding. It also can detect smooth vertical motion, such as when you are tilting the camera vertically to take a movie of a tall building. When the Normal setting is turned on, the camera places a hand icon in the upper right corner of the screen, as shown in Figure 7-15.

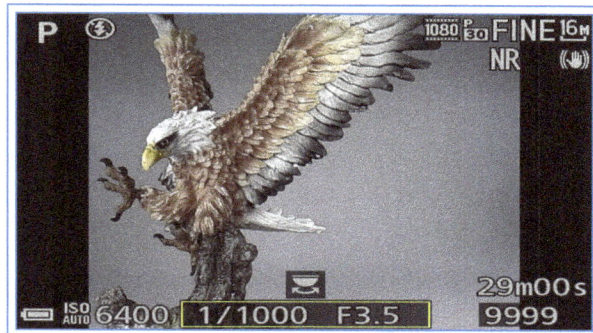

Figure 7-15. Hand Icon on Display for Normal Vibration Reduction

The Active setting is intended for situations in which the camera motion is more erratic and dramatic, such as when you are shooting out of a car window, or from a boat or helicopter, and the camera may be jerked in various directions unpredictably. In this case, the camera does not allow for horizontal motion, but corrects for motion in any direction as well as it can. Of course, the camera cannot erase the effects of violent motion, but it can reduce the blurring effects of milder motion to a fair extent. When the Active setting is turned on, the camera displays the icon shown in Figure 7-16 instead of the plain hand icon.

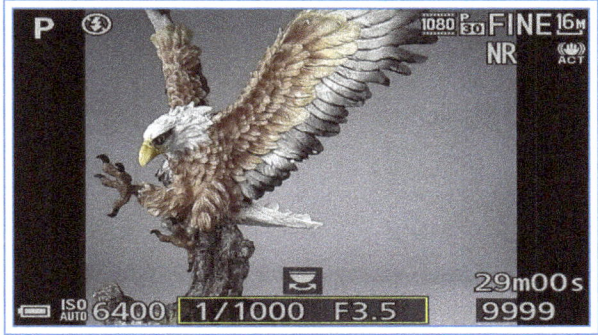

Figure 7-16. Icon for Active Vibration Reduction on Display

The Normal and Active options with (Framing First) added are similar to the Normal and Active options, but they are designed to minimize the mild cropping that the camera uses with those options. With the Normal and Active options, the camera crops the image somewhat, because of the electronic processing it uses to reduce the effects of vibration. If you select the (Framing First) options, the camera places a higher priority on minimizing this cropping than on reducing the effects of vibration. In particular, Nikon recommends using the Normal (Framing First) option when you are panning the camera, because the camera will not attempt to compensate for the smooth, horizontal motion of panning, but only for any vertical motion from shaking.

If you are in a situation in which it is important to include as much of the subject as possible in the frame, choose one of the (Framing First) options. Otherwise, to have the camera place its priority on vibration reduction to reduce motion blur, choose an option without the (Framing First) aspect.

I recommend that you use the Normal setting when handholding the camera in most situations, if you are able to hold the camera quite steady. However, if you are a passenger in a vehicle on a bumpy road or otherwise encountering random motion, you may want to switch to the Active setting to see if it can help even out the jolts to the camera.

AF Assist

This next option on the second screen of the Setup menu lets you turn on or off the reddish light beam that shines from the autofocus assist lamp on the front of the camera. This beam illuminates when the camera is trying to focus in a dark area; the light helps the autofocus mechanism find the patterns and shapes it needs to evaluate in order to achieve proper focus. You should usually leave this setting turned on, but you may want to turn it off when you're taking pictures in a place where the beam could be distracting or annoying to others, or where it might alert the subjects of your candid photography. If the camera then has difficulty in focusing, you can switch to manual focus and adjust the focus yourself.

The choices for this setting are Auto or Off. With the Auto setting, the lamp will work when needed, except with some focus settings and some scene settings, such as Pet Portrait, in which it is disabled and cannot activate. The lamp will always light up when the self-timer or smile timer is used; there is no way to disable the self-timer lamp, though you can cover it with black tape if you need to suppress it. The lamp also serves as the Red-eye Reduction lamp, and lights up when a flash mode with red-eye reduction is selected. That function also is not affected by the setting of the AF Assist menu option.

Digital Zoom

This next item on screen 2 of the Setup menu lets you zoom in on a scene electronically, beyond the magnifying power of the camera's optical zoom. Because it is an electronic zoom and not an optical one, it does not increase the optical information received by the camera; instead, it enlarges the image digitally, which can result in a blocky, pixelated look.

That's not to say that digital zoom is useless. It can help you to compose a scene the way you want to, or to measure the exposure on a small part of the scene before you zoom back out to take the picture without the digital zoom effect, for example. And, in some cases, the use of digital zoom does not actually degrade the quality of the image; it just uses a smaller portion of the image sensor's surface, resulting in a lower-resolution image, but without the pixelation of an artificially magnified image. In addition, Nikon uses a feature called Dynamic Fine Zoom that improves the quality of digitally zoomed images.

There are two settings available on the Setup menu for this option: On and Off. If you choose Off, the camera will be limited to using its optical zoom, which is really not much of a limitation, since the P950's lens has the impressive range of 24mm to 2000mm.

If you choose On, the lens will "zoom" electronically beyond the optical limit of 2000mm, to a maximum of an amazing (though somewhat illusory) 8000mm. With digital zoom, beyond a certain level of magnification the camera will use its circuitry to interpolate pixels—that is, it will create new pixels in between the ones produced by the sensor, in order to expand the image to a greater magnification. When the camera is using interpolation, the image deteriorates to some extent because the camera is using pixels that are not part of the original image.

If you use an Image Size setting smaller than the maximum, you can use digital zoom to a certain extent without image deterioration. This is because the camera needs a smaller number of pixels in order to create the desired image. Therefore, instead of interpolating new pixels among the existing ones, the camera crops out the actual pixels that appear on a portion of the image sensor, and enlarges that portion to fill the entire area of the sensor. In this way, the camera uses only the actual pixels captured through the lens to the image sensor; it does not have to interpolate any new pixels.

Whenever you move the zoom lever, a scale appears in the top center of the image to show how far the lens has been zoomed.

The scale has a small vertical line past the halfway point; that line shows the point where the camera starts using digital zoom instead of optical zoom. As shown in Figure 7-17, when only optical zoom is in use, the zoom scale is white, and the bar stays to the left of that small line.

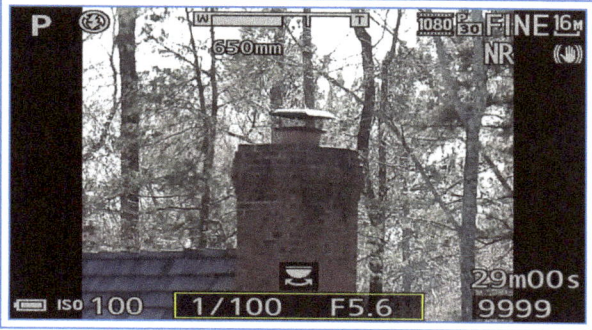

Figure 7-17. Zoom Scale: Optical Zoom Only

If you zoom the lens in so the zoom bar moves past the vertical line, the bar may turn blue, as shown in Figure 7-18, indicating that zoom is being used beyond the normal optical zoom range, but that the picture quality should not deteriorate too much.

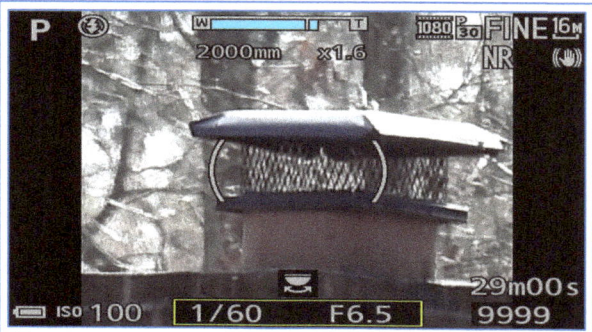

Figure 7-18. Zoom Scale: Zoom Bar in Blue Range

When the zoom bar turns blue, that can mean one of two things. Either the Image Size is set to a value smaller than the maximum of 4608 x 3456 pixels, so the camera can use the extra pixels to magnify the image without loss of quality, or the camera is using what Nikon calls Dynamic Fine Zoom, special processing that increases magnification without compromising image quality in the way that normal digital zoom does. According to Nikon, you can zoom the lens to a focal length of 4000mm, twice the optical zoom range, before image deterioration occurs, even when using the largest Image Size setting.

If you set Image Size to a value smaller than the maximum, the zoom bar will stay blue for longer ranges. If you use one of the smaller options, such as 2272 x 1704 (4M), the bar may stay blue for the entire digital zoom range, because the camera can use the pixels to increase magnification. An example of this effect is seen in Figure 7-19, where digital zoom was used with Image Size set to the 4M size and the zoom bar is blue to the end of its range.

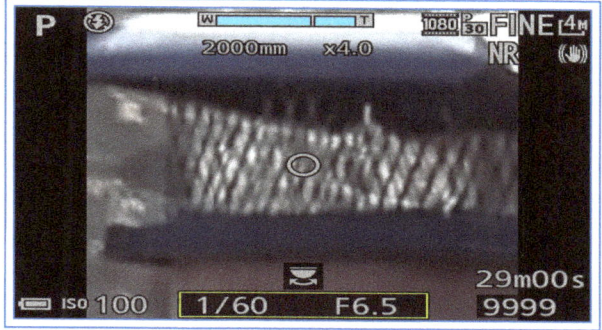

Figure 7-19. Zoom Scale with Smaller Image Size in Use

If you continue to zoom the lens with the largest Image Size settings, the zoom bar may turn yellow, indicating that image deterioration will occur because the camera is adding extra pixels. For example, Figure 7-20 shows the zoom scale with Image Size set to its maximum value, and with the lens zoomed well beyond the optical zoom range.

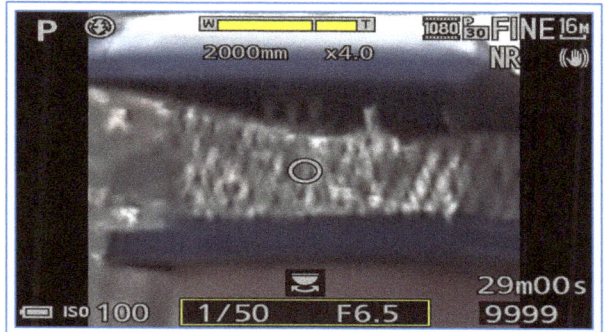

Figure 7-20. Zoom Scale: Zoom Bar in Yellow Range

I rarely use digital zoom. The maximum optical zoom range of the P950's lens is so phenomenal (2000mm) that I seldom find a need to zoom beyond that. It becomes difficult to maintain a completely steady image, even with a tripod, at magnifications greater than that. However, if you are trying to capture an elusive bird or other creature with your lens, or have some other special photographic need, I recommend you use the Digital Zoom menu option if it will help you, bearing in mind that you may want to use some of the smaller image sizes in order to preserve image quality. I suggest you keep the zoom scale in the white range if possible, and let it go into the blue range in some cases. I recommend that you avoid the full digital zoom, with its yellow zoom bar. There is usually no advantage to be gained from pushing the camera to this limit.

Digital zoom is not always available, depending on other settings in use. It cannot be used along with any of the following settings: Raw for Image Quality, smile timer, zoom memory, or AF Area Mode set to Subject Tracking. It also cannot be used with certain scene settings (Portrait, Night Portrait, Pet Portrait, Backlighting with HDR turned on, Easy Panorama, and Time-lapse Movie). Focus will always be in the center of the frame when digital zoom is used. (The focus can be in another part of the frame while the lens is being zoomed through its optical range, but the focus will shift to the center when the digital zoom range is reached.)

Assign Side Zoom Control

I mentioned this menu option briefly in Chapter 5, in discussing the side zoom control. This switch, on the left side of the lens, serves as an alternative zoom control. You may find you can hold the camera steadier by using the side control rather than the zoom lever on top of the camera. (Personally, I don't notice much difference; when using the zoom lever I can hold the camera quite steady.) You also might want to use the side control when you have turned on the zoom memory menu option, because, with that option, the zoom lever can zoom only to specific focal lengths. You might want to use the side control to zoom continuously to all focal lengths when needed.

With this menu option, you can set the speed at which the side zoom control zooms the lens when you are recording a video. You can choose High, Mid, or Low for the speed of zooming. This choice applies only for recording videos. In that situation, the camera operates the zoom at a steady rate, according to the setting of this option. The default setting is High, but you might prefer a slower speed if you are zooming over a scenic area and want to leave time for the audience to enjoy the scenery without being rushed by a quick zooming action.

Snap-back Zoom

As discussed in Chapter 5, when you press the snap-back zoom button, located on the left side of the lens in front of the side zoom control, the camera pulls the zoom lens back to a wide-angle view so you can locate a subject in context quickly. When you release the button, the lens "snaps back" to the previous zoom amount, so you can take the picture after having centered the subject (bird, for example) in the view.

The Snap-back Zoom menu option lets you set how much of the area is included in the view when you press the snap-back zoom button. With the default option, Long, the lens pulls back to a wide-angle view, letting you see a wide area of the scene. With Medium and Short, the lens pulls back to lesser amounts. I usually leave this setting at Long, so I get a clear view of the overall scene when I press the Snap-back button.

Assign Side Dial

This next menu option lets you choose a setting to be assigned to the side dial (located directly behind the side zoom control) when the focus mode selector is set to the AF position, for autofocus. (When that switch is set to MF, for manual focus, the side dial always is assigned to adjust manual focus.) The choices are exposure compensation, ISO sensitivity, white balance, shutter speed, aperture, or none, as shown in Figure 7-21.

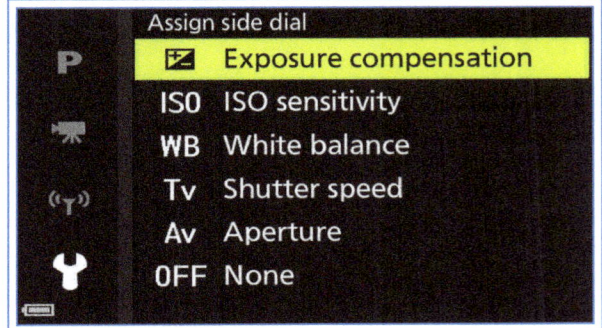

Figure 7-21. Assign Side Dial Menu Options Screen

I generally assign ISO to the side dial, because exposure compensation can be adjusted with the Right button, and I don't have as much need to change the white balance setting. If you assign the dial to control shutter speed or aperture, that setting will be effective only when the assigned value can be controlled, such as when the camera is in Aperture Priority mode, for aperture. If you don't have a need to use the side dial to change settings, you may want to select None, so you don't accidentally change a setting by moving the dial unintentionally.

The options on screen 3 of the Setup menu are shown in Figure 7-22.

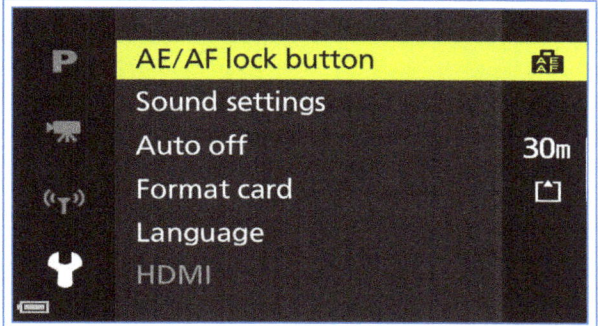

Figure 7-22. Screen 3 of Setup Menu

AE/AF Lock Button

This first item on screen 3 of the Setup menu lets you set the function of the AE-L/AF-L button, which is located at the top of the camera's back, below the mode dial. The choices, as shown in Figure 7-23, are AE/AF Lock, AE Lock Only, AE Lock (Hold), or AF Lock Only.

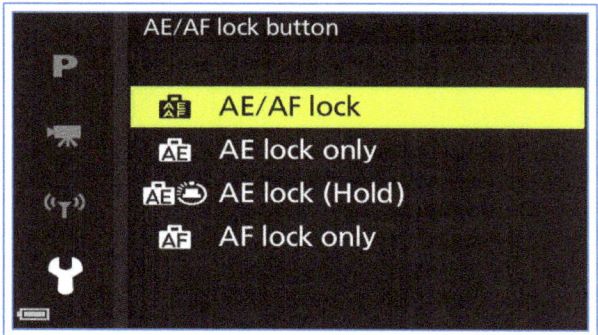

Figure 7-23. AE/AF Lock Button Menu Options Screen

If you choose the first option, the camera locks both exposure and focus when you press and hold the button. With the second option, only exposure is locked. With the third option, you do not have to hold down the button; when you press and release it, exposure is locked, and it stays locked until you press the button again. With the last option, only focus is locked, and you have to hold down the button to keep it locked.

When the camera is recording movies, the AE/AF Lock, AE Lock Only, and AF Lock Only options work differently than described above. For movies, you only have to press the button and release it to engage the lock, then press and release it again to release the lock.

Sound Settings

This next option on the Setup menu, shown in Figure 7-24, gives you a quick way to silence all of the electronic beeps and chirps that are generated when the camera performs certain actions, such as turning on, achieving focus and exposure, or having the shutter pressed to take a picture.

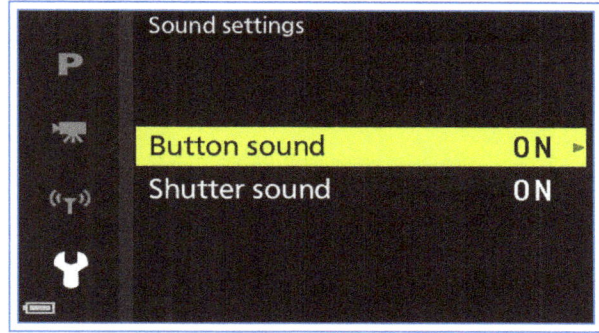

Figure 7-24. Sound Settings Menu Options Screen

There are not many options here—first, you can turn the "Button sound" on or off. This option controls whether or not the camera beeps when it starts up, when settings are made, when it achieves focus, and when an error occurs. When the camera is set to the Bird-watching mode or the Pet Portrait setting of Scene mode, sounds are automatically disabled, regardless of this setting.

The other option for this menu item is to turn on or off the shutter sound, which ordinarily is heard when you press the shutter release button all the way down to take a picture. This sound is automatically disabled with the Bird-watching and Pet Portrait settings, as well as with the Easy Panorama scene type. It also is disabled when using continuous shooting options other than Continuous H and Continuous L, and during movie recording.

Auto Off

This option controls the length of time before the camera enters standby mode to save power. By default, the camera will stay fully powered on for one minute when you are not touching the controls; after that time, it enters standby mode, in which the display goes blank and the green light around the power button blinks about twice per second. After about three minutes in that mode, the camera turns completely off. During standby mode, you can bring the camera back to full-power mode by pressing the power switch, the shutter release button, the Playback button, or the Movie button.

If you want to set a different interval before the camera enters standby mode, you can choose 30 seconds, five minutes, or 30 minutes with this menu item, as shown in Figure 7-25.

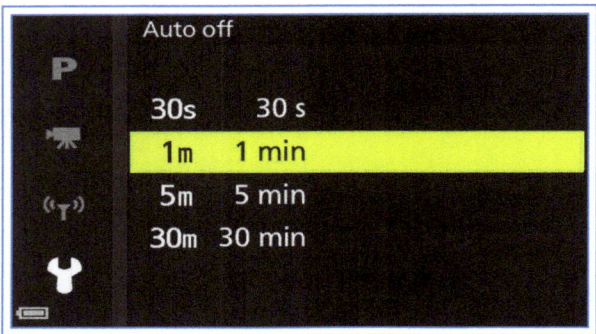

Figure 7-25. Auto Off Menu Options Screen

Note, however, that those times apply only when the camera is in shooting mode, displaying the shooting screen. When menu screens are displayed, the camera will enter standby mode in three minutes, if a shorter setting than that is chosen for Auto Off. Also, during slide show playback, the camera will stay active for up to 30 minutes, and when the AC adapter is connected, the time before entering standby mode will always be 30 minutes.

Format Card

This is an important menu option. Choose this process only when you want or need to completely wipe all of the data from a memory storage card.

When you select the Format Card option, as shown in Figure 7-26, the camera will warn you that all images currently on the card will be deleted if you proceed. Because of the seriousness of this step, the camera displays the selection bar in red if you highlight Format; the bar is yellow if you highlight No.

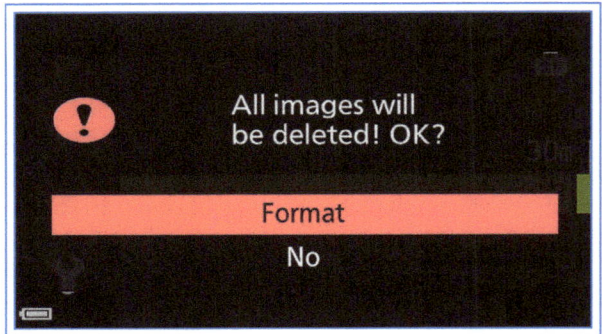

Figure 7-26. Format Card Confirmation Screen

If you highlight Format with the red selection bar and press the OK button to confirm, the camera will format the card that is in the camera, and the result will be a card that is empty of images and videos and properly formatted to store new images from the camera.

With this procedure, the camera will erase all images, including those that have been protected from accidental erasure with the Protect function on the Playback menu. It's a good idea to periodically save your good images and videos to your computer or other storage device and then re-format your memory card, to make sure it is properly set up to start recording new images and videos. It's also a good idea to use the Format Card command on any new memory card when you first insert it in the camera. Even though it likely will work without that procedure, it's best to make sure the card is set up with Nikon's method of formatting.

This menu option may be dimmed and unavailable for selection if a wireless connection is established between the camera and a smart device, even if you are not actively using the connection. If that happens, you can choose Airplane Mode on the Network menu to interrupt the connection while you format the card.

Language

This option gives you a choice of 31 languages for the display of menu screens and other information on the camera's display. Once you have selected this menu item, scroll through the language choices using the multi selector dial or the direction buttons and press the OK button when your chosen language is highlighted, as seen in Figure 7-27.

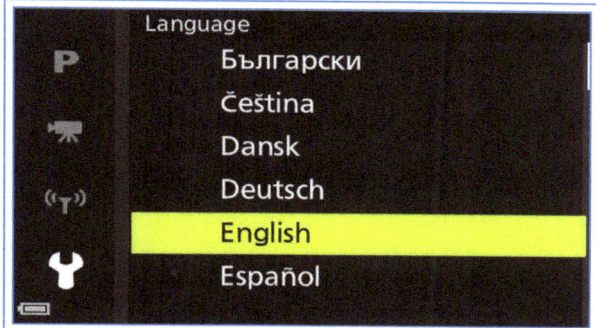

Figure 7-27. Language Selection Screen

HDMI

This menu option has two sub-options: Clean HDMI Output and HDMI Output. The Clean HDMI Output option is for use when you connect the camera to an external video recorder using a micro-HDMI cable. As I will discuss in Chapter 8, with this setup you can record high-quality video to the recorder. In order to do that, you need to set the camera to output the video signal captured through the lens, without added information such as focus frames, shutter speed and aperture values, icons for items such as current white balance setting, etc. This sort of video signal is called "clean" because it contains only the video itself, without the added information.

To use this feature, set Clean HDMI Output to On, connect the camera to the HDMI input of the recorder using a micro-HDMI cable, and set the camera's mode dial to the Movie Manual position. You have to set the focus mode selector to the MF position, and you cannot use some Movie Manual menu options, including Movie Options, Autofocus Mode, and Frame Rate. The camera will output HD video, but not 4K video.

When you are ready to record, press the Movie button on the camera and activate the external recorder. You may have to press the Display button on the camera to reach the screen with the clean HDMI signal.

You can set Clean HDMI Output to Off when you are viewing images and videos in playback mode on an HDTV that is connected to the camera with an HDMI cable. You can also use this setting to view the live image from the camera on an external monitor while you shoot images and videos with the camera.

The second option under the HDMI menu item is HDMI Output. When Clean HDMI Output is On, the camera presents the following options for HDMI Output: Auto, 1080/60p, 1080/50p, 1080/30p, 1080/25p, 720/60p, or 720/50p, as shown in Figure 7-28. You can choose one of these settings for the resolution of the video signal to be sent through the HDMI cable to an external video recorder. When Clean HDMI Output is Off, HDMI Output is fixed at Auto and cannot be changed.

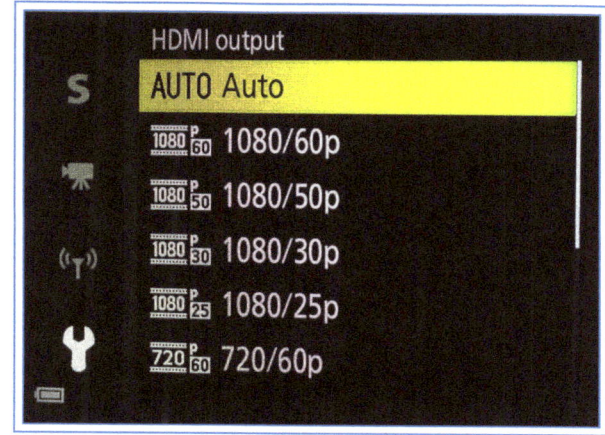

Figure 7-28. HDMI Output Menu Options Screen

The options on screen 4 of the Setup menu are shown in Figure 7-29.

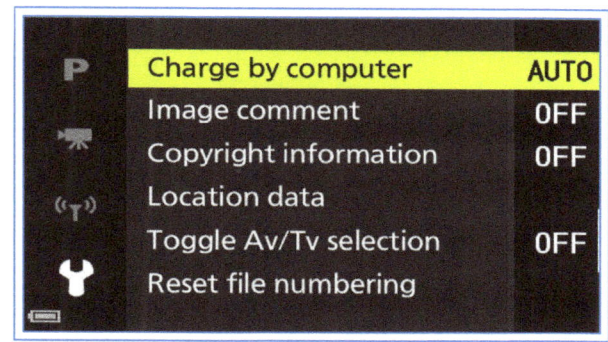

Figure 7-29. Screen 4 of Setup Menu

Charge by Computer

By default, when you connect the Coolpix P950 to a computer using the USB cable, the battery is gradually charged by power from the computer through the cable. To disable this capability, choose Off instead of Auto from this menu item, whose screen is shown in Figure 7-30, and the camera will not get power from the computer.

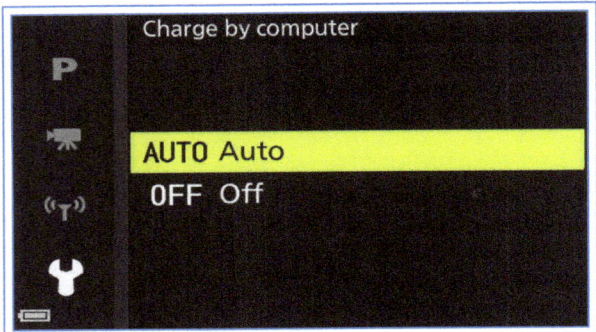

Figure 7-30. Charge by Computer Menu Options Screen

You may want to turn this feature off when you are using a laptop computer and you don't want to run down the computer's battery unnecessarily. Unless you have a particular need to charge your battery by this method, I recommend that you turn this option off.

Image Comment

This menu option gives you a mechanism for creating a comment to be displayed in the metadata for your still images that are captured after you create the comment and attach it to your images with this menu option. The menu option has two sub-options: Attach Comment and Input Comment.

To create a comment that can be attached to your future images, use the Input Comment option. When you highlight that option and press the Right button, the camera displays the screen shown in Figure 7-31, with a virtual keyboard.

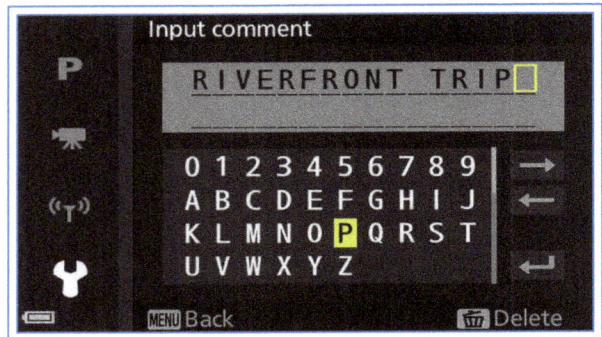

Figure 7-31. Virtual Keyboard for Entering Comment

To use the keyboard, navigate through the letters, numbers, and symbols using the four direction buttons and the multi selector dial. Scroll down past the capital letters to reach the small letters and symbols. The space is located after the small letter z. You can scroll back and forth through the text you are entering using the top two arrows at the right side of the screen. You can enter up to 36 characters. When you have finished inputting the characters, select the Return/Enter arrow at the bottom right of the screen to accept the comment.

Once your comment has been created, highlight the Attach Comment option on the menu screen and press the Right button, to enter a check box beside that option, as shown in Figure 7-32. The comment then will appear on the camera's comment and copyright information screen for all still images that you capture in the future. It also will be readable in software that reads metadata, including the Nikon ViewNX-i software.

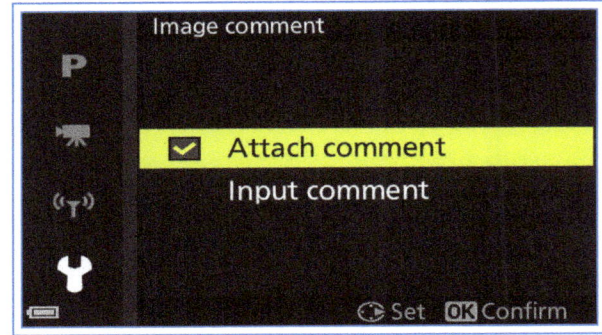

Figure 7-32. Attach Comment Screen with Check Box Checked

Copyright Information

This option works like the previous one. You can input two items: Artist and Copyright. After highlighting either of those two fields, press the Right button to move to the data-entry screen. You can then type in the name of the photographer and the name of the company or person who owns the copyright for still images to be taken in the future with this camera. You can use up to 36 characters for the artist and up to 54 characters for the copyright holder. Once either or both of those fields have been filled in, highlight the Attach Copyright Info item and press the Right button to check its box and attach the information to future images.

Location Data

This menu item, whose options screen is shown in Figure 7-33, enables the camera to download location information from a smartphone or tablet that is connected to the camera using the SnapBridge app.

Chapter 7: The Setup Menu | 115

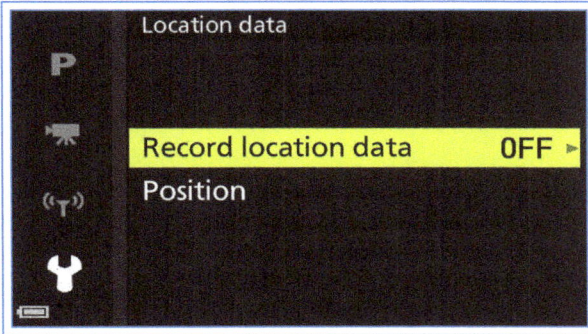

Figure 7-33. Location Data Menu Options Screen

That information can then be added to the metadata for images taken with the camera. I will discuss that process in Chapter 9. Once the information has been downloaded to the camera, you need to select the Position option to cause the camera to display the latest, updated data from the device. If the location changes, you need to select Position again to display the updated location information. Figure 7-34 shows this option in use.

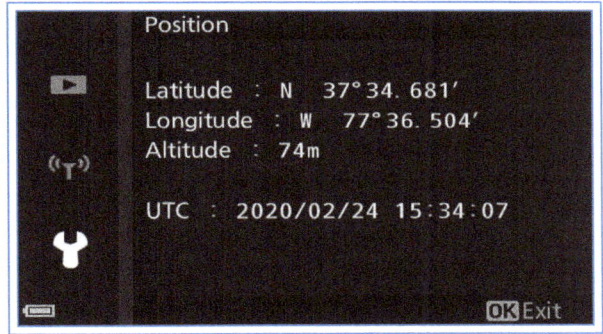

Figure 7-34. Position Option Showing Location Data

Toggle Av/Tv Selection

This menu option has just two possible settings: On or Off. The purpose of this setting is to determine whether the command dial is used to set shutter speed and the multi selector dial is used to set the aperture, as is normally the case, or not. On the menu screen, as shown in Figure 7-35, the two choices are labeled as Do Not Toggle Selection and Toggle Selection.

If you select Do Not Toggle Selection, the dials' assignments are not changed. If you change the setting to Toggle Selection, the camera switches the functions of the command dial and the multi selector dial for setting aperture and shutter speed in Aperture Priority, Shutter Priority, and Manual shooting modes. Ordinarily, the command dial sets shutter speed and the multi selector dial sets aperture. If Toggle Selection is active, the command dial sets aperture and the multi selector dial sets shutter speed.

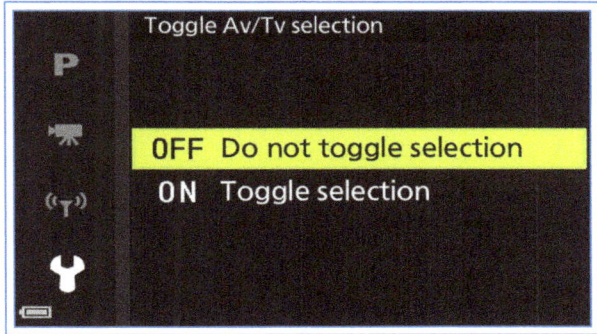

Figure 7-35. Toggle Av/Tv Selection Menu Options Screen

This option also affects the functions of those dials for controlling the flexible program option. Normally, the command dial has that function; you can re-assign that duty to the multi selector dial by setting this menu option to Toggle Selection.

In addition, this setting affects the use of the two dials in Movie Manual mode and for the Multiple Exposure Lighten setting of Scene mode, when you have selected the Nightscape+Light Trails or Fireworks option, for which the camera lets you adjust the shutter speed.

Reset File Numbering

This option resets the file numbering system back to 0001. Ordinarily, the camera assigns increasing file numbers to your images, even when they occupy many folders on the memory card.

For example, when you start out with a new camera and memory card, your first images will be stored in a folder named 100NIKON. (The folder names are visible when you insert the memory card into a card reader and view the contents of the card on a computer.) The first image in the folder will be named 0001.jpg as displayed in the camera in playback mode. On your computer, there will be a prefix such as DSCN, so the name may be DSCN0001.jpg. Once the 100NIKON folder has 999 files stored in it, the camera will automatically create a new folder called 101NIKON.

If none of your files has been deleted, which would interrupt the numbering scheme, the first file in the new folder will be numbered 1000.jpg. That is, each folder can hold only 999 files before a new folder is created, but the individual files' numbers will keep increasing, even over multiple folders, until the individual file numbers reach 9999. Thus, after ten folders are filled with files, the individual numbers start over again at 0001.

If you don't like the idea of your folder and file numbers continuously increasing, you can use this menu option at any time to reset the file numbering back to the beginning. That is, if the file numbers have increased to a number such as 0476.jpg, and you don't want to wait until the numbers reach 9999 before they start over, you can invoke this procedure, select Yes when prompted by the menu, and the camera will start numbering your next image back at 0001.jpg. The folder numbers will continue to increase, however. Whenever the newest folder contains 999 files, a new folder will be created.

The options on screen 5 of the Setup menu are shown in Figure 7-36.

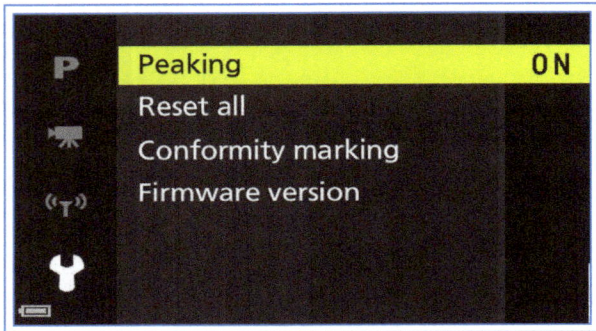

Figure 7-36. Screen 5 of Setup Menu

Peaking

The Peaking feature, which is turned on by default, provides additional assistance for accurate manual focusing with still images. (Peaking does not operate when recording movies.) When Peaking is active and you are using manual focus, the camera displays white pixels in areas that are in sharp focus, as illustrated in Figure 7-37.

As the focus gets sharper, you will see thicker areas of white. Try to adjust the focus to get the white areas to be as thick and obvious as possible.

You can adjust the intensity of the Peaking feature by turning the command dial to choose a value on the scale that appears at the left of the image. The higher the value, the greater the intensity of the feature. If your subject is one with naturally high contrast, such as straight lines and clear differences in color or brightness, you may see the Peaking pixels more clearly with a lower value. If the subject has low contrast, you may do better with a higher Peaking level. If you find the white pixels distracting, you can, of course, just turn the Peaking feature off using this menu item.

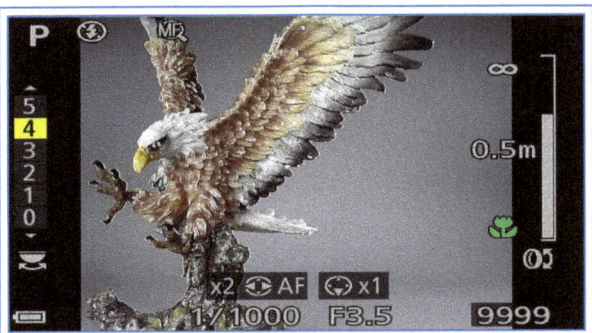

Figure 7-37. Peaking in Use on Shooting Screen

I have found Peaking to be of considerable help with some subjects, particularly those that are dark enough for the white Peaking pixels to show up clearly.

Reset All

Choose this menu option when you want to reset all of the camera's settings to their original (default) values. This action can be useful if you have been experimenting with different settings and you find that something is not working as expected. It will give you a fresh start with known values for all of the major settings on the menus and for shooting.

There are a few settings that will not be reset, including items such as date and time, time zone, and language. In addition, camera settings that you selected for the User Settings shooting mode are not reset by this menu item. To reset those settings, use the Reset User Settings option on screen 3 of the Shooting menu.

Conformity Marking

This option displays information about various industry or regulatory standards that the camera complies with. For my U.S. version of the camera, the only information displayed is about compliance with the rules of the Federal Communications Commission.

Firmware Version

The final entry on the Setup menu is shown in Figure 7-38.

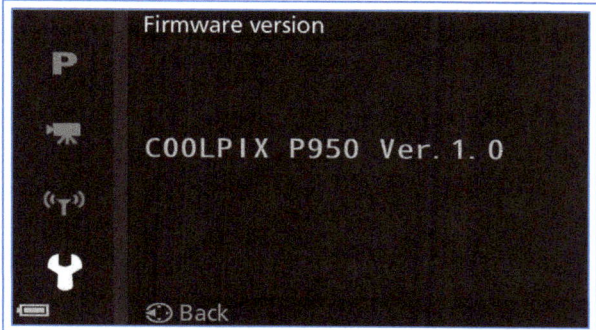

Figure 7-38. Firmware Version Display Screen

This option shows the current version of the firmware installed in your camera. The Coolpix P950, like other digital cameras, is programmed at the factory with firmware, which is a semi-permanent set of computer instructions that are electronically implanted in the camera. These instructions control the camera's operation, including the menus, controls, and in-camera processing of your images. The reason you might want to check to see what version is installed is that, in many cases, the manufacturer will release an updated version of the firmware that may fix problems or bugs in the system, provide minor enhancements, or, in some cases, even provide major improvements, such as including new shooting modes or menu options.

To see what firmware version is currently installed in your camera, highlight this menu option, then press the OK button or the Right button, and the camera will display the version number, as shown in Figure 7-38.

To determine whether any firmware upgrades have been released, I recommend that you visit Nikon's support web site from time to time. For United States customers, the address is http://support.nikonusa.com; for Europe, the site can be found by starting at http://www.europe-nikon.com. Find the Download Center and look for the link to current firmware versions. The site will provide detailed instructions for downloading and installing the new firmware.

Chapter 8: Motion Pictures

The Nikon Coolpix P950 includes high-definition (HD) and 4K (sometimes called Ultra HD) video recording among its capabilities. The P950 also offers extra benefits such as high-speed video recording, which results in slow-motion footage when you view it. I will explain the various options for movie-making in this chapter. Before I discuss the specific settings you can make for your movies, I'll begin with a brief overview of the process.

Movie-making Overview

In one sense, the fundamentals of making videos with the Coolpix P950 can be reduced to four words: "Push the red button." Having a dedicated motion picture recording button makes things easy for the user of the P950, because anytime you see a reason to take some video footage, you can just press the Movie button while aiming at your subject, and you will get results that are very likely to be usable. If you're more of a still photographer and not that interested in movie-making, you don't need to read any further. Be aware that the red button sits on the camera's back just under the AE-L/AF-L button, and if interesting action starts to happen before your eyes, you can press that button and record the events on video with a minimum of effort.

But there are several settings on the P950 that can affect your footage. The shooting mode the camera is set to for still images, and the menu and control-button settings you make, all have some effect on movie recordings. So, it is helpful to be aware of the current settings, even if you just want to capture a brief clip of a scene during your vacation.

Quick Guide to Recording a Movie Clip

I will discuss the details of movie-related settings later in this chapter. For now, here are suggested guidelines for quick settings when you want to record the action and you don't care about fine-tuning menu options and other settings. I'll discuss these steps with extra detail, in case you have turned to this section before reading about the camera's various controls and menus.

1. Turn the mode dial on top of the camera, to the right of the viewfinder, so the green camera icon is at the white indicator mark, putting the camera into the Auto shooting mode, as shown in Figure 8-1.

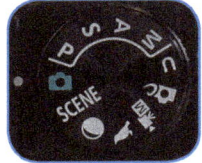

Figure 8-1. Mode Dial at Auto

2. Remove the lens cap and turn on the camera with the power button.

3. Make sure the focus mode selector, the switch surrounding the AE/AF Lock button at the top of the camera's back, is set to the AF position, for autofocus, as shown in Figure 8-2.

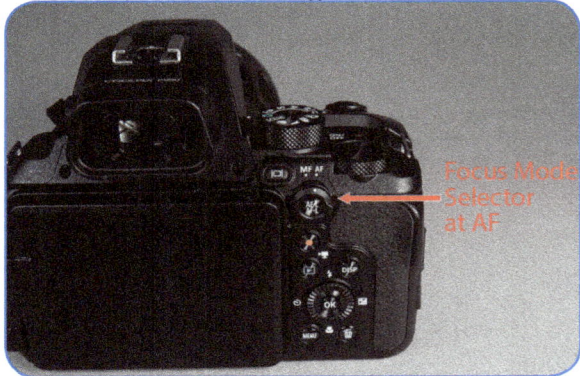

Figure 8-2. Focus Mode Selector at AF

4. Press the Menu button at the bottom left of the control area on the camera's back, and then press the Left button (left edge of the ridged dial that surrounds the OK button), which will move the

Chapter 8: Motion Pictures | 119

yellow selection highlight to the far-left column of menu icons.

5. Press the Down button to move the yellow highlight down to the movie camera icon.

6. Press the Right button to move the yellow selection block into the list of menu options. Using the direction buttons or the multi selector dial (the ridged dial that surrounds the OK button), highlight the top line of the menu, Movie Options.

7. Press the OK button or the Right button to get to the next menu screen, and use the Up or Down button as needed, to highlight the second line with the yellow selection block. It should say 1080/30p, as shown in Figure 8-3. (If it says 1080/25p, see the discussion of Frame Rate later in this chapter.) Press the OK button to select this option.

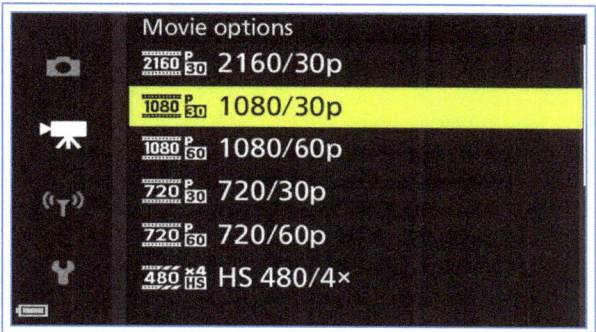

Figure 8-3. 1080/30p Highlighted on Movie Options Menu

8. Press the Menu button to go back to shooting mode.

9. Aim at your subject and use the zoom lever on top of the camera to frame the scene as you want, zooming in or out as needed. Press the shutter button halfway down until you hear a beep, to have the camera evaluate the exposure and focus. When the action starts or you're ready to begin, press the red Movie button to start the recording. Then take your finger off the button and hold the camera as steady as possible.

10. Continue to hold the camera steady, and pan (move the camera from side to side in one direction) slowly and smoothly if appropriate to take in the scene before you. When the scene has ended, press the red Movie button again to end the recording.

Other Settings for Movies

The above steps will get you started recording video with the Coolpix P950 using one of the highest quality recording formats and standard settings for white balance, autofocus, and other options. Once you are familiar with the basic steps for movie-making, though, you may want to experiment with some of the other available settings.

When you record movies with the Coolpix P950 with the mode dial set to a mode other than Movie Manual (indicated by the movie camera icon), the P950 uses largely automatic settings. In particular, it adjusts the exposure automatically and you have little control over it. However, there are some settings you can adjust that do affect the recording of movies in these modes.

WHITE BALANCE, PICTURE CONTROL, AND CREATIVE AND SCENE MODE OPTIONS

If the camera is set to the Program mode, the setting for white balance will be whatever you have set through the Shooting menu, and if you use a Picture Control setting, such as Monochrome, that setting will take effect for movie recording. If you shoot movies with the mode dial set to Creative mode, the movies will take on the appearance of the setting you select, such as Somber, Pure, Denim, Toy, Binary, and others. If you shoot movies in a Scene mode setting that affects the colors of images, such as Sunset, Dusk/Dawn, or Select Color, the movie will be affected just as still images would. With other Scene mode settings, such as Portrait, Food, Easy Panorama and Multiple Exposure Lighten, no special effects will be used; the camera will record a movie as if it were in Auto mode.

FOCUS AND FOCUS LOCK

When the mode dial is at a non-movie setting, such as P, A, S, M, or Auto, the focusing method is determined, first, by the setting of the focus mode selector at the top of the camera's back. If it is set to the MF position, you can adjust manual focus by turning the side dial.

If the focus mode selector is set to the AF position, the autofocus method used during movie recording is determined by the setting of the Autofocus Mode option on the Movie menu. If that menu item is set to AF-S for single AF, focus will be locked when you press the red Movie button to start recording the video. If you need to adjust the focus during the recording, you can press the Left button to cause the camera to refocus.

If Autofocus Mode on the Movie menu is set to AF-F for full-time AF, the camera will automatically adjust its focus during movie recording. You can lock the focus at any point by pressing the AE/AF Lock button, if it has been assigned to lock focus with the AE/AF Lock Button menu option. If that button has not been assigned to lock focus, you can lock focus by pressing the Left button. You do not have to hold down either button to lock focus during movie recording; just press it and release it; press and release again to unlock the focus.

Exposure, Exposure Compensation, and Exposure Lock

You cannot change the exposure mode used by the camera for recording movies in one of the still-shooting modes; it will use automatic exposure adjustment, as if it were in Auto mode, no matter what still-shooting mode is set on the mode dial. Even if you select Manual exposure on the mode dial and make fairly extreme settings for shutter speed and aperture, such as 1/500 second and f/7.1, the P950 will use its autoexposure programming to expose the scene as normally as possible, subject only to whatever exposure compensation and exposure lock functions you employ.

One adjustment you can make that affects video recording in the still-shooting modes is exposure compensation, available in all of those modes except Manual exposure and several settings of Scene mode (Fireworks Show, Multiple Exposure Lighten, and the Night Sky and Star Trails options for Time-lapse Movie).

Whatever exposure compensation adjustment you make before pressing the red Movie button, to brighten or darken the image, will stay in effect during video recording; you will see the effect on the screen in the brightness of the image. You cannot make changes to this setting during the recording.

You also can lock exposure during movie recording. If the AE/AF Lock Button menu option is set to have the AE-L/AF-L button lock exposure, you can use that button to lock exposure. Otherwise, you will see a prompt at the bottom of the display stating that you can press the Right button for AE-L, or autoexposure lock, as shown in Figure 8-4.

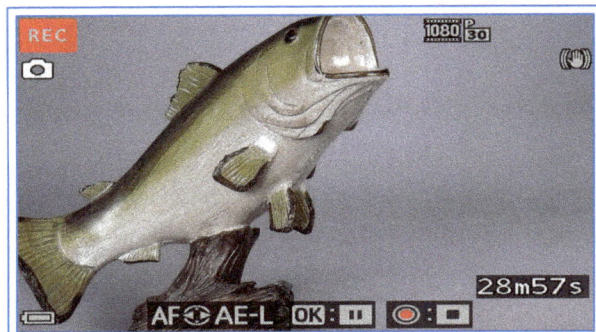

Figure 8-4. Prompt on Screen to Lock Exposure with Right Button

If you press the Right button to lock exposure, the message will change to indicate that you can turn AE-L off by pressing the same button again, and the AE-L label in the lower left corner of the display will indicate that AE-L is in effect, as shown in Figure 8-5.

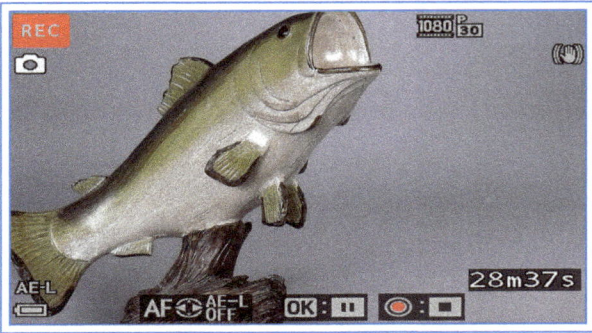

Figure 8-5. Movie Recording Screen When Exposure Locked

Although the Right button is the same one used to adjust exposure compensation, in this situation the button will not affect exposure compensation, only exposure lock. However, any exposure compensation that was in effect before the recording started will remain in effect, even if you use this button to lock the exposure. The locked exposure setting will take into account any exposure compensation value that has been selected.

Self-timer

The self-timer functions for movie recording. Set it as you normally do, by pressing the Left button and selecting either three seconds or ten seconds for the delay. Then, when you press the Movie button, the camera will delay the designated length of time before starting to record.

Vibration Reduction

The Vibration Reduction setting on the Setup menu carries over for movie recording. I recommend that you

Chapter 8: Motion Pictures | 121

usually leave this setting at Normal (Framing First) for movies unless you have the camera on a tripod. When the camera is on a tripod, you can turn VR off, unless you are using a very long focal length. With very long focal lengths, you may need VR even when using a tripod.

When you are handholding the camera, the Normal (Framing First) setting can reduce the shakiness that results from an unsteady hand. You don't need to worry when you are purposely moving the camera in a panning motion, because the camera will detect that motion and ignore it for purposes of vibration reduction; it will attempt to counteract only the vertical shakiness caused by your hand motions.

If you are not concerned about having part of the image cut off by the cropping that results from using VR, and you are not going to be panning the camera, you may want to use the Normal setting, which provides more stabilization than the Normal (Framing First) option.

I don't recommend using the Active settings for movie recording unless you are in a situation such as handholding the camera in a car on a bumpy road, or using a very long focal length without a tripod.

Note that there is another option on the Movie menu, Electronic VR, discussed later in this chapter, that can provide additional stabilization for video footage, though at the cost of further cropping of the edges of the video frame.

ZOOM

The optical and digital zoom both function during video recording. I try to avoid zooming while shooting a video if at all possible, because the zooming motion can be unsettling to the viewer. Also, as Nikon points out in its reference manual, the noise of the zoom mechanism is likely to be audible on the recording. Unless you're following action that requires you to adjust the zoom range, you're probably better off adjusting it before you start recording. (Of course, if you don't mind using editing software, you can later edit out any parts of the movie where you adjust the zoom range.)

The zoom scale is not displayed when the camera is recording a movie, so you will not be able to see what focal length the camera is using as you are recording. You can tell when the optical zoom limit has been reached and digital zoom is being used, because the sound of the zoom mechanism will stop as digital zoom begins to be used. You also may notice a slight pause in the zooming action when the camera shifts from optical zoom to digital zoom while recording a video.

Taking Still Images During Movie Recording

When you are shooting movies with the Coolpix P950, you can capture still images at a limited resolution. When a video sequence is being recorded, the camera will display a camera icon in the upper left corner of the display, as seen in Figures 8-4 and 8-5, meaning that still images can be captured while the recording is in progress.

All you have to do is press the shutter button while the movie is being recorded. This is a useful feature when you want to record an entire event on video, such as a school graduation ceremony, but you also want to capture a few still images at critical moments (such as when the graduate you are most interested in receives his or her diploma). There are several limitations to this feature, as you might expect. First, the sound of the shutter being activated will be recorded. The sound is not too loud and does not interfere with the audio track of the video too severely, but it is a noticeable clicking sound.

A more significant limitation is that all of the images will be recorded at a small size and in the 16:9 aspect ratio. For example, when the Movie Options item on the Movie menu is set to 1080/30p, the resulting still images are about two megapixels in size. These images will not be useful for making large prints, but they will provide a record of the event, and you will have them immediately available for viewing, emailing, or other uses. All images are captured as JPEG files, not Raw.

In addition, this feature is not available in Movie Manual mode or when Movie Options on the Movie menu is set to an HS (high-speed) option. If an HS format is selected, the P950 will display a camera icon with a diagonal line through it during video recording, indicating that still pictures cannot be captured with the current video format.

You also cannot capture a still image while a video recording is paused, or when there are fewer than five seconds of video recording time remaining. There is no preset limit on the number of still images that can be captured during a video recording, except that, when

Movie Options is set to 2160/30p or 2160/25p, there is a limit of 20 images, but the images have the higher resolution of the 3840 x 2160 format.

It also is worth pointing out another option for creating still images from video recording. As is discussed at the end of this chapter, when you are playing a movie in the camera, you can save a still frame from it using the on-screen editing controls. With ordinary HD footage, this action generates a small image that may not suit your purposes. However, if you extract a frame from 4K footage (using the 2160/30p setting for Movie Options), the saved frame will have about 8 megapixels of resolution, and may serve as a more useful still image.

Pausing Recording with the OK Button

When you are recording a video, you can pause the recording by pressing the OK button and resume it by pressing that button again. The camera indicates this capability by displaying at the bottom of the screen two vertical lines for the pause function next to a symbol for the OK button, as shown in Figures 8-4 and 8-5. When the recording is paused, the camera displays the vertical lines at the upper left of the display and places at the bottom of the frame an indication that you can press the OK button to resume recording, as shown in Figure 8-6.

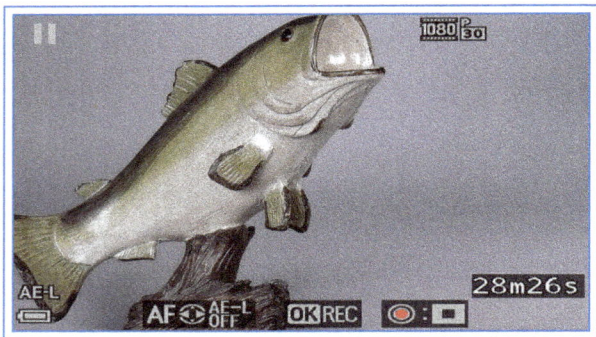

Figure 8-6. Shooting Screen When Movie Recording Paused

This function can be handy if, for example, you are recording a sporting event and you want to pause during a lull in the action, but you don't want to completely stop and re-start the video each time the action stops. The pause cannot last more than five minutes; after that time, the recording will end. This feature is not available with the HS settings of Movie Options.

Fn Button: Does Not Operate During Video Recording

Several of the settings you can program for the Function button are not available for movie recording, such as Image Size, continuous shooting, ISO, and AF Area Mode. However, a few of the settings you can assign to this button do affect video recording, including Picture Control, White Balance, Vibration Reduction, and others. The Function button does not operate while a movie is being recorded. However, you can, of course, press this button before pressing the Movie button, to activate whatever setting is programmed into the Function button.

Limits on Length of Video Recording

Before I discuss the Movie menu and other topics, I will point out a limitation of the Coolpix P950 with respect to the length of its video sequences. Like many modern digital cameras that are not primarily video cameras, the P950 is limited to recording only about 29 minutes or 4 GB of video, whichever comes first, in any single sequence. You can store considerably more than that amount of high-quality video on a large SD card, but you can only record 29 minutes at a time; you have to then stop and re-start your recording. And, as noted, any one sequence cannot exceed 4 GB in size.

If you record using the 2160/30p format, you can record only about seven minutes of video in a single file; the camera will create additional files for longer sequences, and those files cannot be played back continuously. So, in effect, the recording limit is seven minutes for that format and about eight minutes for the 2160/25p option. The limit is about 13 minutes for the 1080/60p format, and 26 minutes for the 1080/30p format. However, you can edit the individual files together in software, so the limit does not necessarily prevent you from recording a sequence of up to 29 minutes in length.

For example, I placed the camera on a tripod and set it to record a movie in the 2160/30p format. The camera continued recording steadily for the full 29 minutes, and then stopped. The result was that the camera created four separate movies, each about 7 minutes and 30 seconds long. You cannot play these four movies back continuously, but you can edit them together

Chapter 8: Motion Pictures | 123

using software on a computer, and the result will be a continuous video of about 29 minutes in length.

The Movie Menu

The Movie menu includes options that affect the recording of movies in the still-image shooting modes, such as Auto, Scene, Program, and others. When the camera is set to one of those modes, you can get access to the Movie menu, represented by the movie camera icon, as shown in Figure 8-7.

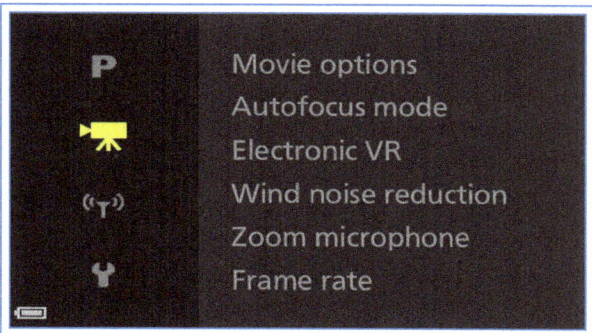

Figure 8-7. Icon for Movie Menu Highlighted at Left

After you have highlighted the movie camera icon, use the Right button to move the highlight back into the list of menu options on the main part of the screen, as shown in Figure 8-8. There are six options on the first screen of this menu. (There is a seventh option that appears on a second screen, but only if an external microphone is plugged in. If no microphone is plugged in, the menu displays only a single screen.)

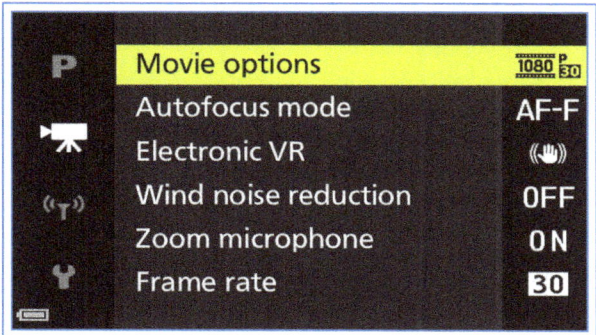

Figure 8-8. First Screen of Movie Menu

Frame Rate

As you can see in Figure 8-8, the six Movie menu items are Movie Options, Autofocus Mode, Electronic VR, Wind Noise Reduction, Zoom Microphone, and Frame Rate. Ordinarily, I would discuss these options in that order. However, the selection you make for Frame Rate determines what choices you can make for the first item, Movie Options, so I will discuss Frame Rate first.

There are two major video standards used in various countries—NTSC and PAL. NTSC is used in the United States, Canada, much of South America, South Korea, and other areas; PAL is used in Europe and some other areas. With the NTSC system, the standard rate for video playback is 30 frames per second; with the PAL system, it is 25 frames per second. These differences are reflected in the Frame Rate and Movie Options menu choices.

If you are using your camera with the NTSC system, the selections for the HD formats will include the number 30 or 60, such as 2160/30p, 1080/30p or 1080/60p. If you are using the P950 with the PAL system, the options will include the number 25 or 50, as in 2160/25p, 1080/25p or 1080/50p. Similarly, the primary choices for the HS (high-speed) options will include numbers that are multiples of 30 for NTSC and 25 for PAL.

Some camera makers sell different versions of a camera for the North American (NTSC) and European (PAL) markets. With the Coolpix P950, though, Nikon provides the Frame Rate menu option to let you set your camera to whichever system you prefer to use. The choices for this menu option are shown in Figure 8-9.

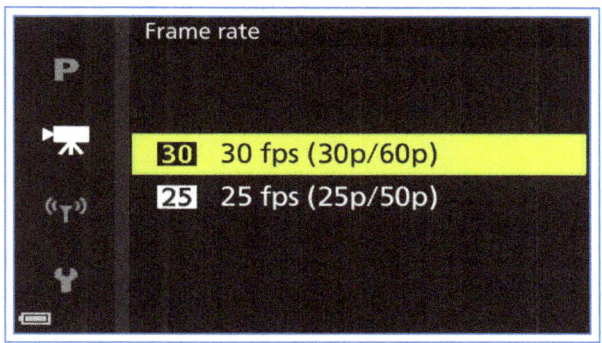

Figure 8-9. Frame Rate Menu Options Screen

If you are located in North America or another area that uses the NTSC system, you should set Frame Rate to 30 fps; if you are in Europe or otherwise using the PAL system, you should set Frame Rate to 25 fps.

Now that I have discussed Frame Rate, I will discuss the first item on the Movie menu, Movie Options. I will assume in this discussion that the NTSC/30 fps system is being used, because that is what is used in the United States, where I am located. If you are using the PAL system, you should substitute 25 or 50 for the number 30 or 60 in this discussion.

Movie Options

The first choice on the Movie menu is Movie Options, whose main screen is shown in Figure 8-10. This item lets you set the aspect ratio, quality, and speed of your video footage from eight possibilities.

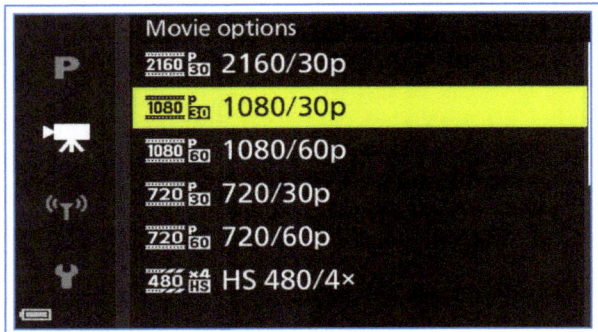

Figure 8-10. First Screen of Movie Options Menu Item

The top option is designated as 2160/30p if Frame Rate is set to 30, or 2160/25p if Frame Rate is set to 25. This option sets the camera to record video in a 4K/UHD format, meaning the format's frames have a horizontal count of roughly 4,000 (4K) pixels, also sometimes designated as UHD for ultra-high definition. (The actual frame size is 3840 by 2160 pixels.) The letter "p" following the number 30 stands for "progressive," which provides higher quality than formats designated with the letter "i," where the "i" stands for "interlaced." (There are no interlaced formats available with the P950 camera.)

This 4K format provides the highest quality of video for the P950 camera, but it also requires the greatest processing power and memory card capability. If you use this format, Nikon recommends that you use a memory card rated in UHS Speed Class 3, the fastest currently available. If you use a slower card, the camera will attempt to record the video, but recording may stutter or halt. As noted earlier, the camera can record only about six minutes of continuous video in this format. With this setting, Electronic VR cannot be turned on, and digital zoom will not function beyond 7200mm. Also, only up to 20 still images can be captured while recording with this option.

To take full advantage of this format, the footage should be displayed on a TV set that is capable of showing 4K video. However, even if you don't have access to a 4K TV, video captured in this format can be viewed on any HDTV set. It also can be edited and down-sampled to a normal HD format such as 1080/30p.

The second selection is designated as 1080/30p, which means it provides high-definition video with 1080 vertical pixels and 1920 horizontal pixels, the same amount as on many HDTV sets. This standard is sometimes called "Full HD" to distinguish it from the lesser-quality HD that provides only 720 vertical pixels and 1280 horizontal pixels.

The third choice for Movie Options, 1080/60p, provides the same quality as the second choice on the menu, but, instead of 30 frames per second, it provides 60 frames per second. This option provides higher quality than the 30p choice, because the camera records more information. The camera records 60 full frames of video each second, but converts the footage internally so it will play back at 30 frames per second without looking slowed down.

However, if you import your 1080/60p footage into video-editing software such as iMovie, Windows Easy Movie Maker, or any other up-to-date program, you can slow it down to one-half normal speed, producing a smooth slow-motion effect. So, if you want higher quality for your HD video or you want to slow it down to half-speed on your computer, you can choose this option.

The next option on the menu, 720/30p, produces footage with 720 vertical and 1280 horizontal pixels, which still provides high-definition video in the 16:9 aspect ratio, but with fewer pixels and somewhat reduced quality. Choose this option if you want HD, but with less-taxing storage and speed requirements for your memory card and computer.

Next, you can choose the 720/60p option, which also records your footage with 720 vertical pixels and 1280 horizontal ones. This choice is similar to the 1080/60p option discussed above, except that it has the reduced resolution of regular HD as opposed to Full HD. Here again, you can slow down the footage to half-speed using editing software.

HS (High-Speed) Movie Options

The next choice on the Movie Options menu, HS 480/4x, is the first one for recording silent HS (high-speed) movies with the Coolpix P950. I have not discussed the HS capabilities of the camera before now, so I will take this opportunity to explain the use of this interesting feature.

First, the abbreviation HS, for high-speed, is really a misnomer, because the HS choices include both high-speed and low-speed options. It would be more accurate to use a term such as "non-standard-speed." HS is a convenient shorthand, but bear in mind that it is not precisely accurate.

Here is a brief explanation of how the HS feature works. The standard rate for recording and playing back video (in the United States) is 30 frames per second. That is, the camera takes 30 individual images each second and then plays them back at that same rate. When your eyes see those images, the pictures follow each other so rapidly that it seems as if the motion in the scene is continuous, rather than 30 separate still photos, which is the actual situation.

If you have seen old silent movies, they sometimes seem unnaturally fast and jerky. That happens because those movies were recorded at a slower speed than movies of today, but sometimes are played back on modern projectors at a faster rate. If a movie was recorded at, say, 15 frames per second, and then played back at 30 frames per second, the action in the movie would appear to be twice as fast as normal, resulting in a jumpy, jerky, speeded-up appearance. Similarly, if you set a camera to record at 60 frames per second and then play back the footage at 30 frames per second, the action will appear to be slowed down to one-half its normal rate.

The Coolpix P950 gives you the ability to either increase or decrease the frame rate at which it records video footage. It's important to note that the video will always play back in the camera at the standard 30 frames per second (or 25 for PAL systems); the only factor you can change is the speed at which the video is recorded.

With that background, I will discuss each of the HS options on the Movie Options menu's two screens. The first screen of options was shown in Figure 8-10.

The first choice, HS 480/4x, sets the camera to record video at 120 frames per second, four times faster than the normal 30 fps. (If you have set Frame Rate to 25 fps, the recording speed will be 100 frames per second.) When this footage is played back in the camera, any movement will appear to be at one-fourth normal speed. This setting provides a capability for slow-motion video, which you can use to analyze a golf swing, slow down the beating of a hummingbird's wings, or for any of a myriad of sports and nature applications. Or, you might just like slow-motion video for its dreamlike, underwater-style appearance.

One major caveat with this setting is that, not surprisingly, its use involves a sharp trade-off of speed against quality. When you set the camera to record 120 frames per second, it automatically reduces the quality to VGA, which provides noticeably lower quality than HD. The aspect ratio is 4:3. There also is another limitation: The camera can only record for 7 minutes and 15 seconds at this rate, which results in a playback time of 29 minutes, the limit for video playback. However, for many applications, that amount of time should be sufficient.

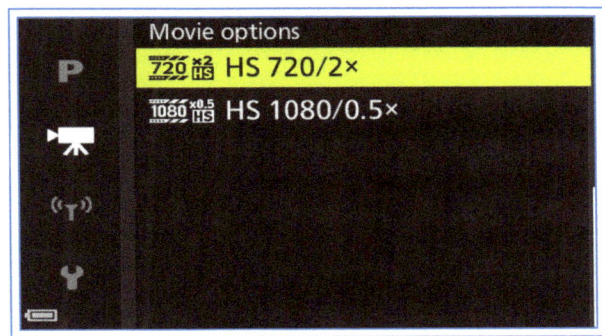

Figure 8-11. Second Screen of Movie Options Menu Item

The last two HS Movie settings are on the second screen of the Movie Options menu screen, shown in Figure 8-11. The HS 720/2x option gives you half as much slowing of motion as the first HS option, with higher image quality. In this case, your footage is recorded at 60 frames per second (50 frames per second if Frame Rate is set to 25 fps), so it will play back at one-half normal speed, and at 720 HD quality. You can record at this speed for 14 minutes and 30 seconds, again resulting in the full 29 minutes of playback time.

Finally, the last option on the list turns the whole exercise in a different direction. This option, HS 1080/0.5x, is the only setting with which the camera records video at a slower than normal speed. In this case, in which the footage is recorded at 15 frames per second (12.5 if Frame Rate is set to 25 fps) and played back at the normal speed (30 or 25 frames per second), the footage will appear to be speeded up to twice the normal speed. And, as a bonus, because the camera is actually doing less work in terms of speed, it can provide higher-quality video: full HD, at 1920 by 1080 pixels, recording for 29 minutes, with a playback time of 14 minutes and 30 seconds.

What would you use this option for? One possibility is to create a movie with the speeded-up look of old silent films, maybe to inject a light touch into a business presentation, or just for fun with footage of the family at the beach. You also could use this mode for some situations in which you need a video record, but you don't need (or want) to have a real-time recording. For example, if you would like to record the patterns of automobile traffic at an intersection near your home or office, you could set up the camera on a tripod, set it to the HS 15 fps mode, and you would then have a video that would reveal the pattern at twice the normal speed, which actually might be easier to interpret than a real-time movie.

Of course, shooting half-speed movies (to show them at double speed) is a mild form of time-lapse photography. If you want to do time-lapse photography for applications such as showing a flower opening up or recording the progress of a construction project, you probably would be better off using the Time-lapse Movie setting of Scene mode, discussed in Chapter 3, or the interval timer function of the Continuous shooting item on the Shooting menu, discussed in Chapter 4.

With all of the HS options, the video is recorded with no sound. The zoom position of the lens, the focus, exposure, and white balance are all set when the Movie button is first pressed; no further adjustments to those settings can be made while the video is being recorded. The HS Movie options are dimmed and unavailable for selection when the Clean HDMI Output option under the HDMI setting on the Setup menu is set to On.

Autofocus Mode

This second choice on the Movie menu controls how the camera focuses when recording videos.

The focus options for movie-making are a bit tricky. First, it's important to remember that the focus mode selector, the small switch at the top of the camera's back, works in any shooting mode to select either AF or MF, for autofocus or manual focus. So, if you want to use the Autofocus Mode option while shooting a movie, make sure you have the focus mode selector set for autofocus, not manual focus. If the camera is set for manual focus, the Autofocus Mode option on the Movie menu will be dimmed and unavailable for selection.

If the focus mode selector switch is set to the MF position, you can focus manually using the side dial.

Assuming you have activated autofocus with the focus mode selector, you have the choice of two options for Autofocus Mode on the Movie menu, as shown in Figure 8-12: AF-S for Single AF, or AF-F for Full-time AF.

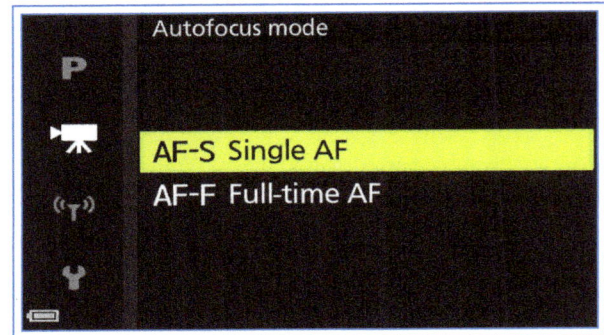

Figure 8-12. Autofocus Mode Menu Options Screen

If you select AF-F, the camera will continually adjust its focus as the scene changes. The camera will focus on any object in the center of the frame. The advantage of this mode is that the focus will remain sharp (with some blurring during focus adjustments) throughout the scene. One disadvantage is that the battery will be drained more quickly because of the demands on the focus mechanism. Another disadvantage is that the camera may shift its focus to an unwanted subject, such as a person who stands up between you and the stage when you are recording at a play or concert.

With the AF-F setting active, you can lock the focus at any time so it will stay fixed at the current distance. The button you use for this function depends on the setting of the AE/AF Lock Button menu option on the Setup menu. If that option is set to AE/AF Lock or AF Lock Only, you can use the AE-L/AF-L button to lock focus. If that option is set to AE Lock Only or AE Lock Hold, you have to use the Left button to lock focus.

The Nikon user's guide says that, with this setting, the camera is likely to record the sounds of the continuous focus adjustments, but I have not found any such sounds to cause problems. The zoom mechanism makes sounds that can be distracting, but the continuous autofocus adjustments have been quiet, in my experience. Therefore, if you are in a situation in which the distance to the subject may change during the recording, I recommend that you use the AF-F setting.

If you select the AF-S setting, the camera will initially focus just once, when you start recording. However, while the recording is in progress, you can force the camera to refocus at any time, by pressing the Left button. You will see a prompt at the bottom of the screen with an icon that shows the Left button next to the letters AF, as shown earlier in Figure 8-4. Once you press the Left button to refocus, the focus will remain locked at the new position unless you press the button again to refocus at another new position.

I recommend that you choose the autofocus setting according to the situation. For example, if you are recording in an environment where the focus distance is likely to keep changing and you have sufficient battery power to last for the entire recording session, I recommend using the AF-F setting so the camera continues to adjust its focus as needed. However, if you are recording a school play or concert, where the focus distance should not change that dramatically and the battery needs to last for a long time, you may be better off using the AF-S setting, with the knowledge that you can adjust the focus at any time by pressing the Left button if necessary.

Electronic VR (Vibration Reduction)

This third option on the Movie menu controls whether the camera uses electronic vibration reduction. This feature is another type of image stabilization, in addition to and independent of the Vibration Reduction setting on the Setup menu. The VR setting on the Setup menu uses lens-shift technology, which means that, when the camera detects image blur from movement, it moves the lens in the opposite direction to counteract the blur.

The Electronic VR setting uses a different method. When the camera detects blur, it uses image processing to eliminate the blur as much as possible. With this method, the resulting image will lose some pixels at the edges as the camera processes the information to remove blur. In other words, the video image will be slightly cropped at the edges when Electronic VR is used.

It is possible to use both Vibration Reduction from the Setup menu and Electronic VR from the Movie menu when shooting movies. My recommendation is to turn off both types of VR when you are using a tripod, unless you are using such a long focal length that the image is still shaky. When you are shooting handheld in normal conditions, I would use VR from the Setup menu. When you are shooting in more unsettled conditions, where more stabilization is needed, you may want to use Electronic VR in addition to the Normal or Active setting for VR on the Setup menu.

Electronic VR is not available when recording movies using any of the HS formats or with the 2160/30p format.

Wind Noise Reduction

This next option controls the use of a feature designed to reduce extraneous sounds that may be recorded in windy conditions. I recommend leaving this option turned off unless the wind noise appears to be a problem, because this feature reduces the sounds that are recorded at certain frequencies. I prefer to record all of the available sounds and adjust them later using editing software if necessary. If you won't be using editing software, you may want to use this feature on a windy day. This option is not available with the HS formats for movie recording.

Zoom Microphone

When this option is turned on, as it is by default, the camera adjusts the angle of the built-in microphone's sensitivity to sound according to the zoom position of the lens. So, when the lens is zoomed back to its wide-angle position, the microphone picks up sounds in a wide pattern. As the lens is zoomed in, the angle of sound recording is narrowed in accordance with the angle of view of the lens.

My recommendation is to leave this feature turned off unless you are certain you want to have it operate. For example, if you are recording a stage play and have zoomed in on the actors, you might want to have this option turned on so the camera will pick up the sounds of the play more clearly than the sounds from the audience. However, if you are recording general scenery, you may want the camera to pick up sounds from every direction, even if you have zoomed in on a distant mountaintop or ship at sea.

This option is not available for selection when an external microphone is attached to the camera's microphone jack or when an HS selection is in effect for Movie Options.

Frame Rate

I discussed the Frame Rate option earlier, because of its importance in determining what movie formats you can choose for your recordings.

External Microphone Sensitivity

This menu option is available for selection only if a microphone is attached to the P950's external microphone jack. When a microphone is attached, this option appears on a second screen of the Movie menu. It has two sub-options, as shown in Figure 8-13: Auto Sensitivity and Manual Sensitivity.

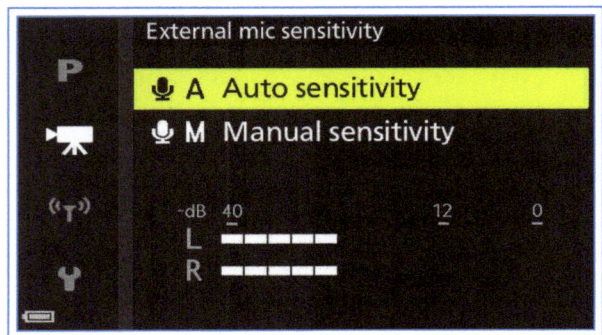

Figure 8-13. External Mic Sensitivity Menu Options Screen

If you choose the Auto option, the camera sets the level for recording sound with the external microphone. With the Manual setting, you choose a setting from 1 to 64 units, using the multi selector dial or the Up and Down arrows to change the value in the yellow bar, which is shown in Figure 8-14.

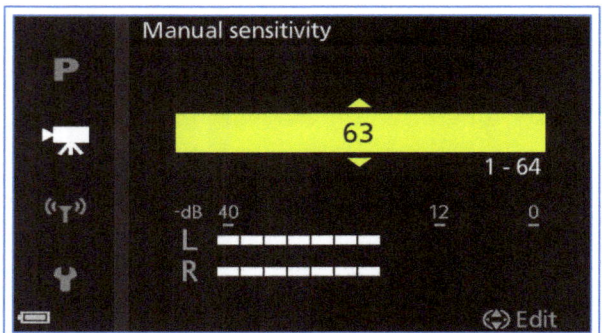

Figure 8-14. Adjustment Screen for Manual Mic Sensitivity

If you are recording a scene with a relatively stable and predictable sound level, such as an interview or concert, I recommend using the Manual setting and making some test shots to get the level set as you want it. If you are recording an event with more variable sound levels, such as people gathered at a picnic, you might want to try the Auto setting so the camera will increase the sound level as necessary to record quieter sounds.

Movie Manual Mode

Up to this point in this chapter, the movie options I have discussed can be used for recording videos in various shooting modes. Now it is time to discuss Movie Manual mode, the special mode that is selected by turning the mode dial to the position marked by a movie camera icon and the letter M, as shown in Figure 8-15.

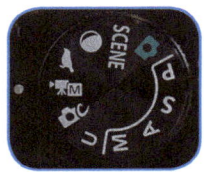

Figure 8-15. Mode Dial at Movie Manual

This is the mode you should use when you need to control the aperture, or the aperture and shutter speed, when you are recording a video. It also is the mode to use when you record video to an external recorder.

When the camera is set to this mode, you can use the shutter button, as well as the red Movie button, to start and stop the recording of a movie. As a consequence, you cannot capture still images when this mode is in effect, either before or during video recording.

Movie Manual Menu

When you select the Movie Manual mode on the mode dial, the Shooting menu and the Movie menu are both replaced by a single menu called the Movie Manual menu. As you can see in Figure 8-16, when the camera is in the Movie Manual mode, there is no separate Movie menu—just the Movie Manual menu, the Network menu, and the Setup menu. The Movie Manual menu incorporates all of the options that appear on the Movie menu in other shooting modes, and also includes several options that are not available on the Movie menu in other shooting modes.

The Movie Manual menu, whose first screen is shown in Figure 8-17, has twelve items, including External Mic Sensitivity, which is available for selection only when an external microphone is attached to the camera:

- Exposure Mode
- Picture Control
- Custom Picture Control
- White Balance
- ISO Sensitivity
- Movie Options
- Autofocus Mode
- Electronic VR
- Wind Noise Reduction
- Zoom Microphone
- Frame Rate
- External Mic Sensitivity

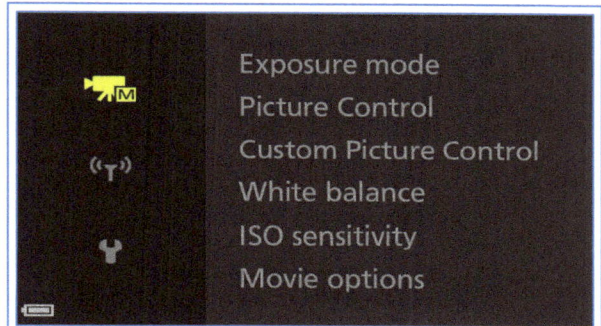

Figure 8-16. Icon for Movie Manual Menu Highlighted at Left

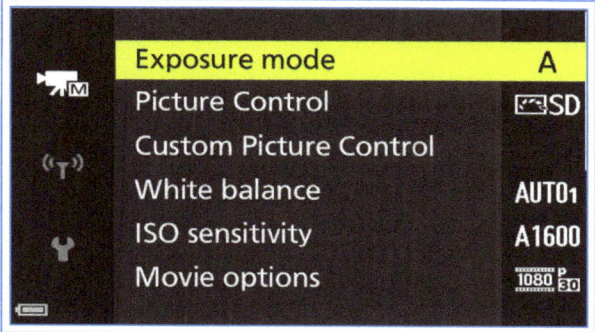

Figure 8-17. First Screen of Movie Manual Menu

All of these options also appear either on the Shooting menu or the Movie menu, and were discussed earlier, with the exception of Exposure Mode, discussed below.

Exposure Mode

The Exposure Mode item, whose options screen is shown in Figure 8-18, has two possible settings: Aperture-Priority Auto or Manual. This setting determines the way the camera controls exposure when you record videos in Movie Manual mode. If you choose Aperture-Priority Auto, you can adjust the aperture value before and during video recording, using the multi selector dial (or the command dial, if the functions of those two controls have been switched using the Toggle Av/Tv Selection item on the Setup menu). You might want to use this mode to blur the background of a video scene by opening the aperture wider, or to keep as much of the scene in focus as possible by using a narrow aperture.

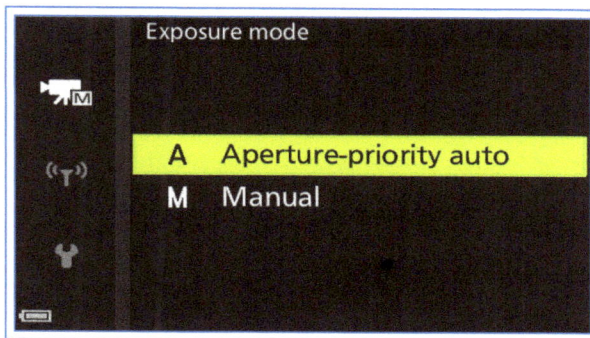

Figure 8-18. Exposure Mode Menu Options Screen

If you choose Manual, you can adjust both aperture and shutter speed during video recording. When recording movies, you can set the shutter speed as fast as 1/8000 second. The slowest shutter speed available is determined by the Frame Rate and Movie Options settings. For example, when Frame Rate is set to 30 fps and Movie Options is set to 1080/30p, the slowest shutter speed available is 1/30 second.

With this capability, you can achieve a dramatic change in the brightness of a scene by starting with a normal shutter speed and adjusting to such a fast value that the scene fades to black. Or, depending on lighting conditions and the ISO setting, you may be able to slow the shutter speed to such an extent that the scene makes a transition to excessive brightness, or even a white screen.

Picture Control and Custom Picture Control

These settings are similar to the items of the same name on the Shooting menu. You can select a value of Standard, Neutral, Vivid, or Monochrome, and shoot a movie with that setting, with or without custom adjustments. For details, see Chapter 4. You cannot adjust this setting during video recording.

White Balance

This setting, also, is similar to the setting of this name on the Shooting menu. It cannot be adjusted during movie recording, even if white balance is assigned to the side dial using the Assign Side Dial menu option.

ISO Sensitivity

This option is similar to the ISO Sensitivity option on the Shooting menu. In Movie Manual mode, the range of available ISO settings is from 100 to 6400, and the Auto ranges are from A400 to A6400, the same as with still shooting, except when an HS value is set for Movie Options. In that case, the setting is fixed at A1600.

In addition, when the ISO setting is assigned to the side dial using the Assign Side Dial item on screen 2 of the Setup menu, you can adjust the ISO setting during movie recording by turning the side dial. This adjustment can be made during movie recording only when the mode dial is at the Movie Manual position.

Other Items on Movie Manual Menu

The remaining options on this menu—Movie Options, Autofocus Mode, Electronic VR, Wind Noise Reduction, Zoom Microphone, Frame Rate, and External Mic Sensitivity—were discussed earlier in this chapter; there is no difference in their operation in Movie Manual mode from that in other shooting modes.

Recording to an External Video Recorder

As I mentioned in Chapter 7 in connection with the HDMI menu option, the Coolpix P950 is equipped with the ability to output a "clean" HDMI video signal through a micro-HDMI cable connected to the camera's HDMI port. You can use that capability to record HD video to an external video recorder. By doing that, you can create a second copy of a movie while recording it to the camera, you can record using a higher quality video format than those used by the camera, and you can take advantage of any features the recorder offers, such as a larger monitor than that of the camera, and special features for evaluating matters like exposure and focus.

I have tried this procedure using an Atomos Shogun 4K video recorder, and I will set forth the steps I used, to illustrate one way of recording video to an external device.

1. On the camera, set the mode dial to the Movie Manual position and set the focus mode selector to the MF position. (This is a technical requirement for recording the clean HDMI signal; autofocus is not available in this situation.)

2. Set Movie Options on the Movie menu to 1080/30p. (You cannot record 4K video to an external recorder from the P950.)

3. Set Electronic VR to On if you are recording handheld, or Off if you are using a tripod.

4. Set Wind Noise Reduction to On if wind noise is an issue.

5. Set Zoom Microphone according to your preference.

6. Set Frame Rate to 30 fps (unless you want to use the PAL system).

7. On the Movie Manual menu, set Exposure Mode to A, and set Picture Control, Custom Picture Control, white balance, and ISO sensitivity as you want.

8. On the camera, set the aperture as you want it.

9. On the Setup menu, make any selections you want for options other than HDMI.

10. For HDMI on the Setup menu, set Clean HDMI Output to On and HDMI Output to 1080/30p.

11. Connect a micro-HDMI cable to the camera's HDMI port and connect the other end of the cable to the recorder's HDMI-In port.

12. Set the recorder for HDMI input with an appropriate recording format, such as ProRes HQ.

13. Press the Display button on the camera, if necessary, to display the screen with no icons or other extraneous information.

14. Turn on the recorder and set it to record.

15. Press the Movie button (or shutter button) on the camera to start the video recording.

With the above steps, the video will be recorded to both the camera and the recorder. You have to adjust focus manually using the side dial. When you are ready to stop recording, press the Movie button (or the shutter button) on the camera and then stop the external recorder.

Movie Playback and Editing

In Chapter 2, I discussed the fundamentals of movie playback. Now it's time to go into more detail about that topic and to discuss how to edit video files in the camera.

Playback

When the camera is in full-screen playback mode, you can recognize a movie by the movie format icon in the lower right corner of the screen, as shown in Figure 8-19. On index screens of 4, 9, or 16 images, you can recognize a movie by the sets of small gray blocks that look like movie film sprocket holes on the sides of the images, as in Figure 8-20.

(With screens of 72 thumbnails, the sprocket holes do not appear, but, when a movie is highlighted, a small movie camera icon appears at the top left of the display.)

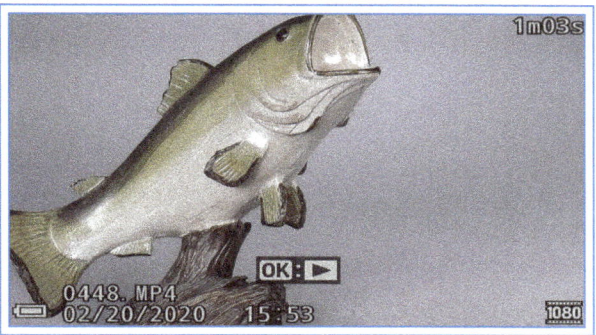

Figure 8-19. Movie Ready to Play in Camera

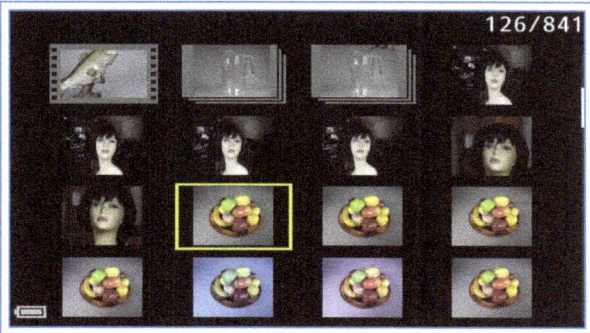

Figure 8-20. Index Screen Including One Movie

With a movie's frame on the display, press the OK button to start it playing. You will see a line of DVR-like icons at the bottom left, as shown in Figure 8-21.

Use the Left and Right buttons to move to any of those icons, then press OK to choose that function. The controls are, from left, stop, rewind, pause, and fast-forward. You have to hold down the OK button while the rewind or fast-forward icon is highlighted in order to activate that function. You can also turn the command dial or multi selector dial to the left or right to rewind or fast-forward the movie. You can press the zoom lever to the right or left at any time to raise or lower the audio volume.

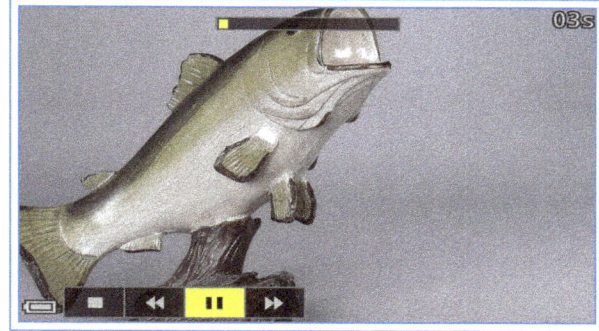

Figure 8-21. Initial Icons for Movie Playback Control

When the pause icon is highlighted, you can press the OK button to pause playback. While the movie is paused, there will be a somewhat different group of icons displayed, as shown in Figure 8-22.

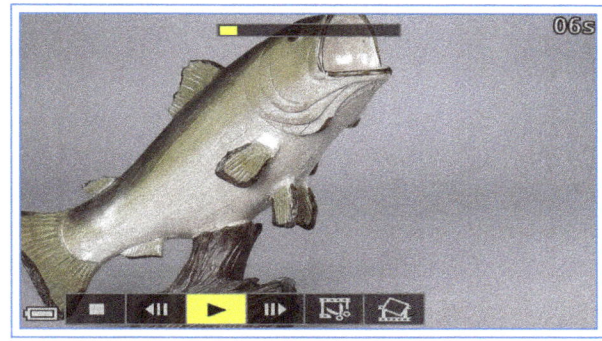

Figure 8-22. Icons for Movie Control When Paused

From the left, those icons represent stop, single-frame back, play, single-frame forward, edit, and extract and save a single frame. If you hold down the OK button while highlighting the single-frame forward or back icon, the frames will move continuously, one at a time, at a slow rate. You can also use the command dial or the multi selector dial to advance or rewind the frames at that rate. If the battery status icon shows only one segment remaining, movie editing functions are not available and the edit icon will not appear.

Editing

Of course, you cannot do full video editing in the camera; if you want to get really involved in editing, you need to import your footage into a program that has serious editing capabilities, like Adobe's Premiere Pro or Premiere Elements, or Apple's Final Cut or Final Cut Express. If you don't want to purchase a dedicated editing program, if you're a PC user you may already have Windows Easy Movie Maker; Mac users often have iMovie available. Finally, you can use Nikon's software suite, which includes ViewNX-Movie Editor software.

However, if you're on a camping trip away from your computer or you need to put together a quick video to play on a hotel's TV screen, you can do basic trimming of your P950 video files in the camera. (As noted earlier, you cannot perform this in-camera editing when the battery power is low.) Here is what you can do.

First, you can save a portion of an original video to a new file by trimming away footage at the beginning and/or end of a clip. To do this, start by playing the video to the approximate location where you want the new, shorter clip to start. Pause the clip by pressing the OK button, then use the Right button to highlight the scissors icon, and press OK to select that icon.

You will see a vertical menu of icons, from top to bottom: Choose Start Point; Choose End Point; Preview; Save; and Back, seen in Figure 8-23. There will be a yellow bar at the bottom of the screen, with a yellow pointer at the left end and a gray pointer at the right end.

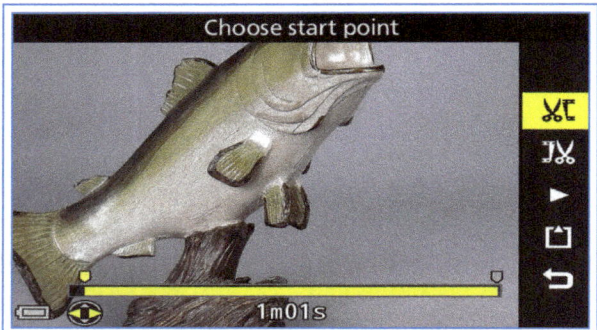

Figure 8-23. Icons on Screen for Movie Editing in Camera

The top icon, Choose Start Point, will be highlighted. Use the Left and Right buttons or the command dial to move the pointer to the starting point for the new clip. It may take some time to move the pointer more than a few seconds, because each press of a button or turn of the dial moves the pointer only a fraction of a second. You can hold down the Left or Right button to move the pointer rapidly.

When you have finished moving the left (start) point, press the Down button to highlight the second icon, for Choose End Point, as shown in Figure 8-24.

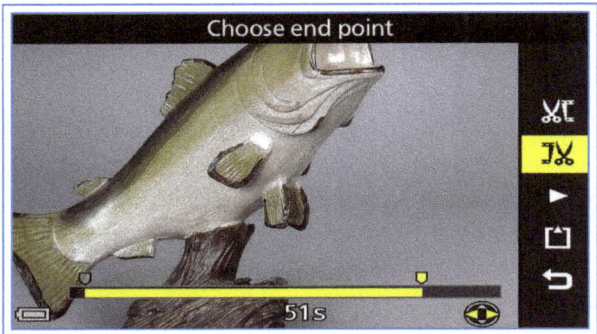

Figure 8-24. Choose End Point Icon Highlighted

Repeat the previous procedure, but move the right (end) point in toward the center of the yellow bar. When both the start and end points are set as you want them, highlight the third icon, which looks like a Play button; this control lets you preview the adjusted clip. If the preview looks okay, press the OK button to stop it if necessary, and move down to the next icon, a rectangle with a small triangle at its top. When that icon is highlighted, as shown in Figure 8-25, press the OK button, and the camera will display a message saying Save OK? asking if you want to save the clip in its new length. The camera will place Yes and No bars at the bottom of this screen.

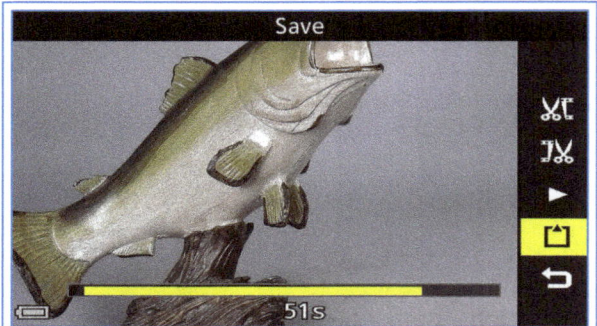

Figure 8-25. Icon to Save Clip Highlighted

If you want to save the clip, highlight the Yes bar and press the OK button. The camera may take quite a while to save the new, shorter version of the clip; the original will remain untouched.

Finally, you can save a single frame from any video clip taken with the P950, except for clips made using any of the HS formats. To do this, start playing the movie to the approximate point where you want to extract a frame, then press the OK button to pause the movie.

You will then, as before, see the icons for playing, advancing, or reversing by single frames, as well as editing and saving a single frame.

Use the advance and reverse controls to move to the exact frame you want to save. Then highlight the icon at the far right that looks like a frame next to some movie footage, and press the OK button. When the camera displays a message asking if you want to copy that frame as a still image, as shown in Figure 8-26, highlight the Yes bar and press the OK button to confirm.

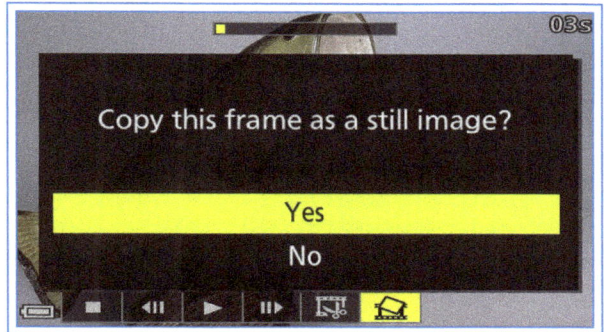

Figure 8-26. Confirmation Screen to Save Still Image from Movie

The camera will display the new still image with a .jpg file name. The still picture will be saved with Normal quality, at the same image size as that of the format of the movie it was extracted from. Because of the relatively high resolution of 4K video, you can save a single frame from a 4K video that may be quite usable as an individual image.

Chapter 9: Wireless Features, Superzoom Lens, and Other Topics

SnapBridge App

The Nikon Coolpix P950 can transfer images to, and can be controlled remotely from, a smartphone or tablet, using a Nikon app called SnapBridge. The SnapBridge app lets the P950 connect to devices that use iOS (such as iPhone, iPad, and iPod Touch) or Android (such as Samsung Galaxy phones and tablets) using a combination of Bluetooth and Wi-Fi. I will not discuss every feature of the app in this book, but I will describe basic procedures for transferring images from the camera to a smart device and for controlling the camera remotely from a smart device. For more information about the app, see the online help at http://nikonimglib.com/snbr/onlinehelp/en/index.html, as well as the SnapBridge Connection Guide pamphlet that is shipped with the camera.

Initial Connection and Transferring Images from Camera to Smart Device

As noted above, the SnapBridge app lets a smartphone or tablet connect to the camera through a Wi-Fi network, as similar apps do for many other cameras. One notable feature of SnapBridge is that it also lets a smart device connect to the camera by Bluetooth, a low-power local network commonly used to connect speakers, headphones, or other devices to a phone or tablet. The Bluetooth connection makes it possible for the camera to upload new images to your phone or tablet as soon as they are taken, automatically. The images will appear in the normal area where images are stored on the device. This connection can remain active even when the camera is turned off, so images stored on the camera's memory card can continue to upload to your phone or tablet.

Following is a summary of steps to set up the connection, which involves pairing the camera with a smartphone or tablet over Bluetooth, using the SnapBridge app. I will illustrate the discussion using an iPhone, though the steps are similar for an Android device.

1. First, download the SnapBridge app from the App Store for Apple devices or from Google Play for Android devices. The icon for the app on an iPhone is shown in Figure 9-1.

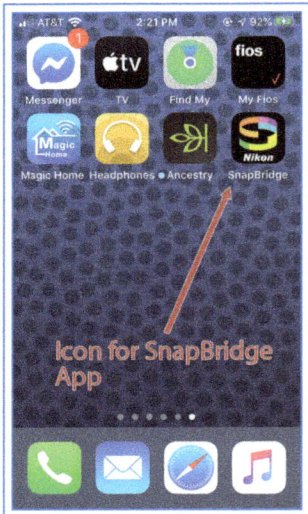

Figure 9-1. Icon for SnapBridge App on iPhone Screen

2. On the camera, go to the Network menu (marked by an antenna icon) and make sure the Choose Connection option is set to Smart Device, as shown in Figure 9-2.

3. On the Network menu, highlight Connect to Smart Device, as shown in Figure 9-3. Press the OK button or the Right button to activate this option.

Chapter 9: Wireless Features, Superzoom Lens, and Other Topics | 135

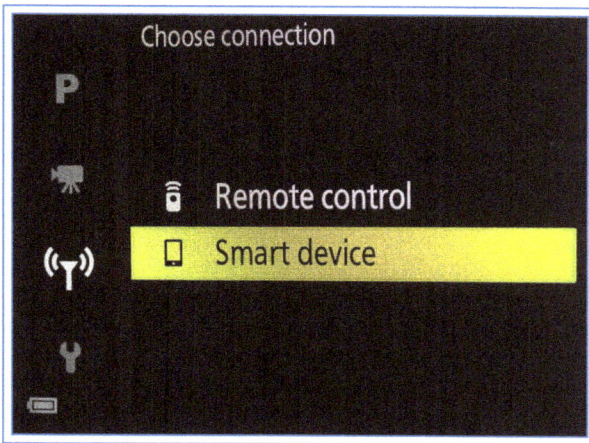

Figure 9-2. Smart Device Highlighted for Choose Connection

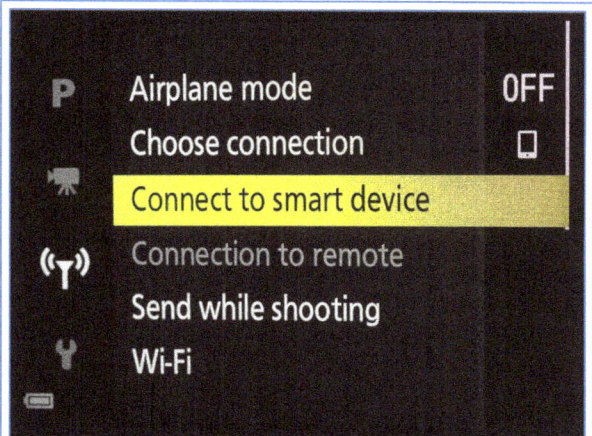

Figure 9-3. Connect to Smart Device Highlighted on Network Menu

4. On the camera, you should see a screen like that shown in Figure 9-4, prompting you to obtain and use the SnapBridge app.

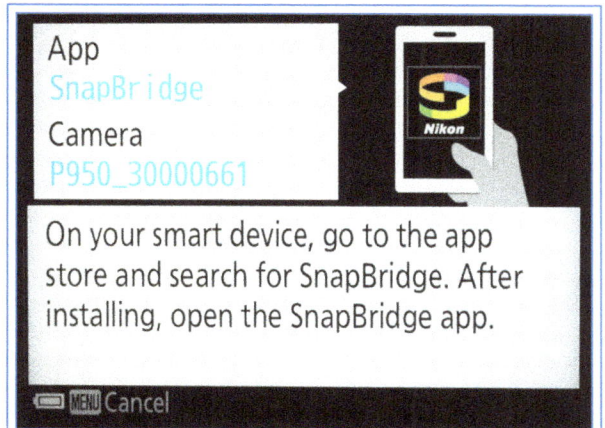

Figure 9-4. Message on Camera to Connect to SnapBridge

5. On your smart device, open the SnapBridge app.

6. In the SnapBridge app, you should see a Connect screen like that shown in Figure 9-5.

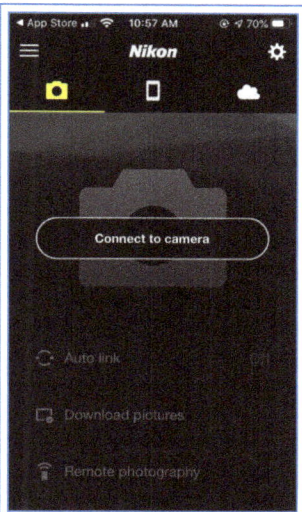

Figure 9-5. Connect Screen in SnapBridge App

7. On that screen, tap the Connect to Camera button. On the next screen, you should see the name of the camera, which should be something like P950_30000661, as shown in Figure 9-6.

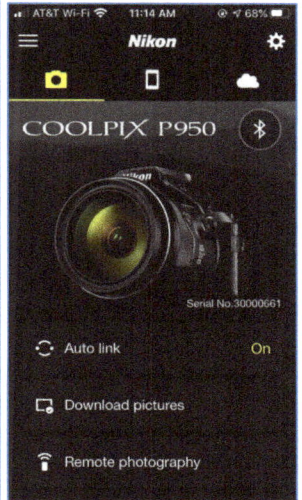

Figure 9-6. Name of Camera on SnapBridge Screen

8. Tap on that name, and a screen with further instructions should appear, as shown in Figure 9-7; tap on Understood to proceed.

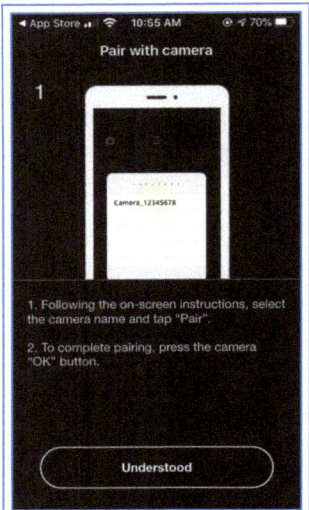

Figure 9-7. SnapBridge App Screen to Proceed to Connect

9. Another screen should appear on the app, asking you to select the Bluetooth accessory to connect to, as shown in Figure 9-8.

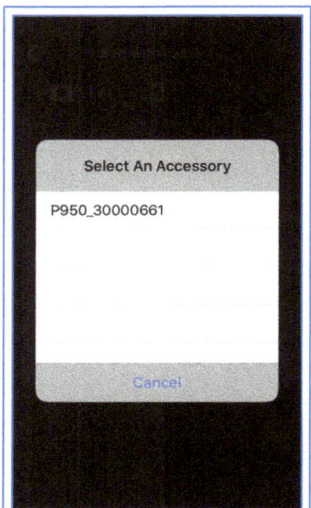

Figure 9-8. Screen in App to Select Camera

10. Tap the name of the camera on that screen, and you should see a screen prompting you to approve the pairing of the two devices. Verify that the authentication code shown on the camera matches that on the smart device, and select Pair on the smart device and OK on the camera. The camera and smart device are now paired.

11. In the SnapBridge app, select the left-most tab at the top of the screen, marked with a camera icon (if necessary), then turn on Auto Link, shown in Figure 9-9, if you want the camera and smartphone to remain linked even when the camera is turned off.

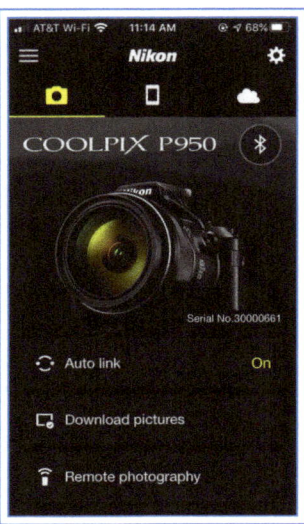

Figure 9-9. Main Screen of App When Connected

12. After selecting Auto Link, you will see the screen shown in Figure 9-10, with options for Auto Download, Synchronize Clocks, and Synchronize Location Data. Check Auto Download if you want to automatically send images directly from the camera to the smart device via Bluetooth, after you have marked the images using the Mark for Upload option on the Playback menu, as discussed in Chapter 6. (The other two options are discussed later in this chapter.)

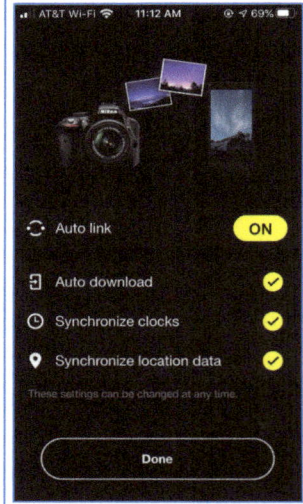

Figure 9-10. Screen in App After Selecting Auto Link

13. On the camera, go to the Network menu and select the Send While Shooting item, which is highlighted in Figure 9-11.

Chapter 9: Wireless Features, Superzoom Lens, and Other Topics | 137

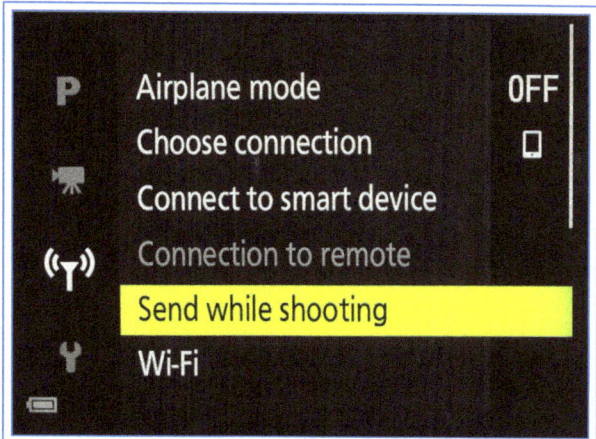

Figure 9-11. Send While Shooting Highlighted on Network Menu

14. On the next screen, shown in Figure 9-12, select Still Images, and set it to On. Then go back to the previous screen and select Upload (Photos). On the next screen, choose whether to upload only single images, all images including every shot in a burst, or just the key frames from bursts.

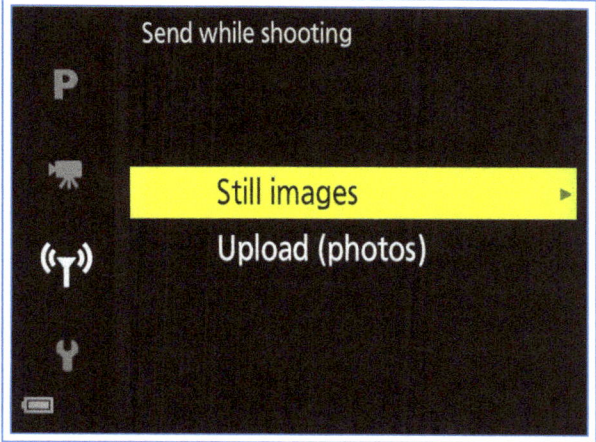

Figure 9-12. Still Images Selected for Send While Shooting

15. On the Network menu, go to the second screen, select Bluetooth and make sure Connection is set to Enable, and set Send While Off to On if you want the camera to continue sending images via Bluetooth even when it is turned off.

16. With the above settings, the camera will start sending images to the connected smart device as soon as they are captured. It may take a while, up to several minutes, for an image to appear on the smart device.

If, instead of sending images to a smart device as they are captured, you want to send images that were previously captured, including larger images and movies (which cannot be sent via Bluetooth), you need to use a different process, which is based on a Wi-Fi connection. The steps for that process are set forth below.

1. With the SnapBridge app installed and activated and the camera turned on, select the Download Pictures item on the app's screen, as shown in Figure 9-9. The app will prompt you to establish a Wi-Fi connection with the camera. Follow the prompts in the app to do so.

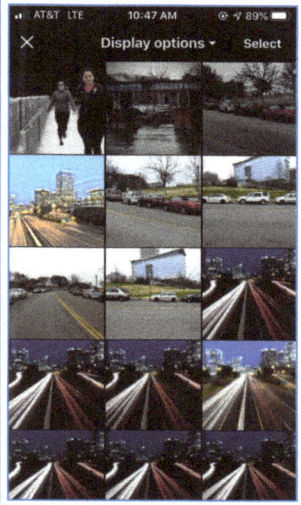

Figure 9-13. App Screen Showing Images for Downloading

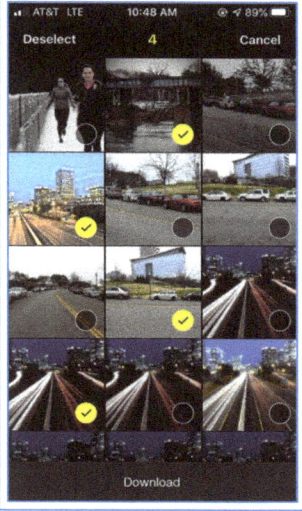

Figure 9-14. App Screen with Images Selected to Download

2. The app will display a screen showing images from the camera, as in Figure 9-13. If you press the Select label in the upper right corner of the app's screen, you can then select the images to download by tapping on them to place a check mark in a yellow circle on each image to download, as shown

in Figure 9-14. Then click on the Download label at the bottom of the screen.

3. The camera will display a screen with choices for the size of the images to download. The choices are two megapixels or original size, as shown in Figure 9-15.

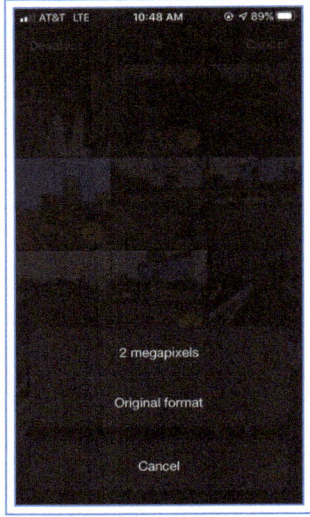

Figure 9-15. App Screen to Select Size of Downloaded Images

4. The downloaded images and videos will appear in the normal area for photos on the smart device. To play a downloaded movie, use the smart device's photo and video viewing app.

REMOTE CONTROL OF CAMERA USING SNAPBRIDGE APP

To control the camera remotely from a smartphone or tablet, follow the steps set forth below. These steps assume that you have previously paired the camera with the smart device, as set forth in the steps above.

1. Turn on the P950 camera in the shooting mode you want to use, with the camera set on a tripod or other support, aiming at the subject you want to shoot.

2. With the SnapBridge app activated, select the camera tab at the top left of the app's main screen. You will then see the screen shown in Figure 9-9, with choices for Auto Link, Download Pictures, and Remote Photography.

3. Select Remote Photography, and the smart device will display a message saying Wi-Fi has been enabled on the camera, and announcing that the app is establishing a Wi-Fi connection to the camera. After a few seconds and some other notices, the app should display a screen like that in Figure 9-16, showing the view through the camera's lens, with a number of control icons. The camera's display will be blank, except for the word "Connected" and a few icons.

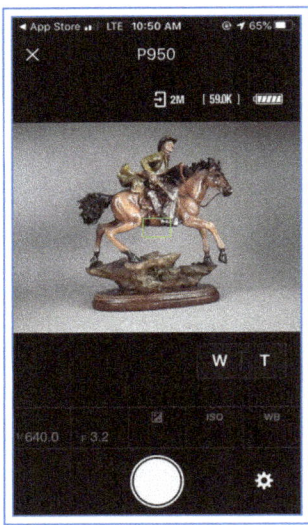

Figure 9-16. App Screen for Remote Control of Camera

4. On this screen in the app, you can use the control icons to capture still images. You can zoom the lens in and out with the T and W buttons at the lower right of the live view, and take a picture with the large white shutter button icon in the lower middle. The app will display current settings for shutter speed, aperture, exposure compensation, ISO, and white balance, but you cannot adjust those settings from the app, or from the camera during remote shooting. Somewhat oddly, you can take a still picture by pressing the large white icon even when the camera is in Movie Manual mode, something you cannot do when the camera is operating on its own.

5. Tap the gear icon at the lower right to open the Camera Settings screen. On that screen, you can choose whether to download images automatically to the smart device after shooting; the download size; and the self-timer. You also can turn off the live view through the camera's lens, though I can't imagine why you would do that.

ADDING LOCATION DATA TO IMAGES

You also can cause a connected smart device to upload location data for your images to the camera. To enable this function, follow the steps below. These steps assume that you previously paired the camera and the smart device using the steps outlined earlier in this chapter.

1. On the camera, go to screen 4 of the Setup menu, select Location Data, then go to the next screen and turn on Record Location Data, as shown in Figure 9-17.

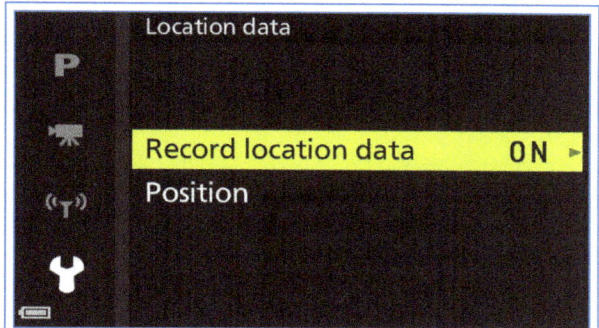

Figure 9-17. Record Location Data Turned On in Camera

2. In the SnapBridge app, on the camera tab screen, select Auto Link.

3. On the next screen, turn on the Synchronize Location Data option, as shown earlier in Figure 9-10.

4. To synchronize date and time information between the camera and the smart device, choose the Synchronize Clocks option on the same screen.

5. Once those settings are in place, images you take with the camera will have location information sent to them from the connected smart device. The information can be viewed in software that reads the metadata for digital images, including Adobe Bridge and Nikon ViewNX-i.

6. For example, Figure 9-18 shows the location information from an image taken using this setup, displayed in Adobe Bridge CC software. Images with location information recorded will display a small GPS satellite icon in the lower left corner when displayed in the camera, as shown in Figure 9-19.

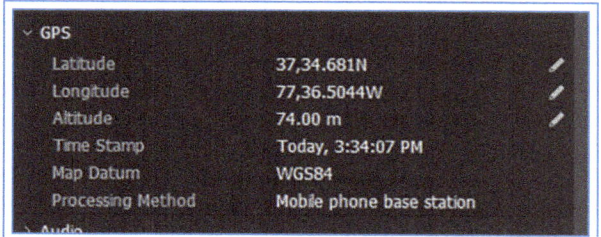

Figure 9-18. Location Information Displayed in Adobe Bridge

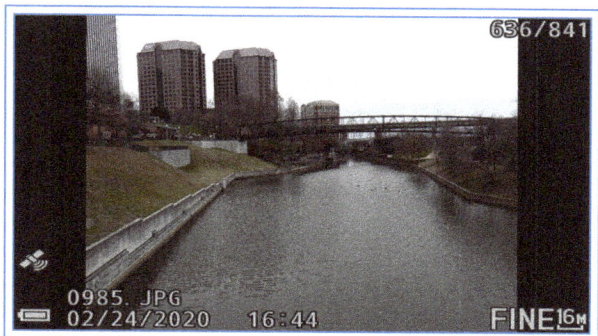

Figure 9-19. Satellite Icon on Image Displayed in Camera

Summary of Options for Transferring Images and Movies to a Smart Device Wirelessly

I found it confusing at first to understand the various options for uploading images and movies to a smartphone or tablet wirelessly, so I have put together a brief summary:

All of the options below assume that the camera has been paired with the smart device by Bluetooth using the SnapBridge app.

To have JPEG still images (not Raw files or movies) sent automatically to a smart device while shooting, on the camera's Network menu, select the Send While Shooting option and choose Yes for Still Images. Using the Upload (Photos) option under that menu item, you can further specify whether to upload only single images, or to include all burst photos, or just the key frames for bursts of photos.

If you have not turned on the Send While Shooting option, you can still have the camera upload JPEG still images automatically to a smart device through the paired connection. To do that, go to the Mark for Upload option on the Playback menu, and select the images you want to have uploaded, as discussed in Chapter 6. The selected images will then be uploaded to the smart device, if you have activated the Auto Link/Auto Download option in the SnapBridge app.

If you have not turned on Send While Shooting and have not marked any images with the Mark for Upload option, you can still upload JPEG (not Raw) images, as well as movies, to a smart device. To do this, go to the SnapBridge app, select the Camera tab at the top left of the screen, and, on the app's main screen, select

Download Pictures. In the dialog box that appears, asking if you want to switch to Wi-Fi, select OK.

Follow the prompts in the app until you see the screen in Figure 9-13. At the top right of the screen, choose the Select option. You should then see thumbnails of all images and movies on the camera's memory card. It may take a long time to load them. When the images are loaded, tap on one or more thumbnails to mark them with check marks, then select Download at the bottom of the app's screen.

Network Menu

The Coolpix P950 has a special menu with several options for controlling the camera's wireless functions. That menu is represented by the wireless network icon, which is highlighted in Figure 9-20.

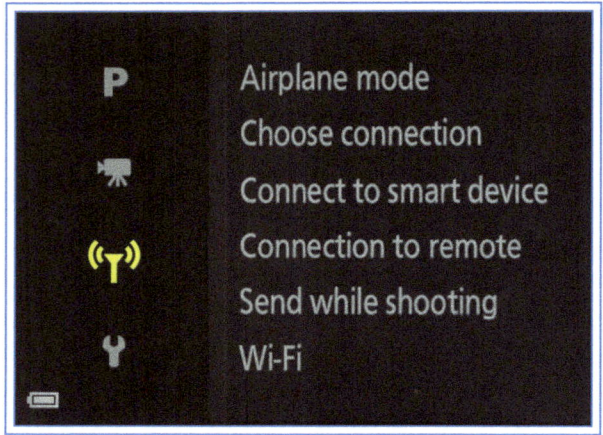

Figure 9-20. Network Menu Icon Highlighted at Left

Once you have highlighted that icon, press the Right button to move the highlight into the list of options on the first screen of the menu, as shown in figure 9-21. I will discuss these menu options in order.

Airplane Mode

This first option gives you a quick way to disable all wireless connections with the camera, including both Bluetooth and Wi-Fi. As the name implies, you can use this menu item when you are on an airplane and need to disable wireless devices. The constant connection between the camera and a smart device will be interrupted, but it will be automatically re-established when you later turn Airplane Mode back off. As noted in Chapter 7, you cannot use the Format Card option when the camera has a wireless connection active. You can use the Airplane Mode option to disable that connection temporarily if you need to format a memory card.

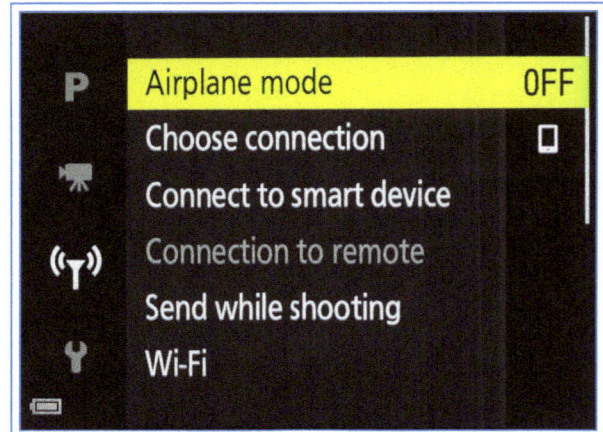

Figure 9-21. Screen 1 of Network Menu

Choose Connection

This next option on the Network menu is for use when you connect the P950 camera with a smartphone or tablet, as discussed earlier in this chapter, or with Nikon's ML-L7 Remote Control, available as a separate option, with which you can control the camera via a Bluetooth connection. You cannot have a smart device and the ML-L7 remote connected to the camera at the same time, so this menu option is provided to let you choose which one to connect. I will discuss that remote control device in Appendix A.

Connect to Smart Device

I discussed this option earlier, in describing the steps for setting up a connection between the camera and a smartphone or tablet. This option will not be available for selection unless the Choose Connection option, discussed immediately above, is set to Smart Device, and the Connection item under the Bluetooth menu option is set to Enable.

Connection to Remote

This option is for use in connecting the P950 camera with the optional Nikon ML-L7 Remote Control. To make that connection, first, set the Choose Connection option, discussed above, to Remote Control. Then select the Connection to Remote option. Once this option is activated, the camera waits to pair with the ML-L7 remote. On that device, press and hold the power button for three seconds or more. Once pairing takes place, you can control several functions of the camera from the remote. See Appendix A for more information.

SEND WHILE SHOOTING

This option, discussed earlier in this chapter, lets you specify what new images, if any, will be automatically uploaded to a smartphone or tablet that is connected to the camera through a Bluetooth connection. This menu item has two sub-options: Still Images and Upload (Photos). The Still Images option can be set to either Yes or No. If you choose No, then no images will be uploaded automatically while you are shooting. In that case, you can use the Mark for Upload option on the Playback menu to mark images to be uploaded automatically from the camera using the SnapBridge app. You also can use the Download Pictures option on the Camera tab in the SnapBridge app to transfer pictures to the smart device later.

If you choose Yes for the Still Images option under the Send While Shooting menu item, you can go to the Upload (Photos) item and choose what types of still images will be automatically uploaded to the connected device: only individual still images; all still images, including ones taken in a burst of continuous shooting; or only key frames from continuous bursts of shots.

Essentially, the Send While Shooting menu option gives you a way to limit the items that are automatically transferred to a smart device when the camera is connected by Bluetooth to such a device. Note that movies cannot be transferred using the Bluetooth connection; they can only be transferred through a Wi-Fi connection using the SnapBridge app.

WI-FI

This next option on the Network menu lets you control the settings the camera uses for establishing a Wi-Fi network to connect to a smart device. As discussed earlier, you can connect the camera to a smart device over a Bluetooth connection that can remain active as you shoot, letting the camera automatically upload still images to the device. However, if you want to upload movies or large volumes of still images, or if you want to control the camera remotely using the smart device, you need to have the camera establish a Wi-Fi network that the device can connect to. Use the settings under this menu option to assist in making that connection.

The first sub-option, Network Settings, is dimmed and unavailable when a wireless connection to a smartphone or tablet is active. To get access to this menu option, you can choose the next menu option, Bluetooth, and then select Connection/Disable to disable the current connection. (You can re-enable it once you have finished using the Network Settings menu option.)

Using the Network Settings item's various sub-options, you can change the SSID (identifying name) of the camera's Wi-Fi network (the default is a name such as P950_30000661); the encryption standard (the default is WPA2-PSK-AES); the password of the network (the default is Nikon_P950); the channel (the default is 6); the subnet mask (the default is 255.255.255.0); and the DHCP server's IP address (the default is 192.168.0.10).I have not found a need to change any of these items, but you may want to change the password or SSID of the network to enhance security in some circumstances.

The Current Settings option under the Wi-Fi item displays the settings that have been established with the Network Settings item.

BLUETOOTH

This next menu item, at the top of the second screen of the Network menu, lets you control how the camera's Bluetooth connection operates. The three sub-options are Connection, Paired Devices, and Send While Off. With the first option, you can choose either Enable or Disable for the current connection. So, if you have paired the camera with a smartphone or tablet using the Bluetooth capability, you can temporarily disable it with this option. You can re-enable it at any time by selecting the Enable option.

The Paired Devices item displays the identification of any device that is currently paired with the camera via Bluetooth. You can use this option to verify that the Bluetooth connection was successfully made (or that a connection was successfully terminated).

The Send While Off option lets you specify whether or not the camera maintains its Bluetooth connection with a smart device while the camera is turned off or in standby mode. If you select On for this option, then the connection stays on when the camera is off, so images can continue to be uploaded. If you want to conserve battery power, you can set this option to Off. In that case, the camera will still upload images to the smart device, but only while the camera remains powered on and active.

RESTORE DEFAULT SETTINGS

This final option on the Network menu lets you reset all wireless settings to their original factory values. This can be useful if you are having problems getting the camera to connect to a smartphone or tablet and you want to get a fresh start with the original settings. This option cannot be selected while a wireless connection is active. You can choose Bluetooth/Connection/Disable to disable a connection so this menu item can be used.

Using the Superzoom Lens

Probably the outstanding feature of the Coolpix P950 is its lens, which has an amazing range of focal lengths, at both the wide-angle and telephoto ends of its zoom. The focal length of a lens determines the width of its view of a scene and the power of its magnification of the view.

A "normal" lens—used for everyday shooting of family scenes, portraits, and the like—is often considered to be a 50mm lens. A "wide-angle" lens is in the range of 35mm or lower, and a "telephoto" lens is one with a focal length of 100mm or greater. The P950, of course, has a zoom lens, which means it can change its focal length. The focal lengths of this lens range from a very wide 24mm to an astounding 2000mm at the telephoto end, for an overall range of 83.3 times optical zoom. (None of this discussion will involve digital zoom, which is not a "real" zoom capability, as discussed in Chapter 7.)

Of course, there are trade-offs for having this zoom range. It is not possible to provide the same quality in a zoom lens of this type as in lenses used by professional photographers at major sporting events, for example. A good Nikon zoom lens for a DSLR can easily cost more than $1,000, and a top-quality telephoto (non-zoom) lens can cost more than $10,000. However, for everyday photography, the P950 provides you with the ability to capture scenes with an array of focal lengths that is practically unmatched in the world of consumer cameras.

At the wide-angle end, the P950's lens gives you several millimeters more than most cameras in its class. A wide-angle range starting at 28mm is often considered quite adequate, and relatively few compact digital cameras offer a zoom range starting as low as 24mm.

The 24mm focal length of the P950 is very useful when you need to photograph a large group of people without standing back a great distance. Also, if you need to photograph the interiors of rooms, this focal length is a great bonus, because you will likely be able to capture an excellent view of the entire room by standing in one corner.

But the telephoto power of its lens is the P950's most dramatic feature, so I will concentrate on its use.

First, the P950's powerful zoom lens captures details you cannot see with the naked eye. For example, Figure 9-22 is a shot I took of a downtown landscape with the lens at its 24mm wide-angle setting. In this image, you can see several buildings, including, if you look closely, one whose top extension is directly in the middle of the image.

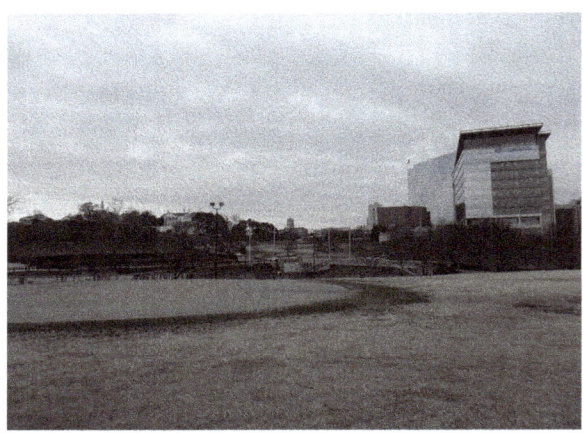

Figure 9-22. View of Scene with 24mm Focal Length

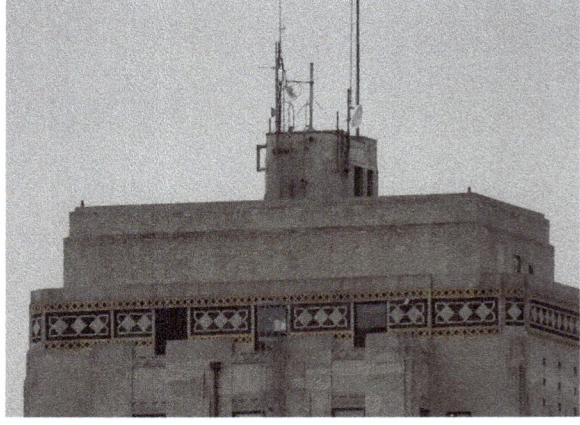

Figure 9-23. View of Scene with 2000mm Focal Length

Now, look at Figure 9-23, taken at the same time and place as the wide-angle shot. This time, the lens was zoomed in to the full 2000mm extent of the optical zoom. In this image, you can clearly see considerable detail at the top of the building in the middle of the first image. This shot includes a level of detail that is not even hinted at in the first image.

When you use the Coolpix P950's powerful zoom lens at its higher settings, you will encounter some issues that you should take into account when deciding whether to rely on the long reach of the lens rather than trying to get closer to your subject.

Figure 9-24. Illustration of Compression of Atmosphere from Long Zoom

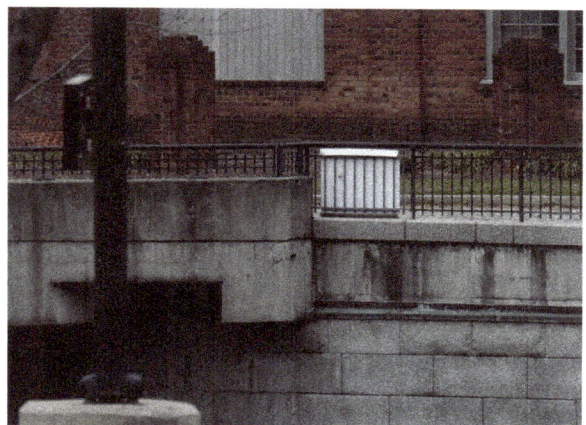

Figure 9-25. Illustration of Flattening of Subjects from Long Zoom

For one thing, as you can see from Figure 9-24 (a telephoto view of a distant water tower), images shot at a long zoom range can suffer from the compression of the atmosphere. In other words, you're shooting through a lot of air, which can add a foggy aura to the image, especially on a hot or hazy day. In this view, the subject appears somewhat faded because of the great distance from the lens and the heat of the day.

In this image, there is a definite haziness caused by the density of the atmosphere between the camera's lens and the subject. (This image was not taken by the P950, and is used just to illustrate the point.)

Figure 9-25, taken by the P950 at the long zoom range of 550mm, illustrates another phenomenon— flattening or foreshortening of the objects you are photographing.

The result of using such a powerful zoom in this case is that objects at different distances from the lens are compressed into a single level, so that it looks as if they are located close to each other, even though they are widely separated in reality.

However, you very well may find good uses for this effect, which can give a distinctive look to your photos.

Another positive aspect of the super-long zoom range is its ability to isolate a single subject. If you use the zoom to focus on a particular person in a crowd or on a particular animal in a pack, you can fill the frame with that single subject, thereby limiting extraneous objects and emphasizing the subject you want to concentrate on. Another advantage can be the ability to take a photo of a subject from a distance without disturbing him, as was the case with Figure 9-26.

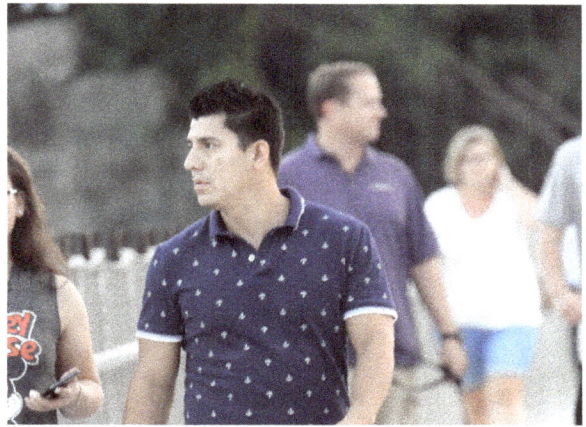

Figure 9-26. Isolation of Subject Using Long Zoom

I wanted to get a picture of this man in the foreground, making it clear that he is the subject, even though he is surrounded by other people. Using the zoom lens at 1500mm, I took this shot from a considerable distance, which isolated him from the people he was walking with and resulted in an image with a nicely blurred background.

Another benefit from using the P950's zoom lens in its telephoto range is that, when the lens is zoomed in, it has a very shallow depth of field. As a result, when you take a picture at the long end of the zoom range, particularly when the lens is fairly close to the subject, the background will be blurred to the point of becoming indistinct. This effect, often called "bokeh," as discussed in Chapter 3, can reduce distractions from the background and emphasize the primary subject in the foreground.

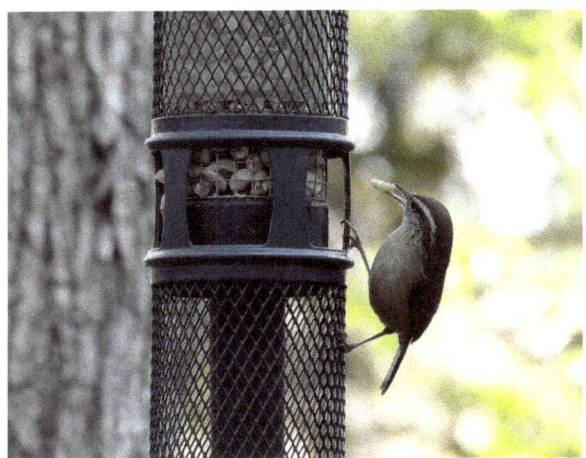

Figure 9-27. Illustration of Blurred Background from Long Zoom

This was the case with Figure 9-27, in which I took a shot of a bird on our backyard feeder with the lens zoomed in to a focal length of 650mm, which blurred the tree and bushes in the distance, resulting in a pleasant and undistracting background. In this case, I was too close to the subject to use the full range of the zoom lens, but the 650mm zoom was sufficient to create substantial blurring of the background, especially because I was fairly close to the subject.

Beyond the specific advantages from the long reach of the zoom lens, perhaps the greatest overall benefit of the superzoom lens on the Coolpix P950 is that it gives you the equivalent of a whole range of focal lengths without the need to carry around a bag filled with heavy lenses. In practical terms, with the P950 you have at your fingertips every focal length that a photographer could reasonably want or need for everyday photography, ranging from the wide-angle 24mm with a strong macro capability to the super 2000mm telephoto.

If you have an opportunity to go on a safari or a cruise around the world and you want to be able to bring back a complete photographic record of your trip using one lightweight, easy-to-use camera, the P950 can fill the bill very nicely.

One major problem that comes along with a superzoom capability is image blur caused by camera movement. When the lens is zoomed in to its full 2000mm focal length or anywhere close to that range, any motion of the camera is multiplied because of the magnification of the image. You will notice how jittery the image looks on the display, and it will be hard to keep the picture steady.

There are several steps you can take to reduce the effects of camera movement. First, if possible, use a tripod. It can be inconvenient to do, but using a solid tripod is one of the best ways to ensure high-quality images. If you can't manage a full-blown tripod, use a lightweight travel tripod, a monopod, or any support available, such as a fence post, or just sit on a bench and hold the camera steady on your lap, folding the LCD display up toward your face to view the image.

Suppose, though, that you are walking through a field in search of wildlife shots and there is no physical support available. There are several things you can do to minimize the effects of camera shake. First, make sure the Vibration Reduction feature is turned on through the Setup menu. This system counteracts camera movement quite effectively, up to a point. As is discussed in Chapter 4, I recommend you use the Normal setting for most situations, but consider using the Active setting if you are shooting in a turbulent environment. Also, you may find you can hold the camera steadier if you use the electronic viewfinder, so you can hold the camera against your forehead and look into that window, rather than using the LCD display at some distance from your face.

Next, use the fastest shutter speed you can. If the shutter is open for only a brief instant, there will not be time for camera motion to register on the image. According to one rule of thumb, when handholding a zoom lens you should use a shutter speed no slower than the fraction of a second with the focal length of the lens as the denominator. So, if the lens of the P950 is zoomed all the way in to 2000mm, you would use a shutter speed of 1/2000 second or faster. In the case of the P950, the choices would be 1/2000 or 1/2500, because the speeds faster than that are not available when the lens is zoomed all the way in.

If you want to control the shutter speed, you should use Shutter Priority as your shooting mode, as discussed in Chapter 3. You also could use Manual mode, if you are willing to accept the added task of setting the aperture correctly. Or, if you use Program mode, you can let the camera set the shutter speed and aperture initially, and then use the flexible program feature, which lets you turn the command dial to select new combinations of shutter speed and aperture that are equivalent to what the camera selected.

However, you are likely to run into a problem if you use the camera's standard settings and try to set a fast shutter speed. One of the limiting characteristics of the superzoom lens on the P950 is that, as was discussed in Chapter 3, its maximum aperture when zoomed in is quite narrow. When the lens is zoomed all the way out to wide-angle, the maximum (widest open) aperture is f/2.8, which is not exceptionally wide to start with, though it is wide enough for most purposes. But, when the lens is zoomed in, it rapidly loses the ability to use a wide aperture.

When the lens is zoomed all the way in, the maximum aperture is f/6.5. In order to use a shutter speed of 1/2000 second or faster at that rather narrow aperture, there will have to be a good deal of light, unless you change some other settings.

Your best option probably is to increase the ISO sensitivity of the camera, which will mean that the camera's image sensor will require less light to expose the picture, at the risk of increased visual noise in the image. Using the ISO Sensitivity setting in the Shooting menu, you may want to try setting ISO to A3200, in which case the camera will set the value as high as 3200 if conditions warrant. If you want to be sure a high ISO is set, you should use a specific level, such as ISO 800, ISO 1600, or even ISO 3200. I don't recommend using ISO 6400 unless absolutely necessary, because of the noise that likely will appear in your images.

If you prefer not to boost the ISO, one approach you can use is to zoom out until the camera can use a wider aperture, such as, say, f/5.0 or f/4.5, so more light is let into the lens. Later on, when editing your photos, you can crop them to achieve the same field of view you originally saw with the zoomed-in lens, though with some loss of quality because of the cropping.

Another tactic for getting good, clear images with the superzoom lens is to take advantage of the P950's continuous-shooting options. With several of these options, the camera will take multiple shots in rapid succession, increasing the likelihood that one or more shots will be usable. You also will experience a decline in image size and quality with some of these settings, though, so you need to consider the balancing factors.

Along the same lines, you might consider recording a sequence at a long distance using the camera's 4K video capability in Movie Manual mode, using a fast shutter speed to avoid motion blur, and then extract one or more of the best frames from that sequence. At a resolution of about 8 megapixels, those single frames may be of excellent quality.

One more note: Don't forget that the Coolpix P950 offers the very useful U slot on the mode dial, for User Settings. If you use the lens zoomed in frequently, you may want to save your preferred settings for those occasions, so you can quickly call them up just by turning the mode dial to the U setting. For example, you may want to set up the camera in Shutter Priority mode, with the lens zoomed all the way in, with a shutter speed of 1/2000 second, with an ISO setting of 1600 and with continuous shooting enabled.

Next, I recommend that you take advantage of the side zoom control on the P950—the switch on the left side of the camera, below the flash pop-up button. As discussed in Chapter 5, with its default function as an alternative to the zoom lever around the shutter button, this switch can help you hold the camera more firmly in both hands. If you zoom with the left-side switch, you can use your right hand to keep a tight grip on the right side of the camera without having to reach up to use the zoom lever.

Finally, you can use the snap-back zoom button to assist with long-telephoto shots. You can use that control to quickly pull back from a zoomed-in view, so you can get your bearings and see exactly where the subject is in relation to its surroundings, before quickly zooming back in to take the picture. It can be very difficult to locate your subject when the lens is zoomed all the way in to its 2000mm maximum; use the snap-back zoom to get the wider view quickly when you need it for orientation.

Macro (Close-up) Photography

Macro photography is the art or science of taking photographs when the subject is shown at actual size (1:1 ratio between size of subject and size of image) or magnified (greater than 1:1 ratio). So if you photograph a flower using macro techniques, the image of the flower on the image sensor may be about the same size as the actual flower. You can get wonderful detail in your images using macro photography, and you may discover things about the subject that you had not noticed before taking the photograph.

The P950 is quite capable of shooting macro photographs. For Figure 9-28, I took a shot from close to the minimum focusing distance of the camera, setting a knight figurine about one inch (2.54 cm) away from the lens and setting the focus mode to macro autofocus. I set the focal length to 30mm, which is within the range at which the closest focusing is possible. The camera focused sharply on the subject.

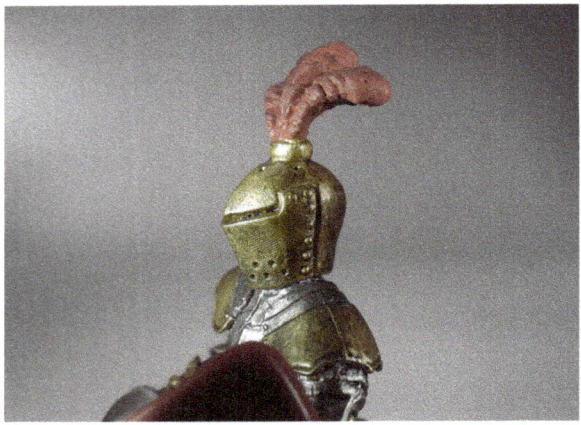

Figure 9-28. Macro Shot Using Macro Autofocus Setting

As discussed in Chapter 5, to activate macro focus, set the focus mode selector to AF, press the Down button to bring up the focus mode menu, then use the Up and Down buttons, the command dial, or the multi selector dial to select the flower icon indicating macro autofocus mode, as shown in Figure 9-29.

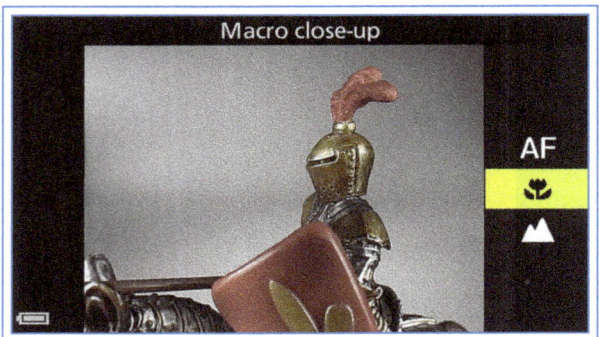

Figure 9-29. Macro Autofocus Selected on Menu

You can choose macro autofocus in Auto mode or in the Program, Aperture Priority, Shutter Priority, or Manual exposure mode, as well as the following Scene mode settings: Beach, Snow, Pet Portrait, and Selective Color. With the Close-up and Food settings, macro focus is selected automatically. Macro focus is available for selection with all settings of the Creative and Movie Manual shooting modes.

With the autofocus mode set to macro, the Coolpix P950 is able to focus as close as 0.4 inch (1 centimeter) when the lens is zoomed out to the wide-angle position or close to that position. The range for which the closest focus is available is indicated on the zoom scale by a small triangle icon, as shown in Figure 9-30.

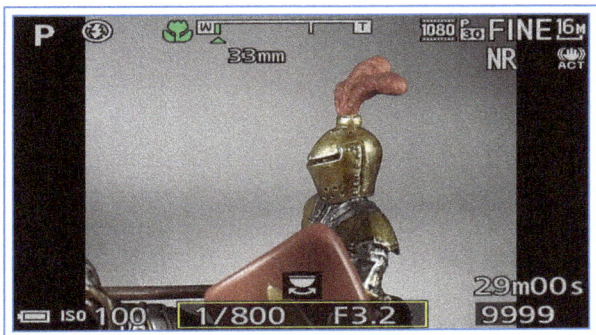

Figure 9-30. Zoom Scale at Point for Closest Macro Shots

When the bar of the zoom scale does not extend past the center of that triangle, the lens can focus down to this minimum distance. Once the zoom bar goes past the triangle, the lens can focus as close as four inches (10 centimeters), as long as the zoom bar stays green. In Figure 9-31, the zoom bar extends as far to the right as possible before it turns white, indicating the end of the macro focus range. When the lens is zoomed in to its full telephoto position in macro autofocus mode, it can focus only as close as 16 feet 5 inches (5 meters).

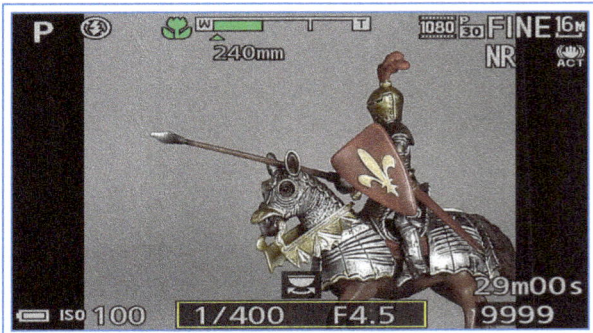

Figure 9-31. Zoom Scale at End of Macro Focus Range

With normal autofocus, the camera can focus as close as about 1 foot 8 inches (50 cm) at the wide-angle position, and as close as about 16 feet 5 inches (5 meters) at the full telephoto position.

If you don't want to have to fine-tune the zoom position to set macro focusing as close as possible, there are two easier methods. First, you can use the Close-up setting in Scene mode (with the Single Shot option). The camera will adjust for the closest possible macro shooting, setting the focus and the zoom position. It also will turn on continuous autofocus and set the AF Area Mode to Manual, so you can adjust the position of the focus frame on the screen. To move the frame, press the OK button and then use the direction buttons or turn the multi selector dial to adjust the frame's position. Press OK to anchor it in place.

Another possibility for close-up focusing is to select the Food setting within Scene mode. This setting is similar to Close-up, except that it adds an adjustment slider so you can fine-tune the hues of the foods (or other items) you are photographing.

You don't have to use the macro autofocus setting or one of the Scene mode settings to take macro shots. If you set the camera to manual focus by turning the focus mode selector to the MF position, you can focus on objects very close to the lens using the side dial. It can be tricky finding the correct focus manually, but you can press the Right button to use autofocus also. In addition, the camera enlarges the view on the screen when manual focus is in use, so you may have good success using manual focus for macro shots.

When shooting extreme close-ups, you should use a tripod or other solid stand whenever possible, because the depth of field is very shallow and you need to keep the camera steady to take a usable photograph. It's also a good idea to take advantage of the self-timer or an optional remote control, as discussed in Appendix A. If you take the picture using the self-timer or the remote, you will not be touching the camera when the shutter is activated, so the chance of camera shake is minimized. Another option is to use the camera's Wi-Fi capability to trigger the shutter from a distance using a smartphone or tablet, as discussed earlier in this chapter. You should also leave the built-in flash retracted so it can't fire, unless you have a system for diffusing the flash to avoid harsh shadows and glare.

Infrared Photography

Infrared photography involves recording images illuminated by infrared light, which occupies a place on the spectrum that is beyond our ability to see. In some circumstances, cameras, unlike our eyes, can record images using this type of light. The results can be spectacular, producing scenes in which green foliage appears white and blue skies appear eerily dark.

Shooting infrared in pre-digital times involved selecting an infrared film and the appropriate filter to place on the lens. With the rise of digital imaging, you need to find a camera that is capable of "seeing" infrared light. Many cameras nowadays include internal filters that block infrared light. However, some cameras do not, or block it only to a relatively small extent. (You can do a quick test of any digital camera by aiming it at the light-emitting end of an infrared remote control while pressing a button on the remote; if the remote's light shows up in the camera as bright white, the camera can "see" infrared light at least to some extent.)

The Coolpix P950 can take good infrared photographs. In order to unleash this capability, you need to get a filter that blocks most visible light, but lets infrared light reach the camera's light sensor. (If you don't, the infrared light will be overwhelmed by the visible light, and you'll get an ordinary, non-infrared picture.) The P950's lens is threaded to accept filters with a screw-in diameter of 67mm. The filter I use most often is the Hoya R72, which is a very dark red and blocks most visible light, letting in mainly infrared light rays in a part of the spectrum that produces interesting images. In Figure 9-32, this filter is shown on the lens of the P950.

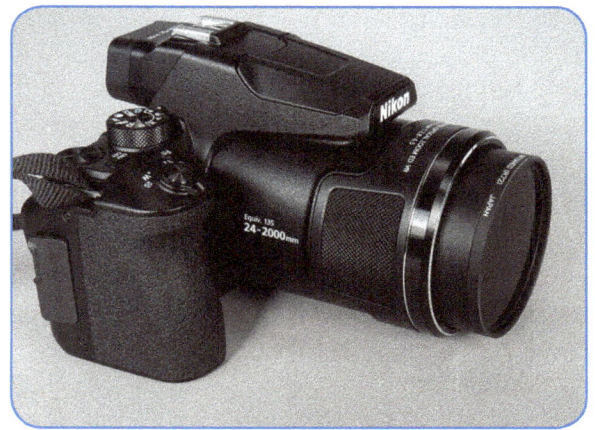

Figure 9-32. Infrared Filter on Coolpix P950 Lens

For the image shown in Figure 9-33, I set a custom white balance, using brightly sunlit green foliage as the base. On the screen for setting a Preset Manual white balance, I aimed the camera at the green foliage and pressed the OK button. For exposure, I set the camera to shoot in Manual exposure mode and experimented with shutter speeds and aperture until I found good settings at f/3.5 and 0.8 second, with ISO set to 400. I set the camera on a tripod and used the three-second self-timer to minimize vibration during the long exposure. The results were essentially what I expected from infrared photography—grass, leaves, and bushes that look white, and other unusual but pleasing effects.

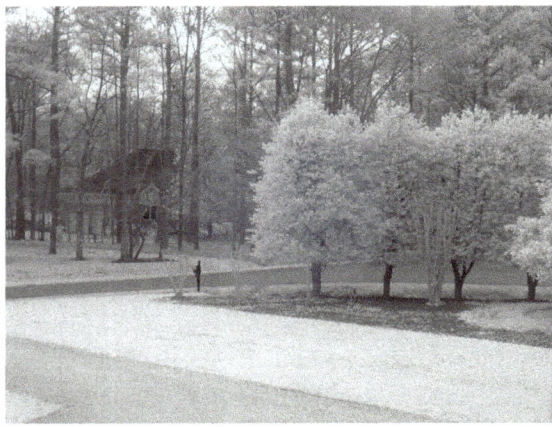

Figure 9-33. Infrared Image

You can often get interesting results if you shoot on a sunny day with a good amount of green grass and trees in the image, as well as blue sky and white clouds. One issue that affects infrared images taken with the P950 is the possibility of a "hot spot" of overexposure, often near the middle of the image. If this problem occurs, you may need to compose the scene with the most important subject matter away from the center, or be prepared to adjust the brightness in the center of the image with editing software.

Street Photography

The Coolpix P950 is not the first camera that would come to mind for street photography—shooting candid pictures in public settings, often without the subject's knowledge. Many cameras that are well-suited for this type of work are small, lightweight, and unobtrusive in appearance, so they can easily be held casually or hidden in the photographer's hand. The P950 is somewhat bulky and not that easily concealed from view. However, it has its good points for this type of photography.

The P950's 24mm wide-angle lens is excellent for taking in a broad field of view, for shooting from the hip without framing the image carefully on the screen. The P950's LCD screen is useful for street photography, because, if you fold it out so it is parallel to the ground, you can look down at the screen to frame your shots without drawing attention to yourself. With this system, I can zoom in on a subject a considerable distance away and keep the framing accurate while looking down at the screen. Also, the camera shoots quickly and performs well at high ISO settings, so you can use a relatively fast shutter speed to avoid motion blur. Options for continuous shooting give you good ways to get sharp images under difficult circumstances. And, you can silence the camera by turning off beeps and shutter sounds through the Setup menu.

As far as the best settings for street photography with the P950 are concerned, I will mention some guidelines as a starting point. The answer depends in part on your style of shooting, such as whether you will talk to your subjects and get their agreement to being photographed, or just fire away from across the street with a zoomed-in lens and accept the risk of blurry photos from camera shake at such a long focal length.

Here are a couple of approaches you can start with and modify as you see fit. Some photographers like to shoot in color at the highest quality and image size and then use post-processing software such as Photoshop or Lightroom to convert their images to black-and-white, along with any other effects they are looking for, such as extra grain to achieve a gritty look. (Of course, you don't have to produce your street photography in black-and-white, but that is a common practice.) I recommend you shoot in Shutter Priority mode at a fairly fast shutter speed, say, 1/100 second or faster, to stop action on the street and to avoid blur from camera movement. You can set ISO to A1600, or possibly use a high ISO setting, in the range of 800 or so, if you don't mind some visual noise. You may want to set the aspect ratio to 16:9 (by selecting an image size of 4608 x 2592 pixels) in order to take in a wide field of view for street scenes. (You could shoot at the maximum image size and crop down to this size, but then you would not have the benefit of seeing the 16:9 aspect ratio on the screen as you compose your shots.)

Another option is to set image quality and size to their highest settings and set the Picture Control feature on the Shooting menu to the Monochrome option. You can use the standard settings for Monochrome, or you can go beyond the standard screen by pressing the Right button, and tweak the settings a bit. For example, you may want to try boosting contrast by one unit and reducing sharpening the same amount. To get the gritty "street" look, you also could try setting the camera's ISO to 1600 or 3200 to include some visual grain in the image while boosting sensitivity enough to stop action with a fast shutter speed.

You also might consider turning the mode dial to the Creative position and choosing one of the offerings from the Noir group of settings, which provide monochrome options with varying degrees of contrast.

Also, consider using continuous shooting so you'll get several images to choose from for each shutter press. For the best combination of quality and speed, choose Continuous H.

For Figure 9-34, I was shooting images on a pedestrian bridge across the river when I saw these two people jogging. I captured this image from a fairly long distance with the lens zoomed in to 650mm.

I generally use normal autofocus for this type of shooting, though some photographers like to use manual focus with the range set for the approximate distance where you expect your subjects to be. If I am shooting at street level, fairly close to my subjects, I often leave the lens zoomed back to its full wide-angle position to maintain a broad depth of field and keep most of the image in focus.

With the P950, you may want to at least experiment with long-range street photography, taking advantage of the superzoom lens. This approach has the advantage of letting you stay at a comfortable distance from your subjects. It has the disadvantage of producing a shallow depth of field, so it is harder to keep the entire scene in focus. Also, you may find that the foreshortening effect of a powerful zoom lens is not the look you are seeking for street photographs. And, you may find it difficult to get really sharp images at a long focal length unless you use a tripod, which limits your options for candid shots. On a bright day, though, or at high ISO settings, you should be able to use a fast enough shutter speed to avoid blur from a shaky camera, even without a tripod.

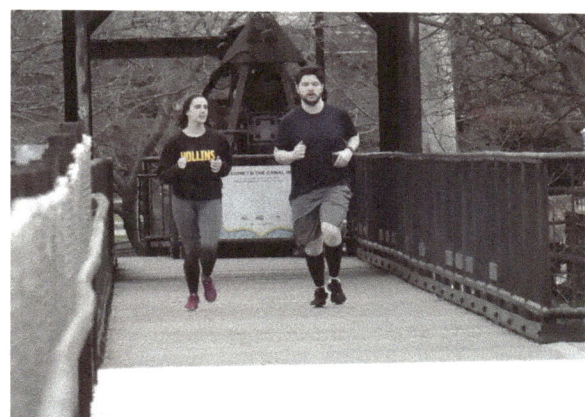

Figure 9-34. Street Photography Example

Connecting to a Television Set

To connect the Coolpix P950 to a television set, you need to purchase an optional HDMI cable and connect the camera to a high-definition set. You can use any cable, as long as one end has a micro-HDMI (type D) male connector, and the other end has a standard HDMI male connector, as shown in Figure 9-35.

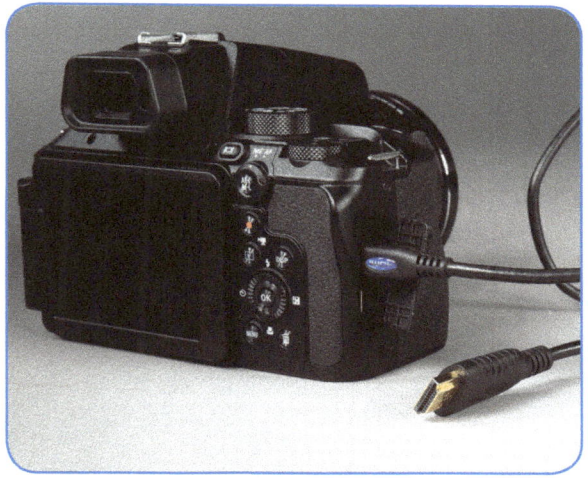

Figure 9-35. Coolpix P950 with HDMI Cable Connected to HDMI Port

Once you have connected the Coolpix P950 to a TV set, the camera operates much the same way it does on its own. Of course, depending on the size and quality of the TV set, you will get a much larger image, possibly better quality (on an HD set), and certainly better sound for your movies.

Also, as discussed in Chapter 8, you can use an HDMI cable to connect the camera's HDMI port to an external monitor or video recorder, to view or record HD video generated by the camera.

Appendix A: Accessories

Cases

There are many types of camera cases on the market. At least for me, there is no "perfect" case for the P950. The type of case I use with this camera depends on what my purpose is for carrying the camera at a given time.

One case that fits the P950 somewhat snugly but has excellent features is the Lowepro Inverse 100 AW, shown in Figure A-1. The upper flap of this case closes securely with its zipper. The case has extra compartments to hold filters, batteries, and other small items. One of its best features is that it has straps on the bottom where you can attach a sturdy tripod—a very useful item when doing long-zoom photography with the P950. It also has flexible outer pouches where you can carry water bottles or other small items.

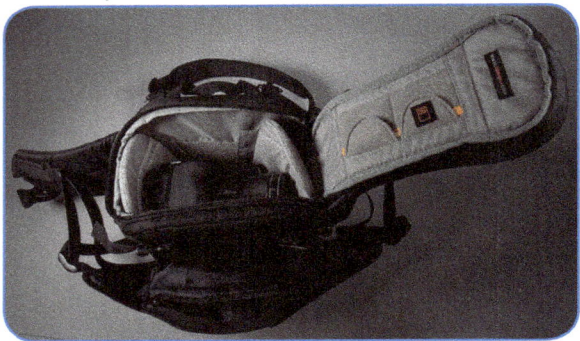

Figure A-1. Lowepro Inverse 100 AW Case with P950

Figure A-2 shows the Lowepro Toploader Zoom 55 AW II, one of many top-loading bags that are available, designed mainly for DSLR cameras with long lenses attached. This model fits the P950 with room to spare. It is intended to hold the camera with the lens pointing downward into the bag, so you can grab the camera body and quickly pull it out to start shooting.

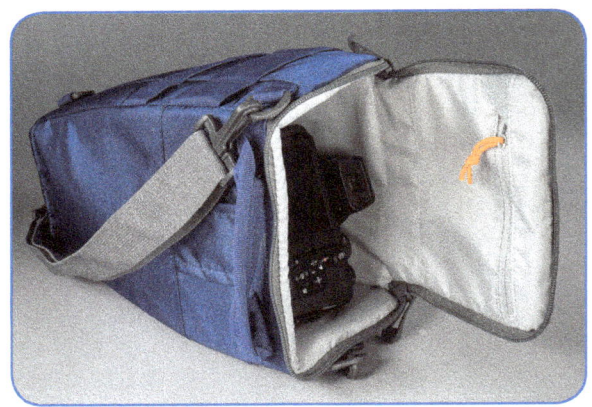

Figure A-2. Lowepro Toploader Zoom 55 AW II Case with P950

Batteries and Chargers

I use the camera heavily, and I find it runs through batteries quickly, especially when Wi-Fi and Bluetooth functions are activated. So, unless you are going to limit yourself to short shooting sessions, you need to have some options available to use the camera beyond the limits of a single charged battery.

One solution is to purchase additional Nikon batteries, model number EN-EL20a, which cost about $50 each as I write this. In order to charge them outside of the camera, you can use the optional Nikon external charger, model Number MH-29, which costs about $39.95 currently.

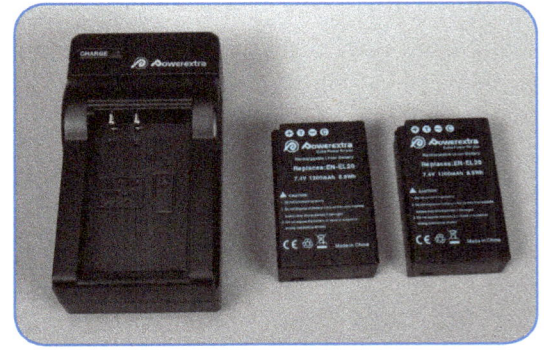

Figure A-3. Generic Battery and External Battery Charger

Appendix A: Accessories

You also can find generic replacement batteries, as well as chargers to charge the batteries outside the camera, inexpensively from Amazon.com and elsewhere. I purchased a package including two generic replacement batteries and a charger for $18.00 from Amazon.com, and the batteries and the charger, shown in Figure A-3, work fine. With this setup, I can have one battery charging while another is in the camera.

Another option is to operate the camera with power from its supplied charger. This system works with the charger that ships with the camera, which is model number EH-73P with my camera. With this system, the camera will operate, but the battery will not be charged. I found that this system also works when using the Nikon charger with a longer, generic micro-USB cable, although, as discussed below, Nikon strongly discourages the use of non-Nikon products for charging the battery or powering the camera.

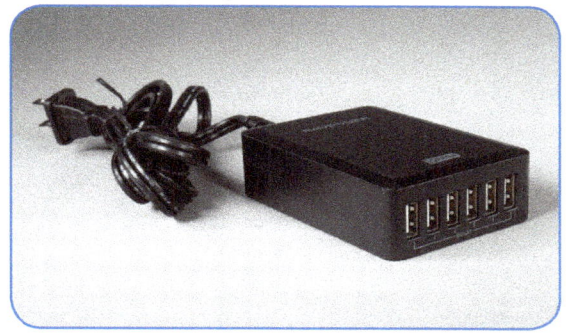

Figure A-4. RavPower 6-Port Desktop USB Charger

This system apparently does not work with non-Nikon chargers. I tried charging the battery with the RavPower 6-Port Desktop USB charger, model number RP-UC10, shown in Figure A-4, and that device did successfully recharge the battery inside the camera while the camera was turned off. However, the camera would not operate when the RavPower device was plugged into the camera's USB port.

Similarly, I tried to recharge the battery with the Mophie PowerStation XL portable USB battery, shown in Figure A-5, while operating the camera. Again, that device recharged the battery, but the camera could not be operated with power coming from that device.

So, if you want to charge the battery while it's in the camera, you can, in theory, use a standard desktop or portable USB charger like those shown here. However, the camera cannot be operated when powered by such a device. Second, and perhaps more important, Nikon issues a stern warning, at page 42 of its user manual, against the use of a "commercially available USB-AC adapter or a battery charger for a mobile phone," saying that "[f]ailure to observe this precaution could result in overheating or damage to the camera."

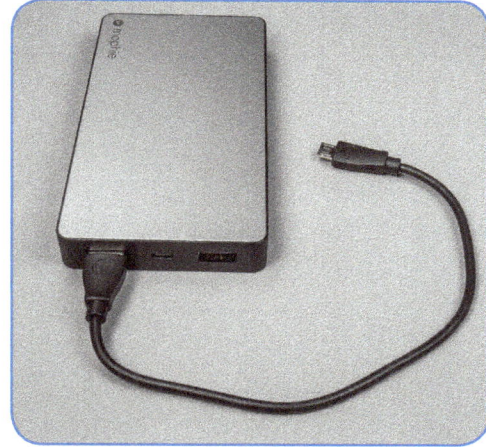

Figure A-5. Mophie PowerStation XL Portable USB Battery

So, although I have found these devices useful for charging the battery while the camera is turned off, I cannot recommend their use, because that use could cause damage and could void your warranty from Nikon.

AC Adapter

If you want to supply power to the camera for operating it over a long period of time, you can use the AC adapter kit, Nikon model number EH-5b, along with the EP-5C Power Connector, shown in Figure A-6. (These are two separate items; I had difficulty locating them, and eventually purchased them from two separate vendors. Nikon lists the model number for the AC adapter as EH-5d in the user manual, but I used one marked with model number EH-5b with no problems.)

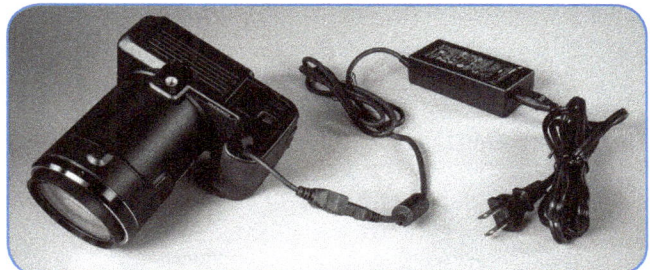

Figure A-6. Nikon EH-5b AC Adapter with EP-5C Power Connector

This pair of accessories provides a constant source of power to the camera. The EH-5b AC adapter includes a standard-sized AC cord that you plug into a power brick and into an AC outlet.

The power brick is attached to a long cable that is then connected to the separate EP-5C Power Connector, which terminates in a plastic piece the same size and shape as the camera's battery. You insert that plastic piece into the battery compartment. Before you close the battery compartment door, you have to pull down a small rubber flap that covers an opening next to the battery compartment door. You then place the cable from the Power Connector into that opening, so you can close the battery compartment door fully, leaving the flap sticking up slightly, as shown in Figure A-7.

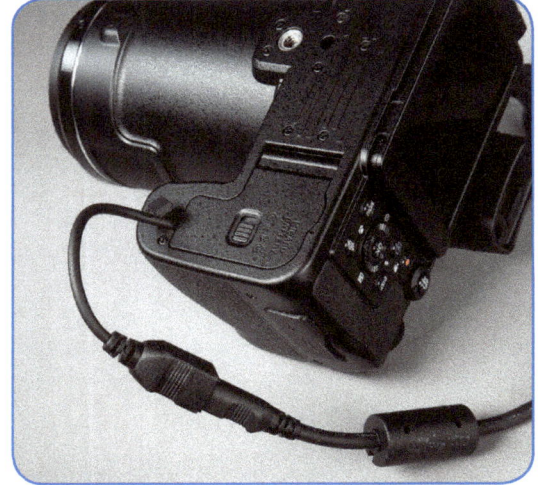

Figure A-7. Cord of AC Adapter Going into P950 Battery Compartment

Providing power to the camera is all this adapter does. It is not a charger, either for batteries outside of the camera or for batteries while they are installed in the camera. It is strictly a power source for the camera. It is useful if you are using the interval timer or working in a studio or laboratory setting, to eliminate the trouble of constantly charging and replacing batteries. It also could be useful if you are recording many images or movie scenes in a setting where you have access to AC power. However, the AC adapter's cables and power brick are bulky, so using the adapter can be inconvenient. If you don't have a real need for this setup, I recommend that you invest in extra batteries, and perhaps an extra battery charger, so you can always have a couple of batteries ready for action.

Remote Controls

As discussed in Chapter 9, you can control the P950 camera remotely from a smartphone or tablet, using the SnapBridge app with the camera's built-in Wi-Fi capability. Nikon also has provided two other options for remote control of the camera, with several available accessories to take advantage of those options.

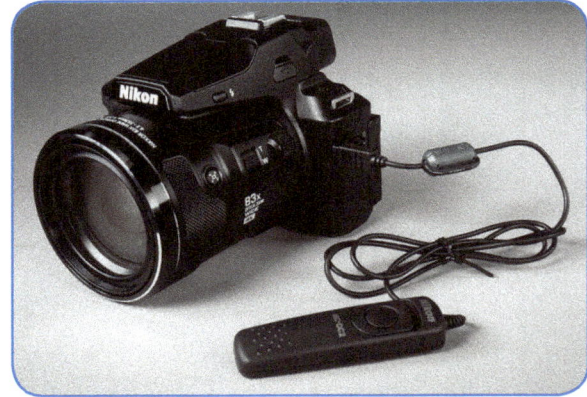

Figure A-8. Nikon MC-DC2 Remote Cord with P950

First, Nikon offers remote control devices that plug into the accessory terminal on the left side of the camera. The MC-DC2 Remote Cord, shown in Figure A-8, is a very simple device. It has a single button that functions as the shutter button, which you can press halfway to evaluate focus and exposure, and press all the way down to capture an image. You also can slide it forward when pressed down, to lock it in place for a Bulb exposure when the camera is in Manual exposure mode.

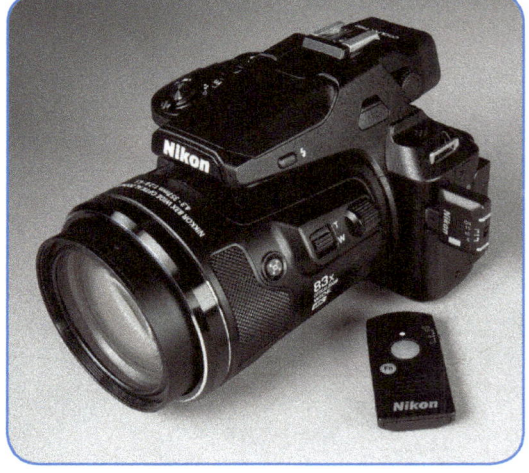

Figure A-9. Nikon WR-T10 and WR-R10 Remote Devices

Next, Nikon sells a pair of devices that work together, the WR-R10 Wireless Remote Controller and the WR-T10 Wireless Remote Controller. The R10 is a small radio receiver that plugs into the accessory terminal on the camera, and the T10 is a comparably small transmitter. Both devices are shown in Figure A-9. Once the devices are set to the same channel and paired, you can control the camera wirelessly using the R10 transmitter, from a distance of up to 164 feet (50 meters). As with the wired remote discussed above, the R10 transmitter provides

Appendix A: Accessories

only a shutter button. (This remote has a Fn button, but that button does not appear to function with the P950 camera, as of this writing. It appears that that button has to be assigned to a function using a menu option that this camera does not have.)

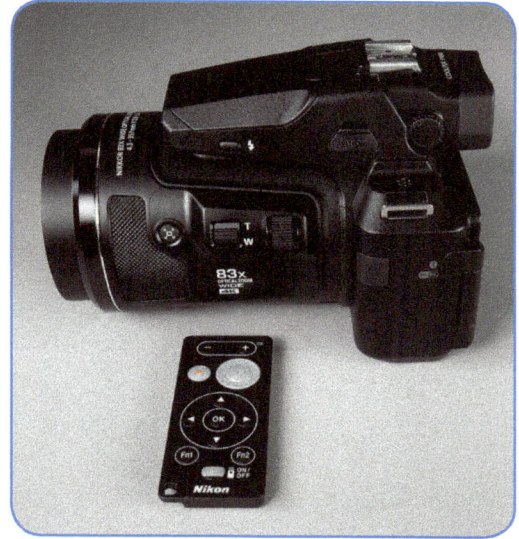

Figure A-10. Nikon ML-L7 Remote Control with P950

The Nikon ML-L7 Remote Control, shown in Figure A-10, which connects to the camera wirelessly via Bluetooth, provides multiple functions, including shutter button, zoom control, movie recording button, and multi selector control, with buttons corresponding to the four direction buttons on the camera, as well as an OK button that lets you apply selections made using the four multi selector buttons. You can use the top and bottom direction buttons to adjust manual focus. The controller also has two function buttons, Fn1 and Fn2, and they can each be assigned to a different option, as discussed below.

To use this control with the P950, on screen 1 of the Network menu go to Choose Connection, and select Remote Control. Then go to the Connection to Remote option on the same menu screen and select it. Then press and hold for three seconds or more the power button on the remote control. A remote control icon will appear in the lower left corner of the camera's screen, as shown in Figure A-11, once the pairing of the device with the camera is successful.

Once the control has been paired with the camera, you can assign the two function buttons on the remote to operate different options on the camera. To do this, for each button, press the button to call up the function menu on the camera, scroll down to the Fn item at the bottom of the list, and choose an option for that button to control, using the multi selector arrows and OK button on the remote control. In this way, you actually can have three function buttons assigned to three different options at the same time: one on the camera itself, and two on the ML-L7 remote control.

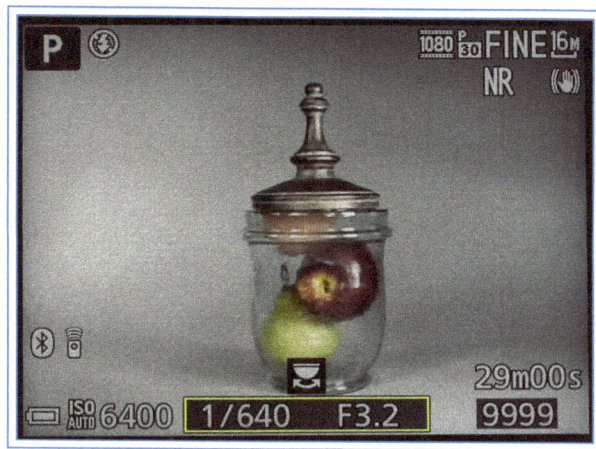

Figure A-11. Icon on Camera Screen When Paired with Remote

This control can communicate with the camera from a distance up to about 33 feet (10 meters), depending on obstacles in the environment.

Dot Sight

Another useful accessory is the Nikon DF-M1 Dot Sight, an item that can be placed in the camera's accessory shoe, as shown in Figure A-12. This item generates a reticle, which is a small, bright, red or green circle with a dot in its center. When you have calibrated the sight properly, you can position the reticle over your subject to help you center it in the camera's view. The sight is intended to be helpful when you are using the lens at telephoto settings.

I have not used the sight extensively, and I find the camera's built-in features, such as snap-back zoom and the special subject-locating frames for Bird-watching and Moon mode, to be adequate for locating subjects. Here is a link to a detailed discussion of the sight by members of the Nikon Coolpix Talk forum at dpreview.com: https://www.dpreview.com/forums/post/61764145.

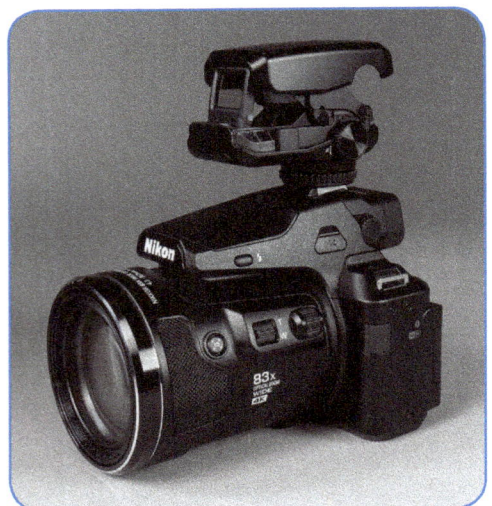

Figure A-12. Nikon DF-M1 Dot Sight on P950

I have also seen discussion of the Olympus EE-1 red dot sight, which may be less expensive than the Nikon version, with similar features. I have not used that device myself.

External Flash

The Coolpix P950, unlike some of the earlier models in the Coolpix line of cameras, is equipped with an accessory shoe where you can install an external flash. According to Nikon, three of its Speedlight flash units are compatible with the P950: the SB-500, the SB-700, and the SB-5000. All three of these units communicate with the camera through the accessory shoe and provide automatic flash exposure control.

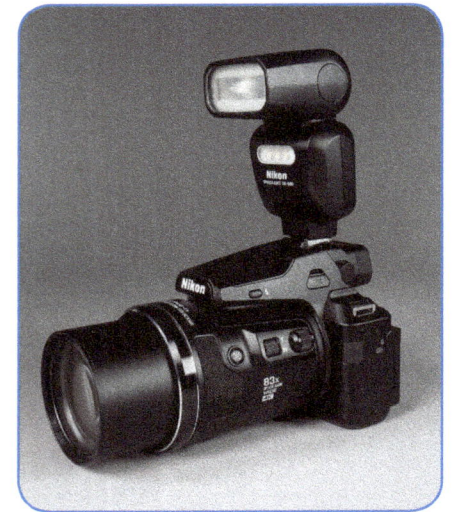

Figure A-13. Nikon Speedlight SB-500 on P950

The SB-500, shown in Figure A-13, is an excellent choice for a basic flash, because of its compact size and good features. It tilts up 90 degrees and swivels from left to right. Besides its flash features, it has a video light mode, which provides a beam of continuous light. However, it is not very powerful and does not have a built-in diffuser.

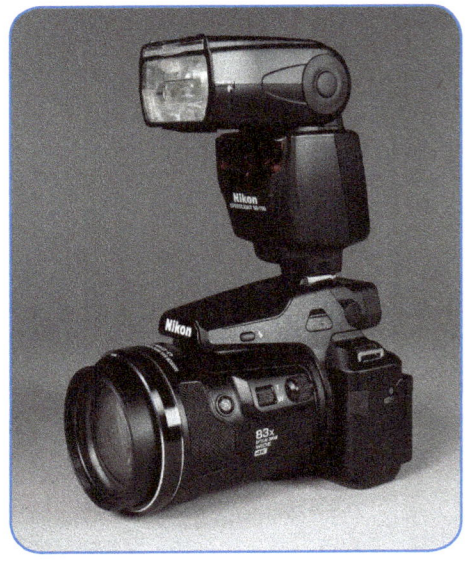

Figure A-14. Nikon Speedlight SB-700 on P950

The SB-700, shown in Figure A-14, is a step up from the SB-500, with greater power and a built-in diffuser. It tilts and swivels like the SB-500, but does not have a video light feature like that model.

The SB-5000, not shown here, is considerably more expensive than the other two models, costing almost twice as much as the SB-700. It offers greater power and more advanced features, including wireless control, but you need to purchase additional equipment to control the flash wirelessly.

There are other flash units available from third-party companies such as Nissin, Godox, and others, that presumably will work with the P950, though I have not tested any of those. I have read that the Godox TT685N works well with the P950, for example.

External Microphones

Another excellent feature of the Coolpix P950 is the external microphone jack, which lets you use the microphone of your choice rather than rely on the built-in microphone. Nikon offers two microphones that are compatible with this camera. First, the ME-1, shown in Figure A-15, is a standard shotgun microphone that attaches to the hot shoe and plugs into the microphone jack. It receives its power from the camera, so it does

Appendix A: Accessories | 155

not need a battery. It comes with a windscreen, shown lying beside the camera in Figure A-15.

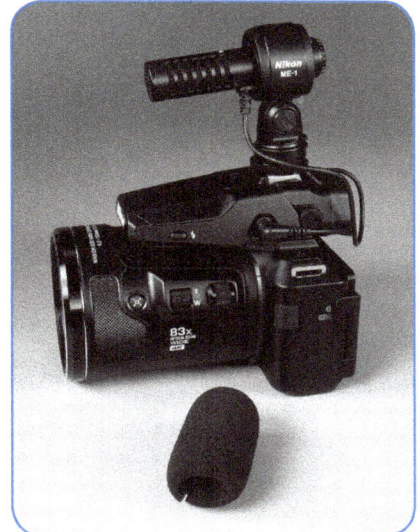

Figure A-15. Nikon ME-1 Microphone on P950

Another option, which offers greater flexibility, is the Nikon ME-W1, which is a wireless microphone and receiver set, shown with the receiver attached to the camera by the included cable in Figure A-16.

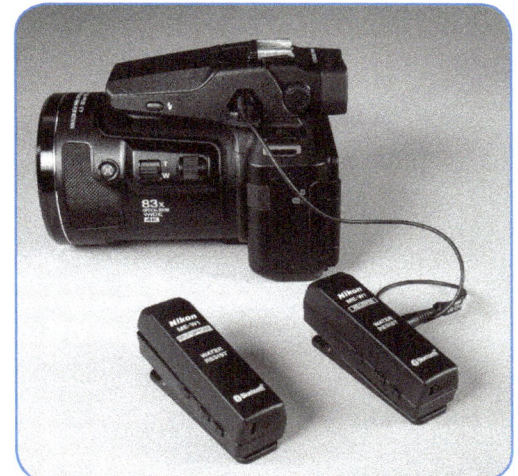

Figure A-16. Nikon ME-W1 Wireless Microphone and Receiver

It operates using Bluetooth, and, according to Nikon, provides a range of up to 164 feet (50 meters). Both the receiver and the microphone, which are very similar in construction, have clips that make it easy to attach them to clothing or to a camera strap. Also, both units have microphones built into them, so you can record sound from both the microphone and the receiver, and you can use the two units for two-way communication between the photographer and the remote subject who is wearing the microphone.

You also can use any other standard microphone with a 3.5mm stereo plug, such as the Rode VideoMic Pro, shown in Figure A-17.

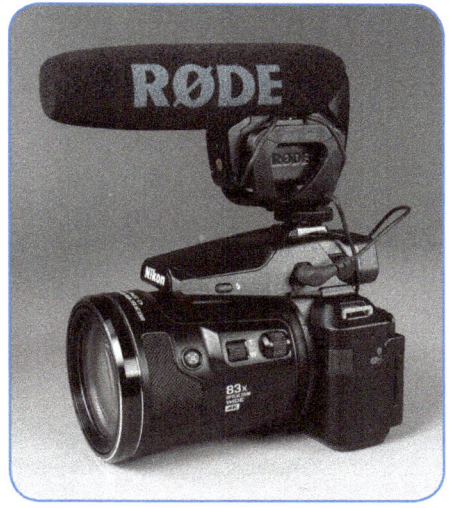

Figure A-17. Rode VideoMic Pro on P950

Filters

A nice feature of the Coolpix P950 is that its lens is threaded to accept standard accessories with a 67mm screw-in diameter, so you can attach items such as filters and closeup lenses. Figure A-18 shows the camera with a neutral density filter that cuts down the amount of light entering the lens, so you can use a slow shutter speed in bright light to smooth out the appearance of flowing water, for instance. You can use polarizing filters to improve the appearance of the sky. As discussed in Chapter 9, you can use an infrared filter to take infrared photographs.

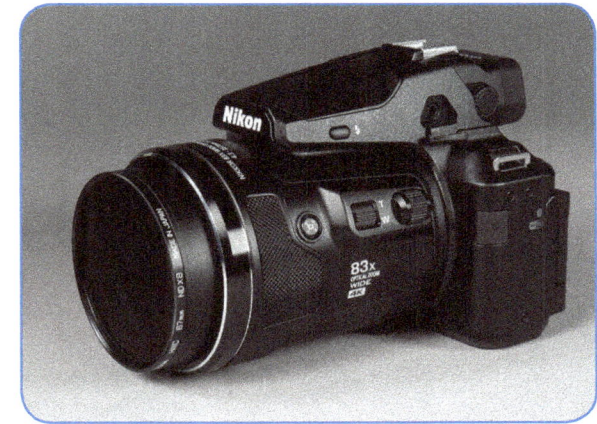

Figure A-18. Neutral Density Filter on Lens of P950

Some photographers like to screw on an ultraviolet filter just to protect the lens from damage. You also can use closeup filters that enable the lens to focus on closer subjects, although the camera has such a strong macro focus capability that I have so far not found the need for such filters.

Lens Hood

This is not an optional accessory, because it ships with the camera, but I am mentioning it here because it is easy to forget you have it. When you are shooting with the lens exposed to direct sunlight, it is a good idea to attach the lens hood, as shown in Figure A-19, to avoid flare from the sun's rays. The hood also can provide some protection against bumping or scratching the lens, so it is a good idea to have it with you at all times.

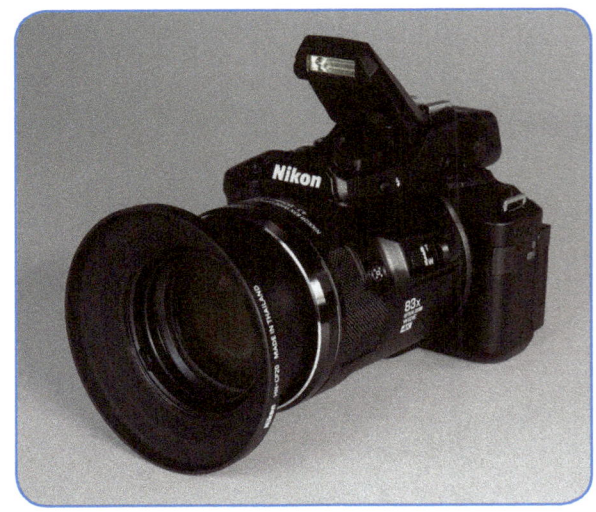

Figure A-19. Lens Hood on P950

Appendix B: Quick Tips

This section includes tips and facts that might be useful as reminders, especially to those who are new to digital cameras like the Coolpix P950. I have tried to include bits of helpful information that you might not remember from day to day, especially if you don't use the P950 constantly.

Use continuous shooting. The P950 has burst-shooting capabilities that can capture images other cameras might not manage. I recommend you consider using continuous shooting as a matter of routine in some situations, unless you are running out of memory storage or battery power, or have a particular reason not to use it. Even with stationary portraits, you may get the perfect expression on your subject's face with the fourth or fifth shot. Go to the Continuous item on the Shooting menu (or press the Function button if it is assigned to this menu item), scroll down the list of options, and turn one of them on. Continuous shooting is not available in the Auto or Creative shooting modes, in most of the Scene modes, or in some other situations, such as when the flash is used.

Take advantage of the User Settings mode. Use this feature to store your most important group of settings. For example, you could set up the U slot with these settings for street photography: Shooting mode = Program; Image Quality = Fine; Image Size = 4608 x 2592; Picture Control = Monochrome; Metering = Matrix; Continuous = Continuous H; ISO = 800; Sound Settings = Button Sound and Shutter Sound off.

Use the in-camera HDR setting. It's not immediately obvious how to get to the HDR setting on the P950. As a reminder, turn the mode dial to the SCENE position and then press the Menu button. Scroll through the list of scene types to Backlighting, press the OK or Right button, and select On for HDR on the next screen. When you take a picture with this setting, the camera will capture several images and process them to achieve a good balance of light and dark areas in the final image.

Explore the P950's creative potential. The Coolpix P950 has several advanced features that let you explore experimental photographic techniques. Some suggestions: Use Manual exposure mode with its settings for bulb and time exposures to take night-time shots with trails of lights from automobiles, storefronts, and other sources. Use shutter speeds as fast as 1/4000 second to freeze moving motorcycles, track and field runners, skateboarders, and other speedy subjects in mid-motion. Try zooming in or out during a multi-second exposure. Use long exposures (on a tripod) to turn night into day.

Adjust the camera's color settings. The Coolpix P950 has several settings for color-related adjustments: Picture Control, White Balance, the Creative shooting mode, and the Food setting in Scene mode, which lets you adjust a hue slider. The Selective Color setting in Scene mode lets you retain a single color in an image that is otherwise black and white. You can achieve unusual effects by purposely setting a custom white balance while aiming at a colored surface, rather than a white or gray one. Remember that you can make further adjustments to the Picture Control and Creative mode settings.

Use a neutral density (ND) filter for some shots. There are times when you need a slow shutter speed, but, in bright light, you can't achieve it, because the aperture can only go as narrow as f/8.0. One solution is to use an ND filter to cut down on the light reaching the sensor, resulting in slower shutter speeds. You might want to do this to slow down the rush of a waterfall to a smooth, blended look, or to achieve a motion blur in a shot of a passing runner or walker. The P950 accepts filters with a 67mm diameter.

Diffuse your flash or reduce its intensity. If you find the built-in flash produces light that's too harsh for close subjects or other shots, try using translucent plastic pieces from milk jugs, other food containers, or broken ping-pong balls as homemade flash diffusers. Just hold the plastic up between the flash and the subject. Another approach when using flash outdoors is to use flash exposure compensation to reduce the intensity of the flash by about -2/3 EV.

Use Creative mode and Scene Mode for recording movies. Don't overlook the fact that you can shoot movies in these modes, with their image-altering settings such as Selective Color, Charcoal, Bleached, Sepia and others. See Chapters 3 and 8 for details.

Use the self-timer or remote to avoid camera shake. The Coolpix P950 has a self-timer that is easy to use; just press the Left button and choose your setting. This feature is not only for group portraits; you can use it whenever you'll be using a slow shutter speed and you need to avoid camera shake. It can be useful when you're doing macro photography or using the superzoom lens, also, because those are both sensitive to camera motion. You also can use a Nikon remote control device, as discussed in Appendix A, or remote shooting using the camera's wireless connection ability, as discussed in Chapter 9.

Set zone focusing. If you're doing street photography or are in any other situation when you want to set the camera on manual focus for a general distance, here is a quick way to do so. Set the focus mode to autofocus, then aim the camera at a subject at approximately the distance you want to be able to focus on quickly. Once focus is set, turn the focus mode selector to MF to select manual focus, and press the Down button to lock the focus. Now you are ready to shoot any subject at that distance without the need to refocus.

Leave good settings in place when you end a shooting session. Several settings on the Coolpix P950 are "sticky"—they will remain set to their current values when the camera is powered off and then on again. Some examples are exposure compensation, ISO, and continuous shooting. It is a good idea to check the camera when you stop shooting to make sure you have not left any settings in place that could cause problems if you have to start shooting again in a hurry. For example, you might want to leave the Scene mode set to the Selective Color option, with no color selected, which results in normal shots. Then, if you pick up the camera in a hurry and turn the mode dial to the Scene position, you will get normal-looking shots, rather than shots with the unusual coloration of Dusk/Dawn or some other unwanted setting.

Be aware of the Movie Options setting when recording movies. When you press the Movie button to record a movie, the camera will use whatever setting is currently selected for Movie Options on the Movie menu. If you have this menu item set to one of the HS (High Speed) settings, the resulting movie will be either in slow motion or speeded up, and will have no sound. If you want to be ready to record a good-quality, normal movie, leave Movie Options set to the second setting from the top of the menu screen, which is 1080/30p (or 1080/25p if you have set Frame Rate to 25 fps).

Shoot larger panoramas. When you are shooting a horizontal panorama using the Easy Panorama setting as discussed in Chapter 3, you can increase its height using a simple technique. Select your setting, such as Normal, and then hold the camera vertically, as if you were shooting a tall building, but pan it horizontally. With this approach, the dimensions of the panorama will be 1536 pixels tall by 4800 pixels wide, instead of the normal dimensions of 920 by 4800.

Use the Filter Effects setting on the Playback menu. With this setting, you can add interesting and attractive processing to your recorded images, including Cross Screen, Painting, Fisheye, Miniature Effect, Photo Illustration, and several others. One nice bonus is that you can add these effects even to images that were taken with the Creative or Scene mode. In that way, you can use two effects with the same image, such as Binary with Fisheye or Night Landscape with Painting, as shown in Figure 6-23.

Use a pull-focus effect when recording a movie. When recording a movie, you can lock focus with the AE-L/AF-L button if the AE/AF Lock Button option on the Setup menu is set to AF Lock Only and Autofocus Mode on the Movie menu is set to AF-F for Full-time Autofocus. With those settings in place, while recording a movie in autofocus mode, let the camera focus on the first subject, such as an object in the fairly distant background, and press the AE-L/AF-L Button to lock focus on that subject. Then, with the second subject centered in the scene in the foreground, press the button again to release the focus lock, and the camera will "pull" its focus from the background subject to the foreground subject.

Appendix B: Quick Tips

Create an in-camera fade-in effect when recording a movie. Set the AE-L/AF-L button to lock exposure using the AE/AF Lock Button menu option. Then, before starting the video recording, aim the camera at a bright light or other bright scene, and press the button to lock exposure. Then press the Movie button to start recording a normally exposed scene, which should appear quite dark or black. When you are ready, press the AE/AF Lock Button and the scene should fade in quickly from black to normal exposure.

Use Auto ISO settings with Manual exposure mode. Set the mode dial to M and set the ISO Sensitivity option to a setting such as A1600. Then, you can select the shutter speed and aperture you want, and the camera will adjust the ISO setting to achieve a normal exposure if possible. In this way, you can control your settings but still take advantage of the camera's automatic exposure capability.

Save the settings for the ML-L7 remote control's two function buttons. As discussed in Appendix A, you can save one setting to each of the two function buttons on the optional Bluetooth remote control. If you then use the Save User Settings menu option to save a group of settings, those settings for the two function buttons on the remote will be saved as part of that group. The buttons will retain those settings as long as the mode dial is set to the U position.

Use the self-timer with the Continuous H: 120 fps or Continuous H: 60 fps setting. Although the self-timer does not function fully with some other Continuous settings, it does function with these. So, for example, you can set the camera on a tripod with one of these settings in place and set the self-timer for ten seconds. Then press the shutter button and position yourself in front of the camera to swing a golf club or do some other action to be analyzed. The camera will take a group of 60 images very rapidly, so you can analyze your swing or other action quite closely. When viewing the images in playback mode, after opening up the sequence with the OK button, you can move through the sequence rapidly by turning the multi selector dial.

Use a remote control when making time or bulb exposures. When the camera is in Manual exposure mode, you can make long exposures using the Time or Bulb setting for shutter speed, as long as ISO is set to 1600 or lower. You should set the camera on a tripod and, if possible, use a remote control device to trigger the shutter. The available devices are discussed in Appendix A.

Appendix C: Resources for Further Information

Photography Books

A visit to any large bookstore or an online search will reveal the vast assortment of books about digital photography that is currently available. Rather than trying to compile a long bibliography, I will list a few books that I consulted while writing this guide, which are useful resources for further exploration.

J. Gulbins & R. Gulbins, *Photographic Multishot Techniques* (Rocky Nook, 2009)

C. Harnischmacher, *Closeup Shooting* (Rocky Nook, 2007)

C. Harnischmacher, *The Wild Side of Photography* (Rocky Nook, 2010)

H. Horenstein, *Digital Photography: A Basic Manual* (Little, Brown 2011)

J. Paduano, *The Art of Infrared Photography* (4th ed., Amherst Media, 1998)

D. Sandidge, *Digital Infrared Photography Photo Workshop* (Wiley, 2009)

Digital Photography Review

http://www.dpreview.com/forums/1007

This is the current web address for the "Nikon Coolpix Talk" forum within the dpreview.com site. Dpreview is one of the most established and authoritative sites for reviews, discussion forums, technical information, and other resources concerning digital cameras.

Reviews of the Coolpix P950

The links below lead to reviews of the Coolpix P950 by several sites.

https://www.imaging-resource.com/PRODS/nikon-p950/nikon-p950A.HTM

https://www.photographyblog.com/reviews/nikon_coolpix_p950_review/news

https://www.ephotozine.com/article/nikon-coolpix-p950-review-34459

https://www.digitalcameraworld.com/reviews/nikon-p950-review

https://camerajabber.com/reviews/nikon-coolpix-p950/

The Official Nikon Site

The United States arm of the Nikon company provides resources on its web site, including the downloadable version of the user's manual for the Coolpix P950 and the Nikon ViewNX-i software. The last link in this group is for the Nikon SnapBridge app manuals and online help.

http://www.nikonusa.com/en/Nikon-Products/Product/Compact-Digital-Cameras/COOLPIX-P950.html

https://downloadcenter.nikonimglib.com/en/products/540/COOLPIX_P950.html

https://downloadcenter.nikonimglib.com/en/products/363/SnapBridge.html

Appendix C: Resources for Further Information | 161

Videos

The links below lead to videos with information that may be useful to users of the Nikon Coolpix P950.

https://youtu.be/d-06jgLiYZ4

This first link, above, leads to a general overview of the P950, going through pros, cons, and general impressions.

https://youtu.be/4PONo3nf_wE

The link above points to general overview of the P950 by Jessops Camera in England.

https://youtu.be/3ir32waNfWo

The link above leads to a good overview of the camera by Clifton Cameras in England, with some good sample photographs.

https://youtu.be/d49WAvF430Y

The link above is to an unboxing video for the P950, which provides some good insights about the camera and its features.

https://youtu.be/F3HmLSjb9u0

The link above leads to a detailed video discussion of how to attach the Nikon P900 (not the P950) to a Sky-Watcher AZ-GTi mount for tracking celestial objects.

Photography Information

The site below provides some helpful information about infrared photography with digital cameras.

http://www.wrotniak.net/photo/infrared/

This next site has excellent information and tutorials about many aspects of photography.

http://www.cambridgeincolour.com/

This site has some brief, but useful tips on improving your photographs of birds.

http://www.allaboutbirds.org/page.aspx?pid=1109

Index

Symbols

4K option for motion picture recording 124
  incompatibility with other settings 124

A

AC adapter
  Nikon model EH-5b or 5d 151–152
  Nikon Power Connector, model number EP-5C 151–152
    inserting cord through channel in battery compartment door 152
Accessory shoe 6
Accessory terminal 8, 76, 152
Active D-Lighting menu option 66–67
  incompatibility with other settings 67
  relationshiop to HDR setting 35
Adobe Bridge CC software
  reading location data with 139
Adobe Camera Raw software 46
AE/AF Lock Button menu option 7, 76, 111
AE-L/AF-L button 7, 76
  controlling action of 111
  using to lock focus or exposure during motion picture recording 111, 158
  using to refocus during motion picture recording 127
AF Area Mode menu option 63–65
  Face Priority option 63
  Manual (Spot, Normal, or Wide) 63–64
  Subject Tracking option 64
  Target Finding option 64–65
AF Assist menu option 88, 108
Airplane Mode menu option 140
Aperture
  procedure for setting 24
  relationship to depth of field 23
Aperture Priority mode 22–24
Aperture setting
  effect on range of available shutter speeds 21
Aperture values
  available range of 8, 20, 22, 24, 26, 145
    limited by focal length of lens 1, 24
Aspect ratio 47–49
  comparison images 48
  relationship to Image Size setting 47
Assign Side Dial menu option 7, 75, 110–111
Assign Side Zoom Control menu option 7, 75, 110
Atomos Shogun 4K video recorder 130

Auto Flash setting 83
Autofocus
  selecting with focus mode selector 76
Autofocus Mode menu option (movies) 16, 126–127
Autofocus Mode menu option (still images) 65
  not available with infinity focus setting 65
Auto Link option in SnapBridge app 136, 139
Auto mode 19
  incompatibility with other settings 19
  settings available for adjustment 19
Auto Off menu option 112
Auto with Red-eye Reduction flash setting 83

B

Backlighting/HDR setting 34–36
Battery charger
  generic model for charging outside of camera 151
  Mophie PowerStation XL portable USB battery 151
  Nikon model number EH-73P 4
    using to power camera 151
  Nikon model number MH-29 150
  RavPower 6-Port Desktop USB Charger 151
Battery/memory compartment door
  flap for inserting cord from AC adapter 8, 152
Battery, Nikon EN-EL20a 3, 150
  charging 3–4
    length of time for full charge 4
    using USB cable connected to computer 4, 113
  inserting into camera 3
  using generic replacement 151
Beach setting 31
Bird-watching mode
  selecting focal length for framing option 28–29
  using continuous shooting with 28
Blinking aperture number on display
  meaning of 22
Bluetooth menu option 137, 141
Blurred background 144
  how to achieve 24
Bokeh. See Blurred background
Bulb setting for shutter speed 26
  using remote control device for 159
Button sound
  silencing 111

C

Calendar screen in playback mode 90–91
Cases
   Lowepro Inverse 100 AW beltpack 150
   Lowepro Toploader 55 AW II Bag 150
Charge by Computer menu option 4, 113–114
Choose Connection menu option 134, 140, 153
Clean HDMI Output menu option 113
   using to record video to external recorder 113
Close-up photograph. See Macro photography
Close-up setting 33, 147
Command dial 7, 79
   icon on shooting screen 78, 79
   switching functions of with multi selector dial 79
   using to adjust Peaking level 78
   using to change enlargement factor in playback mode 79, 91
   using to set shutter speed 79
Comments
   creating and attaching to still images 114
Conformity Marking menu option 116
Connection to Remote menu option 140, 153
Connect to Smart Device menu option 134–135, 140
Continuous menu option 56–59
   assigning to Function button 73
   Continuous H: 60 fps 58
   Continuous H: 120 fps 58
   high-speed shooting 57
   Interval timer setting 58–59
      compared to Time-lapse Movie setting 59
      folder names for images 59
   low-speed shooting 57
   Pre-shooting Cache setting 56, 57–58
   single shots setting 57
   turning off continuous shooting 57
   using self-timer with 57, 86, 159
Continuous shooting
   advantages of using 56, 157
   flashing display on screen when data being written 6
   in general 56
   playback of continuous shots 17, 57, 93–94, 101
Contrast
   adjusting for images as they are shot 50
      unavailable when Active D-Lighting in effect 67
Controls on back of camera 6–7
Controls on front and sides of camera 7–8
Controls on top of camera 6
Copyright Information menu option 114
Creative mode 39–41
   comparison charts 41
   incompatibility with other settings 40
   list of settings 41
   making adjustments to settings 40
   resetting after adjustments 40, 80
   selecting a setting for 39–40, 41
   using for motion picture recording 158

Cropping images in camera 80, 91
Cross Screen setting for Filter Effects 97
Custom Picture Control menu option 51
Custom Picture Control menu option (movies) 129
Custom white balance
   how to set 53

D

Date and time
   imprinting on images 106
   setting 9–10, 102–103
Date format
   setting 103
Date Stamp menu option 106
   incompatibility with other settings 106
Daylight Saving Time
   setting 102–103
Delete/Trash button 7, 80
   using to delete images and videos 80
   using to reset Creative mode adjustments 40
Depth of field 23
Digital Zoom menu option 108–110
   incompatibility with other settings 110
   using with motion picture recording 121
   using with smaller image sizes 108–109
Dimmed items on menu screens 44
Diopter adjustment wheel 8, 76
Direction buttons 81–87
   general uses of 81
   in general 7
Display button 7, 78–79
Display screens
   playback mode 78, 91–93
   shooting mode 78–79
D-Lighting menu option 96
   distinguished from Active D-Lighting 96
Dot Sight accessory
   Nikon DF-M1 153–154
   Olympus EE-1 154
Down button
   using to call up focus mode menu 85
   using to toggle manual focus screen 86
Dusk/Dawn setting 32
Dynamic Fine Zoom feature 108–109

E

Easy Panorama setting 36
   dimensions of panoramic images 36
   incompatibility with other settings 36
   scrolling panorama with OK button 36
   shooting taller panoramas 158
Electronic VR menu option 16, 127
   incompatibility with other settings 127
Enlarging images in playback mode 17, 73, 91
EVF Auto Toggle menu option 7, 76, 105–106
EVF Options menu option 104

Exposure
   locking. See Locking exposure
Exposure bracketing 62–63
   incompatibility with other settings 62–63
   using for HDR photography 36
Exposure compensation
   activating with Right button 85
   display of histogram with 14, 105
   incompatibility with other settings 85
   procedure for using 13–14, 85
   using with motion picture recording 120
Exposure Mode menu option (movies) 129
External flash units
   Godox TT685N 154
   Nikon SB-500 154
   Nikon SB-700 154
   Nikon SB-5000 154
External microphone jack 8, 75
External microphones
   adjusting sensitivity of 128
   Nikon ME-1 154–155
   Nikon ME-W1 155
   Rode VideoMic Pro 155
External Mic Sensitivity menu option 128
External video recorder
   recording video to through HDMI port 130
Eye sensor 7, 76

F

Faces
   setting autofocus to detect 63
Fade-in effect for motion picture recording 158
Fade-out effect for motion picture recording 129
Fill Flash/Standard flash setting 83
Filter effects
   adjusting for monochrome images as they are shot 50
Filter Effects menu option 96–98
   using to add second effect to image 98, 158
Filters
   using with P950 155–156
Fireworks Show setting 34
Firmware
   checking for updates 117
Firmware Version menu option 117
Flash, built-in 7
   can't fire unless manually popped up 14, 74, 82
   diffusing 157–158
   general procedure for using 14–15
   incompatibility with other settings 82
Flash Exposure Compensation menu option 65–66, 85
   using to reduce harshness of flash 65, 158
Flashing display of remaining images number
   meaning of 6
Flashing parts of image in playback mode 93
Flash mode menu 12, 15, 82–85
Flash pop-up button 7, 74

Flexible program feature 20, 145
Focal length range of lens 8
Focal Length Selection option on Bird-watching mode menu 28
Focal Length Selection option on Moon mode menu 28
Focus
   basic procedures for adjusting 11–12
   controlling in Auto mode 13
   locking. See Locking focus
   manual. See Manual focus
Focus frame
   moving on display 63–64
Focus mode
   selecting 13, 86
Focus mode menu 13, 85–86
   unavailability of some settings in some shooting modes 85
Focus mode selector 7, 76–78
   using to select manual focus 13
Food setting 33–34, 147
Format Card menu option 112
   unavailable when wireless connection is active 112
Frame Rate menu option 15, 123, 128
Function button 6, 73–74
   cannot be used during motion picture recording 122
   changing option assigned to 74
   incompatibility with other settings 74
   on remote control device 153
   settings that can be assigned to 73

G

GPS location ability, built-in
   lacking in Coolpix P950 1
Grid
   displaying in shooting mode 78–79, 104

H

HDMI cable
   using to connect camera to television set 149
HDMI menu option 113
HDMI Output menu option 113
HDMI port 8, 88
HDR (high dynamic range) photography
   in general 34
   using HDR setting of P950 camera for 34–36, 157
Histogram
   displayed when using exposure compensation 14, 105
   playback mode 79, 92–93
   shooting mode 78–79, 105
      incompatibility with other settings 71, 105
      relationship to Manual Exposure Preview option 71, 105
HS (high-speed) movie options 124–126
   unavailable when Clean HDMI Output is turned on 126

I

Image Comment menu option 114
Image numbers

resetting 115–116
Image Quality menu option 45–47
Image Review menu option 90, 104
Image Size menu option 47–49
   relationship to zoom range 108–109
Index screens in playback mode 73, 90–91
Infinity focus modes 13, 86
   differences between two infinity modes 34
Infrared filter
   Hoya R72 147
Infrared photography 147–148
Interval timer setting 58–59
ISO Sensitivity menu option 59–61
   Auto settings 60
     using with Manual exposure mode 26, 159
   deciding on value to choose 60
   effect on range of available shutter speed settings 20, 21, 26
   incompatibility with other settings 62
   listing of available values 60
   Minimum Shutter Speed setting 61–62
   negative effects of very high setting 61
   procedure for making setting 60
   using to enable use of fast shutter speed 60, 145
   using with Manual exposure mode 26
ISO Sensitivity menu option (movies) 130
   adjusting during motion picture recording 130

K

Kelvins 53–54
   used to measure color temperature 52
Key Picture Selection menu option 101

L

Landscape setting 30
Language
   setting 10, 112
Language menu option 112
LCD monitor
   adjusting brightness and color of 104
   resolution of 89
   switching view by folding in against camera 76, 106
   switching view to and from 76, 105–106
   tilting and swiveling features of 89–90
Left button
   using to adjust manual focus magnification 87
   using to call up self-timer/smile timer/ Pet Portrait Release menu 86
   using to cause camera to focus when recording video 87, 120, 127
Lens
   specifications of 8
   using superzoom capability of 142–145
Lens hood 156
Level. See Virtual Horizon menu option
Location data
   adding to images using SnapBridge app 138–139

Location Data menu option 114–115, 139
   using Position option to display location data for image 114
Locking exposure 72, 111
   with motion picture recording 120
Locking focus 72, 111
   with motion picture recording 87, 119–120, 126–127
Long Exposure NR menu option 66

M

Macro autofocus setting 13, 146
Macro photography 145–147
   using manual focus for 147
Manual exposure mode 24–26
   incompatibility with other settings 26
   procedure for making settings 25
   using Auto ISO setting with 26, 159
   using to create HDR images 24, 35
Manual Exposure Preview menu option 71
Manual focus
   adjusting magnification with 77
   adjusting with side dial 7, 13
   general use of 13, 77–78
   reasons for using 77
   selecting with focus mode selector 77
   using autofocus with 77
   using Down button to toggle magnified screen 77
   using for macro photography 147
   using Left button to toggle enlargement factor 77
Mark for Upload menu option 95, 139, 141
Memory card
   formatting 112
   inserting into camera 5
   largest capacity usable in Coolpix P950 5
   need for high-speed card for highest-quality video formats 5, 124
   number of images that can be stored 5
   operating camera without 4
   types and capacities of 4
Menu button 7, 79
   using to save cropped version of image in playback mode 80, 91
Menus
   listing of 44
   navigating through 43–44
   unavailable items on 44
Metering menu option 54–56
   incompatibility with Active D-Lighting setting 56
Microphone, built-in 74
Microphone, external
   plugging in disables built-in microphone 74
   port for plugging in 8, 75
     ability to provide power for microphone 75
micro-SD card
   using in Coolpix P950 5
Miniature setting for Filter Effects 97–98
Minimum focus distance of lens 146–147

Minimum Shutter Speed menu option 61–62
Mode dial 6, 73
Monitor button 76
   using to switch between LCD and viewfinder 7, 76
Monitor Options menu option 104
Monitor Settings menu option 104–105
   using to add histogram in shooting mode 78
Monochrome Picture Control setting
   adjustments to 51
Moon mode 27–28
   incompatibility with other settings 28
   selecting focal length for framing option 28
   using color filter options with 28
Motion picture recording
   effects of mode dial position 119
   exposure control in still-shooting modes 120
      autoexposure lock 120
      exposure compensation 120
   focus options 119–120, 126–127
   general procedure for 118–119
   limitations on length of recording 122
   locking focus 120, 126, 127–128
   overview 118
   pausing with OK button 122
   slow-motion options 125
   speeded-up motion option 125–126
   still photo settings available 119–121
   taking still images during recording 121–122
      incompatibility with other settings 121
   using Creative and Scene modes for 158
   using exposure compensation 120
   using optical and digital zoom 121
Motion pictures
   editing in camera 131–133
      not available when battery level is low 132
   editing with computer 17
   identifying on index screens in playback mode 131
   playback 17–18, 131–132
      adjusting sound volume 17
   saving single frame from 122, 132–133
      using this feature as an alternative to continuous shooting 145
Movie button 7, 78
Movie Manual menu 128–130
Movie Manual mode 128–130
Movie menu 15, 123–128
   list of items on 129–130
Movie Options menu option 15–16, 119, 124–126
Moving subject
   tracking with autofocus 64
Multiple Exposure Lighten setting 38
   using for images of light trails, star trails, or fireworks 38
Multiple Exposure menu option 68
Multi selector dial 7, 80–81
   general uses 80
   switching functions with command dial 81
   using to set aperture value 80

N

Network menu 140–142
Neutral density filter 157
Night Landscape setting 32
Night Portrait setting 31
Nikon Capture NX-D software 46
   using to process Raw images 46
   where to download 3
Nikon Coolpix P950 camera
   advantages of 1
   drawbacks of 1
   items that come in the box 3
   new features of 1
Nikon Reference Manual for Coolpix P950
   where to download 1
Nikon ViewNX-i software
   where to download 3
Nikon ViewNX-Movie Editor software 3
No card present error message 4
Noise Reduction Filter menu option 66
NTSC video system 123

O

Off-center subject
   setting exposure for 72
   setting focus for 64, 72
OK button 7
   functions of 81

P

Painting setting for Filter Effects 98
PAL video system 123
Panorama photography. See Easy Panorama setting
Party/Indoor setting 31
Peaking feature for manual focus 78, 116
   adjusting level with command dial 116
   not available with motion picture recording 116
Peaking menu option 116
Pet Portrait Auto Release feature 37, 87
Pet Portrait setting 37
Photo Illustration setting for Filter Effects 98
Picture Control menu option 49–51
   adjustments to settings 50–51
      incompatibility with other settings 50
   comparison images 49–50
   saving custom settings 51–52
   using with motion picture recording 129
Picture Control menu option (movies) 129
Playback button 7, 17, 78
   using to turn on camera 78
Playback menu 94–101
   need to have camera in playback mode to get access 94
Playback of images and videos
   calendar screen 90–91
   checking tone levels of images 93

Index

continuous burst of shots 17, 57, 93–94
  choosing key picture for 101
  displaying as individual images 94, 101
  cropping image with Menu button 91
  enlarging image 91
  general procedures 16–17, 90
  index screens 90–91
  motion pictures 17, 131–132
Portrait (Color + B&W) setting for Filter Effects 98–99
Portrait setting 30
Power saving mode. See Auto Off menu option
Power switch 72
Program mode 20
Program shift. See Flexible program
Protect menu option 99–100
Pull-focus effect for recording movies 158

Q

Quick Retouch menu option 95–96
  incompatibility with other settings 96

R

Raw + Fine and Raw + Normal settings 46–47, 48
Raw format for images 45–47
  advantages and disadvantages of 45–46
  compared to JPEG format 45–46
  incompatibility with other settings 46
  using to adjust shooting settings after the fact 45–46
Rear-curtain Sync flash setting 84–85
Remote control of camera
  Using Nikon Bluetooth remote, ML-L7 153
  using SnapBridge app 138
Remote control units
  Nikon MC-DC2 Remote Cord 152
  Nikon ML-L7 Remote Control 140, 153
    saving settings for its two function buttons 159
  Nikon WR-R10 and WR-T10 Wireless Remote Controllers 152–153
  port for plugging in wired remote 8
  using with Time or Bulb setting for shutter speed 159
Reset All menu option 116
  using to help resolve conflicts among camera settings 116
Reset File Numbering menu option 115–116
Reset User Settings menu option 69
Resolution of images 47
Restore Default Settings option on Network menu 142
Right button
  using for autofocus in manual focus mode 85
  using for exposure compensation 85
  using to lock exposure when recording video 85, 120
Rotate Image menu option 100

S

Saturation
  adjusting for images as they are shot 50
Save User Settings menu option 42, 69

Scene modes
  in general 26–27
  limitations of 27
SCENE setting on mode dial 29–39
  incompatibility with other settings 27
  listing of scene types 26
SD cards. See Memory card
Selective Color setting 37
Selective Color setting for Filter Effects 97
Self-timer 86
  controlling whether it remains set after use 106
  general procedure for using 86
  using to avoid camera shake 86, 158
  using with continuous shooting options 57, 86, 159
  using with motion picture recording 86, 120
Self-timer/AF Assist/Red-eye Reduction lamp 8, 87–88
  disabling 88, 108
Self-timer: After Release menu option 106
Send While Off menu option 141
Send While Shooting menu option 136–137, 139, 141
Sequence Display menu option 94, 101
Setup menu
  in general 102
Sharpening
  adjusting for images as they are shot 50
Shooting menu
  in general 43–44
Shooting modes
  names of 19
Shutter Priority mode 20–22
Shutter release button 6, 72–73
  operating when no memory card in camera 4, 103
  using to start or stop movie recording 6, 73, 128
Shutter sound
  silencing 111
Shutter speed
  display of fractional values 21
  procedure for setting 21–22
  range of available settings 19, 20, 21, 22, 129
    limitations when using Continuous menu option 22, 57
Shutter Speed Equivalents 21
Side dial 7, 75
  assigning function to for use in autofocus mode 75, 110–111
  using to adjust manual focus 75
Side zoom control 7, 75
  not affected by Zoom Memory setting 75
  setting speed of zoom with Assign Side Zoom Control menu option 75, 110
  using for telephoto shots 145
Skin Softening menu option 96
Slide Show menu option 99
Slot Empty Release Lock menu item 4, 103
Slow motion video
  how to record 124–126
Slow Sync flash setting 83
Small Picture menu option 100–101

Smile timer 87
   incompatibility with other settings 87
Snap-back zoom button 7, 75
   not available for use when recording movies 75
   setting degree to which it widens view of scene 110
   using for telephoto shots 75, 145
Snap-back Zoom menu option 75, 110
SnapBridge app 134–140
   overview of use 134
   procedure for connecting to camera 134–137
   summary of options for transferring images and videos 139–140
   using for image transfer and remote control of camera 134–138
   where to find online help 134
Snow setting 31
Soft Portrait setting for Filter Effects 96–97
Sound Settings menu option 111
Sounds made by camera
   automatically silenced in some situations 28, 111
   silencing 111
Speaker
   location of 6, 74
Speeded-up video
   how to record 125–126
Sports setting 30
Startup Zoom Position menu option 70, 73
Step-by-step tutorials
   adding location data to images using SnapBridge app 139
   basic picture-taking 11
   motion picture recording 15
   quick guide to motion picture recording 118
   recording to an external video recorder 130
   remote control of camera using SnapBridge app 138
   setting up SnapBridge connection and transferring images by Bluetooth 134
   transferring images to smartphone or tablet 134
   using SnapBridge to transfer images and videos by Wi-Fi 137–138
Still images
   taking during motion picture recording 121–122
      incompatibility with other settings 121
Street photography 148–149
Sunset setting 32

T

Tables
   fractional shutter speed equivalents 21
   limits on shutter speed settings 21
Television set
   connecting camera to 149
Time-lapse Movie setting 38–39
   compared to interval timer setting for Continuous shooting 38, 59
   list of available scenarios 39
Time-lapse photography 38–39, 58–59, 126

Time setting for shutter speed 26
   using remote control device for 159
Time zone
   changing for travel 103
   setting 103
Time Zone and Date menu option 9, 102–103
Toggle Av/Tv Selection menu option 21, 115
   using to switch functions of command dial and multi selector dial 115
Tone levels in image, checking 93
Toning
   adjusting for monochrome images as they are shot 50
Transferring images and videos from camera to smart device via W-Fi connection 137–138
Transferring images from camera to smart device via Bluetooth connection 134–137
Tripod socket 8

U

UHD (ultra-high definition) motion picture recording. See 4K option for motion picture recording
UHS-3 speed class for memory cards
   requirement to use card of that speed for high-quality video formats 124
Up button
   using to call up flash mode menu 82
USB port 8
   uses of 88
User Settings mode 41–42, 69, 145, 157

V

VGA resolution for images 58
Vibration Reduction menu option 106–108
   using with long telephoto shots 144
   using with motion picture recording 120
Video recording. See Motion picture recording
Viewfinder 6–7, 76
   adjusting brightness and color of 104
   adjusting for user's vision 8, 76
   switching view by folding LCD screen in against camera 6–7, 76, 106
   switching view to and from 6–7, 76, 105–106
View/Hide Framing Grid menu option 104
View/Hide Histograms menu option 71, 105
Vignette setting for Filter Effects 98
Virtual Horizon menu option 105
Volume
   adjusting for motion picture playback 17, 131

W

White balance comparison chart 54
White balance menu option 52–54
   Choose Color Temperature setting 53–54
   list of available settings 52–53
   making adjustments to preset settings 53
   Preset Manual setting

Index

    using to set custom white balance 53
    using with motion picture recording 119
White balance menu option (movies) 130
Wi-Fi menu option 141
Wind Noise Reduction menu option 127

Z

Zone focusing 158
Zoom lens
    flattening of subjects into single plane 143
    haze effect from compression of atmosphere 143
    isolating subject through telephoto shot 143
    rule of thumb for choosing shutter speed for telephoto shots 144
    shallow depth of field at telephoto settings 143–144
    using telephoto power of 142–143
    ways to avoid image blur at telephoto settings 144–145
Zoom lever 6, 73
    using to display index screens 73, 90
    using to enlarge image in playback mode 73
    using to operate zoom lens 73
Zoom Memory menu option 69–70, 73
    not applicable to side zoom control 70–71
Zoom Microphone menu option 16, 127
    incompatibility with other settings 127
Zoom range 8
Zoom scale
    display when using various zoom amounts 108–109
    not displayed during motion picture recording 121
Zoom speed
    changing with Assign Side Zoom Control option 7

www.ingramcontent.com/pod-product-compliance
Lightning Source LLC
Chambersburg PA
CBHW040540220526
45473CB00016B/2986